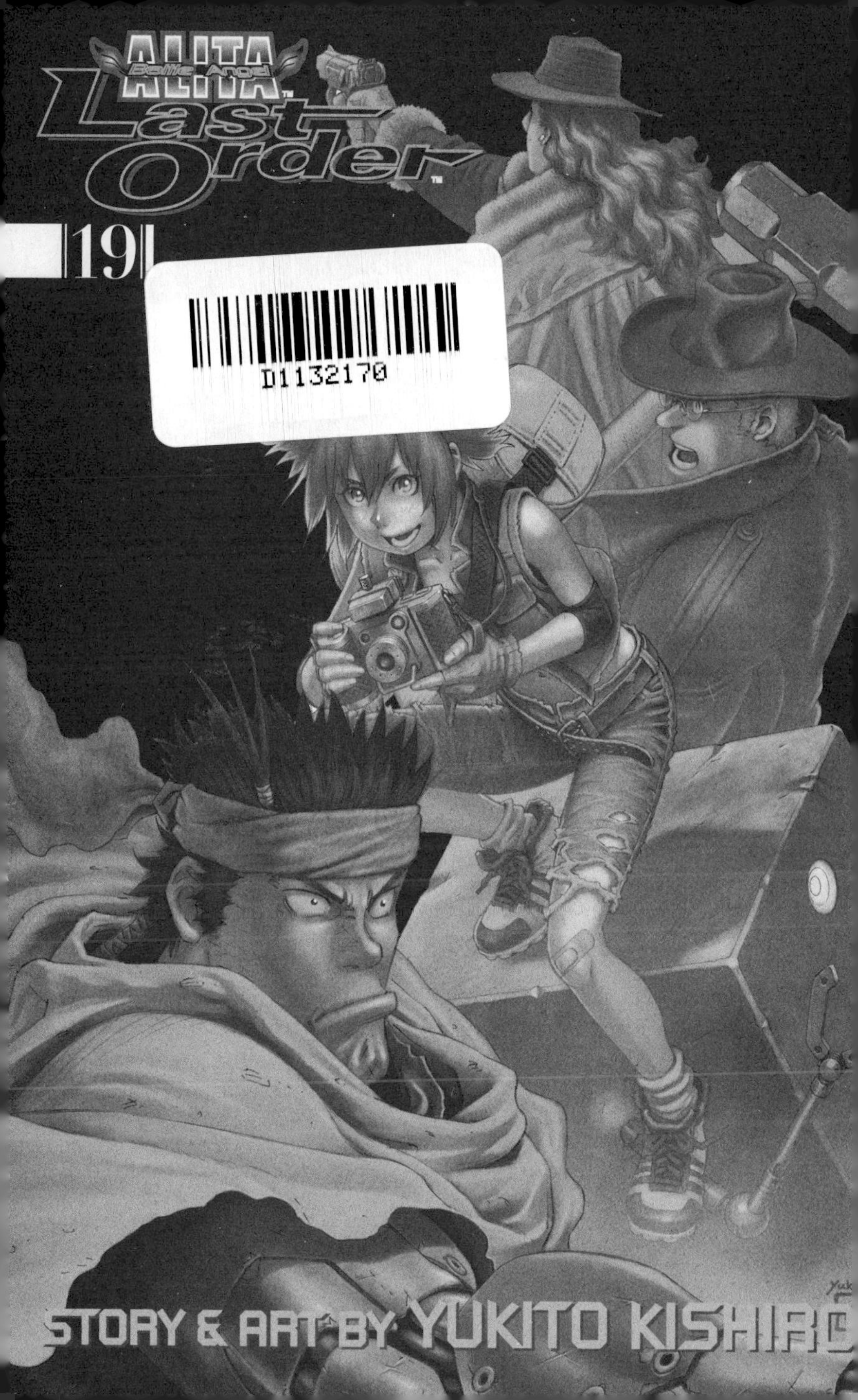

ALITA Battle Angel Last Order™

19

STORY & ART BY YUKITO KISHIRO

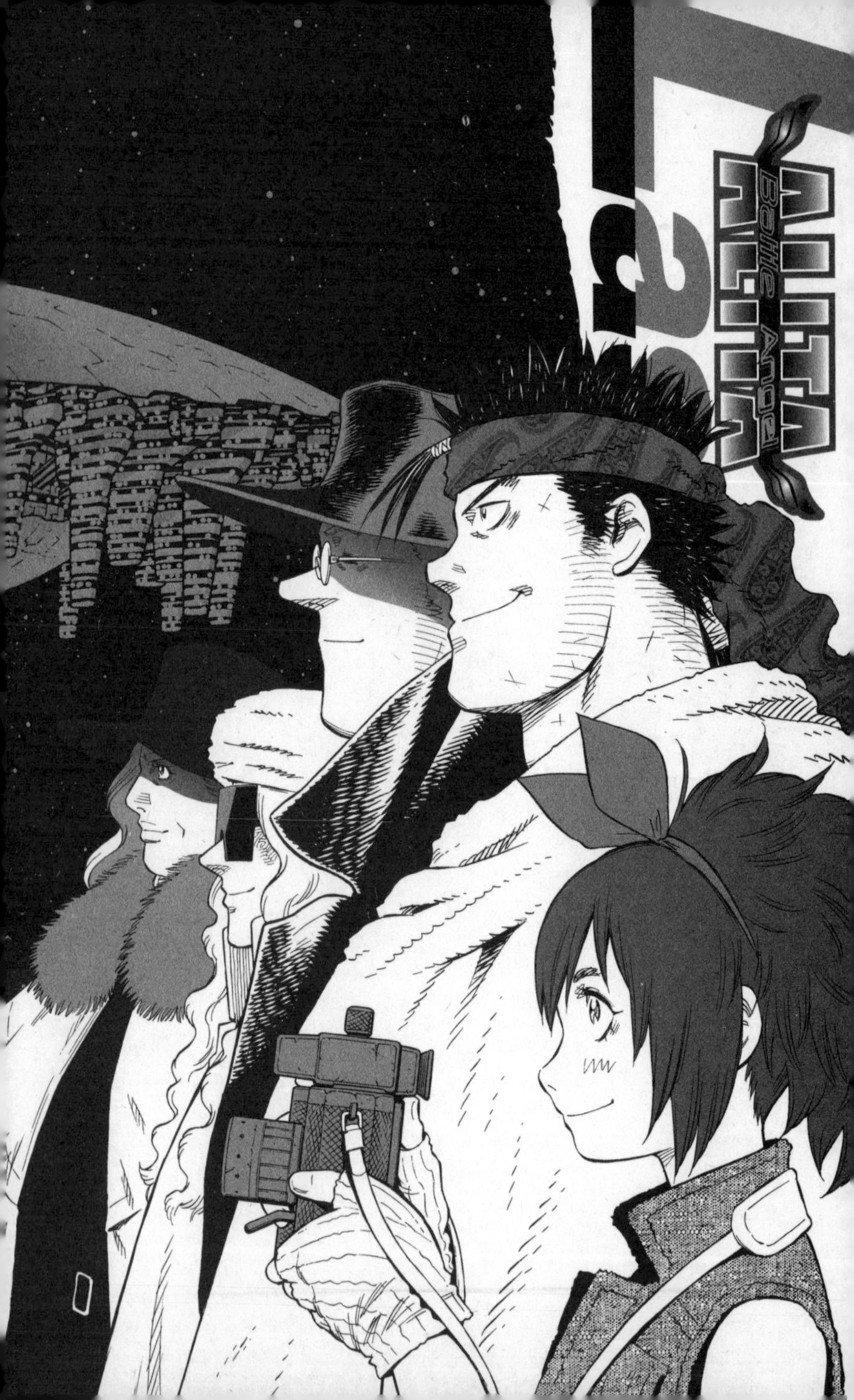
ALITA
Battle Angel

OUTLINE

The Future.

The development of cyborg technology has cheapened the value of human life. Ido, a cybernetic doctor in the Scrapyard, finds the head of a cyborg, hundreds of years old, in a pile of rubble. Miraculously resurrected, the girl was called Alita.

Alita had lost her memory, but her flesh remembered the legendary martial art, Panzer Kunst and with Ido by her side, she became a bounty hunter. An incident triggered a hunt for the mad scientist Nova, ending in a battle against Tipharean oppression. (See Battle Angel Alita.)

Alita went into space. To save her friend and her homeland, she participates in the ZOTT, the solar system's grandest combat tournament. Alita's team, the Space Angels, defeat the Space Karate Forces, struggle through Mbadi's interference, and narrowly emerge as victors. However, Mbadi ejects the entire arena towards the moon. At this rate, it will crash into the cities on the lunar surface. To prevent this from happening, Alita activates her Imaginos body...

Meanwhile, on the surface, Figure awaits the return of his love, Alita. He hears reports of the Angel of Death's demise, and leaves his village in search of Alita. Tracing her footsteps and in search of Ido, Kayna, Nova and other acquaintances, he wanders through the wasteland. Will he ever reach Alita...?

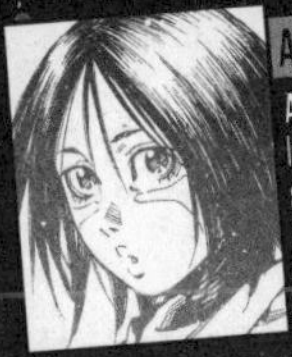

Alita: A cyborg girl who lost her memory, she is a master of the legendary art of Panzer Kunst.

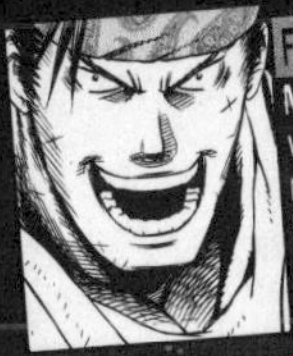

Figure: Met Alita when he was a mercenary and fell in love.

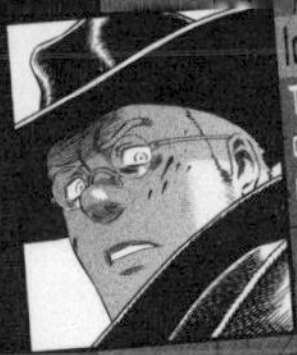

Ido: The cybernetic doctor who resurrected Alita.

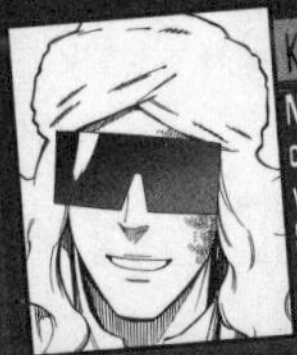

Kaos: Nova's son with psychometric abilities, who dreams of the Scrapyard unifying with Tiphares.

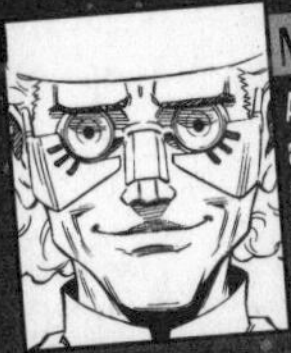

Nova X: A mad scientist and dangerous man willing to do anything for his karmic research.

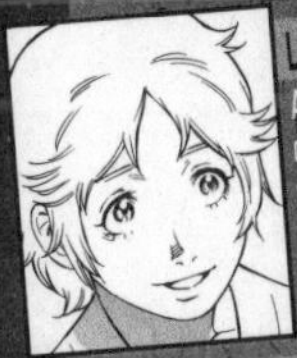

Lou: Alita's friend and operator while she was a TUNED agent. Only her brain exists.

CONTENTS

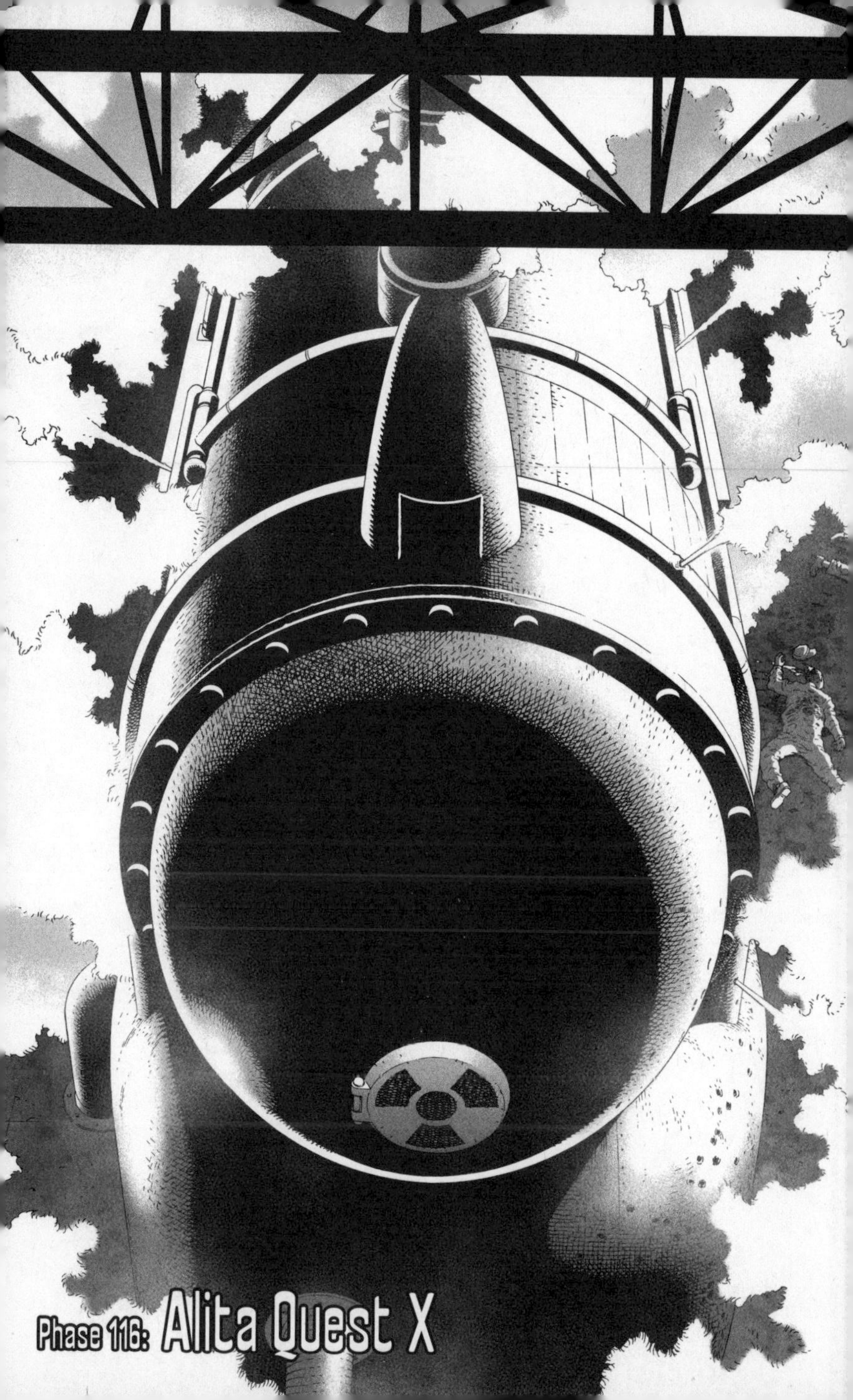
Phase 116: Alita Quest X

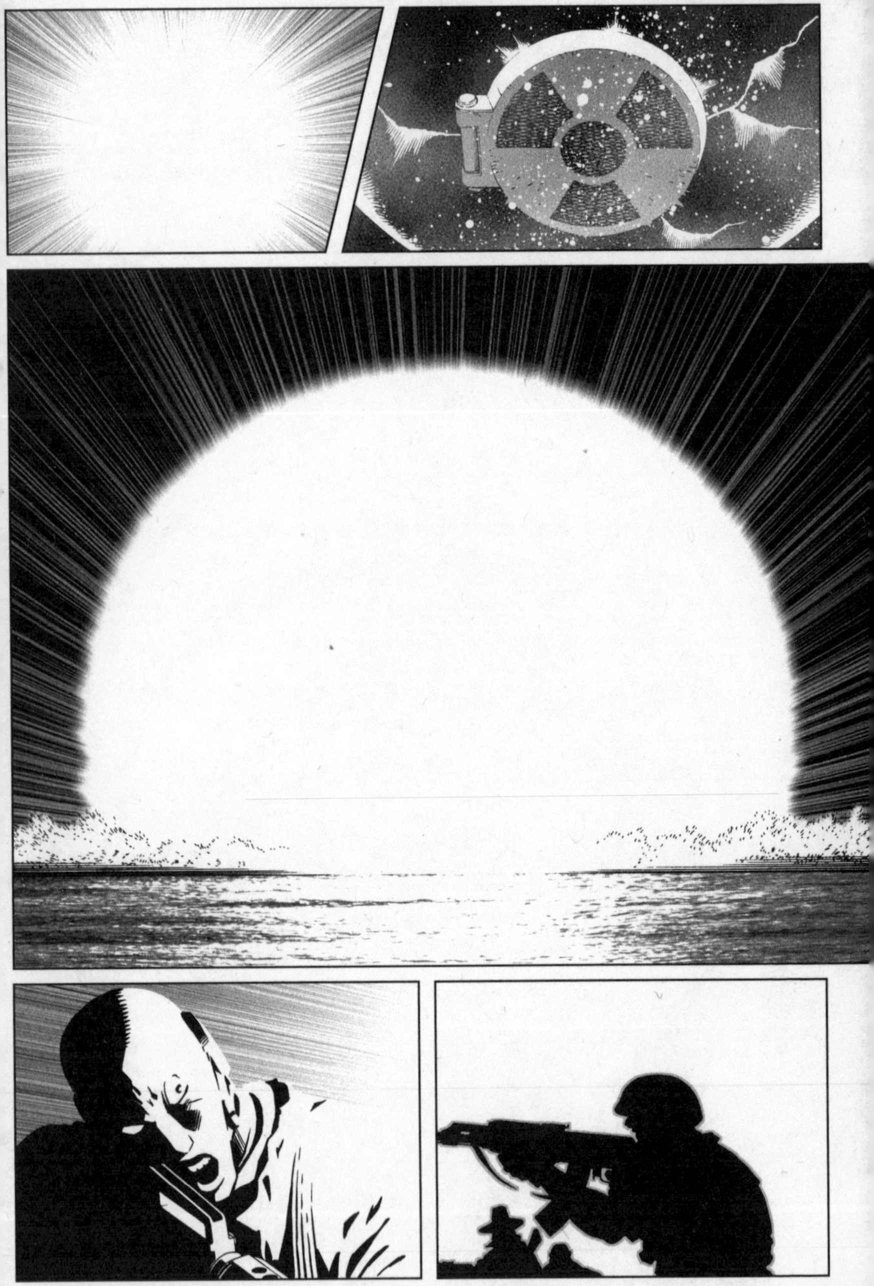

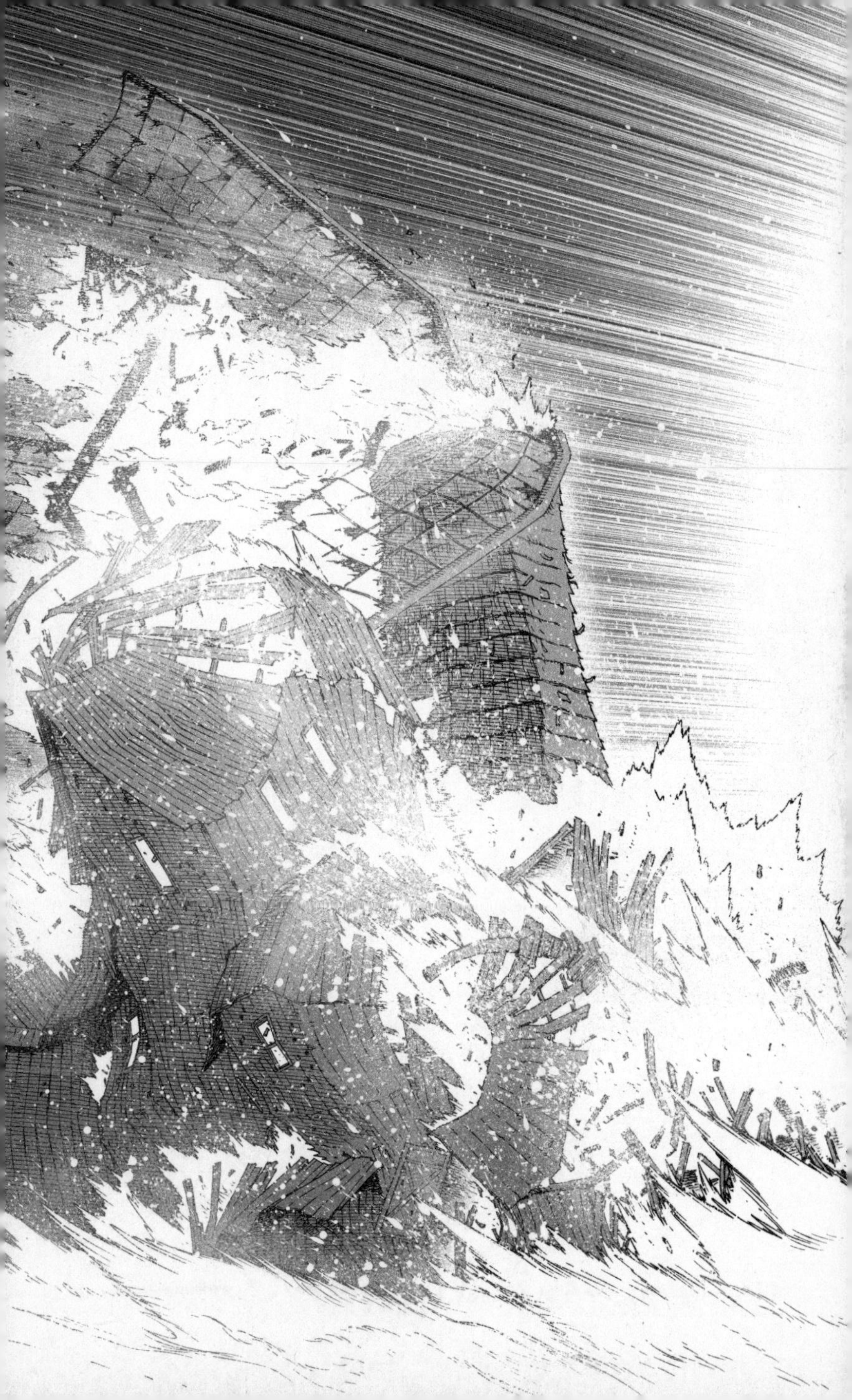

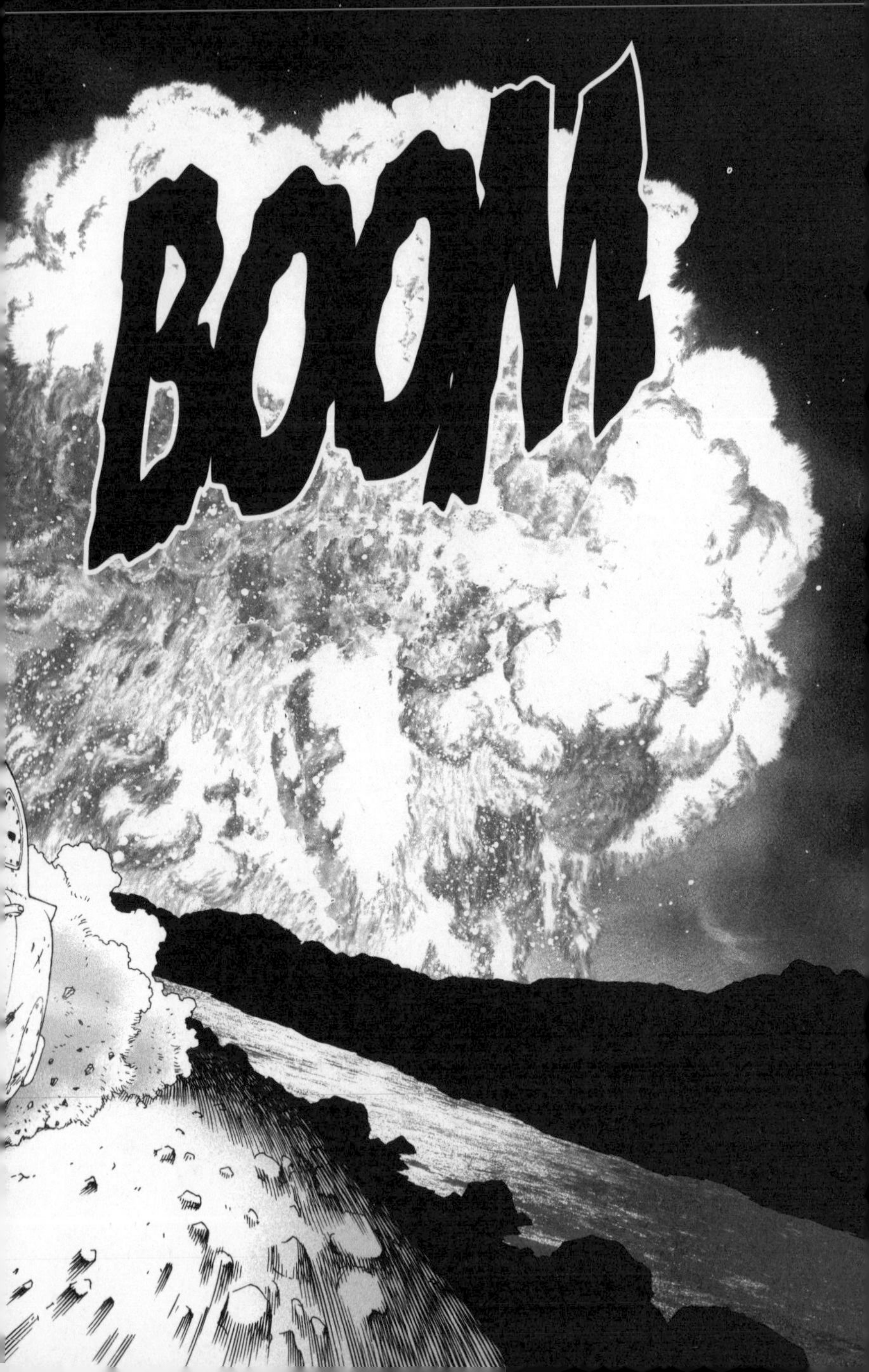
BOOM

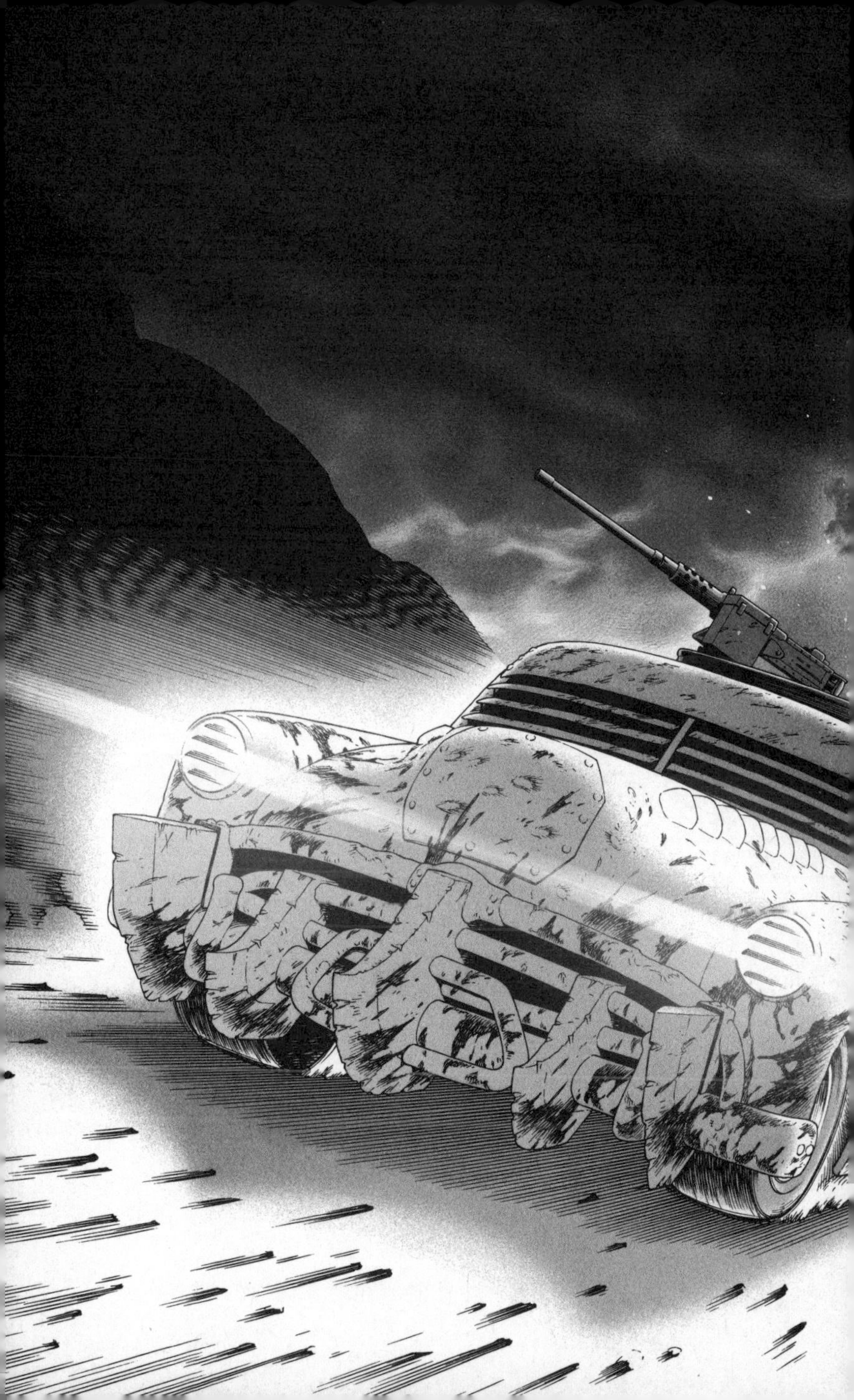

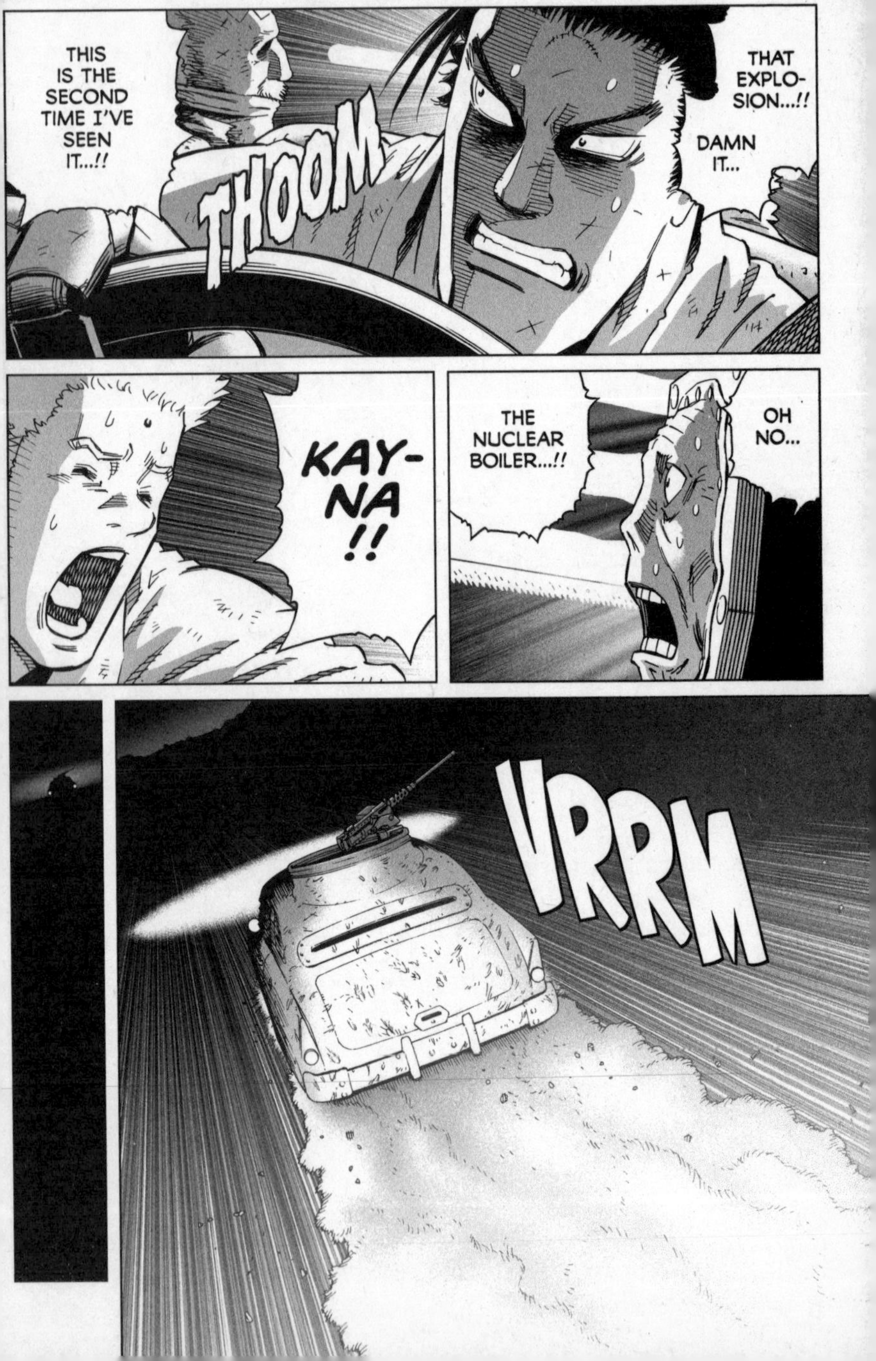
THAT EXPLOSION...!!
DAMN IT...
THOOM
THIS IS THE SECOND TIME I'VE SEEN IT...!!
OH NO...
THE NUCLEAR BOILER...!!
KAY-NA!!
VRRM

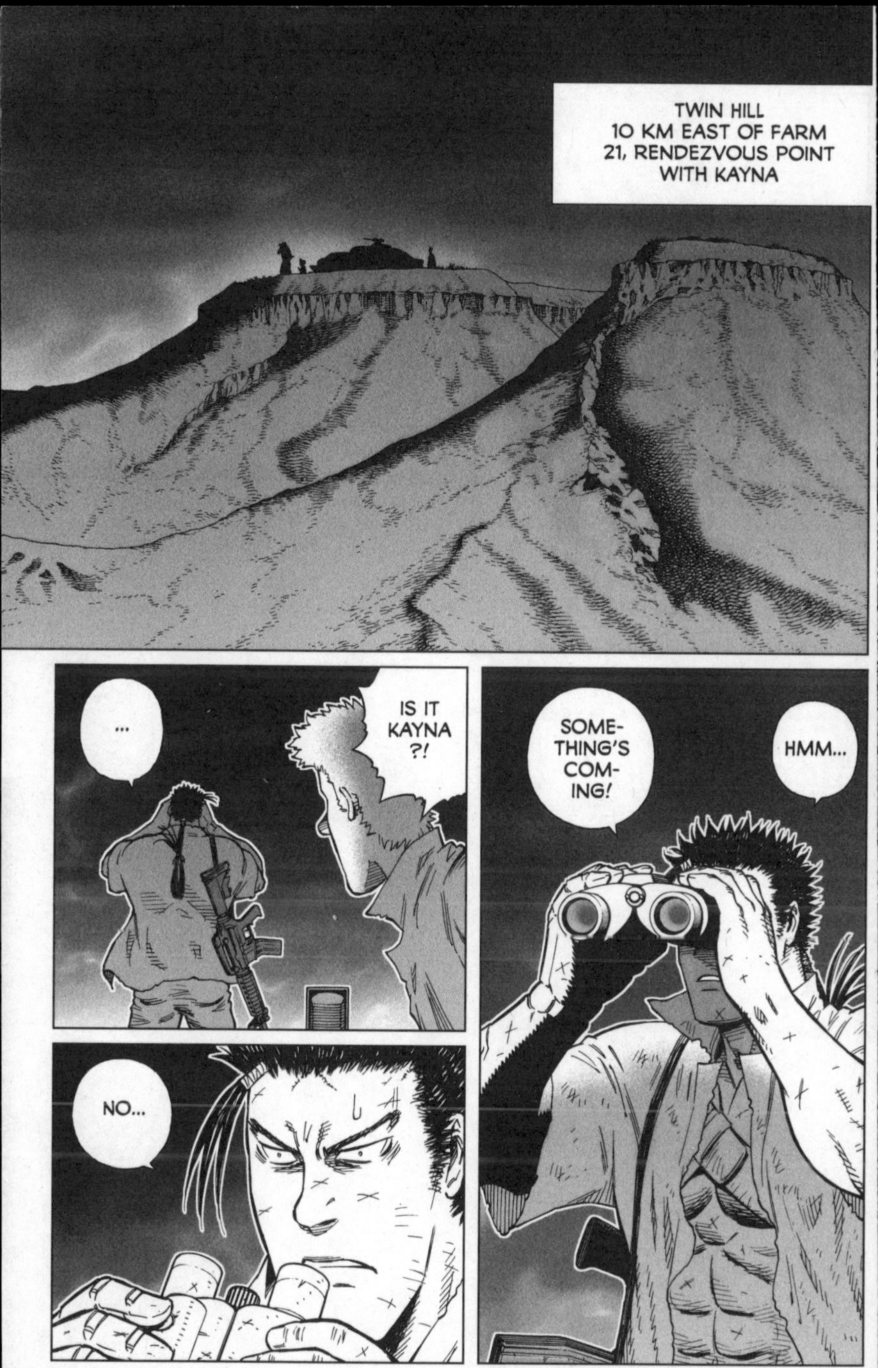
TWIN HILL 10 KM EAST OF FARM 21, RENDEZVOUS POINT WITH KAYNA
HMM...
SOME-THING'S COM-ING!
IS IT KAYNA ?!
...
NO...

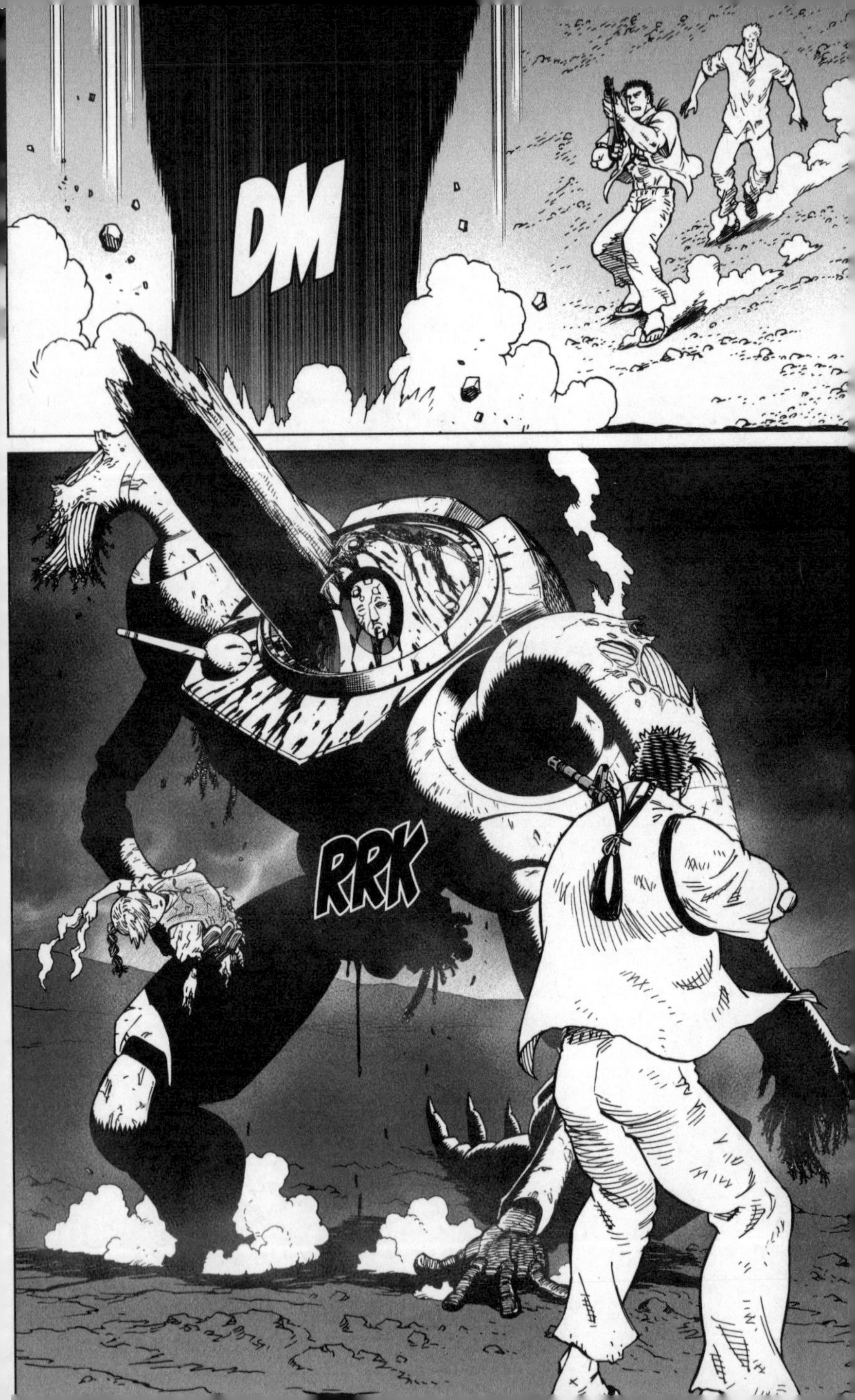
DM
RRK

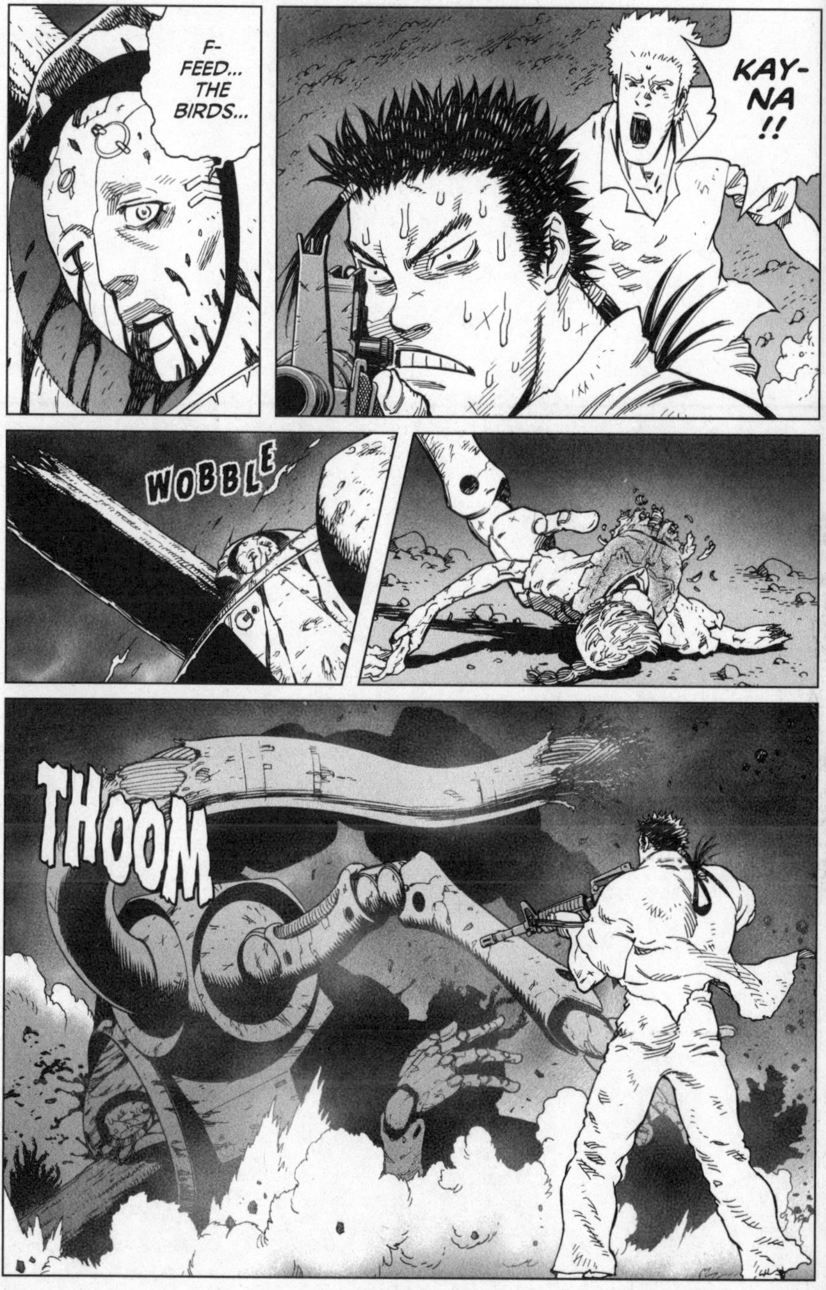
KAY-
NA
!!
F-
FEED... THE BIRDS...
WOBBLE
THOOM

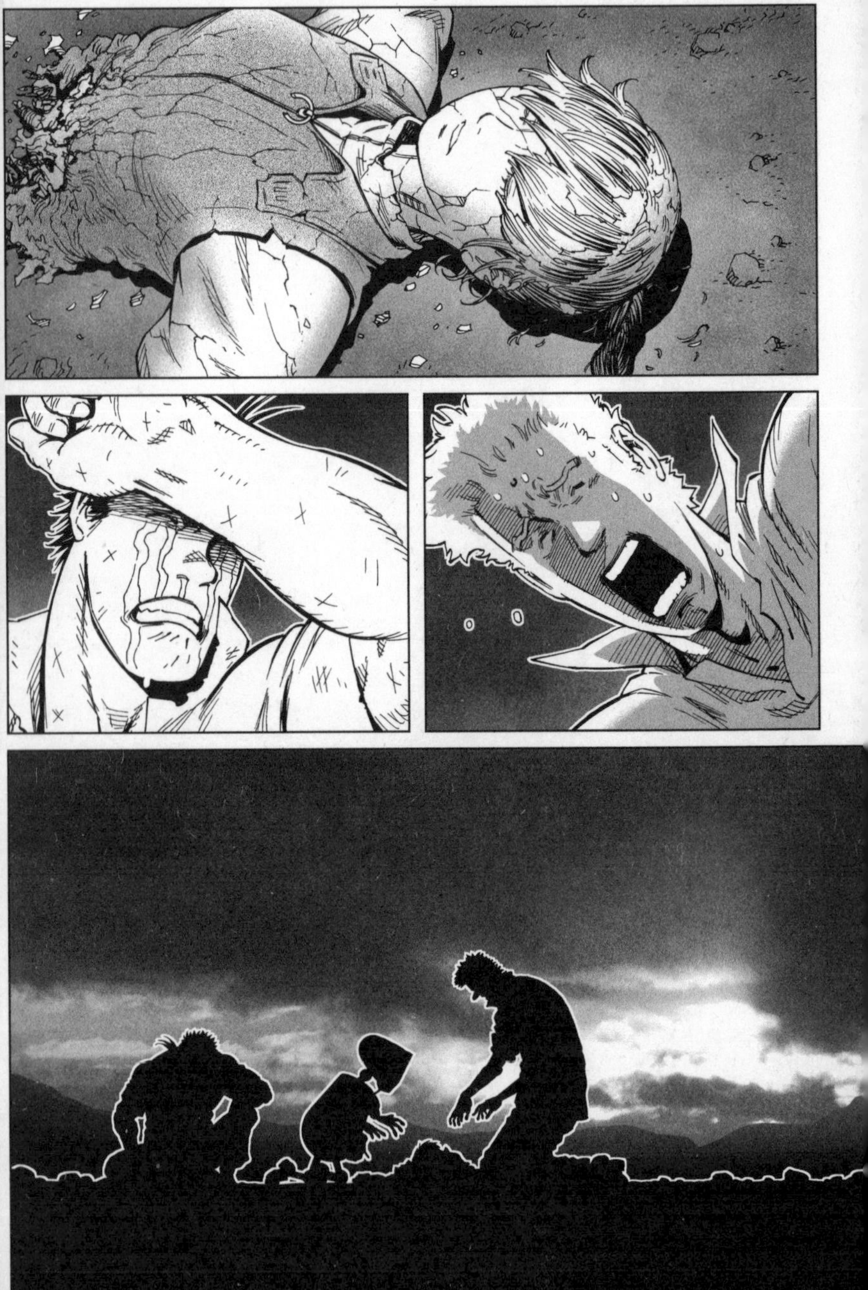

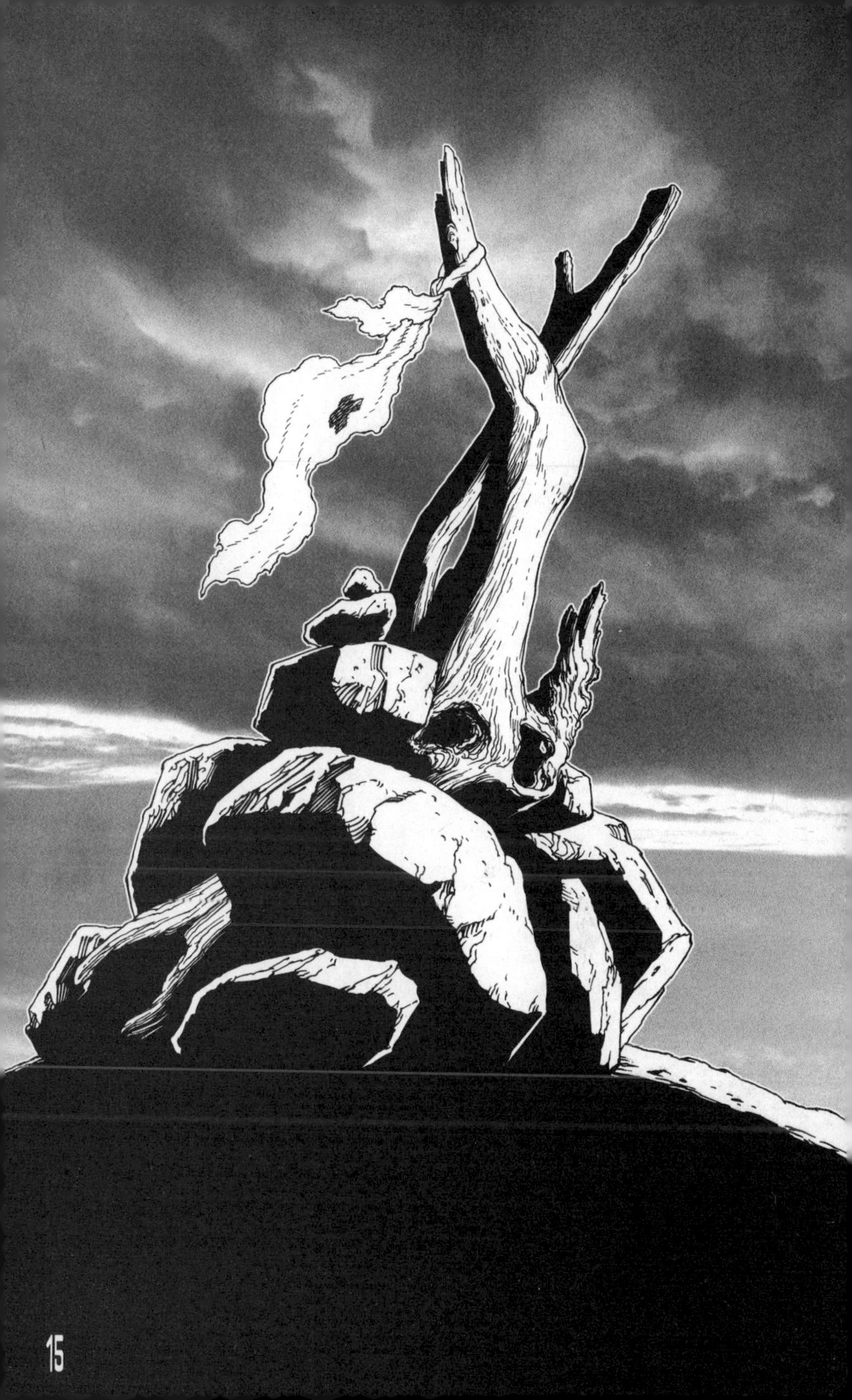

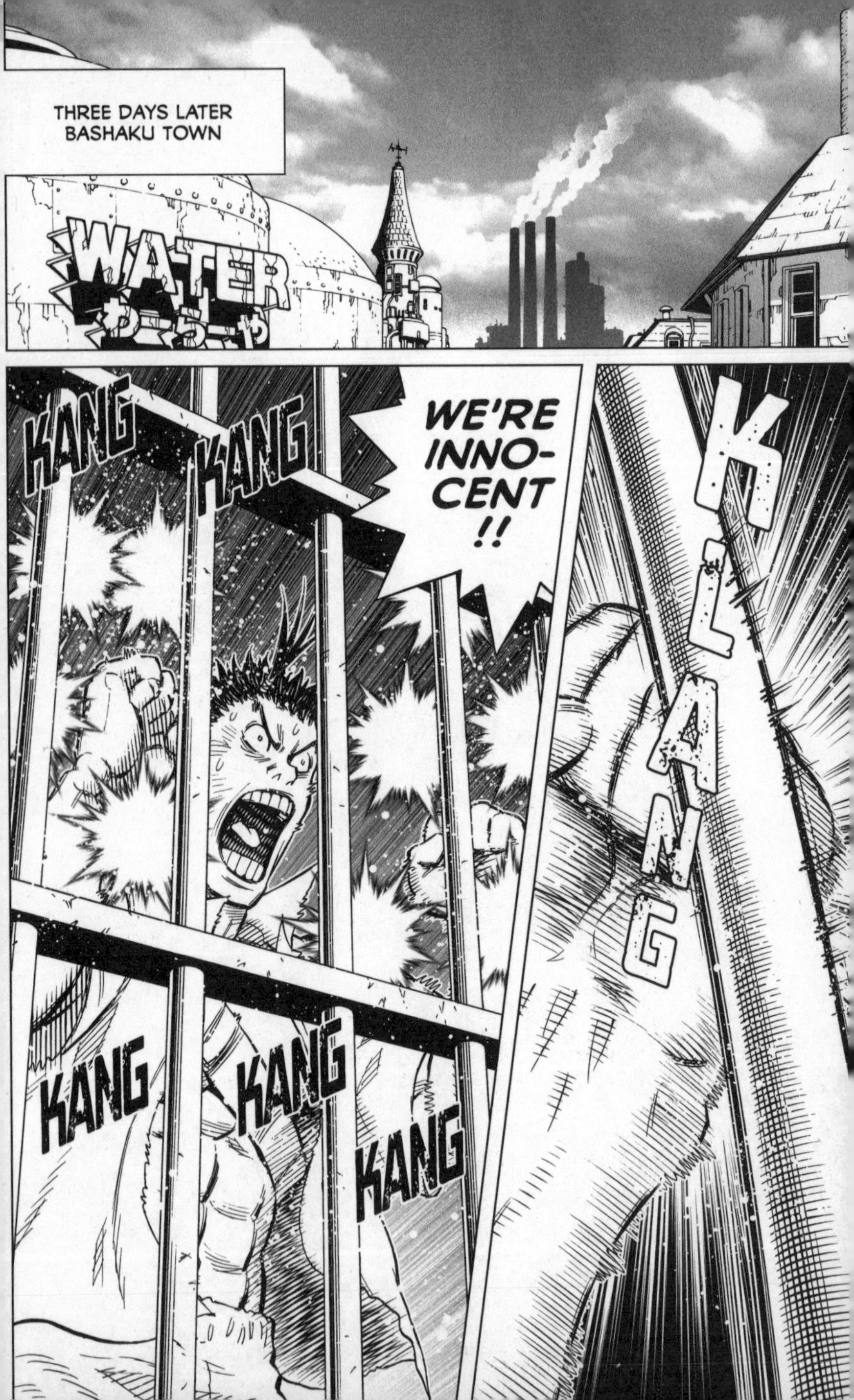
THREE DAYS LATER
BASHAKU TOWN
WATER
KLANG
KANG
KANG
WE'RE INNO-CENT!!
KANG
KANG
KANG

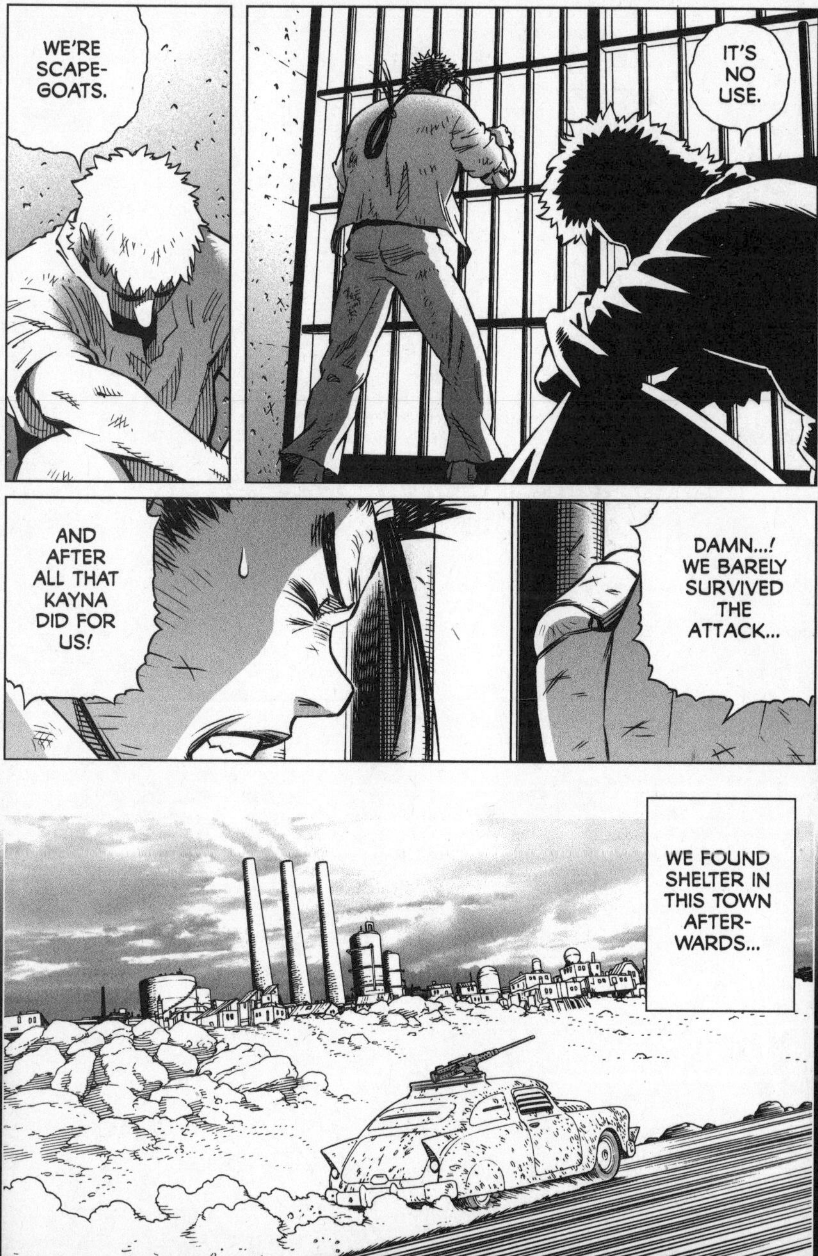
IT'S NO USE.
WE'RE SCAPE-GOATS.
DAMN...! WE BARELY SURVIVED THE ATTACK...
AND AFTER ALL THAT KAYNA DID FOR US!
WE FOUND SHELTER IN THIS TOWN AFTER-WARDS...

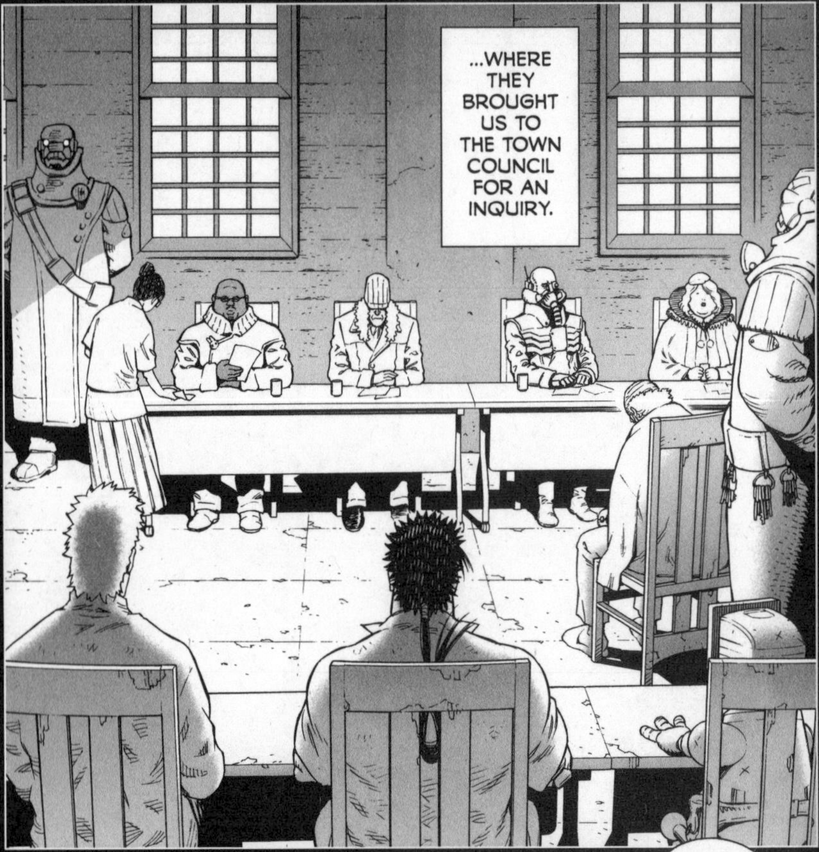
...WHERE THEY BROUGHT US TO THE TOWN COUNCIL FOR AN INQUIRY.
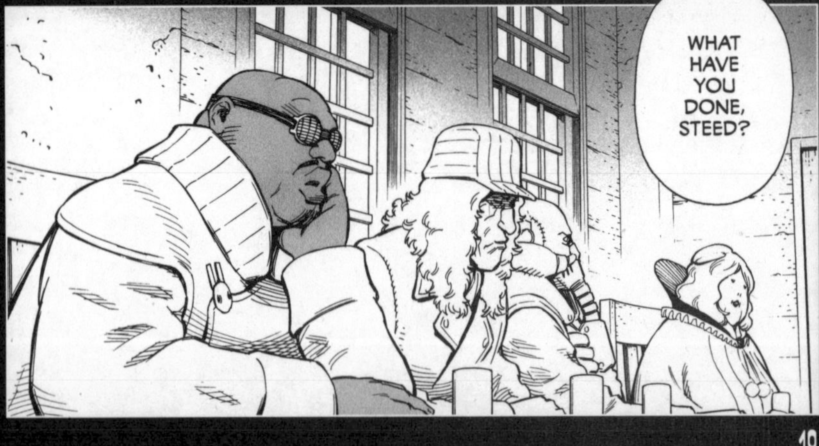
WHAT HAVE YOU DONE, STEED?

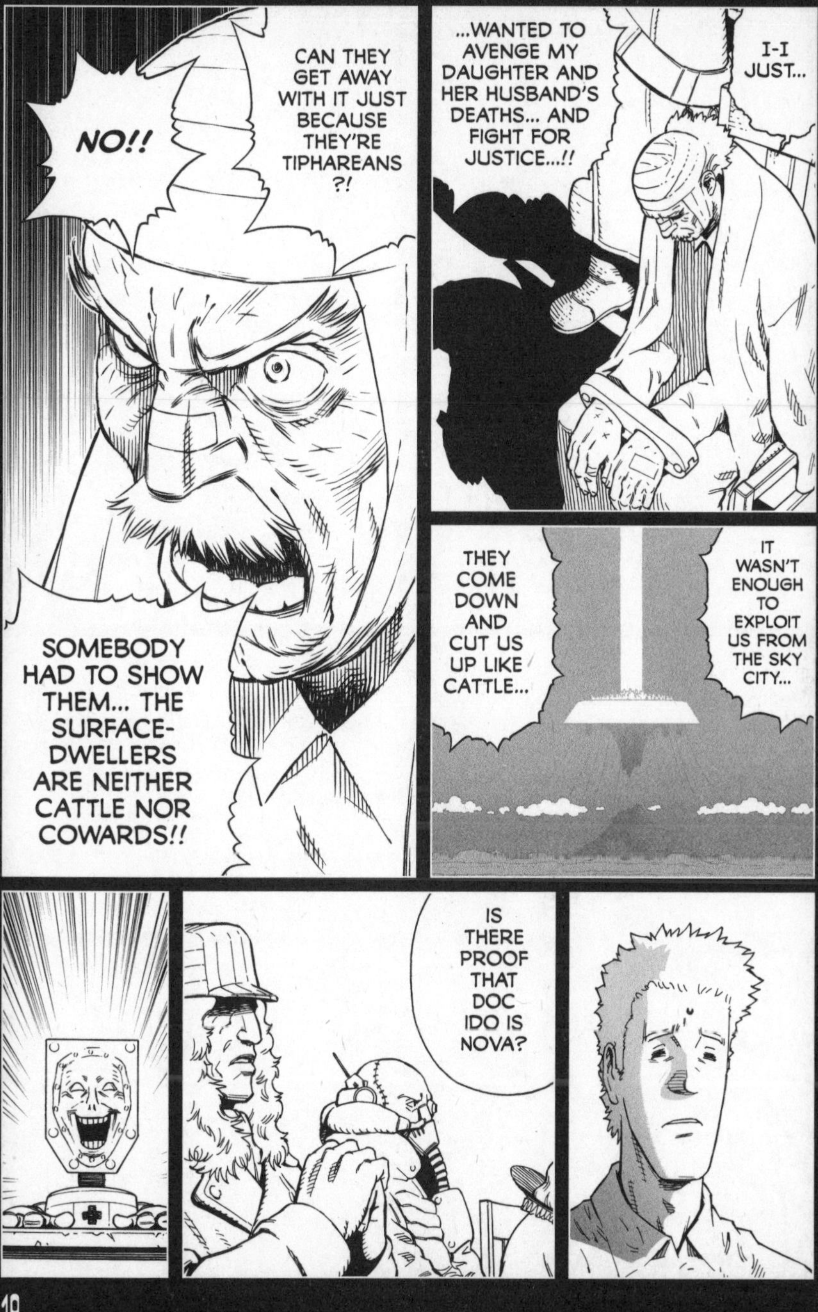

I-I JUST...
...WANTED TO AVENGE MY DAUGHTER AND HER HUSBAND'S DEATHS... AND FIGHT FOR JUSTICE...!!
IT WASN'T ENOUGH TO EXPLOIT US FROM THE SKY CITY...
THEY COME DOWN AND CUT US UP LIKE CATTLE...
CAN THEY GET AWAY WITH IT JUST BECAUSE THEY'RE TIPHAREANS ?!
NO!!
SOMEBODY HAD TO SHOW THEM... THE SURFACE-DWELLERS ARE NEITHER CATTLE NOR COWARDS!!
IS THERE PROOF THAT DOC IDO IS NOVA?

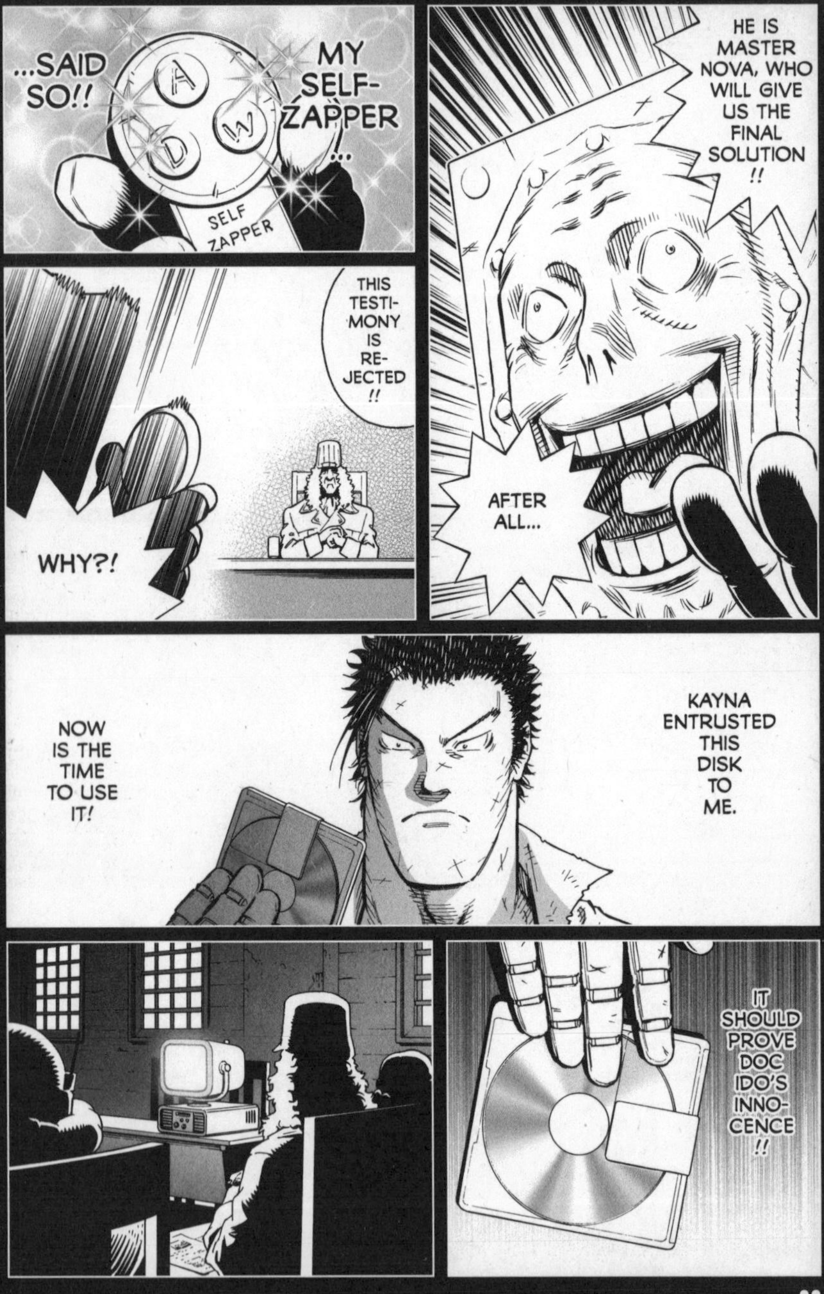
HE IS MASTER NOVA, WHO WILL GIVE US THE FINAL SOLUTION!!
AFTER ALL...
MY SELF-ZAPPER...
SELF ZAPPER
...SAID SO!!
THIS TESTIMONY IS REJECTED!!
WHY?!
KAYNA ENTRUSTED THIS DISK TO ME.
NOW IS THE TIME TO USE IT!
IT SHOULD PROVE DOC IDO'S INNOCENCE!!

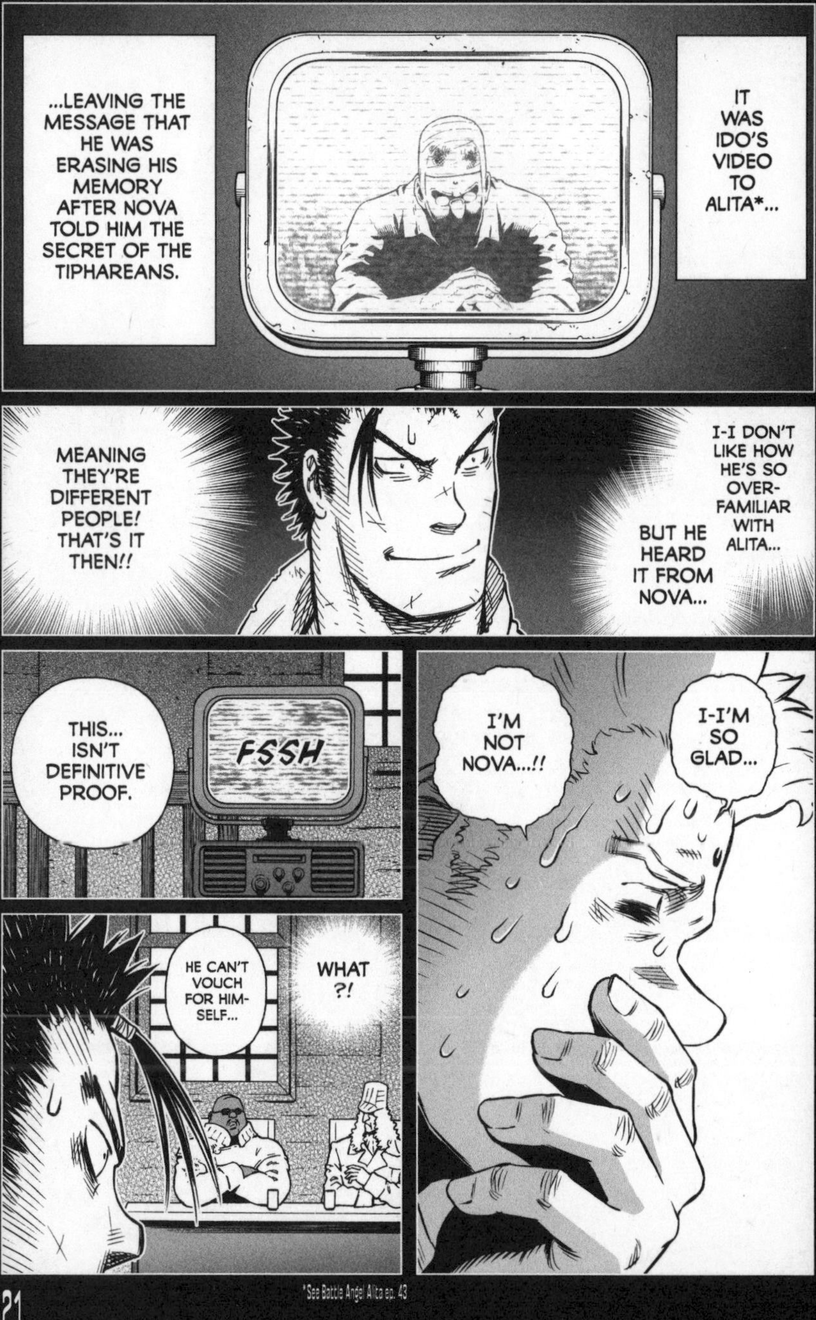
IT WAS IDO'S VIDEO TO ALITA*...
...LEAVING THE MESSAGE THAT HE WAS ERASING HIS MEMORY AFTER NOVA TOLD HIM THE SECRET OF THE TIPHAREANS.
I-I DON'T LIKE HOW HE'S SO OVER-FAMILIAR WITH ALITA...
BUT HE HEARD IT FROM NOVA...
MEANING THEY'RE DIFFERENT PEOPLE! THAT'S IT THEN!!
I-I'M SO GLAD...
I'M NOT NOVA...!!
THIS... ISN'T DEFINITIVE PROOF.
FSSH
WHAT ?!
HE CAN'T VOUCH FOR HIM-SELF...

*See Battle Angel Alita ep. 43

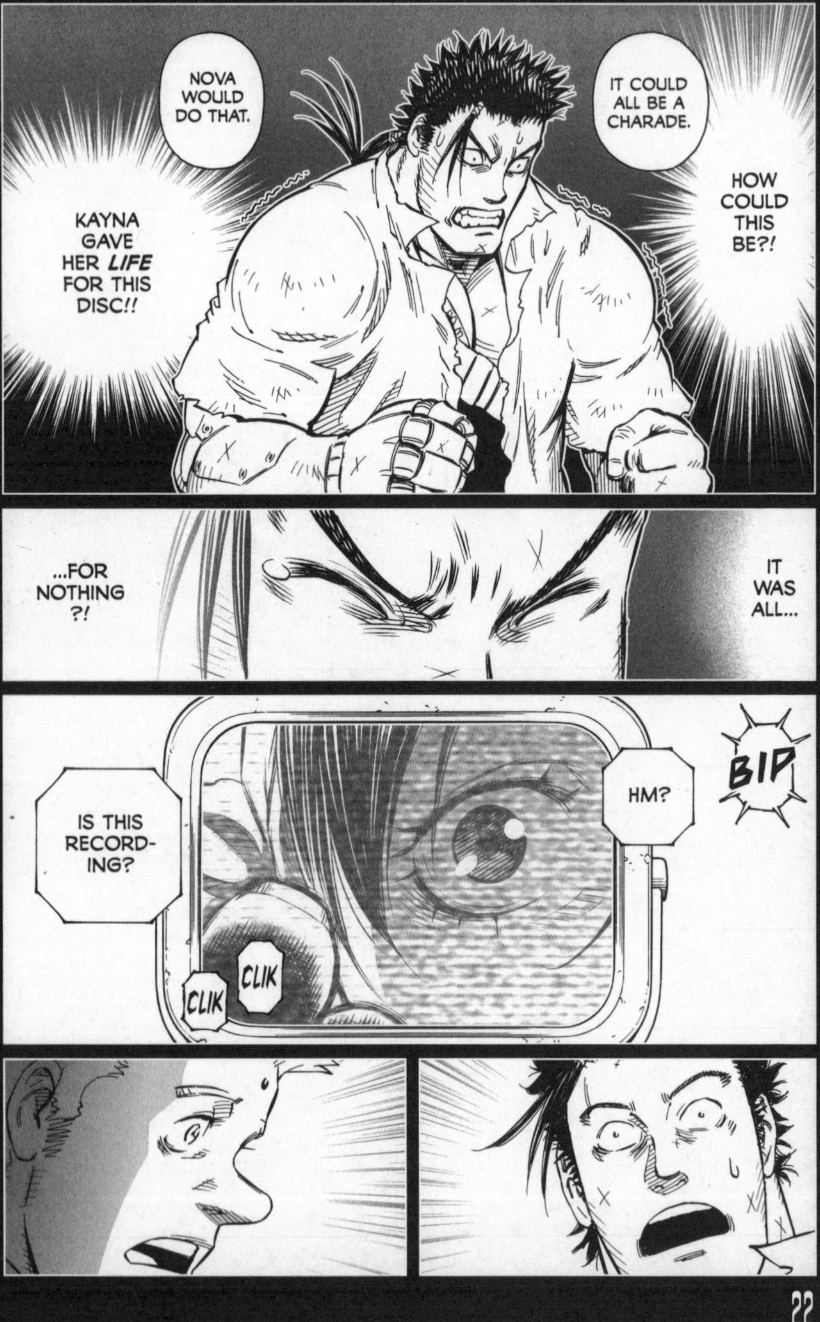
IT COULD ALL BE A CHARADE.
HOW COULD THIS BE?!
NOVA WOULD DO THAT.
KAYNA GAVE HER *LIFE* FOR THIS DISC!!
IT WAS ALL...
...FOR NOTHING ?!
BIP
HM?
IS THIS RECORD-ING?
CLIK
CLIK

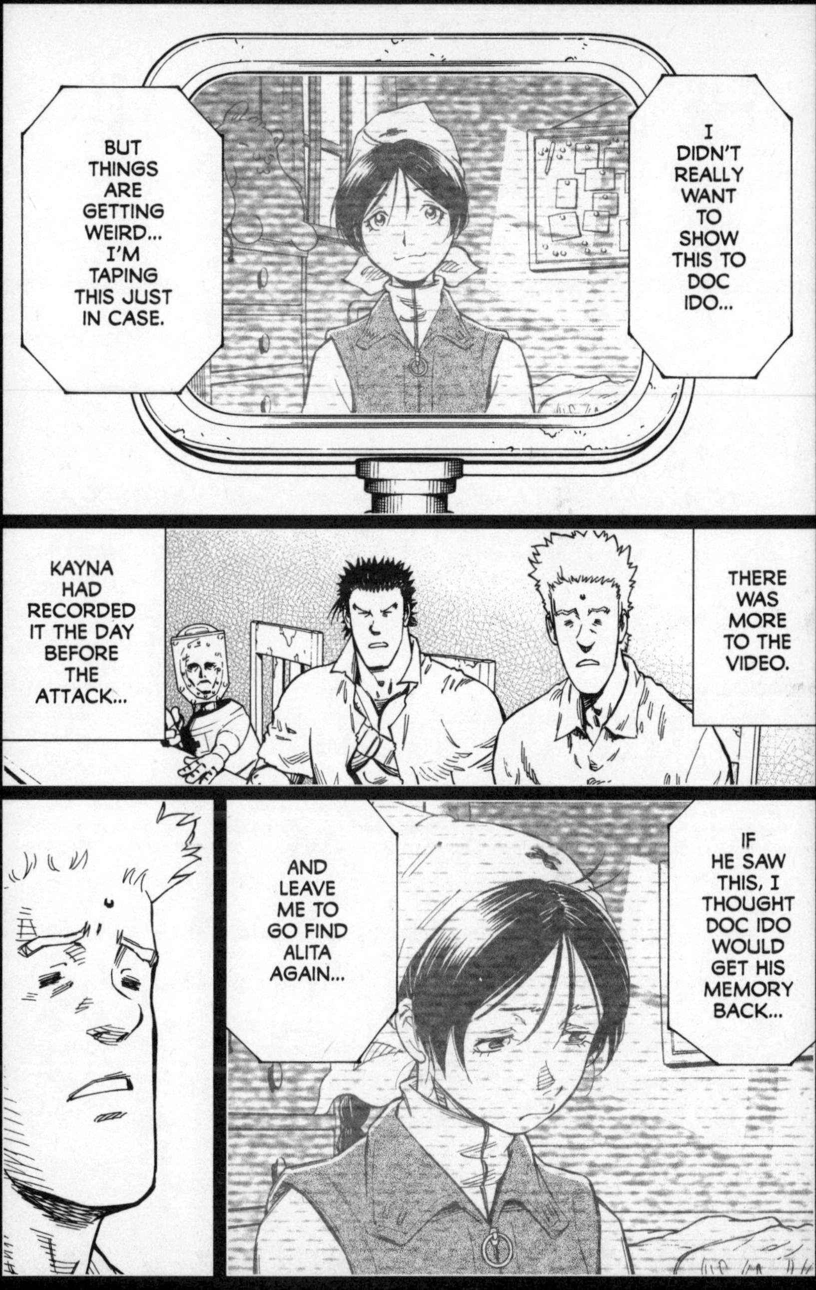
I DIDN'T REALLY WANT TO SHOW THIS TO DOC IDO...
BUT THINGS ARE GETTING WEIRD... I'M TAPING THIS JUST IN CASE.
THERE WAS MORE TO THE VIDEO.
KAYNA HAD RECORDED IT THE DAY BEFORE THE ATTACK...
IF HE SAW THIS, I THOUGHT DOC IDO WOULD GET HIS MEMORY BACK...
AND LEAVE ME TO GO FIND ALITA AGAIN...

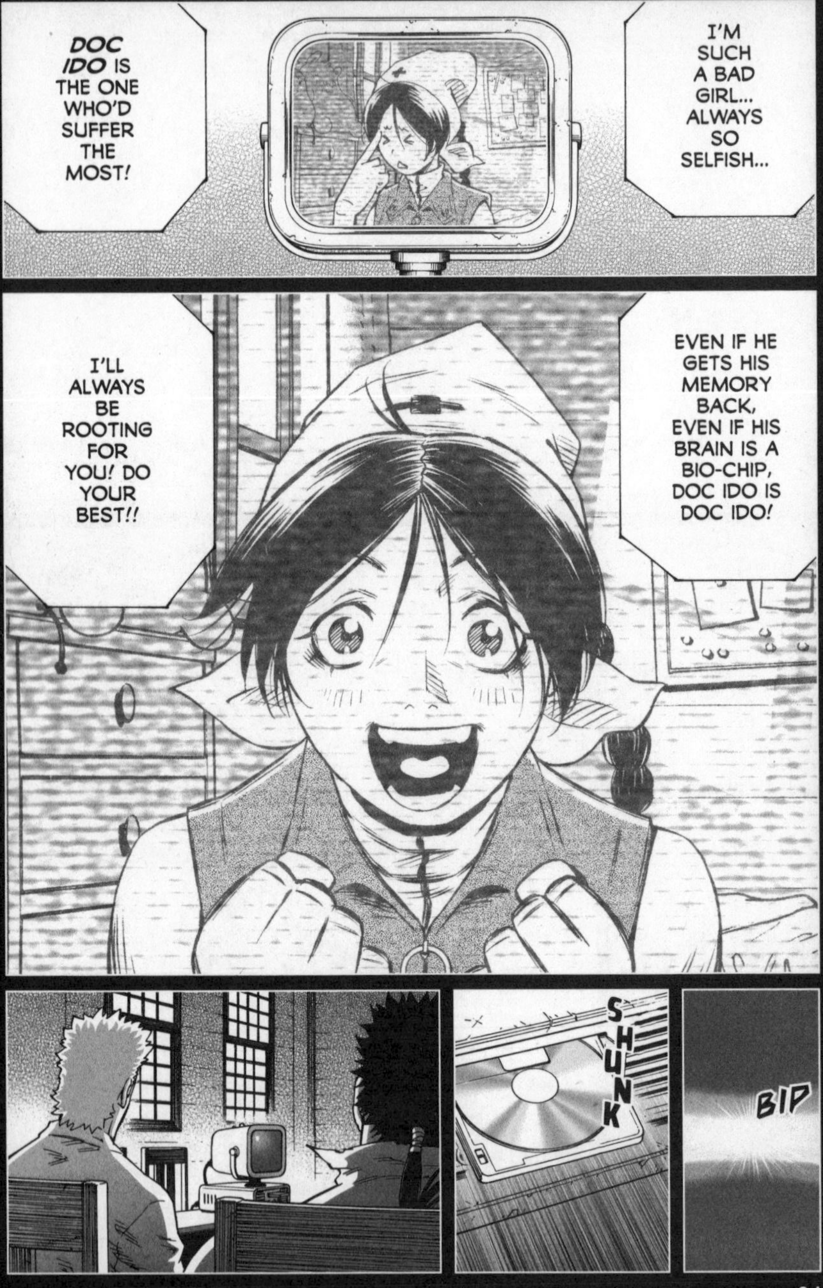
I'M SUCH A BAD GIRL... ALWAYS SO SELFISH...
DOC IDO IS THE ONE WHO'D SUFFER THE MOST!
EVEN IF HE GETS HIS MEMORY BACK, EVEN IF HIS BRAIN IS A BIO-CHIP, DOC IDO IS DOC IDO!
I'LL ALWAYS BE ROOTING FOR YOU! DO YOUR BEST!!
BIP
SHUNK

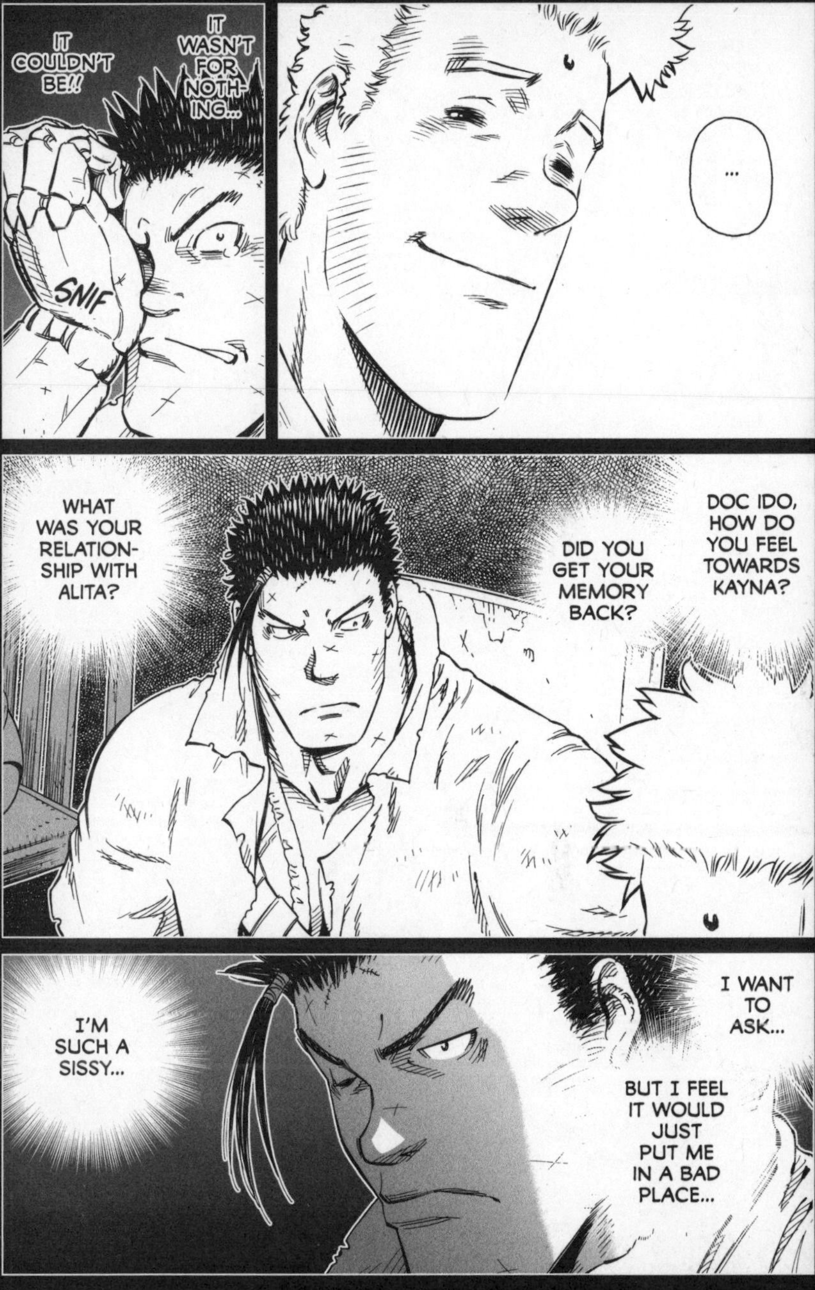
...
IT WASN'T FOR NOTHING...
IT COULDN'T BE!!
SNIF
DOC IDO, HOW DO YOU FEEL TOWARDS KAYNA?
DID YOU GET YOUR MEMORY BACK?
WHAT WAS YOUR RELATIONSHIP WITH ALITA?
I WANT TO ASK...
BUT I FEEL IT WOULD JUST PUT ME IN A BAD PLACE...
I'M SUCH A SISSY...

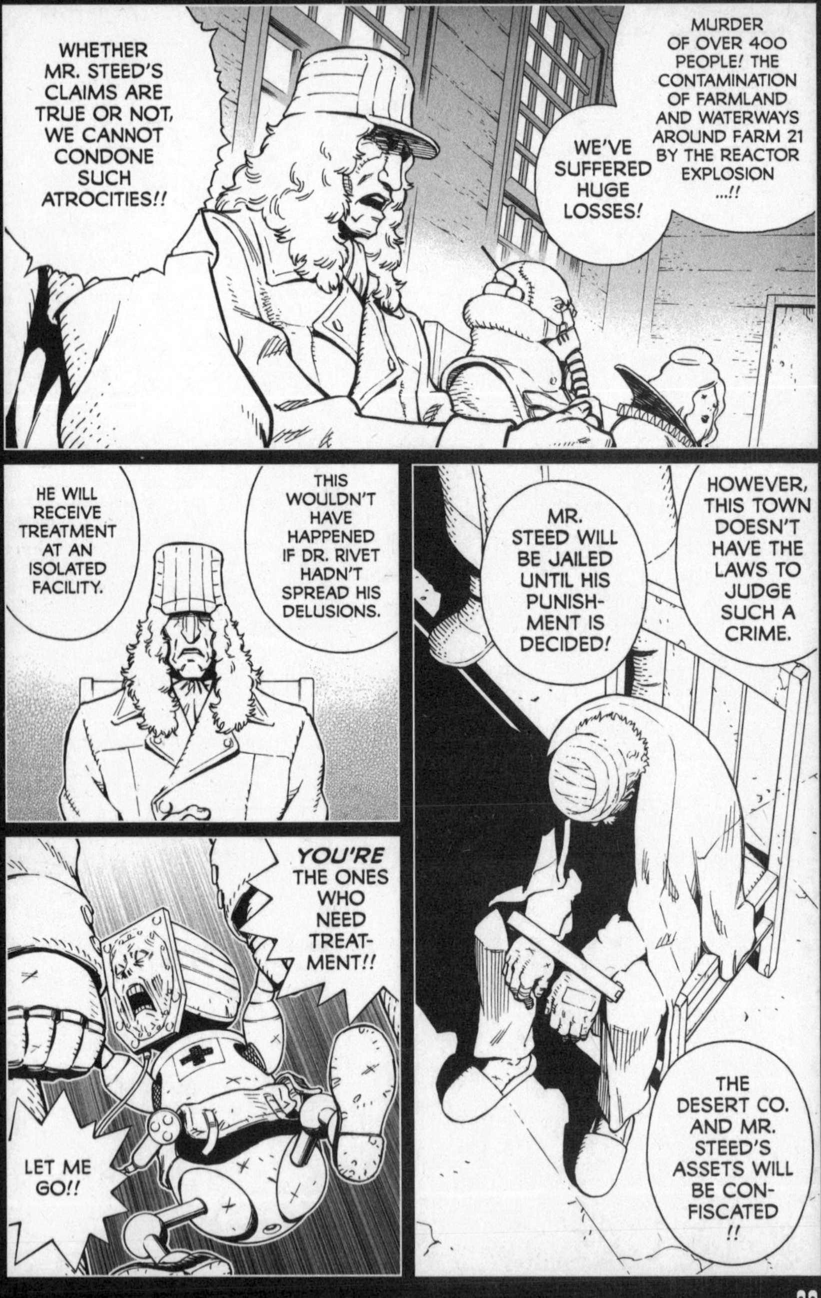
MURDER OF OVER 400 PEOPLE! THE CONTAMINATION OF FARMLAND AND WATERWAYS AROUND FARM 21 BY THE REACTOR EXPLOSION ...!!
WE'VE SUFFERED HUGE LOSSES!
WHETHER MR. STEED'S CLAIMS ARE TRUE OR NOT, WE CANNOT CONDONE SUCH ATROCITIES!!
HOWEVER, THIS TOWN DOESN'T HAVE THE LAWS TO JUDGE SUCH A CRIME.
MR. STEED WILL BE JAILED UNTIL HIS PUNISHMENT IS DECIDED!
THE DESERT CO. AND MR. STEED'S ASSETS WILL BE CONFISCATED !!
THIS WOULDN'T HAVE HAPPENED IF DR. RIVET HADN'T SPREAD HIS DELUSIONS.
HE WILL RECEIVE TREATMENT AT AN ISOLATED FACILITY.
YOU'RE THE ONES WHO NEED TREATMENT!!
LET ME GO!!

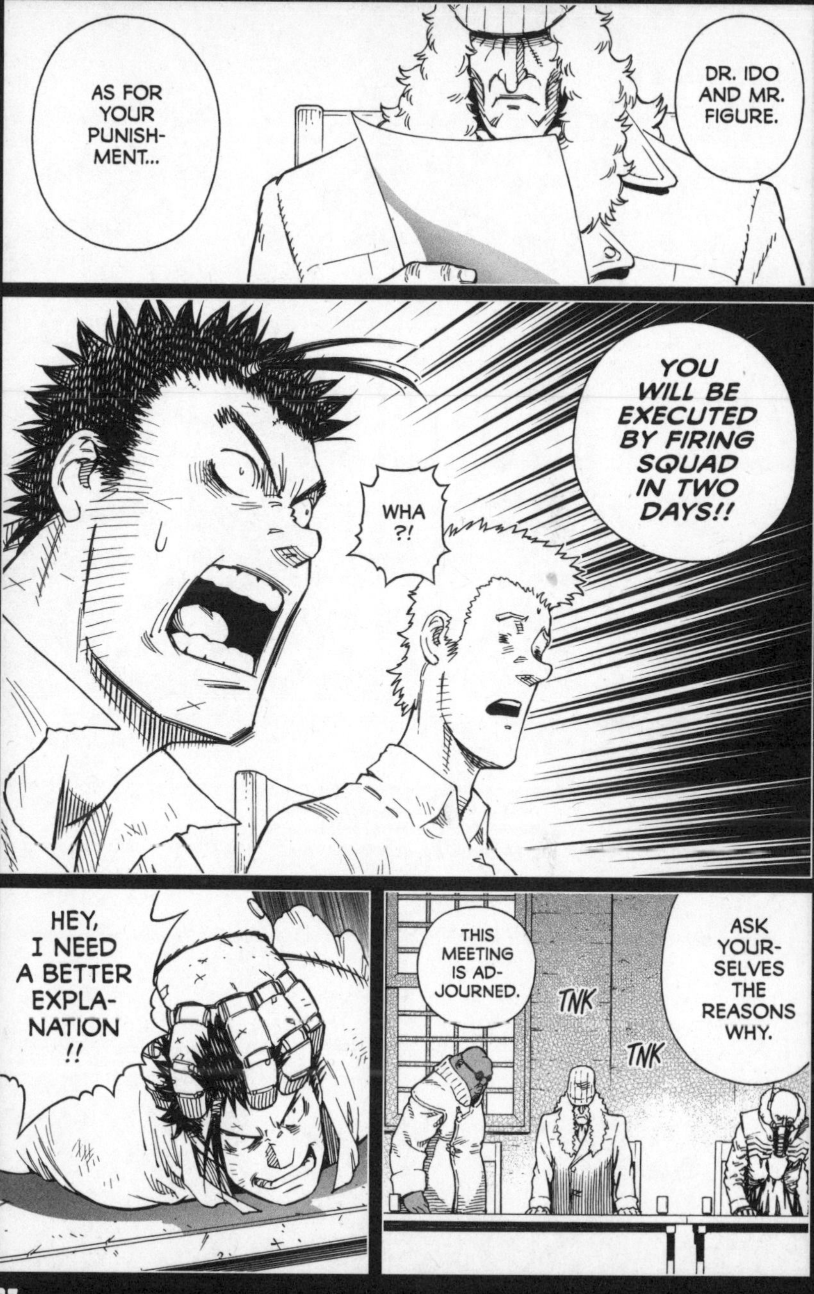
DR. IDO AND MR. FIGURE.
AS FOR YOUR PUNISHMENT...
YOU WILL BE EXECUTED BY FIRING SQUAD IN TWO DAYS!!
WHA ?!
ASK YOURSELVES THE REASONS WHY.
THIS MEETING IS ADJOURNED.
TNK
TNK
HEY, I NEED A BETTER EXPLANATION !!

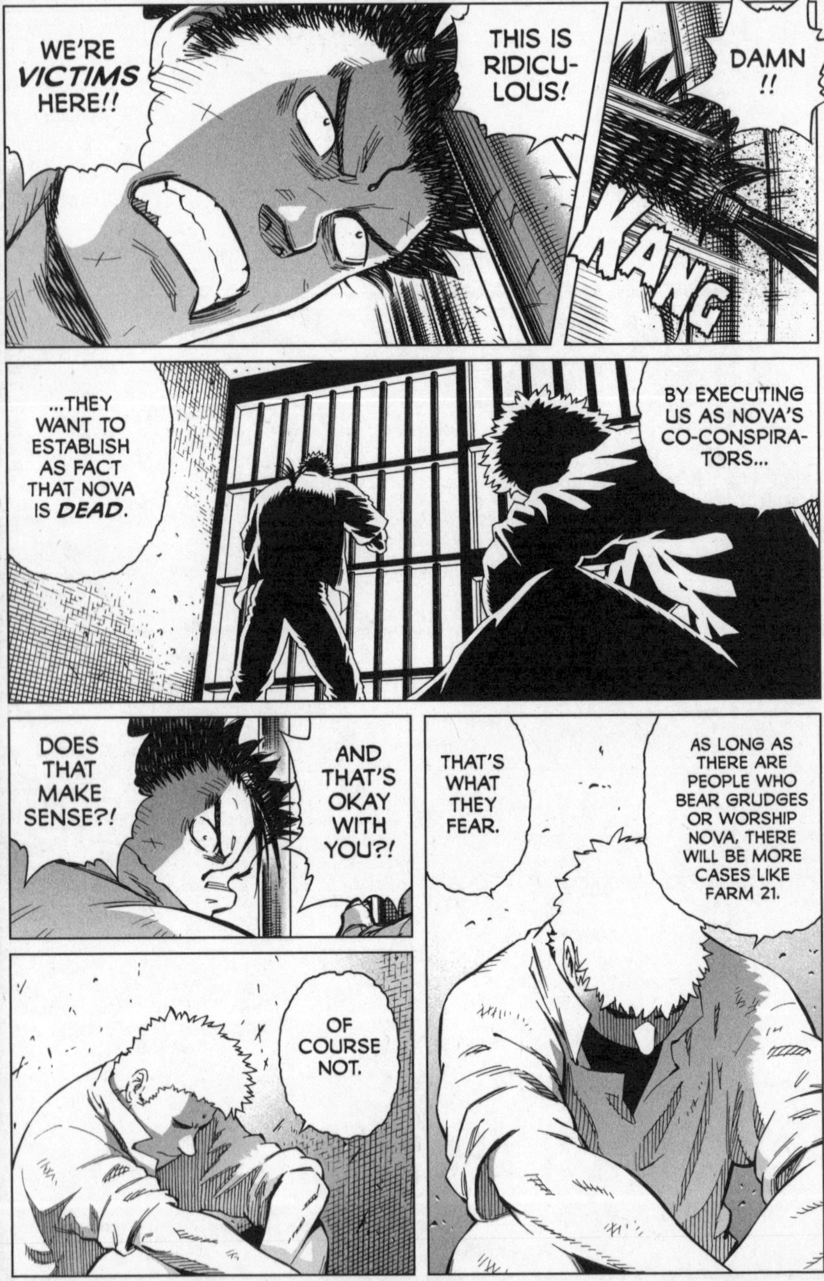
DAMN!!
KANG
THIS IS RIDICULOUS!
WE'RE VICTIMS HERE!!
BY EXECUTING US AS NOVA'S CO-CONSPIRATORS...
...THEY WANT TO ESTABLISH AS FACT THAT NOVA IS DEAD.
AS LONG AS THERE ARE PEOPLE WHO BEAR GRUDGES OR WORSHIP NOVA, THERE WILL BE MORE CASES LIKE FARM 21.
THAT'S WHAT THEY FEAR.
AND THAT'S OKAY WITH YOU?!
DOES THAT MAKE SENSE?!
OF COURSE NOT.

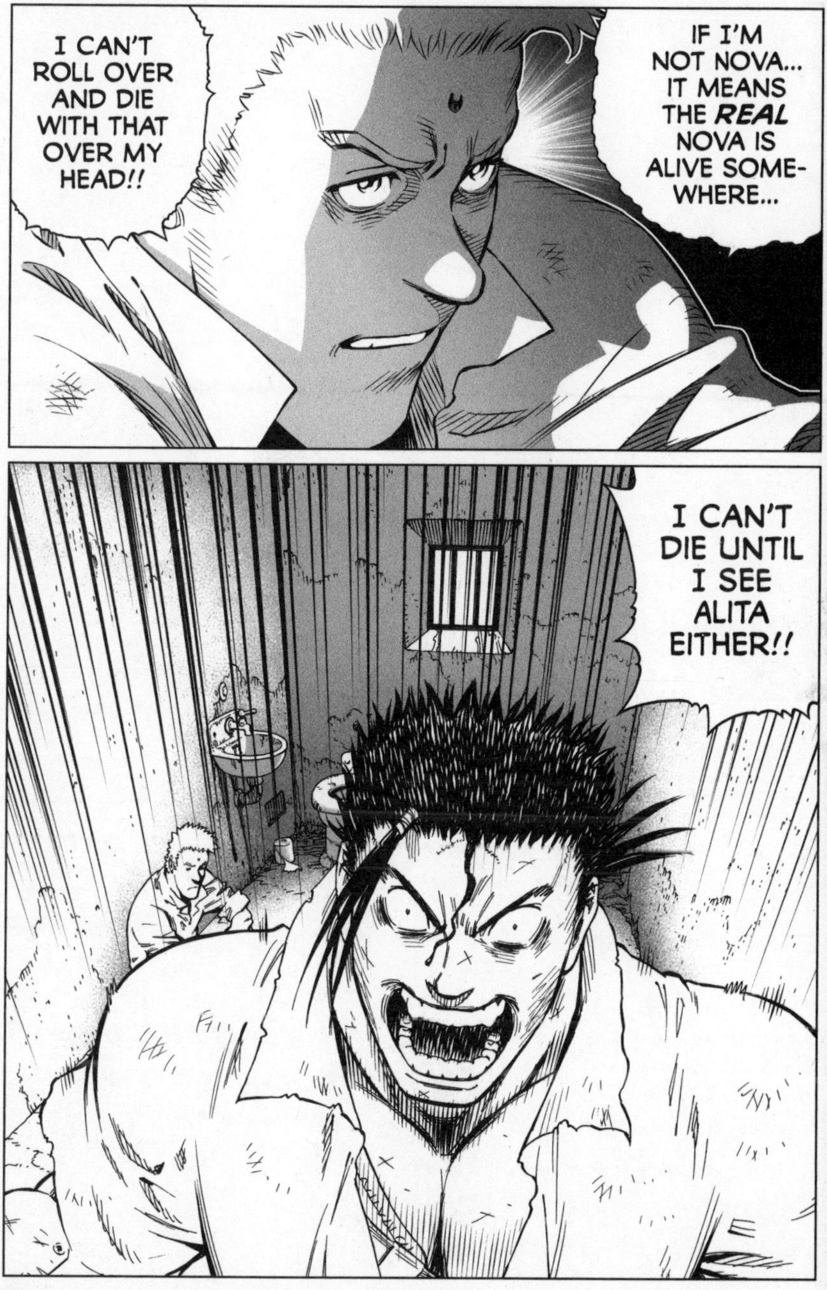
IF I'M NOT NOVA... IT MEANS THE *REAL* NOVA IS ALIVE SOME-WHERE...
I CAN'T ROLL OVER AND DIE WITH THAT OVER MY HEAD!!
I CAN'T DIE UNTIL I SEE ALITA EITHER!!

Phase 117: Alita Quest XI

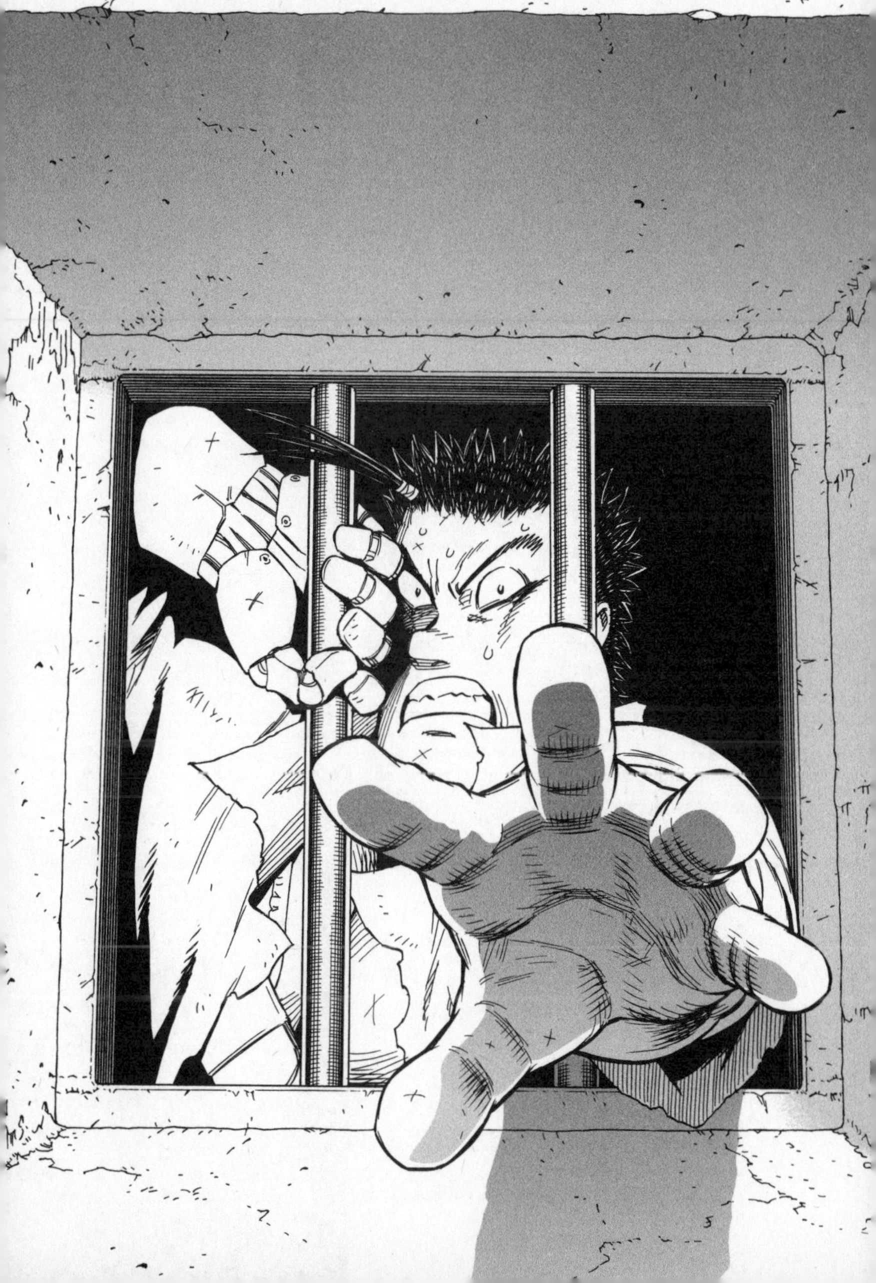

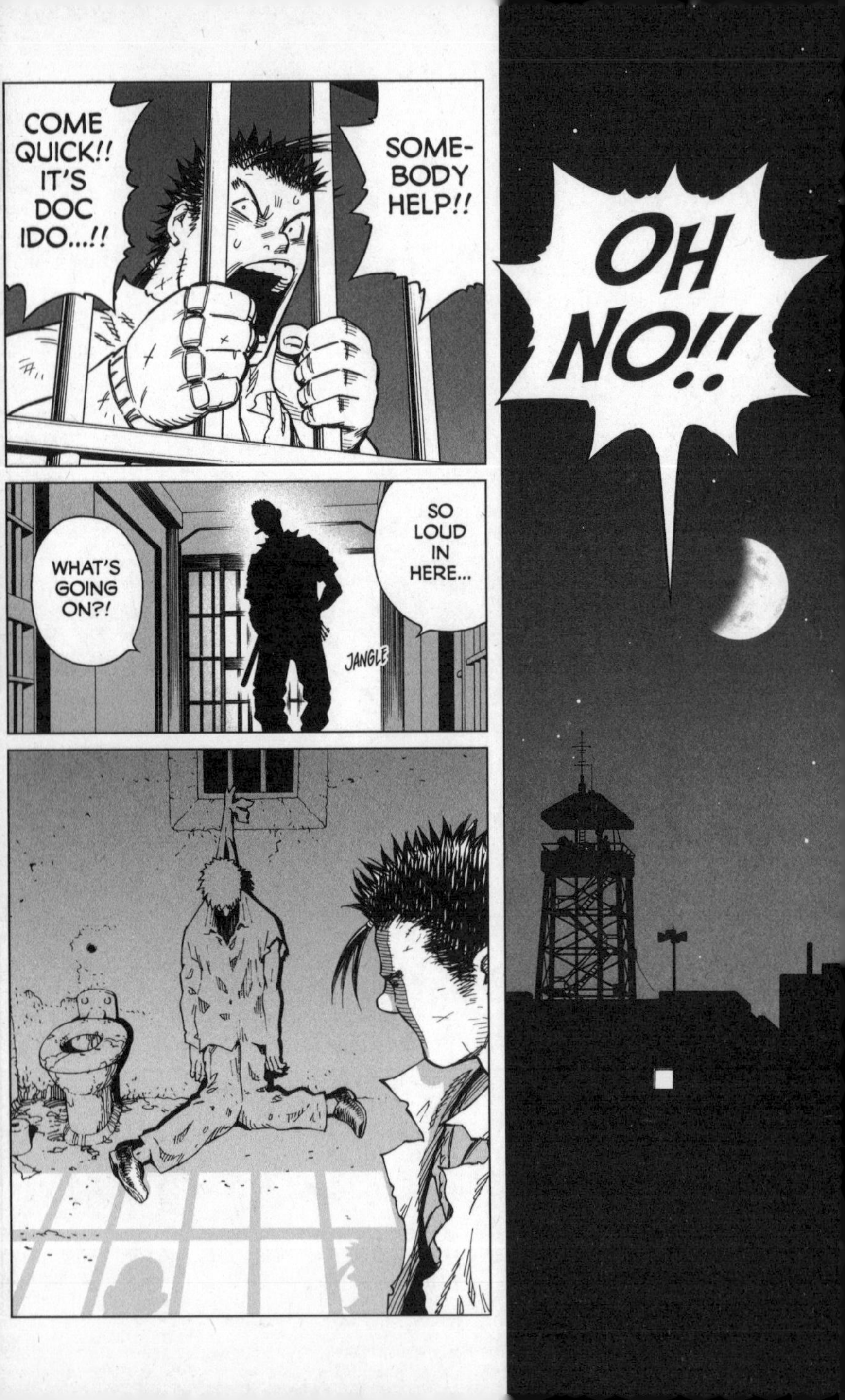
OH NO!!
SOME-BODY HELP!!
COME QUICK!! IT'S DOC IDO...!!
SO LOUD IN HERE...
JANGLE
WHAT'S GOING ON?!

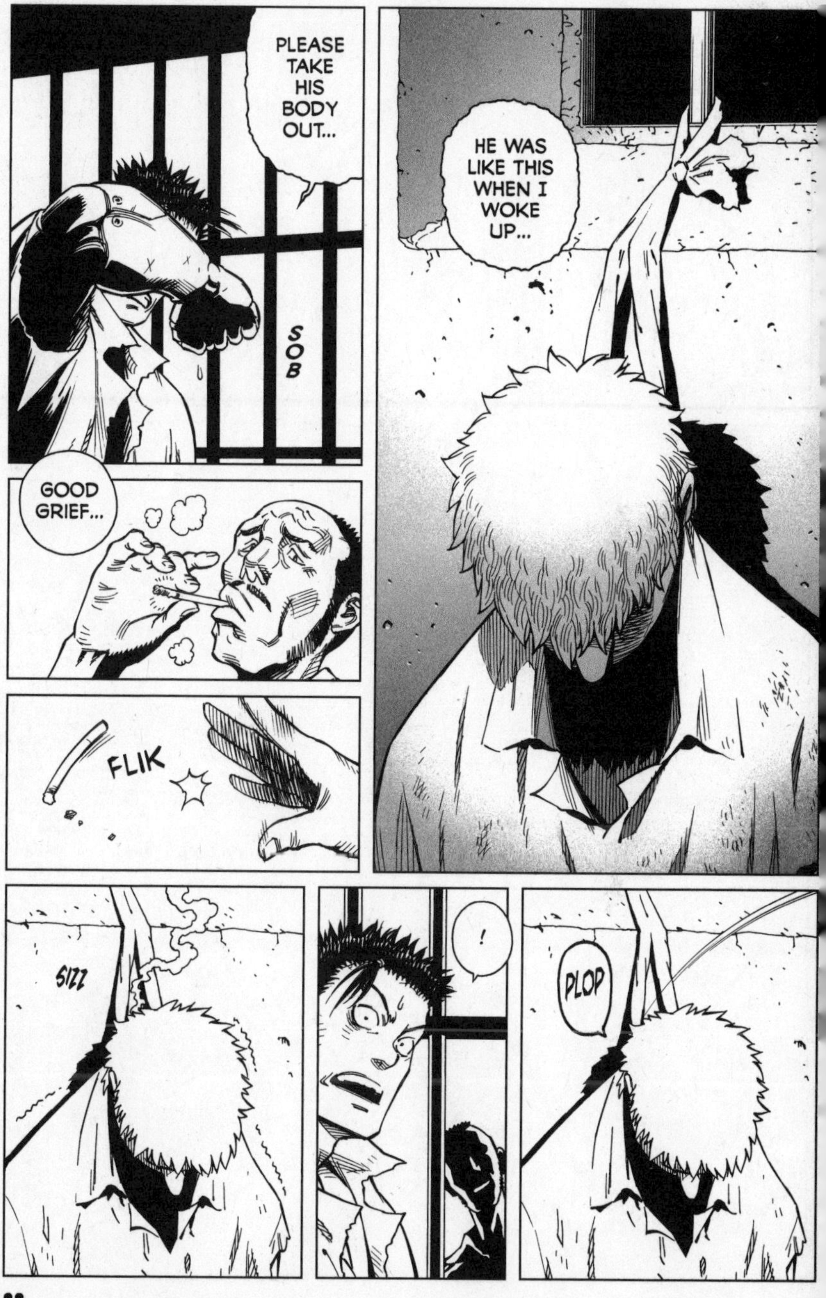

HE WAS LIKE THIS WHEN I WOKE UP...
PLEASE TAKE HIS BODY OUT...
SOB
GOOD GRIEF...
FLIK
PLOP
!
SIZZ

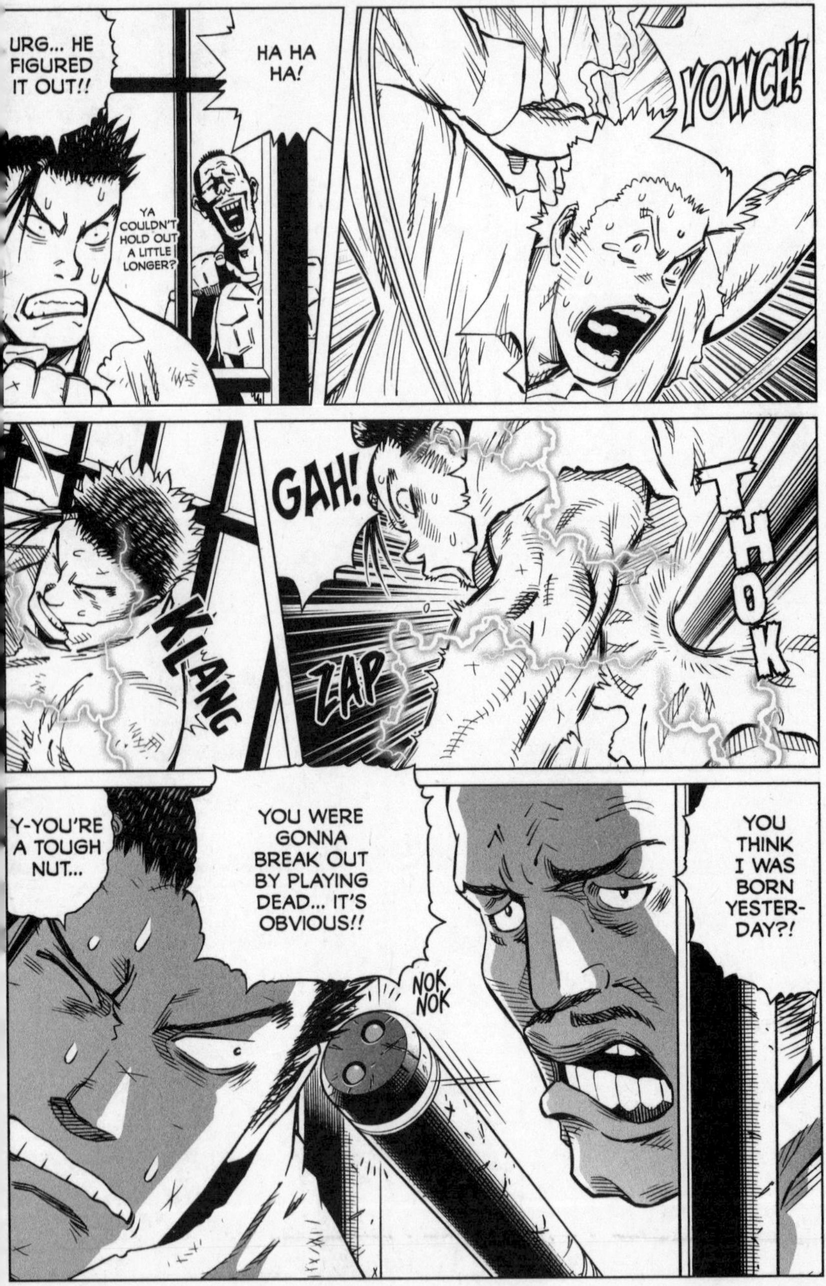
YOWCH!
HA HA HA!
URG... HE FIGURED IT OUT!!
YA COULDN'T HOLD OUT A LITTLE LONGER?
THOK
GAH!
ZAP
KLANG
YOU THINK I WAS BORN YESTER-DAY?!
YOU WERE GONNA BREAK OUT BY PLAYING DEAD... IT'S OBVIOUS!!
Y-YOU'RE A TOUGH NUT...
NOK NOK

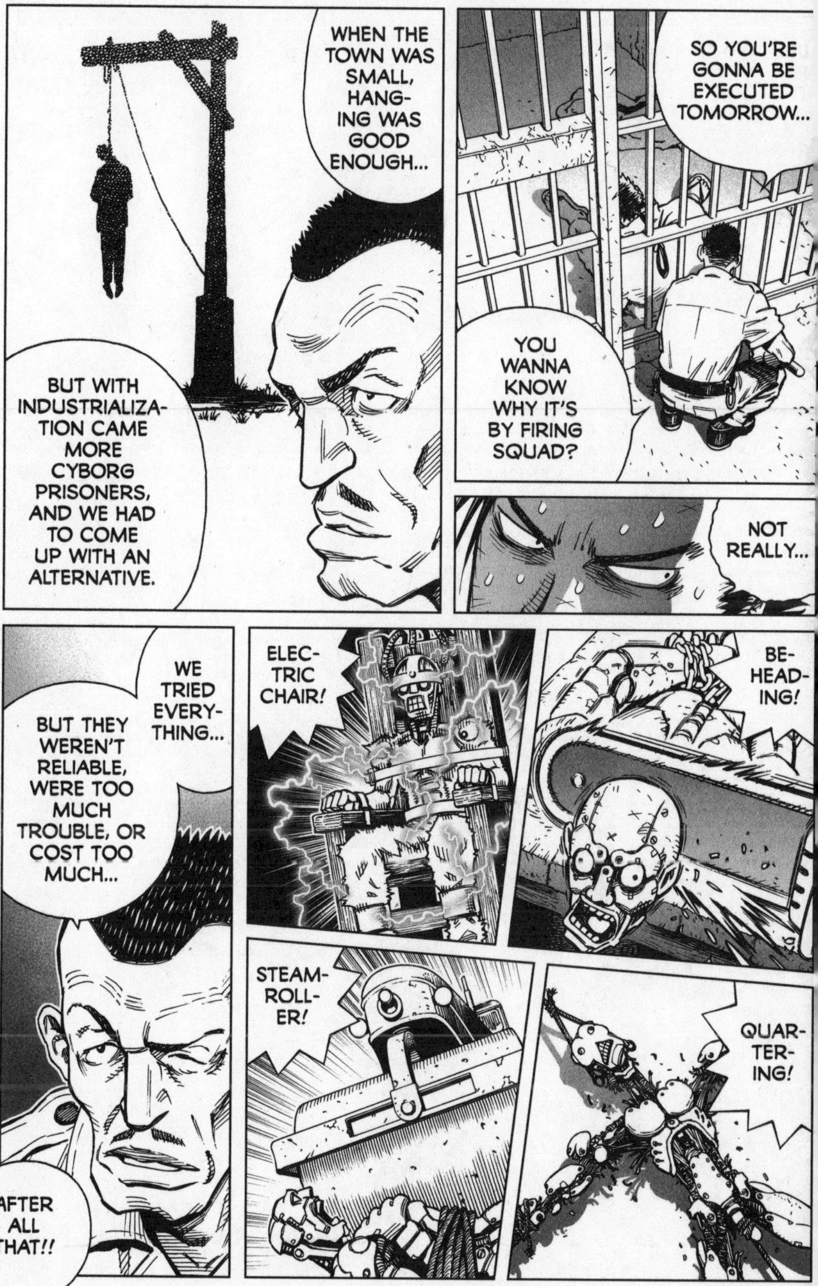
SO YOU'RE GONNA BE EXECUTED TOMORROW...
YOU WANNA KNOW WHY IT'S BY FIRING SQUAD?
NOT REALLY...
WHEN THE TOWN WAS SMALL, HANG-ING WAS GOOD ENOUGH...
BUT WITH INDUSTRIALIZA-TION CAME MORE CYBORG PRISONERS, AND WE HAD TO COME UP WITH AN ALTERNATIVE.
BE-HEAD-ING!
ELEC-TRIC CHAIR!
QUAR-TER-ING!
STEAM-ROLL-ER!
WE TRIED EVERY-THING...
BUT THEY WEREN'T RELIABLE, WERE TOO MUCH TROUBLE, OR COST TOO MUCH...
AFTER ALL THAT!!

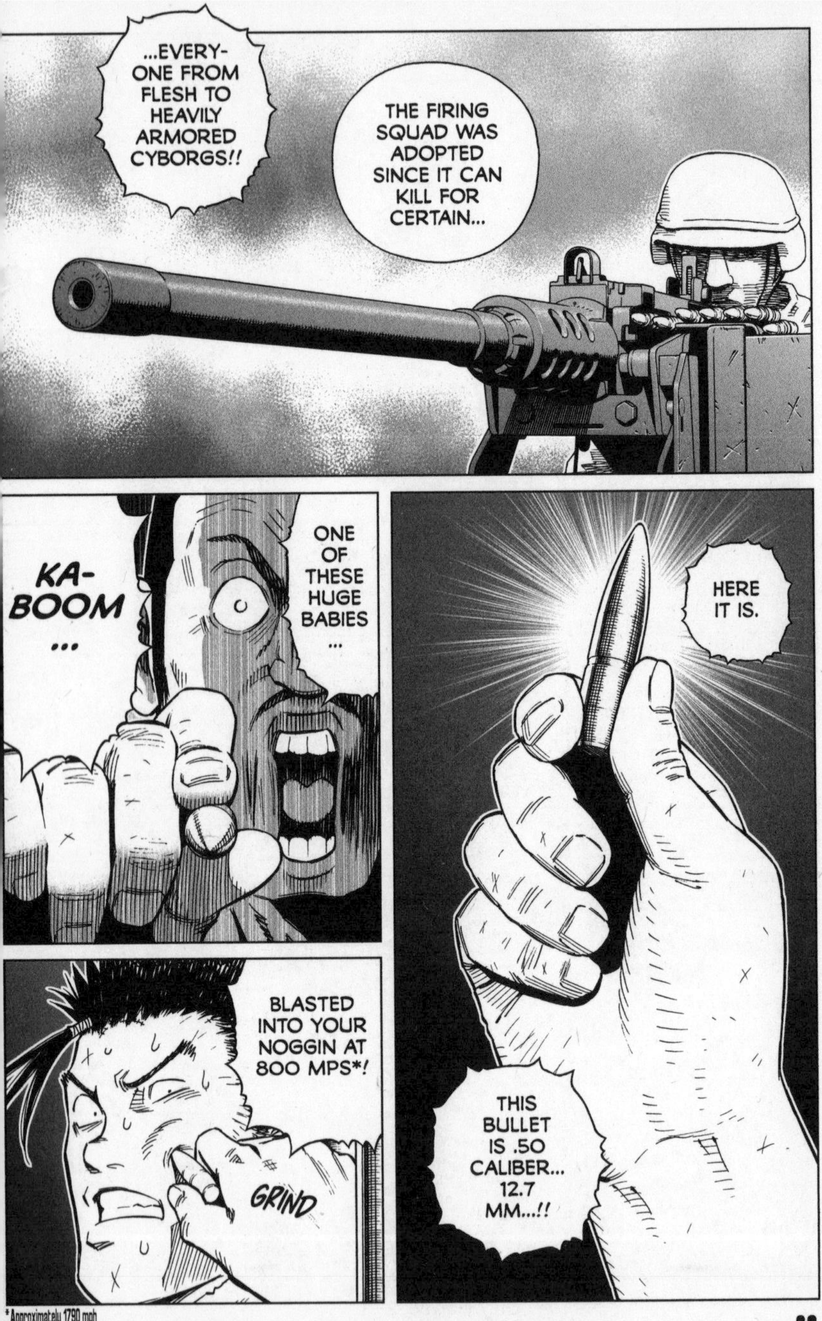
THE FIRING SQUAD WAS ADOPTED SINCE IT CAN KILL FOR CERTAIN...
...EVERY-ONE FROM FLESH TO HEAVILY ARMORED CYBORGS!!
HERE IT IS.
THIS BULLET IS .50 CALIBER... 12.7 MM...!!
ONE OF THESE HUGE BABIES ...
KA-BOOM ...
BLASTED INTO YOUR NOGGIN AT 800 MPS*!
GRIND

*Approximately 1790 mph

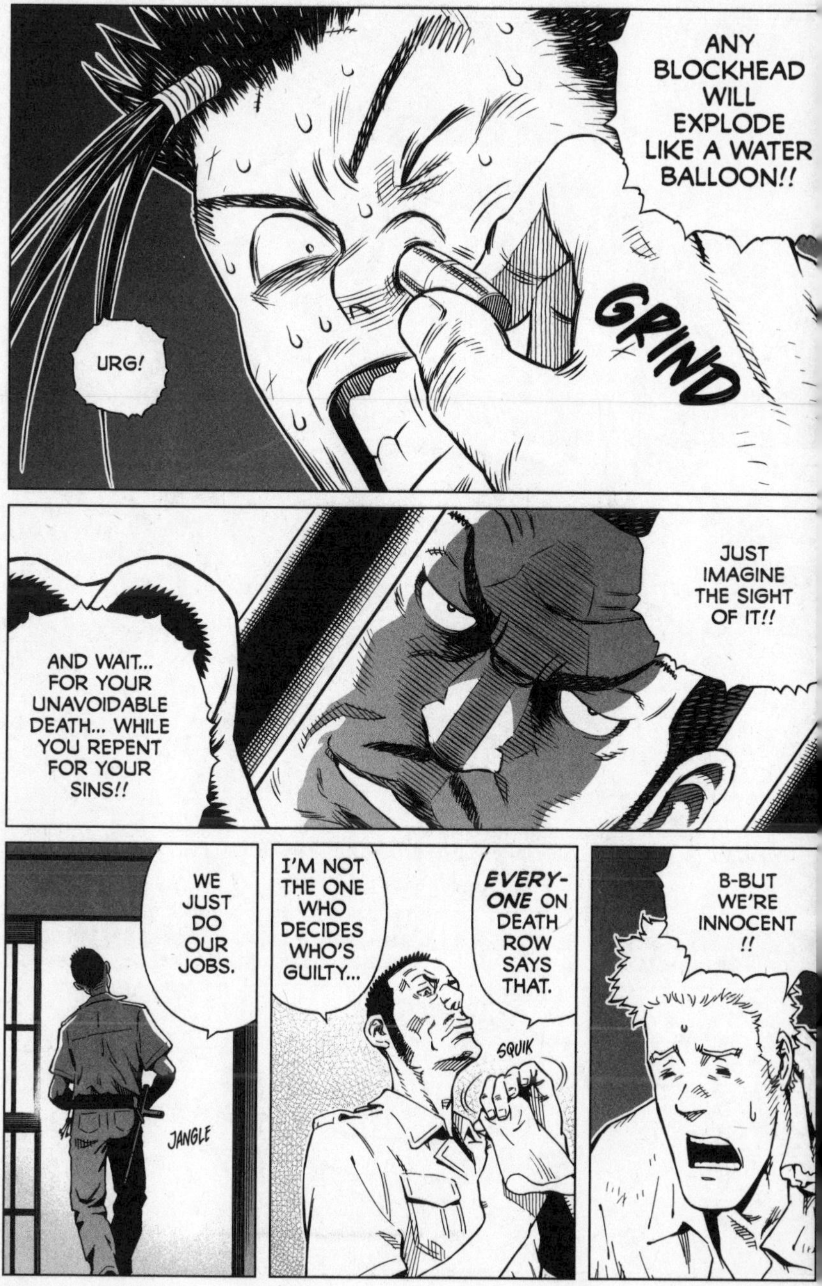
ANY BLOCKHEAD WILL EXPLODE LIKE A WATER BALLOON!!
GRIND
URG!
JUST IMAGINE THE SIGHT OF IT!!
AND WAIT... FOR YOUR UNAVOIDABLE DEATH... WHILE YOU REPENT FOR YOUR SINS!!
B-BUT WE'RE INNOCENT!!
EVERYONE ON DEATH ROW SAYS THAT.
I'M NOT THE ONE WHO DECIDES WHO'S GUILTY...
SQUIK
WE JUST DO OUR JOBS.
JANGLE

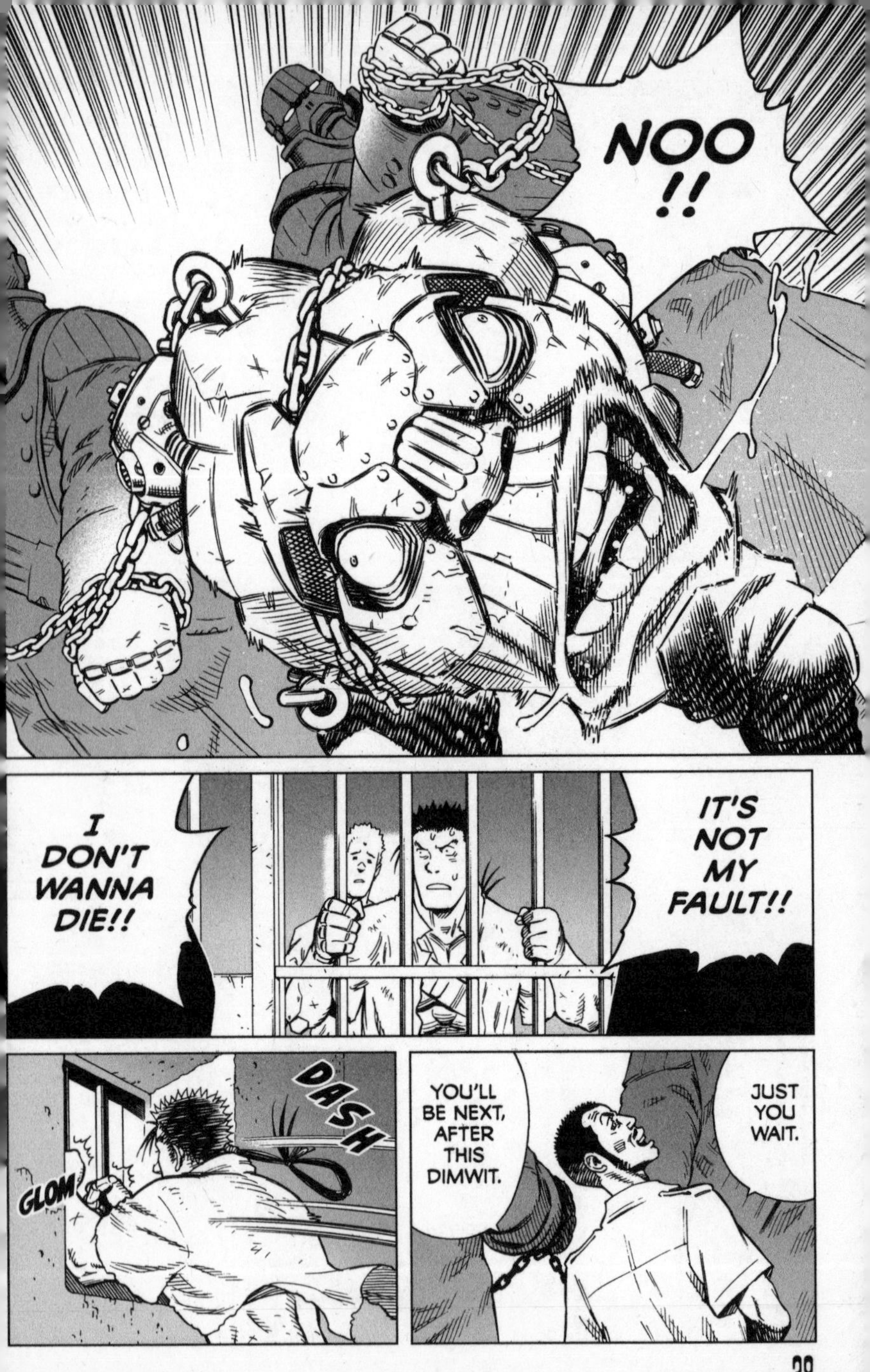
NOO!!
IT'S NOT MY FAULT!!
I DON'T WANNA DIE!!
JUST YOU WAIT.
YOU'LL BE NEXT, AFTER THIS DIMWIT.
DASH
GLOM

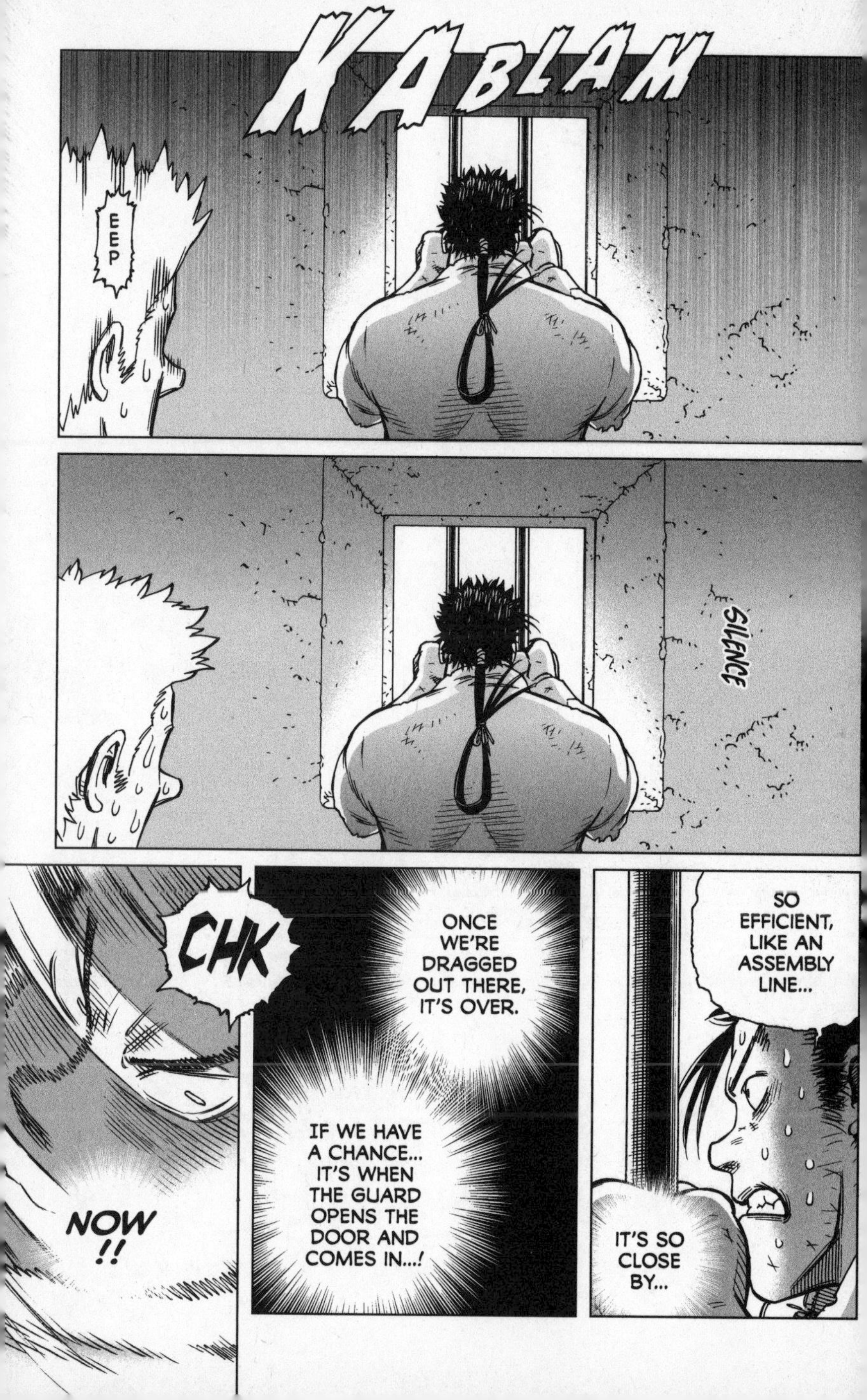
KABLAM
EEP
SILENCE
SO EFFICIENT, LIKE AN ASSEMBLY LINE...
IT'S SO CLOSE BY...
ONCE WE'RE DRAGGED OUT THERE, IT'S OVER.
IF WE HAVE A CHANCE... IT'S WHEN THE GUARD OPENS THE DOOR AND COMES IN...!
CHK
NOW!!

URK

?!

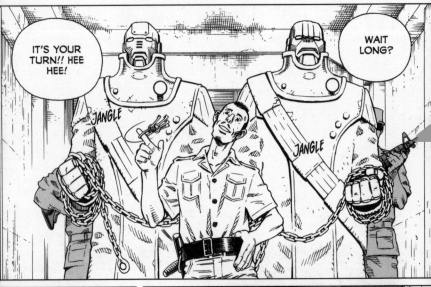

IT'S YOUR TURN!! HEE HEE!

JANGLE

JANGLE

WAIT LONG?

THEY ESCAPED!!

FIND THEM!!

HEY!

EMPTY

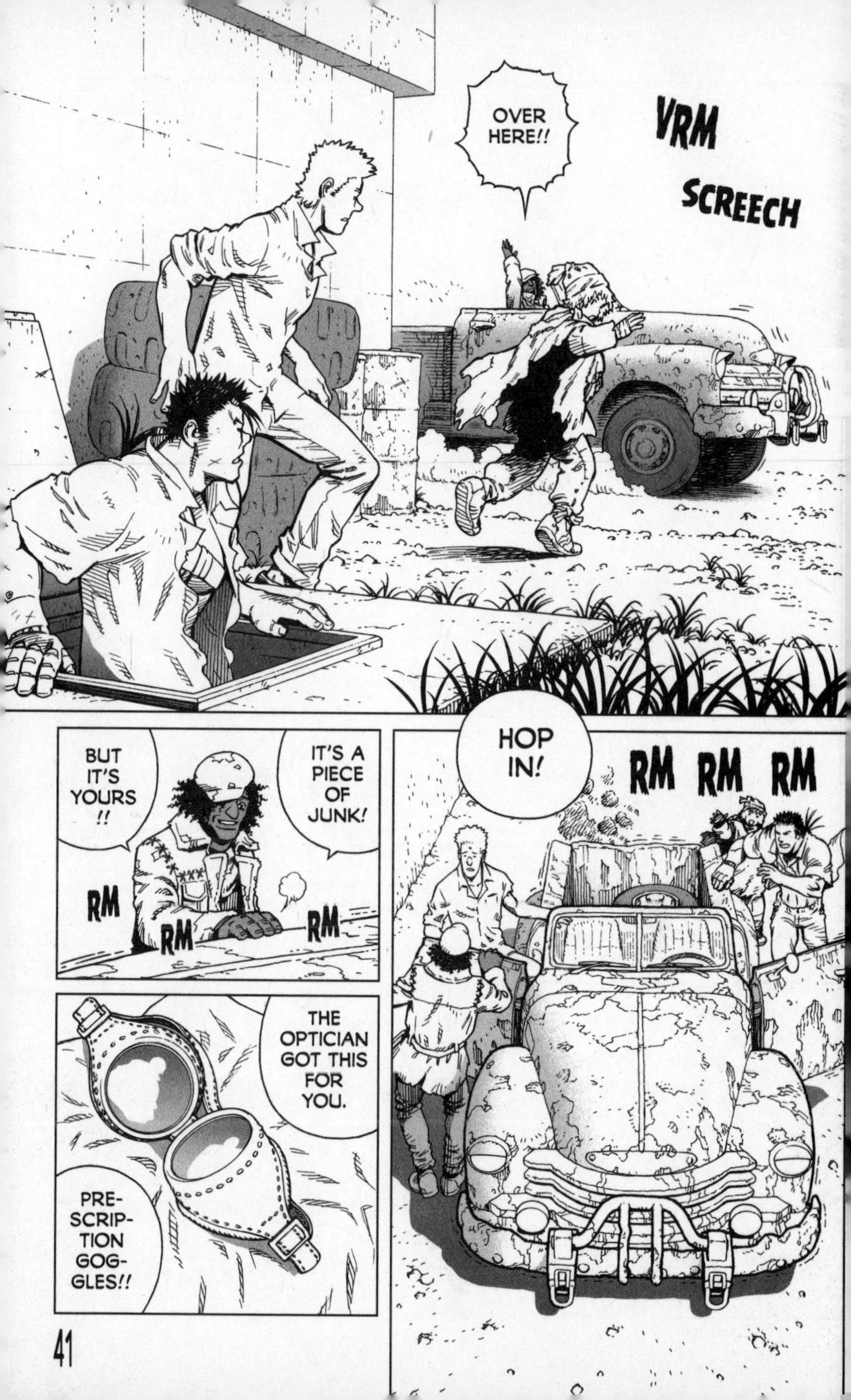
OVER HERE!!
VRM
SCREECH
HOP IN!
RM RM RM
IT'S A PIECE OF JUNK!
BUT IT'S YOURS!!
RM
RM
RM
THE OPTICIAN GOT THIS FOR YOU.
PRE-SCRIP-TION GOG-GLES!!

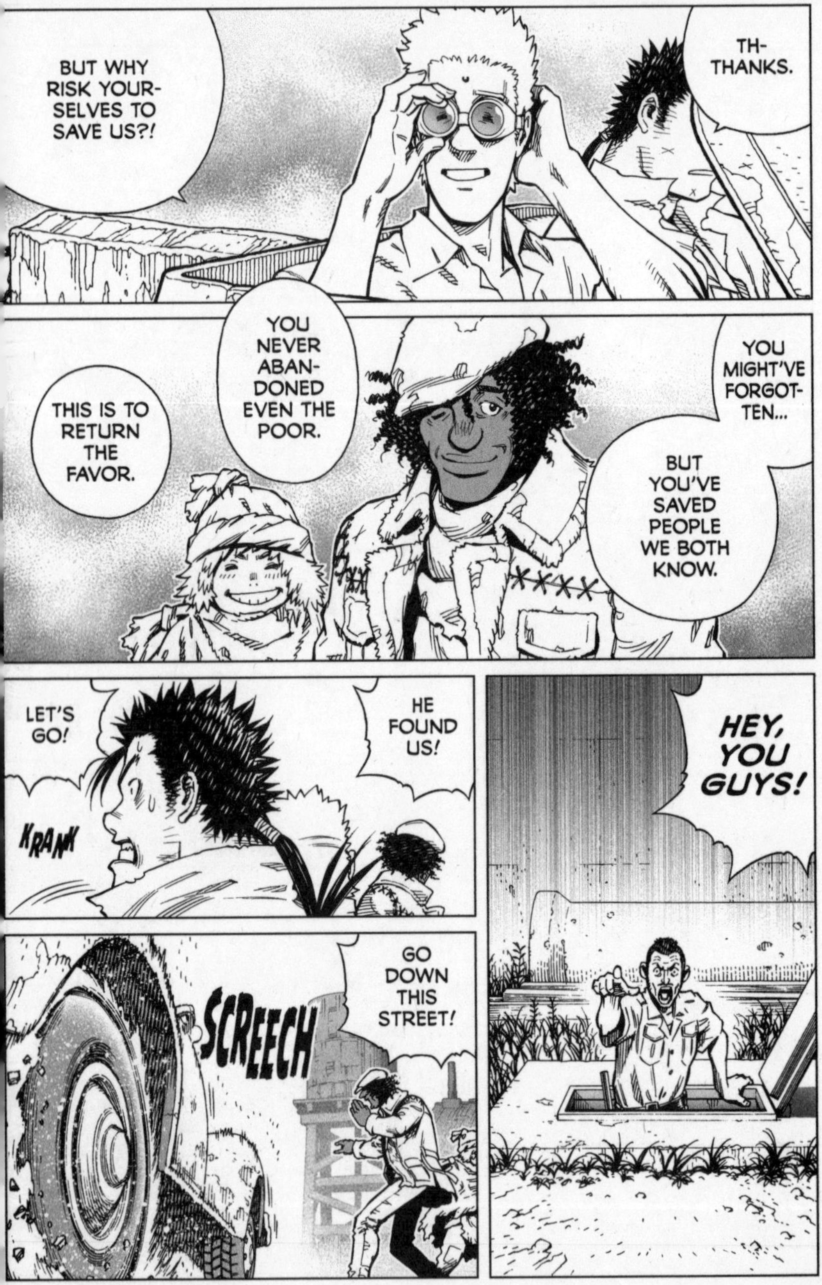
TH- THANKS.
BUT WHY RISK YOUR-SELVES TO SAVE US?!
YOU MIGHT'VE FORGOT-TEN...
BUT YOU'VE SAVED PEOPLE WE BOTH KNOW.
YOU NEVER ABAN-DONED EVEN THE POOR.
THIS IS TO RETURN THE FAVOR.
HEY, YOU GUYS!
HE FOUND US!
LET'S GO!
KRANK
GO DOWN THIS STREET!
SCREECH

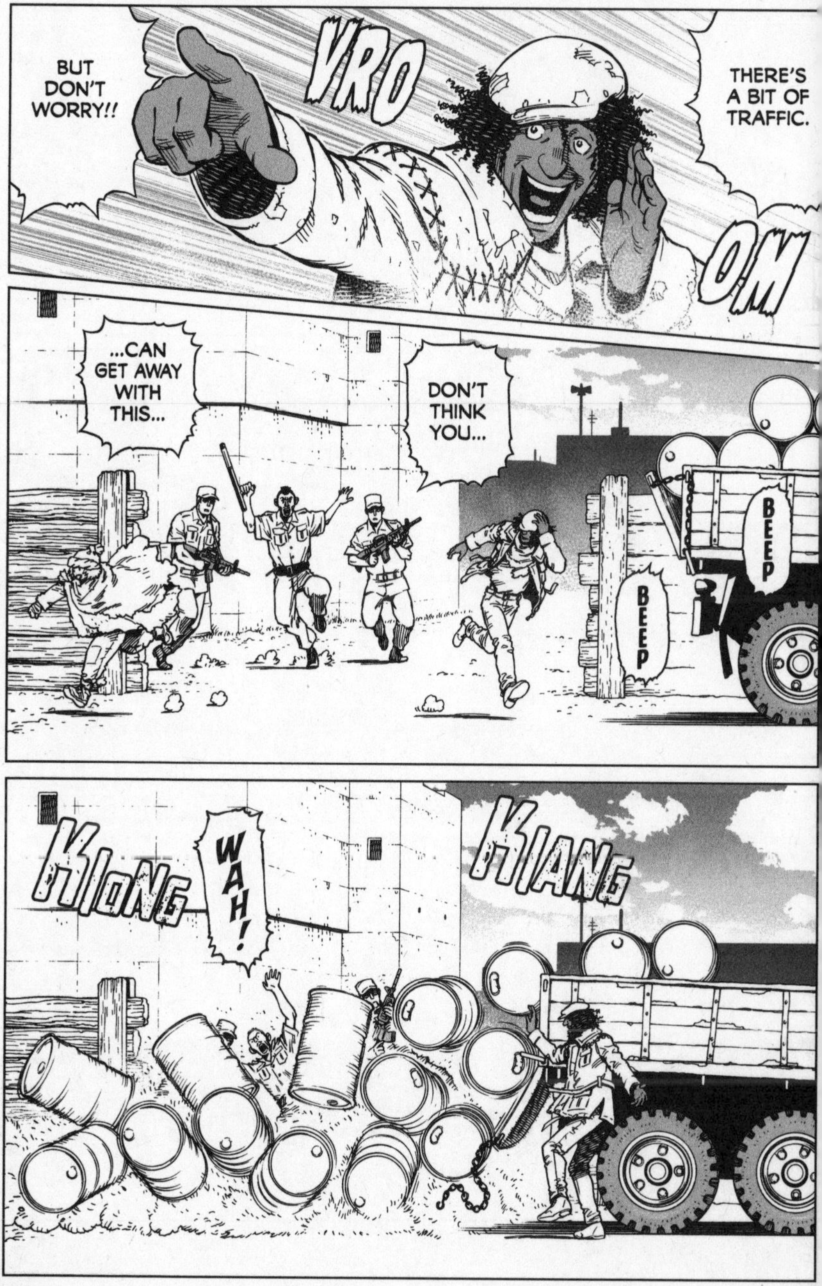
THERE'S A BIT OF TRAFFIC.
VRO
OM
BUT DON'T WORRY!!
DON'T THINK YOU...
...CAN GET AWAY WITH THIS...
BEEP
BEEP
KIANG
WAH!
KIONG

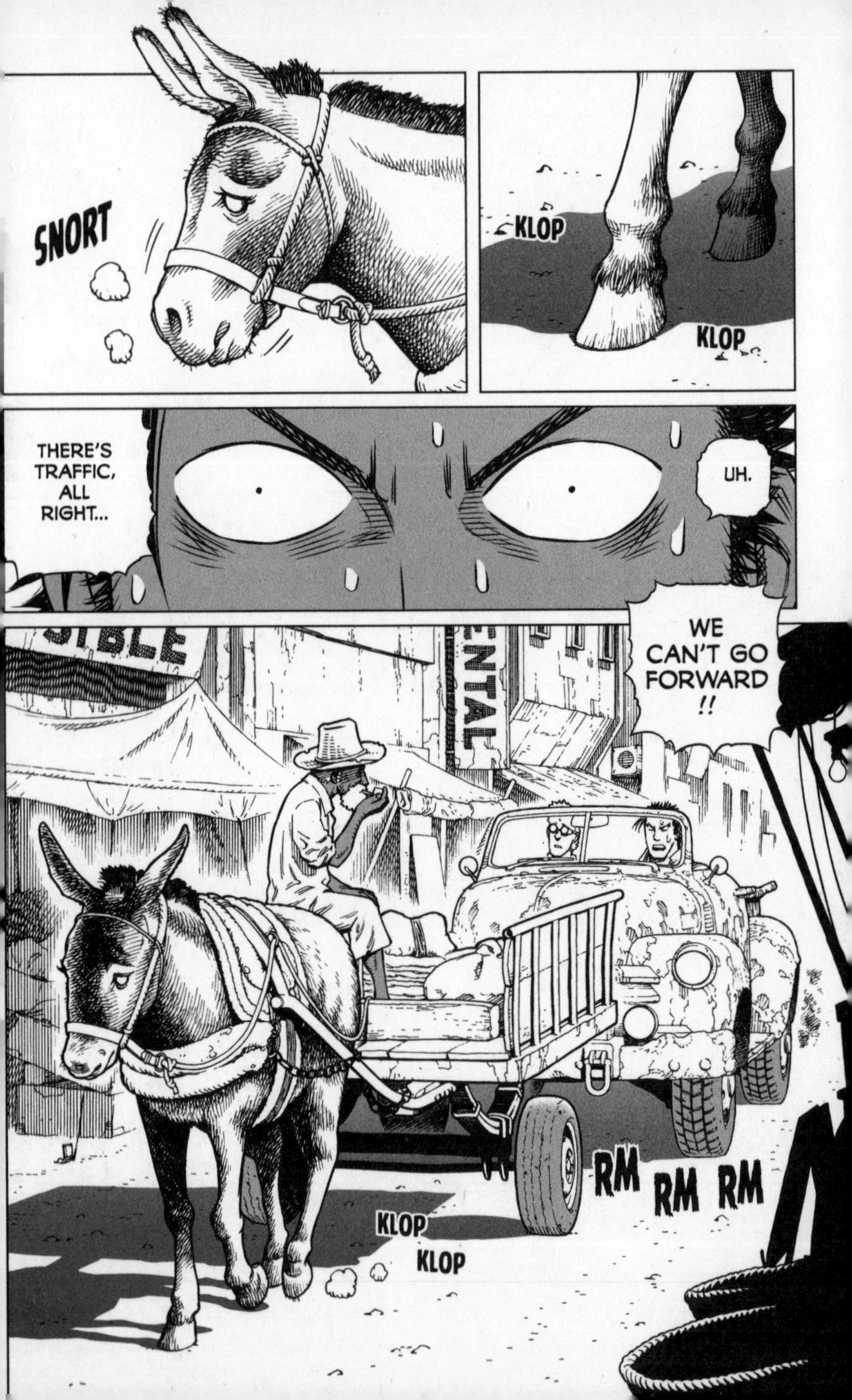
KLOP
KLOP
SNORT
UH.
THERE'S TRAFFIC, ALL RIGHT...
WE CAN'T GO FORWARD !!
RM RM RM
KLOP KLOP

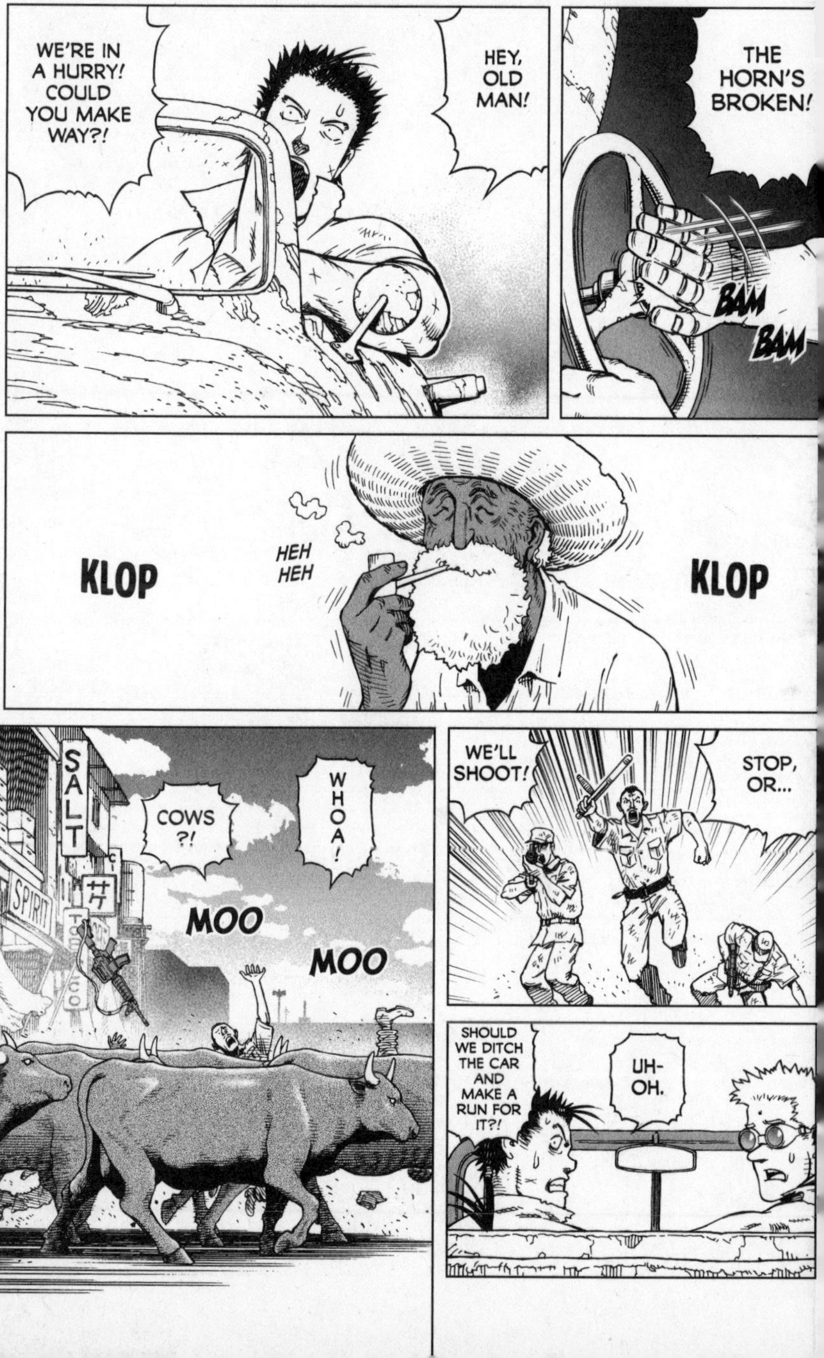
THE HORN'S BROKEN!
BAM
BAM
HEY, OLD MAN!
WE'RE IN A HURRY! COULD YOU MAKE WAY?!
KLOP
HEH HEH
KLOP
STOP, OR...
WE'LL SHOOT!
UH-OH.
SHOULD WE DITCH THE CAR AND MAKE A RUN FOR IT?!
WHOA!
COWS?!
SALT
サケ
SPIRIT
MOO
MOO

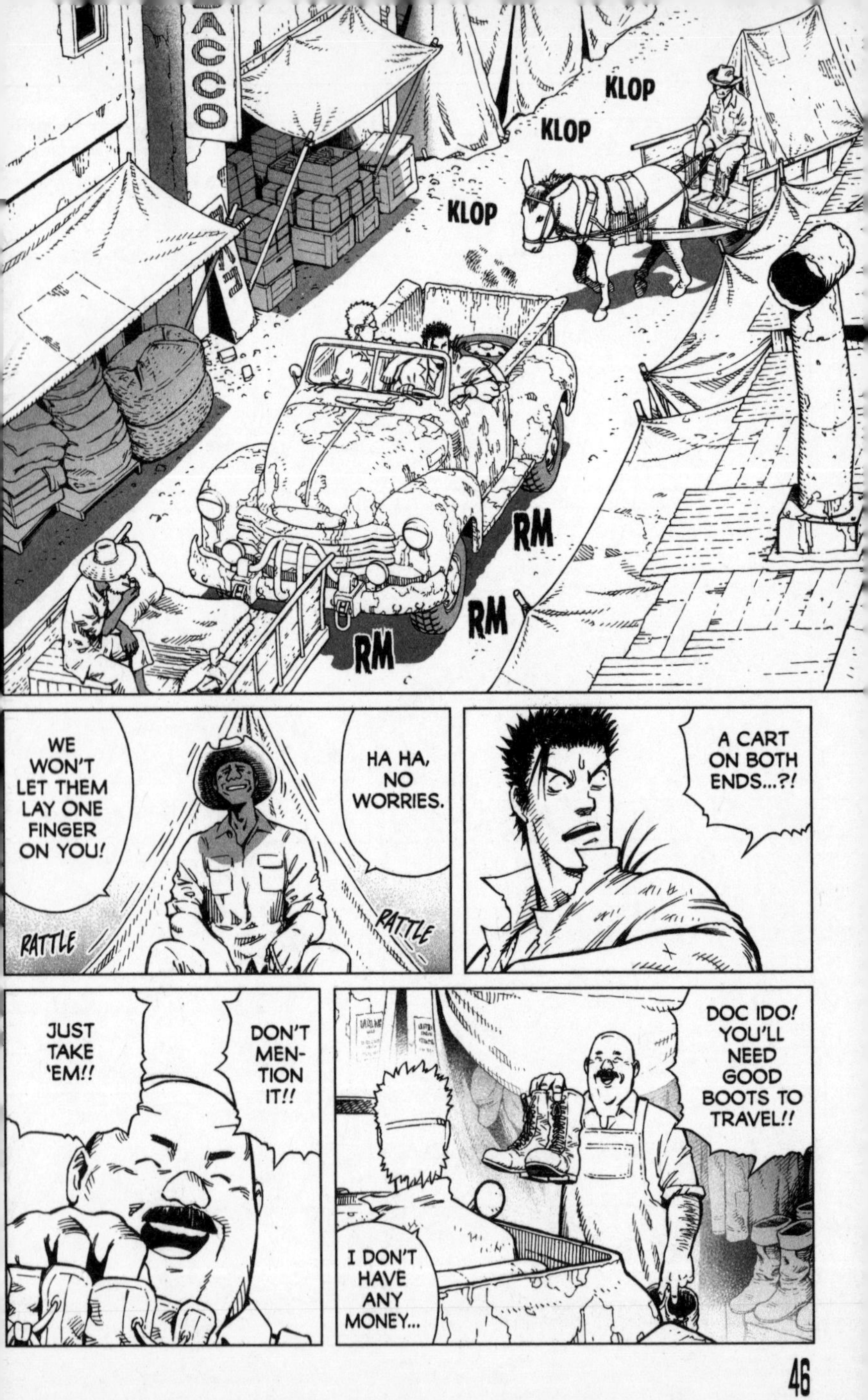

ACCO
KLOP
KLOP
KLOP
RM
RM
RM
A CART ON BOTH ENDS...?!
HA HA, NO WORRIES.
WE WON'T LET THEM LAY ONE FINGER ON YOU!
RATTLE
RATTLE
DOC IDO! YOU'LL NEED GOOD BOOTS TO TRAVEL!!
I DON'T HAVE ANY MONEY...
DON'T MEN-TION IT!!
JUST TAKE 'EM!!

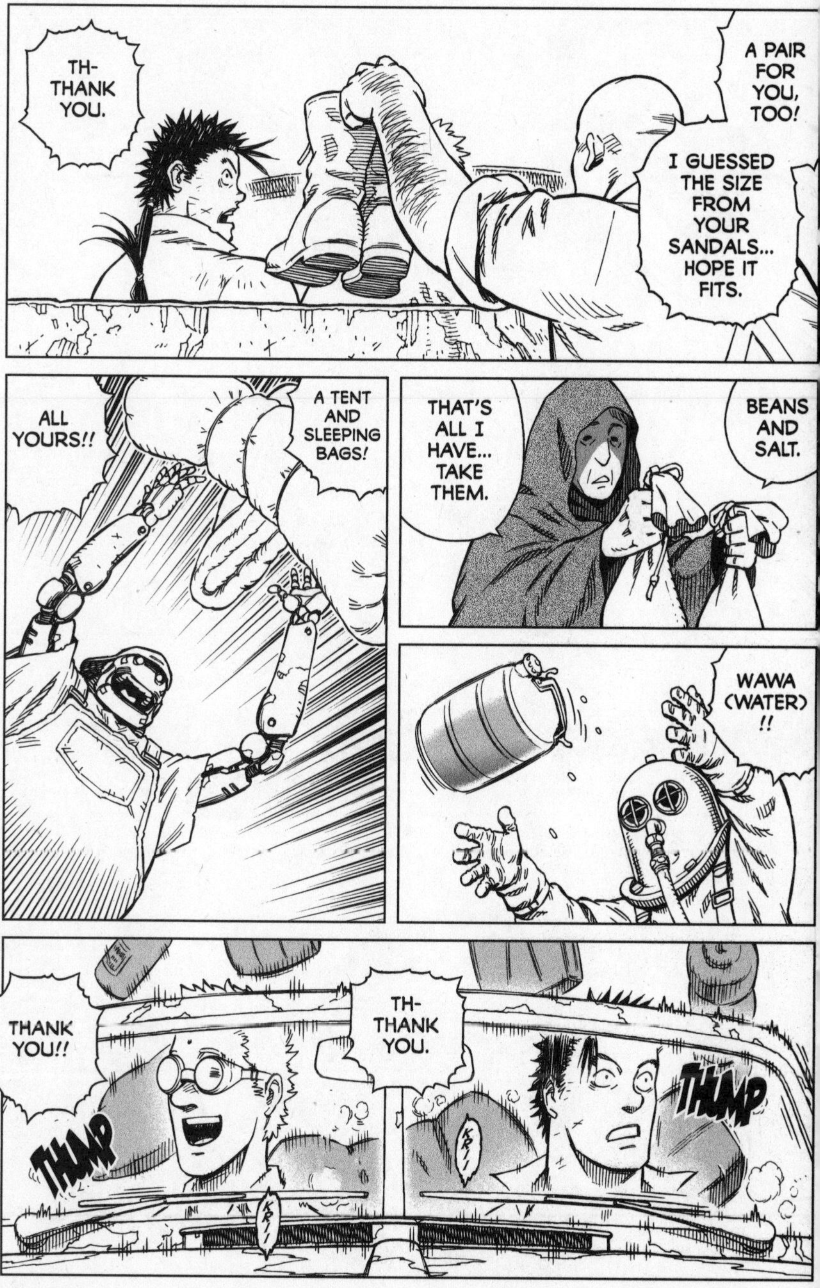
A PAIR FOR YOU, TOO!
I GUESSED THE SIZE FROM YOUR SANDALS... HOPE IT FITS.
TH- THANK YOU.
BEANS AND SALT.
THAT'S ALL I HAVE... TAKE THEM.
WAWA (WATER) !!
A TENT AND SLEEPING BAGS!
ALL YOURS!!
TH- THANK YOU.
THUMP
KRI
THANK YOU!!
THUMP
KRI

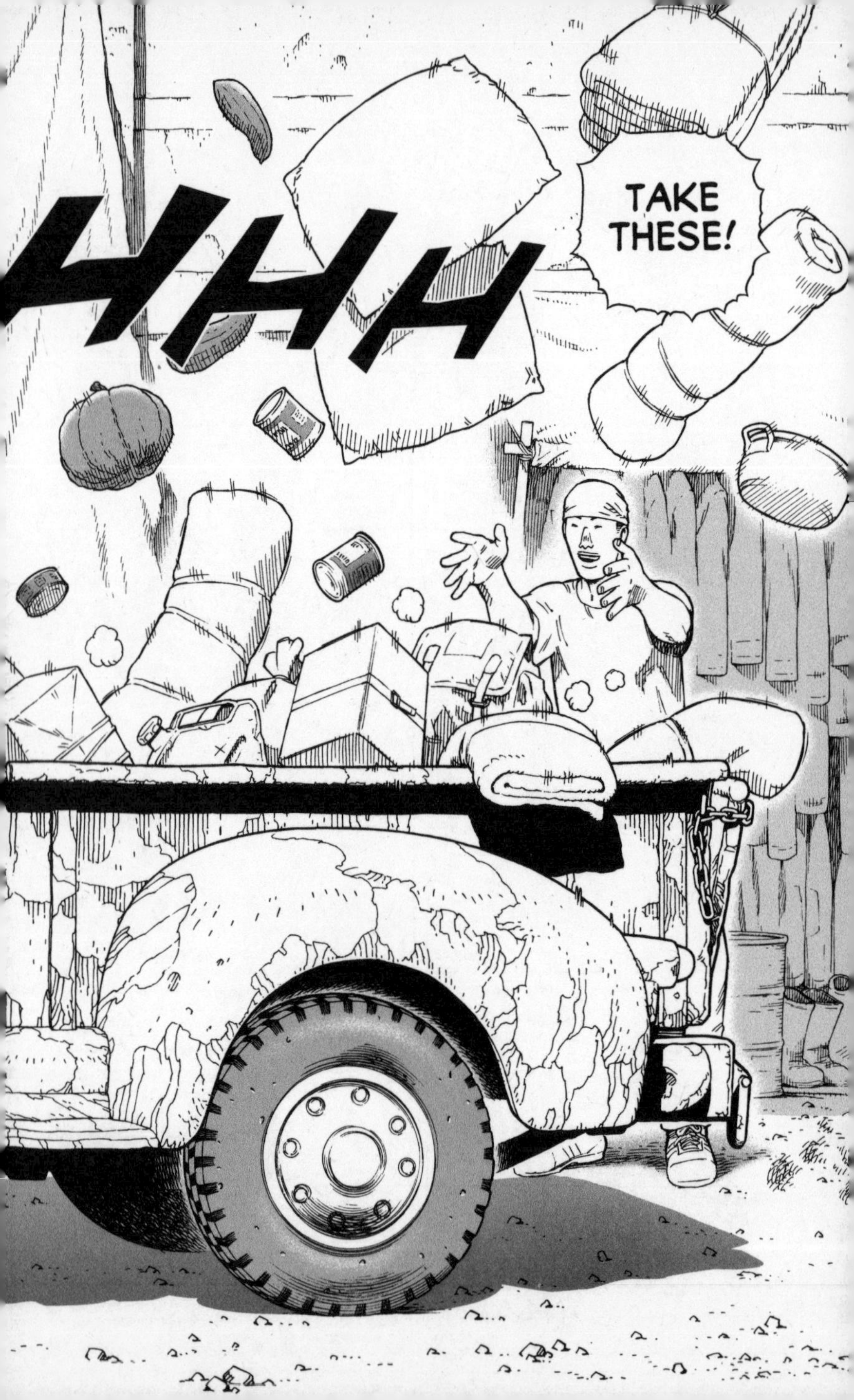
TAKE THESE!

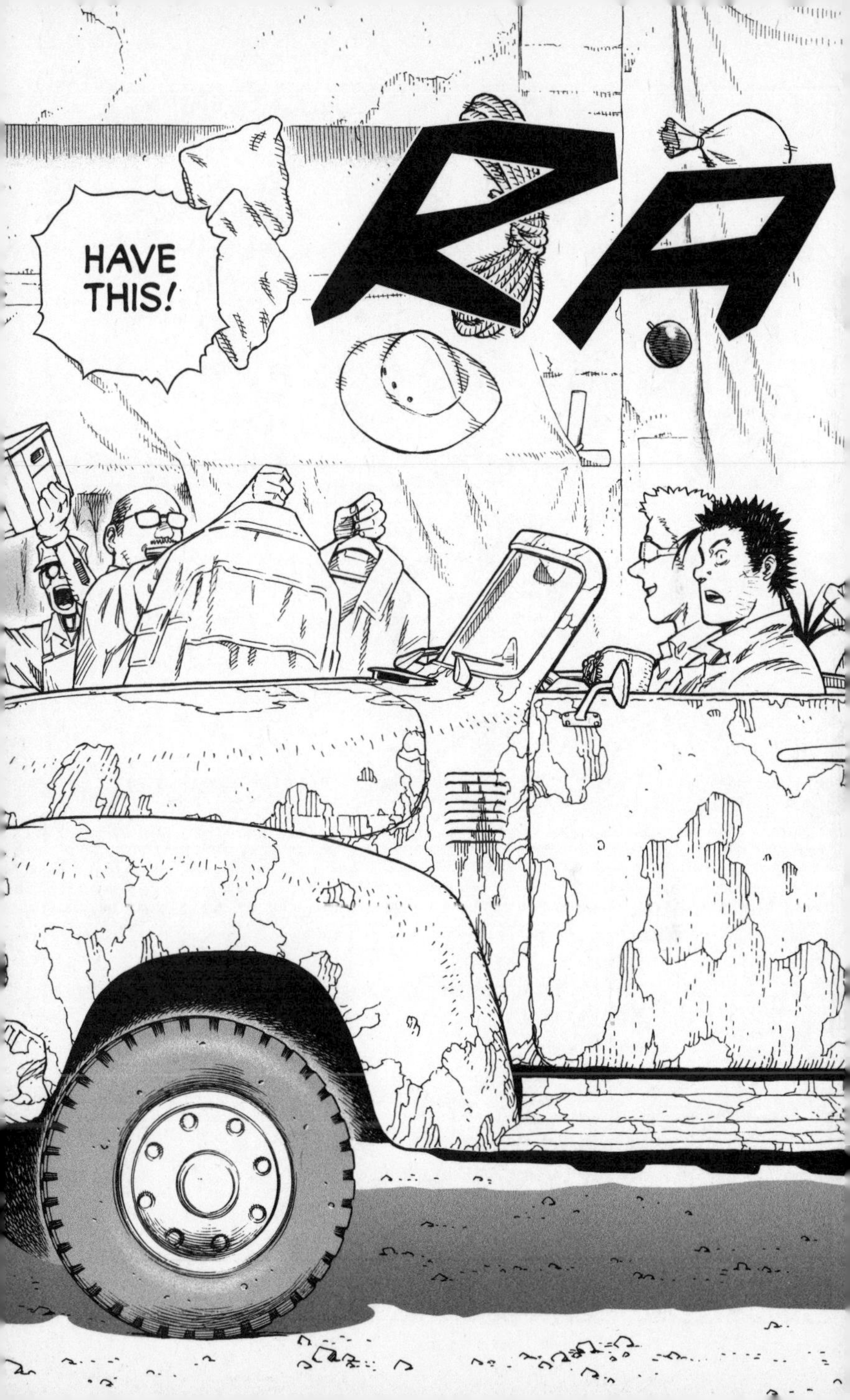
RA
HAVE THIS!

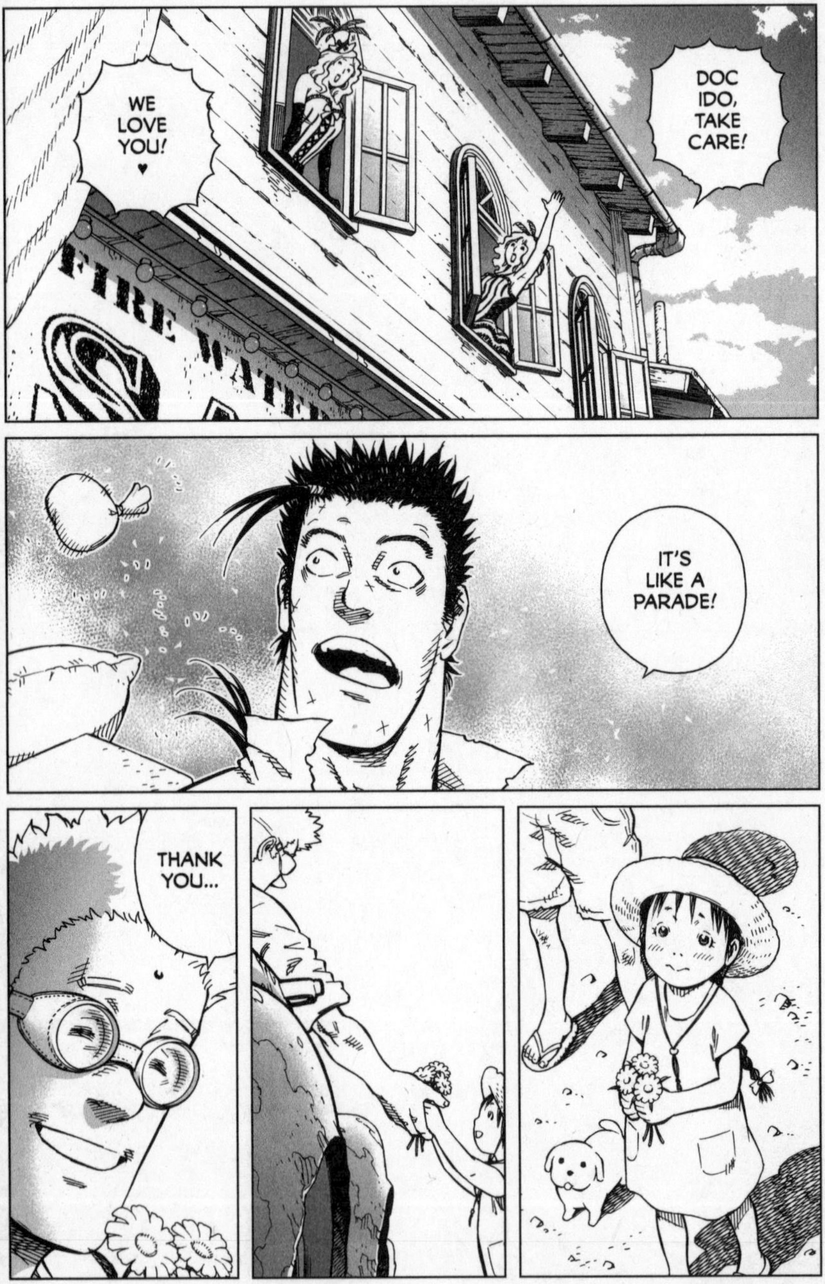
DOC IDO, TAKE CARE!
WE LOVE YOU! ♥
IT'S LIKE A PARADE!
THANK YOU...

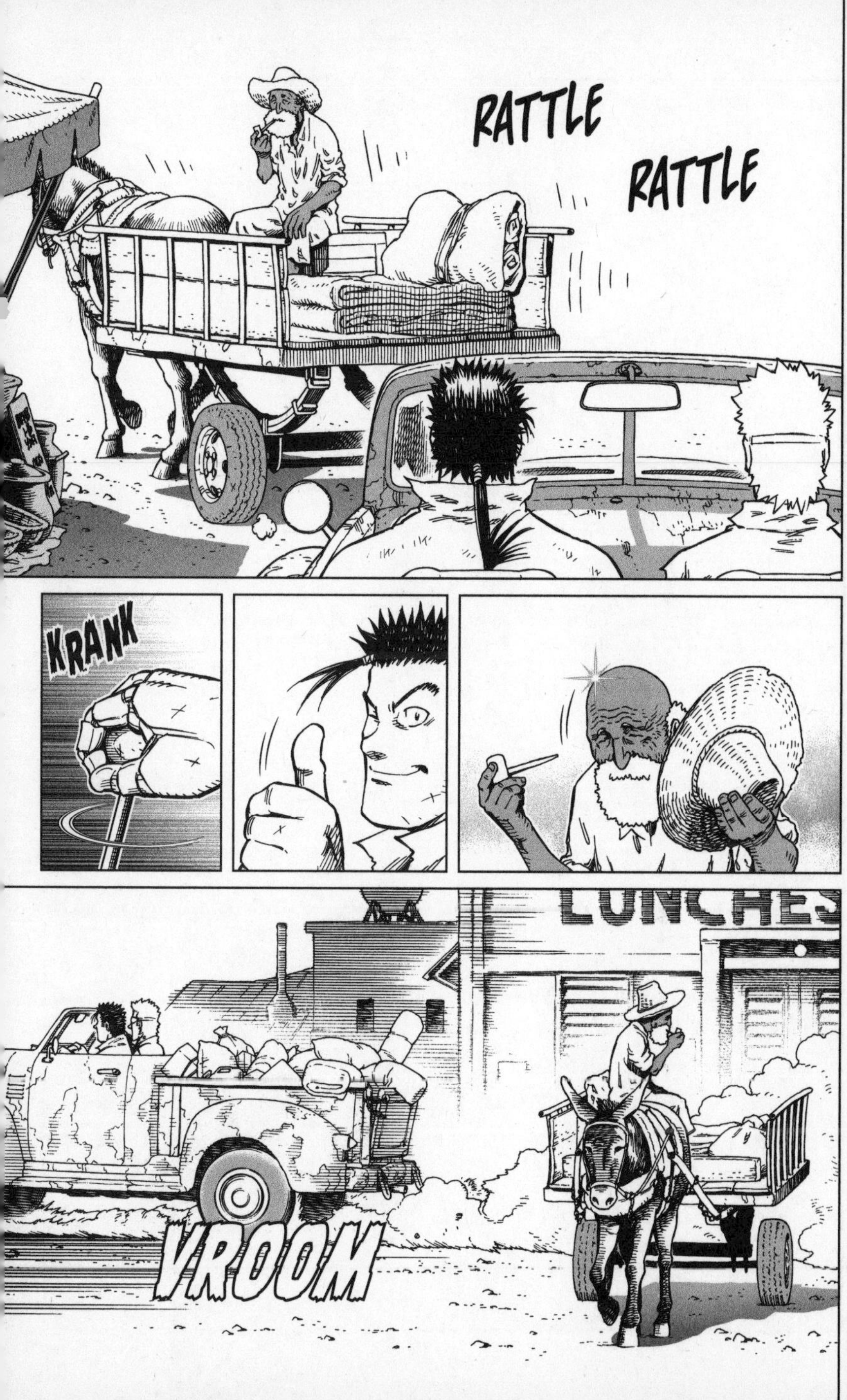
RATTLE
RATTLE
KRANK
LUNCHES
VROOM

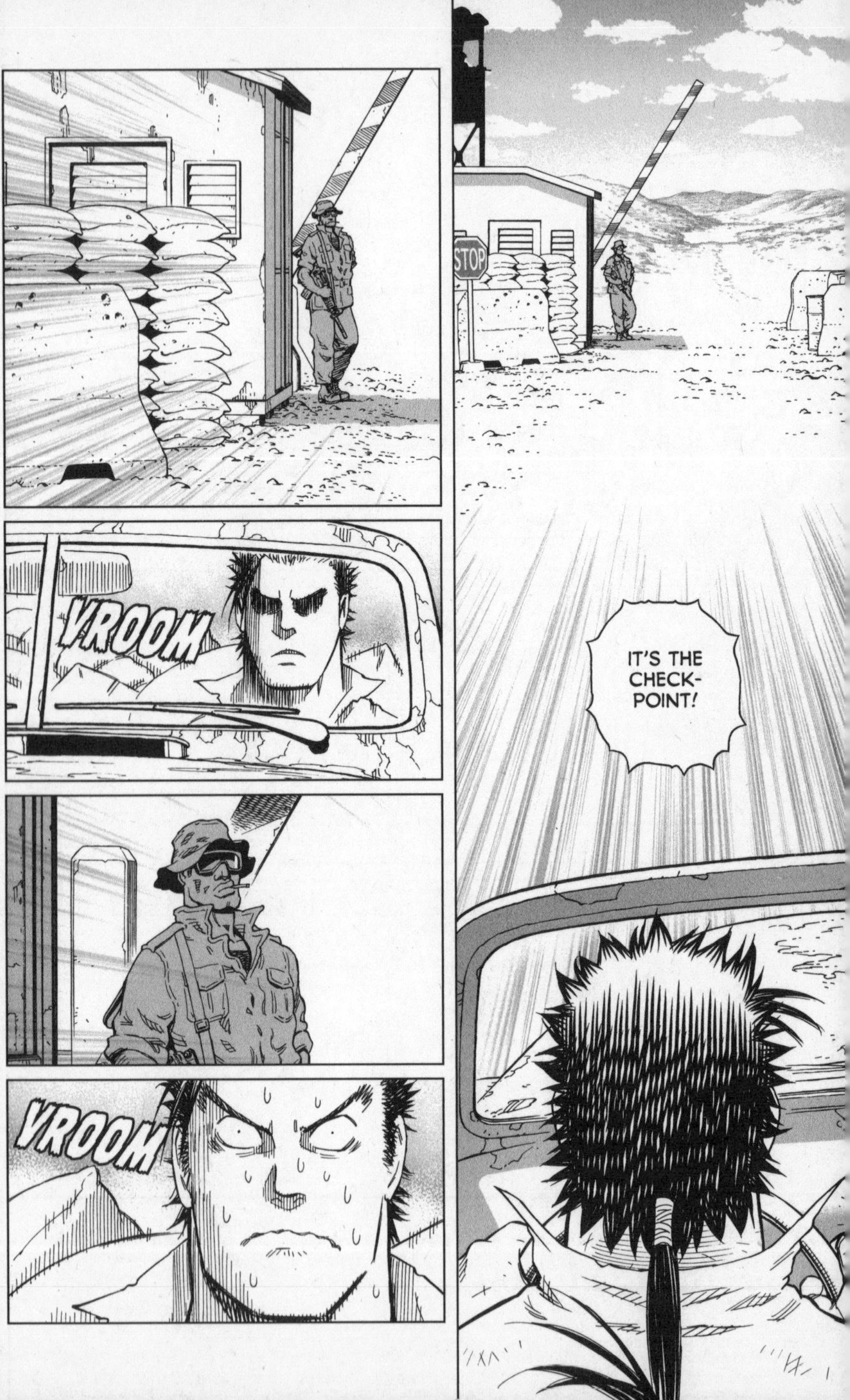
IT'S THE CHECK-POINT!
VROOM
VROOM

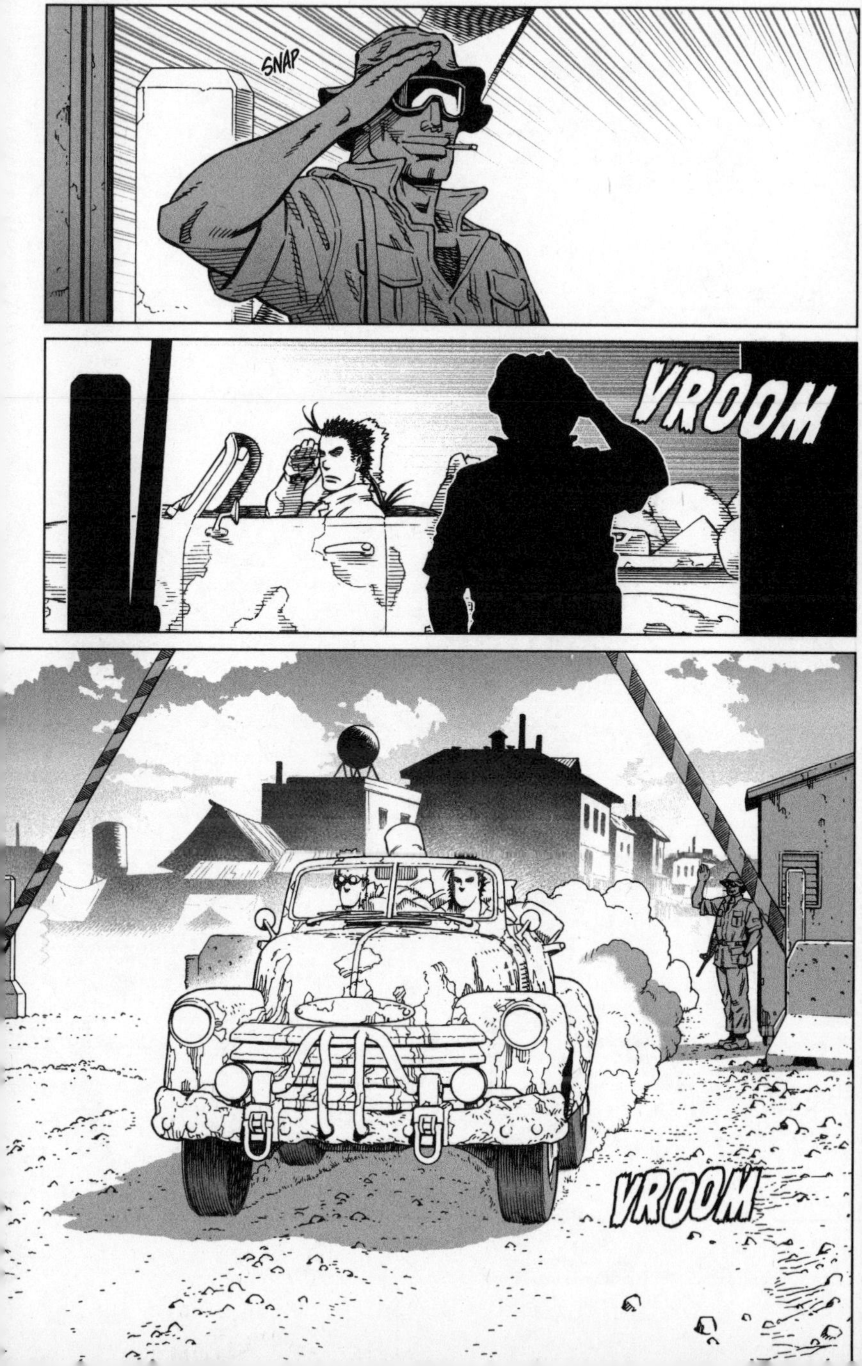
SNAP
VROOM
VROOM

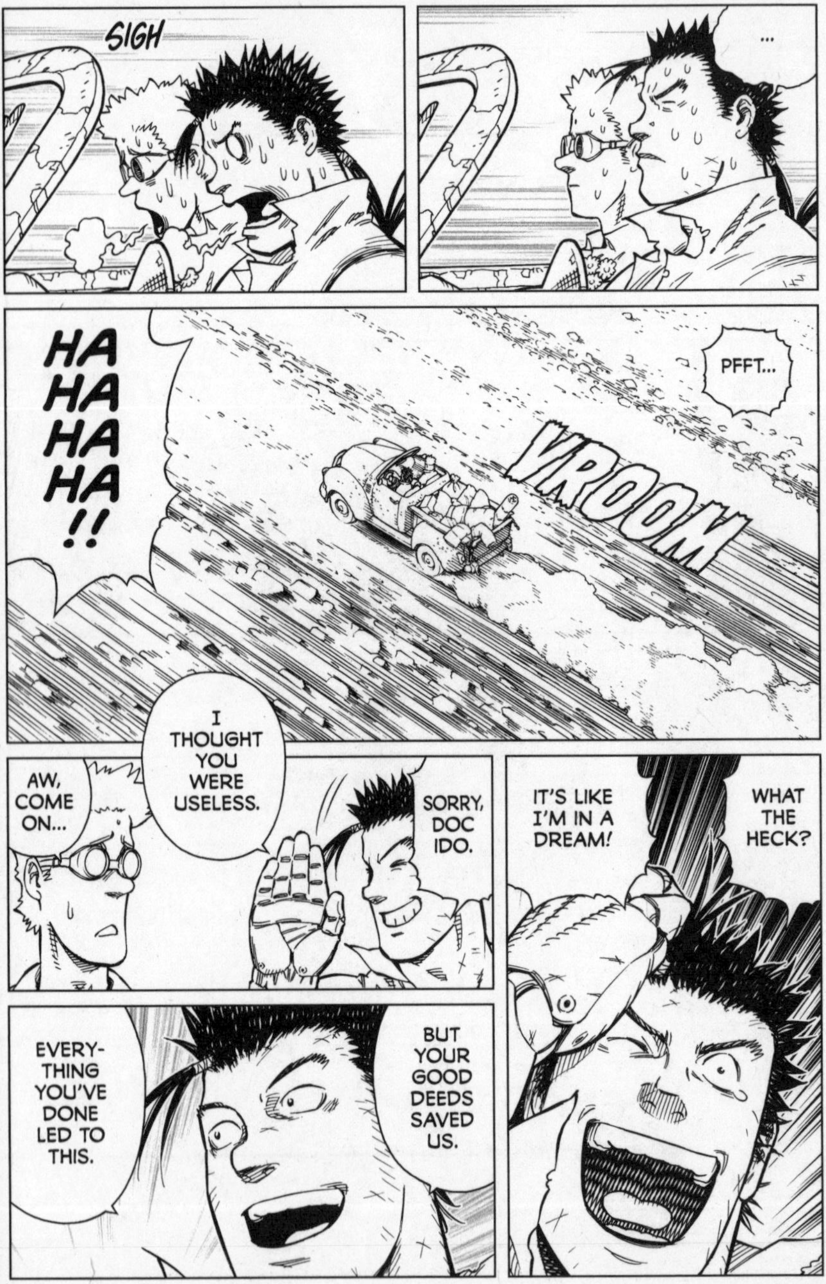
...
SIGH
PFFT...
VROOM
HA HA HA HA!!
WHAT THE HECK?
IT'S LIKE I'M IN A DREAM!
SORRY, DOC IDO.
I THOUGHT YOU WERE USELESS.
AW, COME ON...
BUT YOUR GOOD DEEDS SAVED US.
EVERY-THING YOU'VE DONE LED TO THIS.

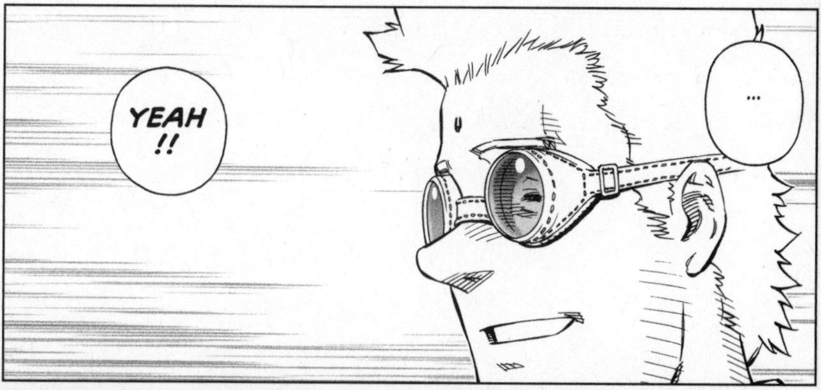
...
YEAH !!

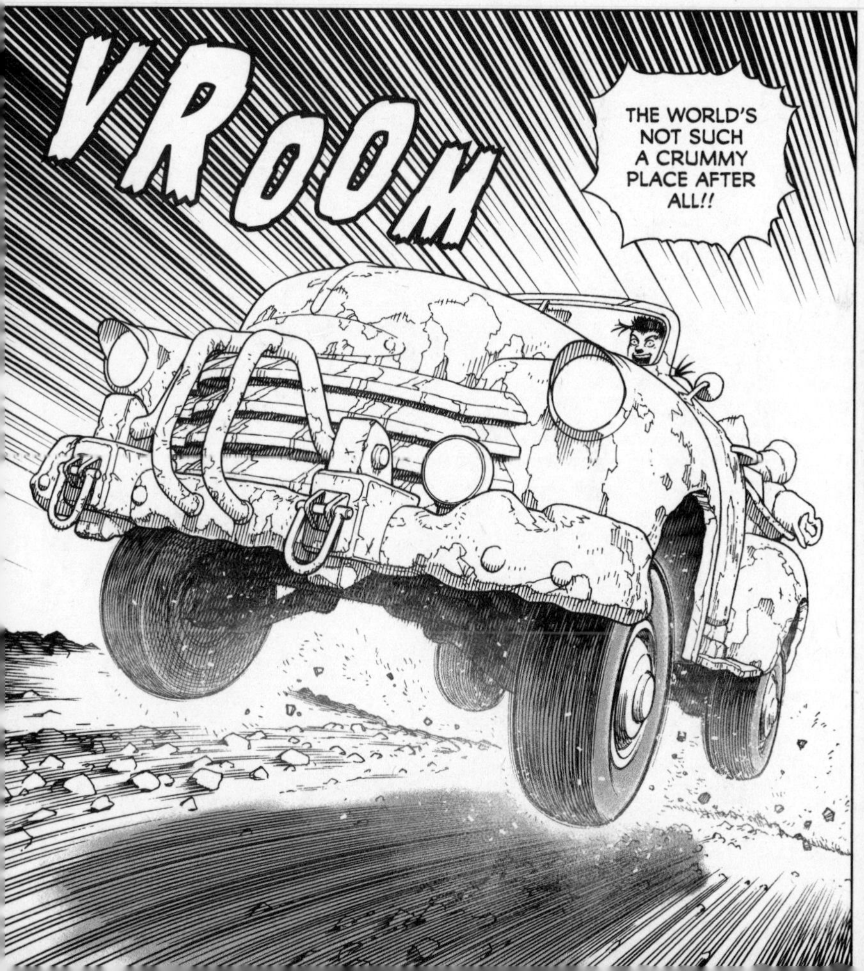
VROOM
THE WORLD'S NOT SUCH A CRUMMY PLACE AFTER ALL!!

Phase 118: Alita Quest XII

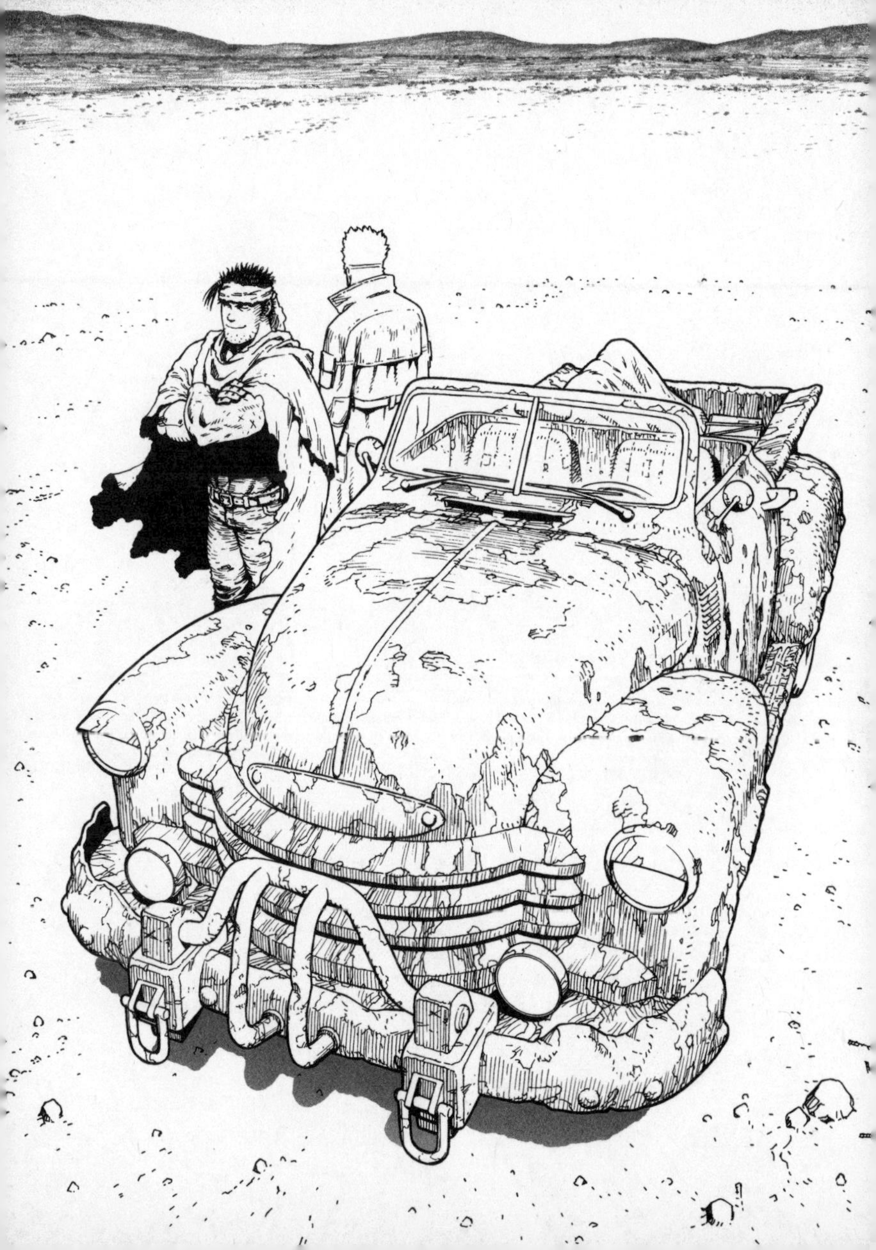

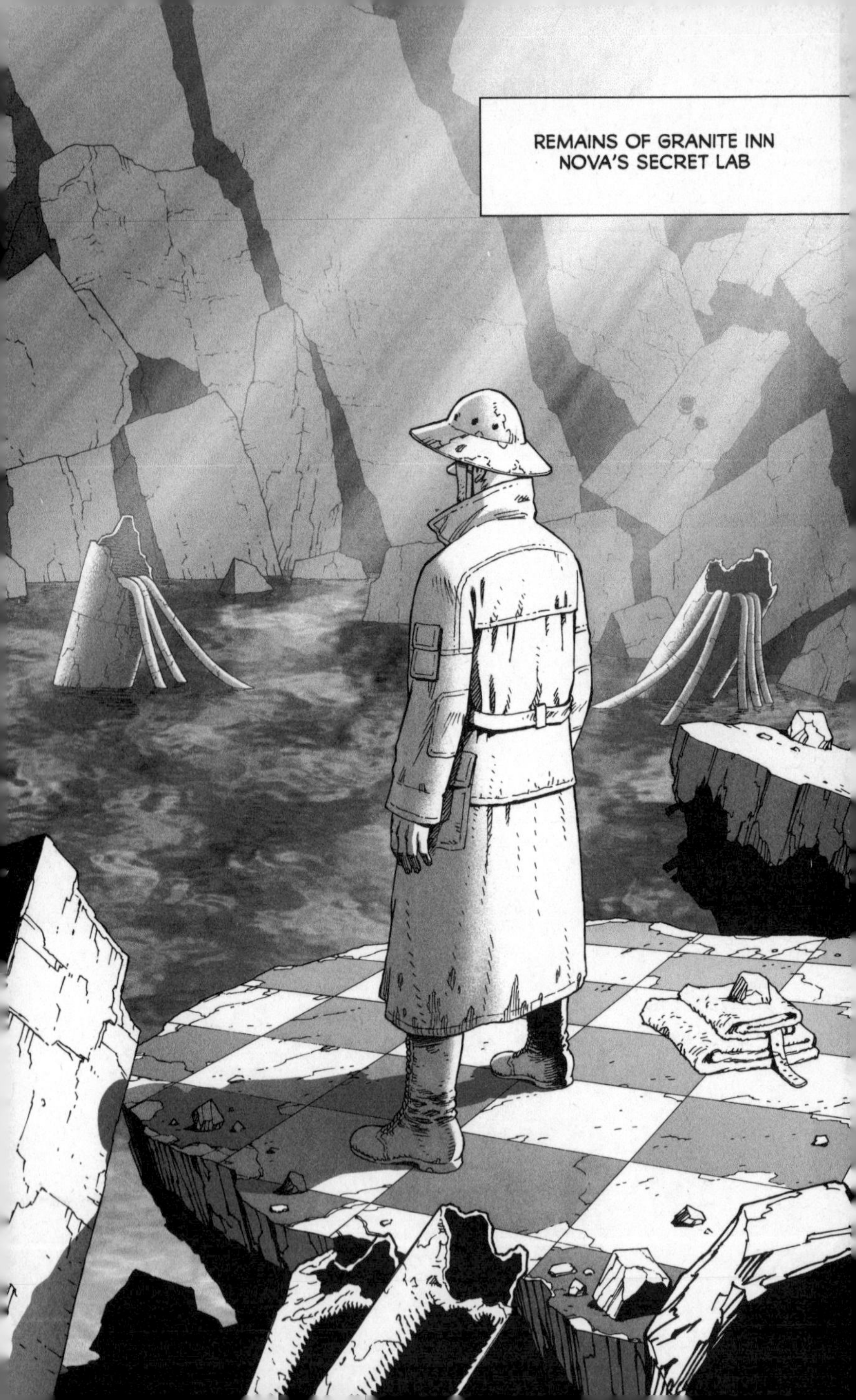
REMAINS OF GRANITE INN
NOVA'S SECRET LAB

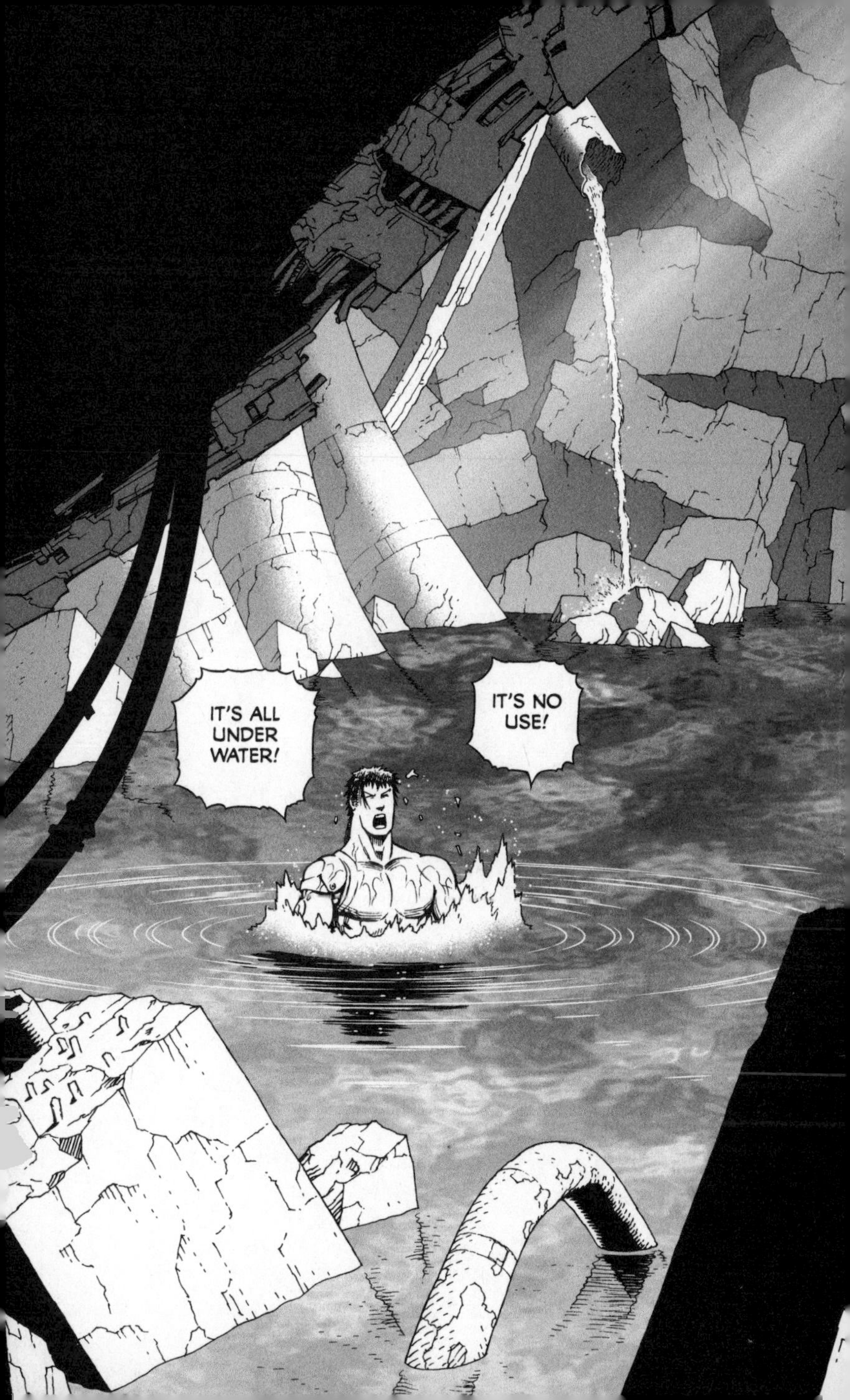
IT'S NO USE!
IT'S ALL UNDER WATER!

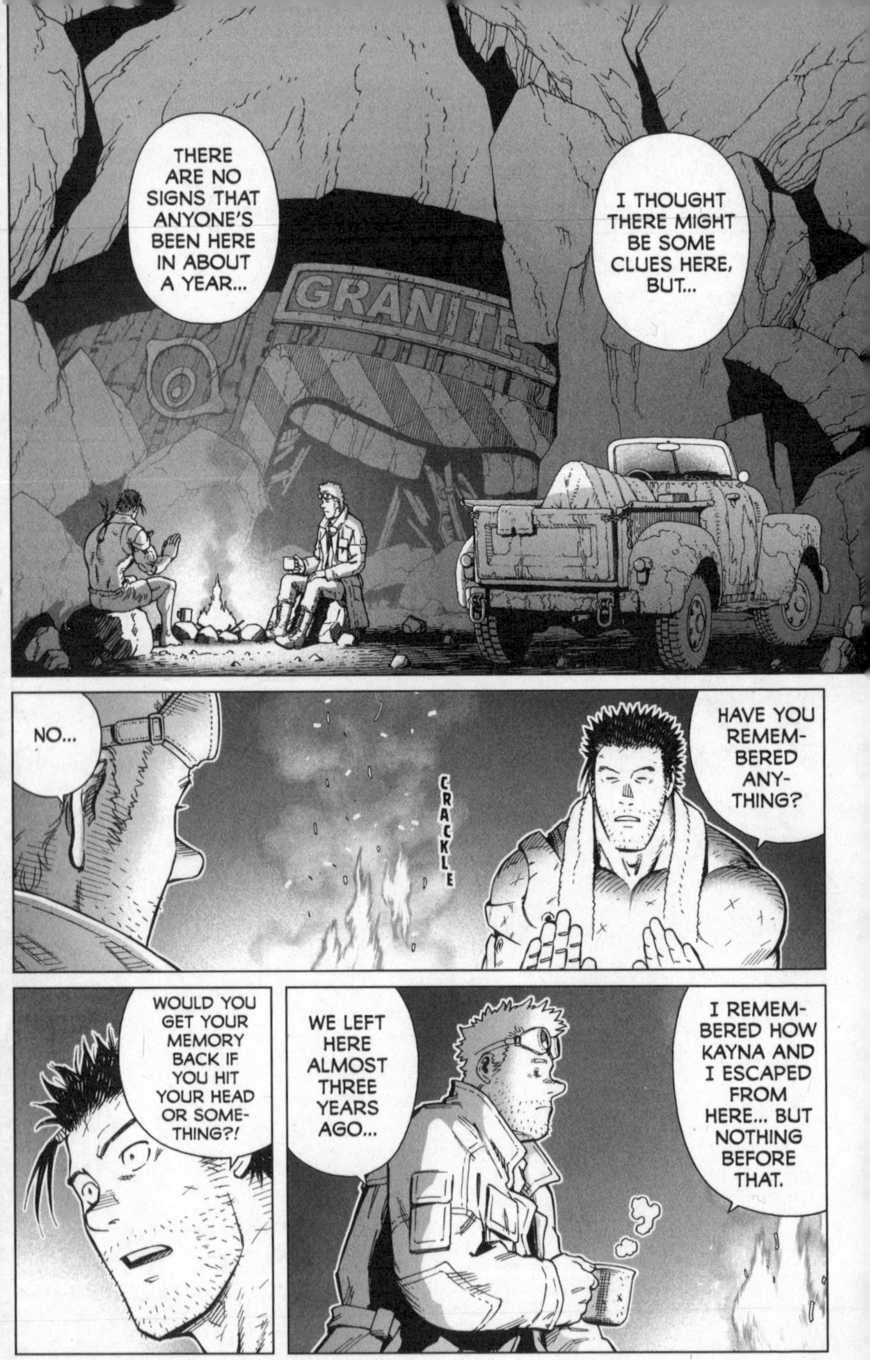
I THOUGHT THERE MIGHT BE SOME CLUES HERE, BUT...
GRANITE
THERE ARE NO SIGNS THAT ANYONE'S BEEN HERE IN ABOUT A YEAR...
HAVE YOU REMEMBERED ANYTHING?
CRACKLE
NO...
I REMEMBERED HOW KAYNA AND I ESCAPED FROM HERE... BUT NOTHING BEFORE THAT.
WE LEFT HERE ALMOST THREE YEARS AGO...
WOULD YOU GET YOUR MEMORY BACK IF YOU HIT YOUR HEAD OR SOMETHING?!

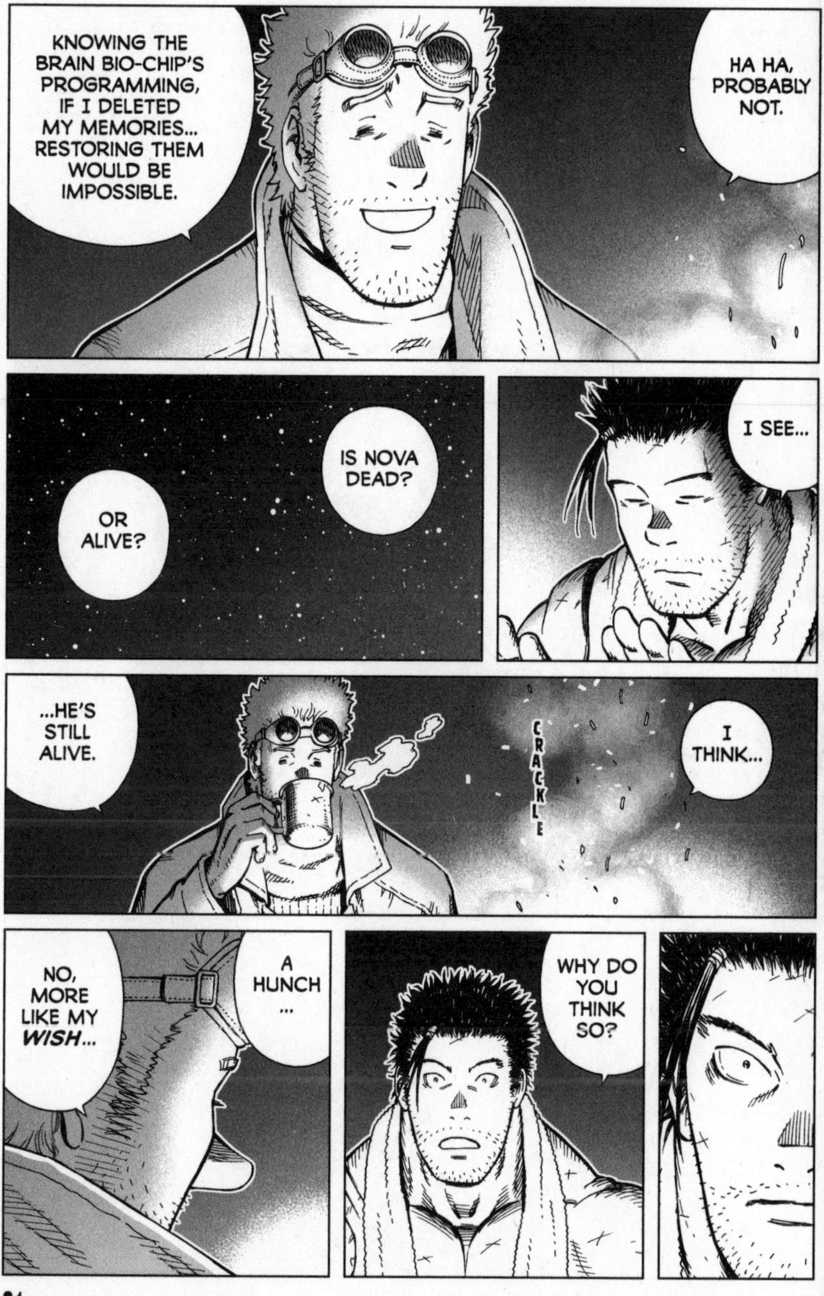
HA HA, PROBABLY NOT.
KNOWING THE BRAIN BIO-CHIP'S PROGRAMMING, IF I DELETED MY MEMORIES... RESTORING THEM WOULD BE IMPOSSIBLE.
I SEE...
IS NOVA DEAD?
OR ALIVE?
I THINK...
CRACKLE
...HE'S STILL ALIVE.
WHY DO YOU THINK SO?
A HUNCH ...
NO, MORE LIKE MY *WISH*...

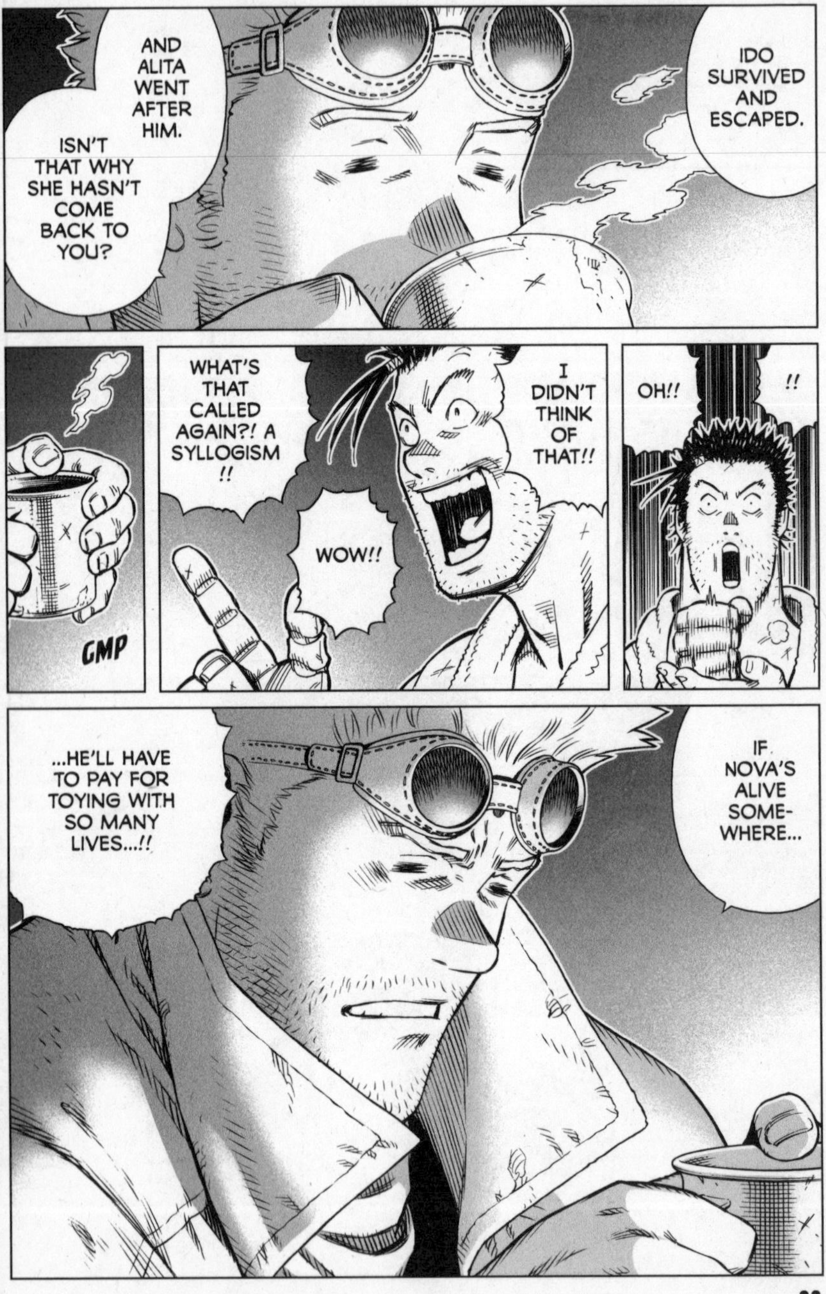
IDO SURVIVED AND ESCAPED.
AND ALITA WENT AFTER HIM.
ISN'T THAT WHY SHE HASN'T COME BACK TO YOU?
OH!!
!!
I DIDN'T THINK OF THAT!!
WHAT'S THAT CALLED AGAIN?! A SYLLOGISM!!
WOW!!
GMP
IF NOVA'S ALIVE SOME-WHERE...
...HE'LL HAVE TO PAY FOR TOYING WITH SO MANY LIVES...!!

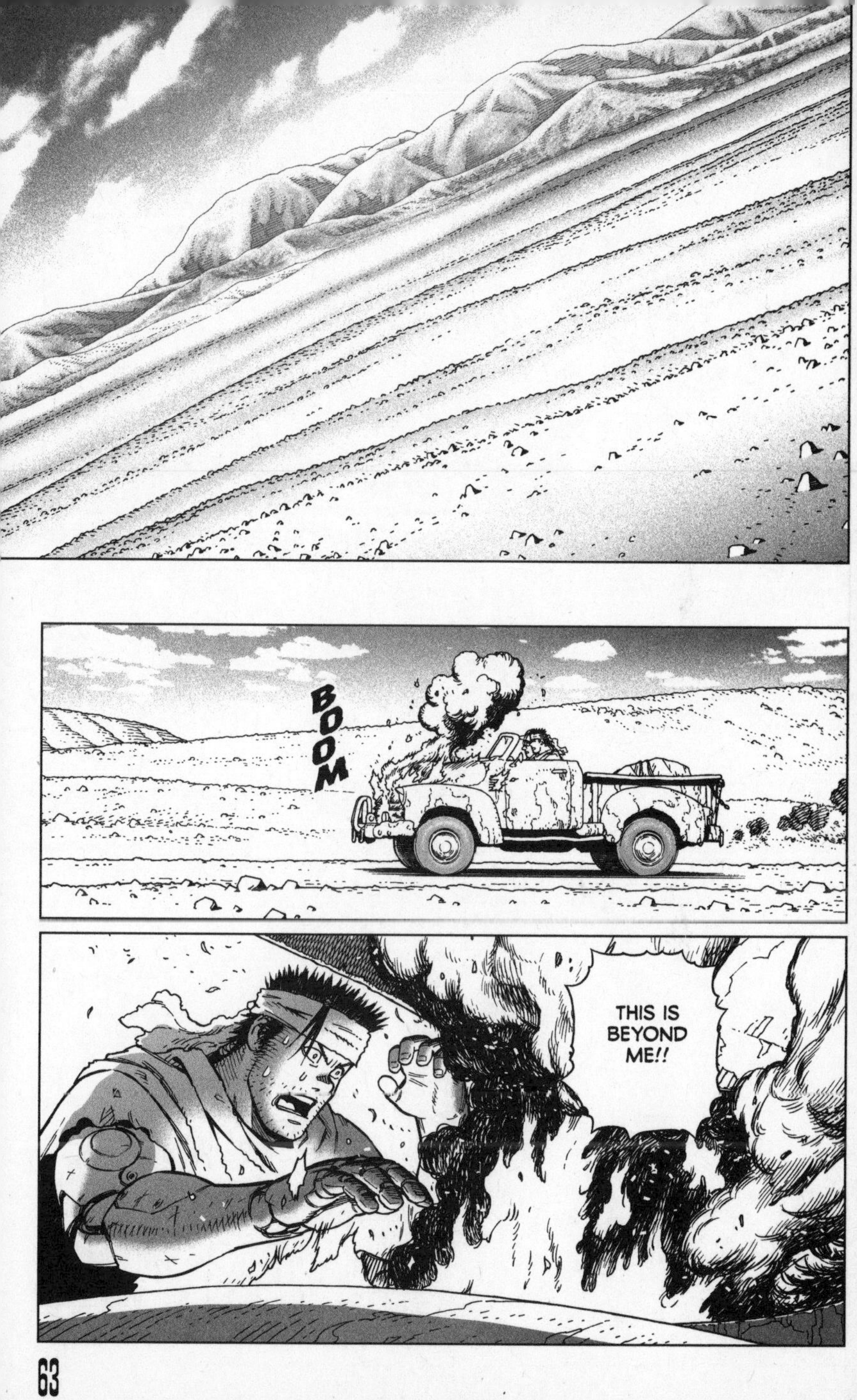
BOOM
THIS IS BEYOND ME!!

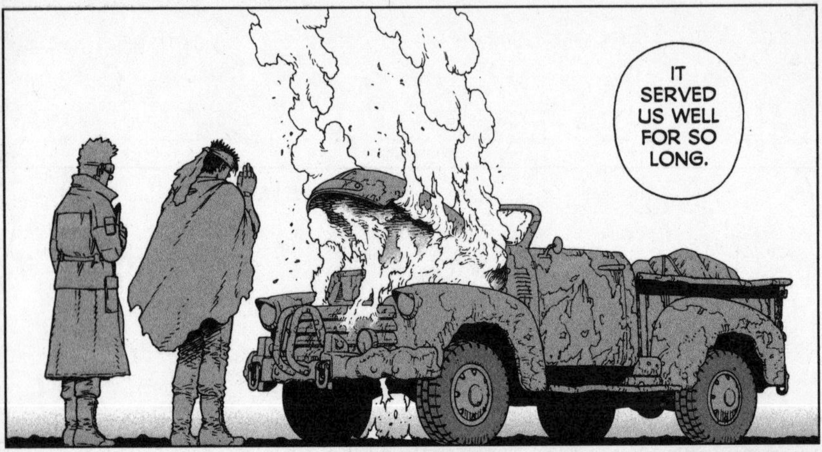
IT SERVED US WELL FOR SO LONG.
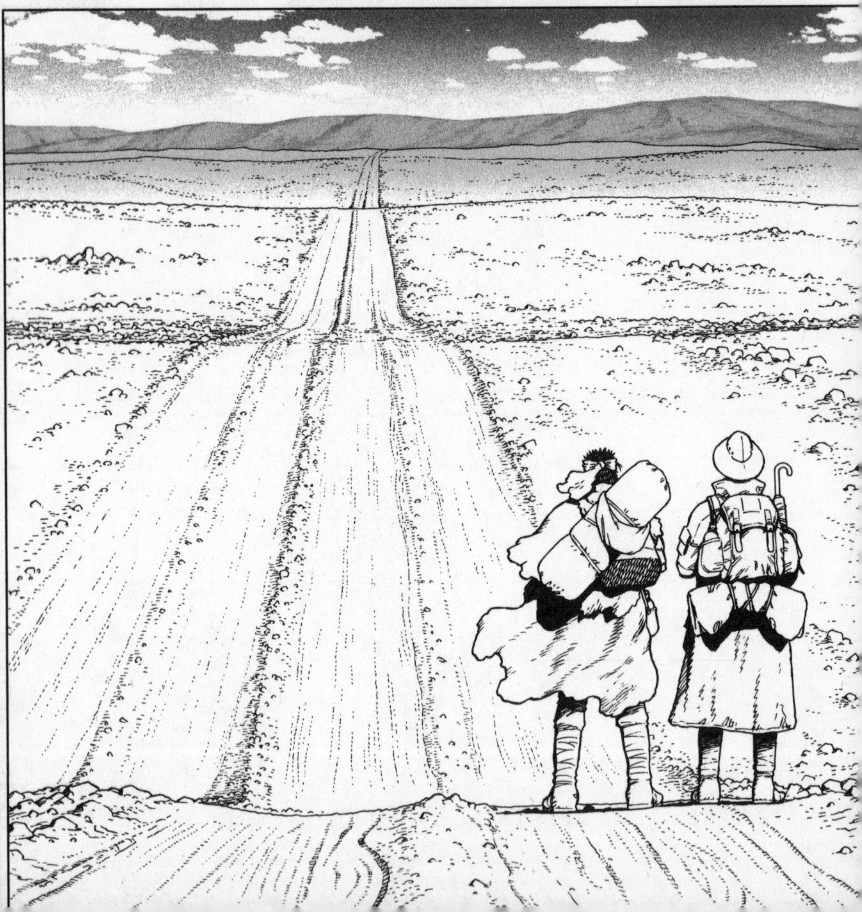

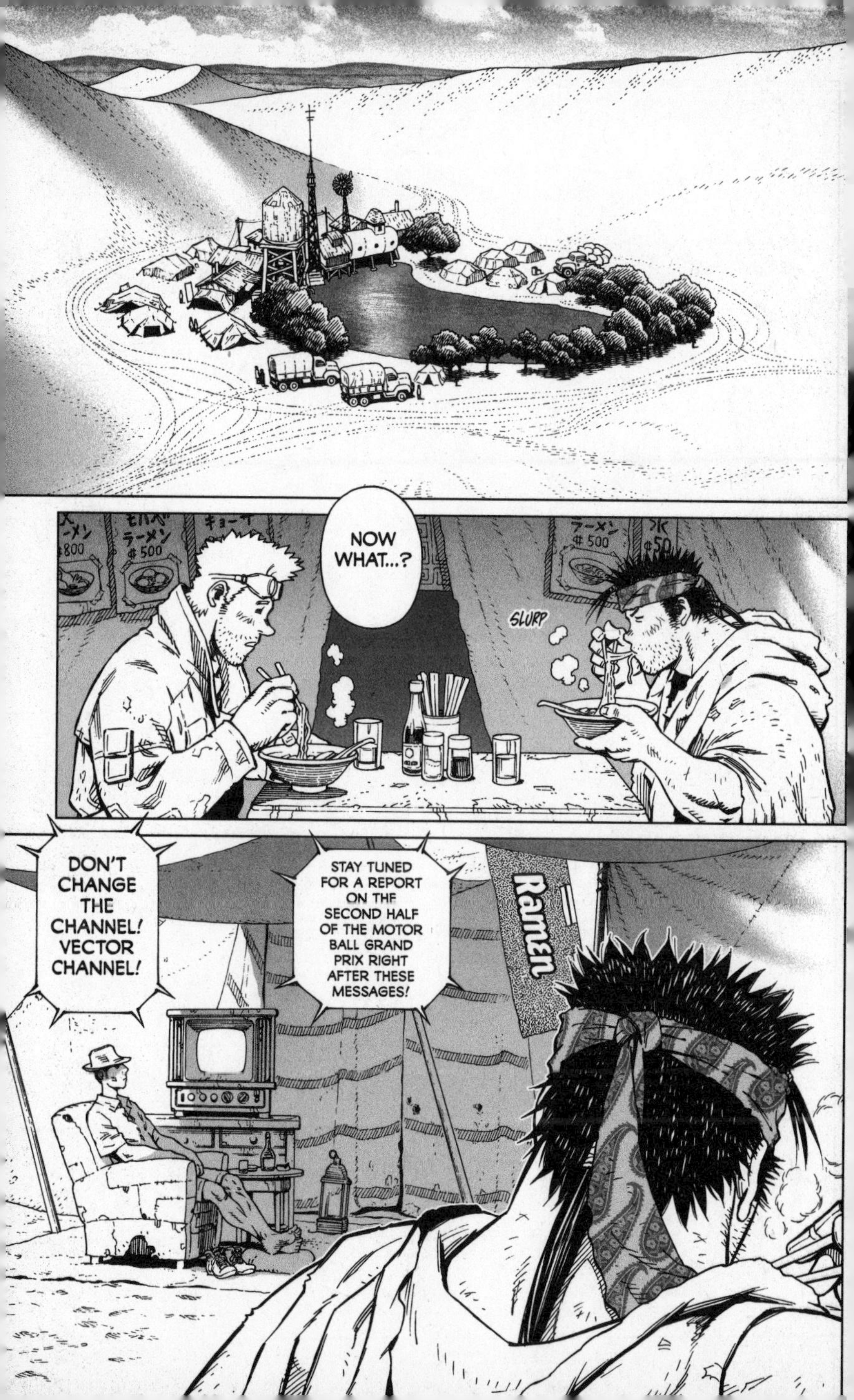

NOW WHAT...?
SLURP
Ramen
STAY TUNED FOR A REPORT ON THE SECOND HALF OF THE MOTOR BALL GRAND PRIX RIGHT AFTER THESE MESSAGES!
DON'T CHANGE THE CHANNEL! VECTOR CHANNEL!

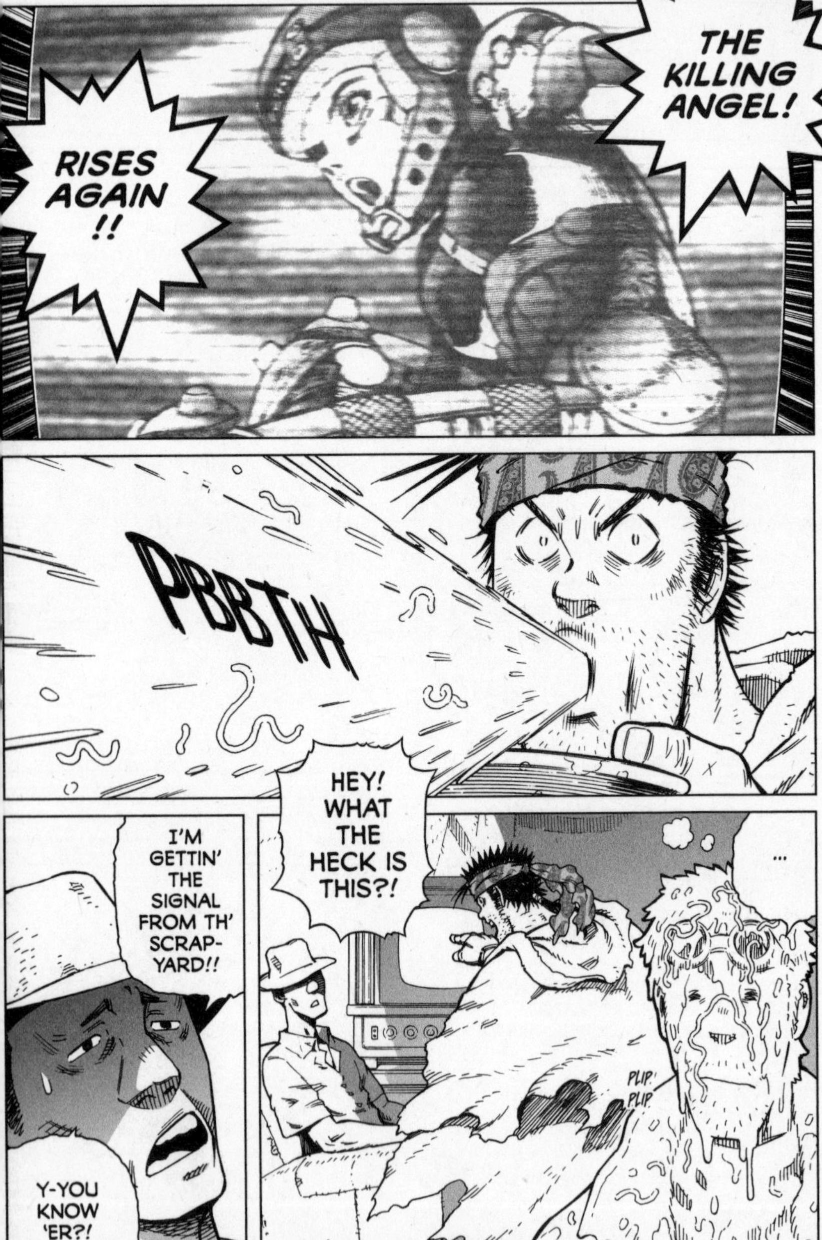
THE KILLING ANGEL!
RISES AGAIN !!
PBBTH
HEY! WHAT THE HECK IS THIS?!
...
PLIP PLIP
I'M GETTIN' THE SIGNAL FROM TH' SCRAP-YARD!!
Y-YOU KNOW 'ER?!

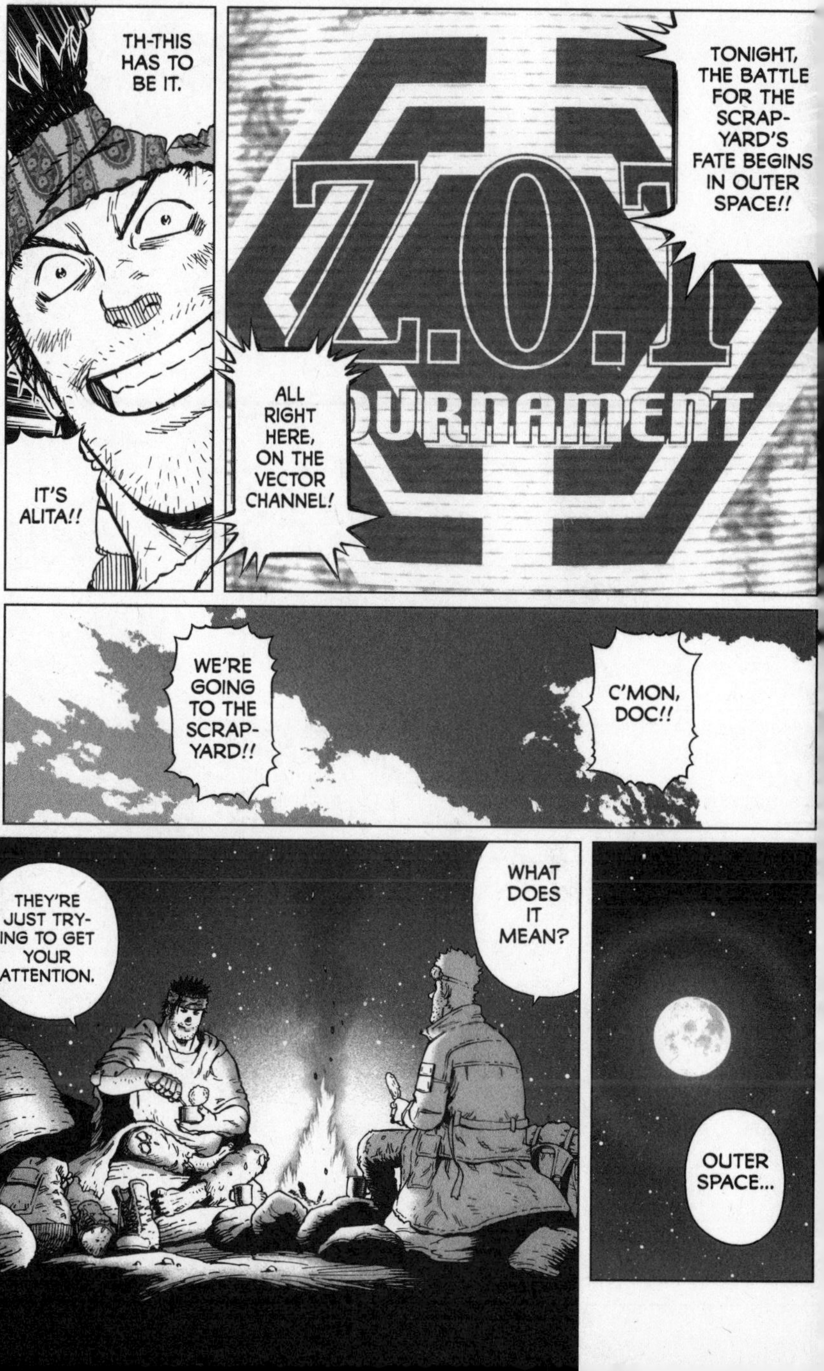
TONIGHT, THE BATTLE FOR THE SCRAP-YARD'S FATE BEGINS IN OUTER SPACE!!
Z.O.T.
OURNAMENT
ALL RIGHT HERE, ON THE VECTOR CHANNEL!
TH-THIS HAS TO BE IT.
IT'S ALITA!!
C'MON, DOC!!
WE'RE GOING TO THE SCRAP-YARD!!
OUTER SPACE...
WHAT DOES IT MEAN?
THEY'RE JUST TRYING TO GET YOUR ATTENTION.

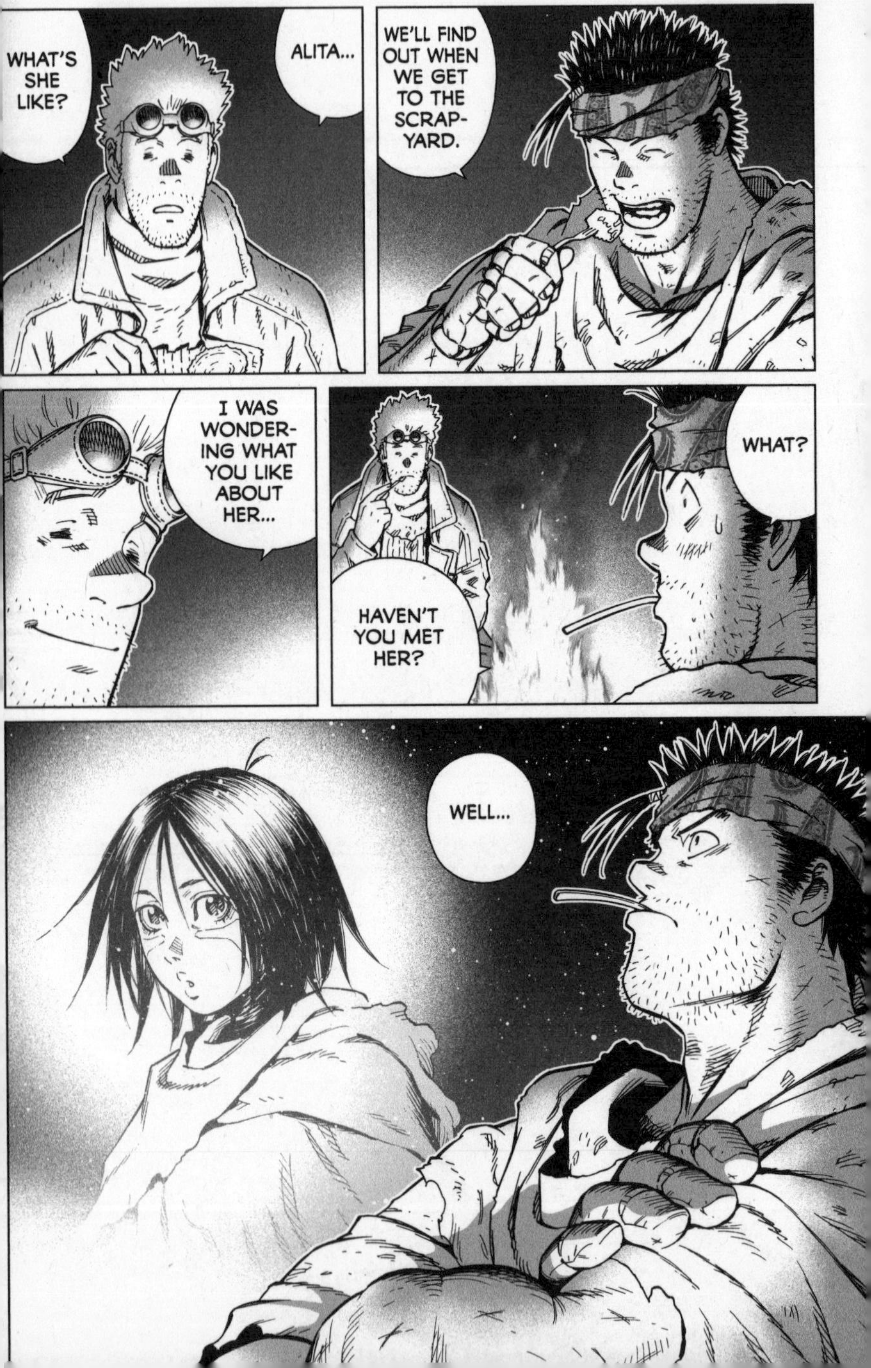
WE'LL FIND OUT WHEN WE GET TO THE SCRAP-YARD.
ALITA...
WHAT'S SHE LIKE?
WHAT?
HAVEN'T YOU MET HER?
I WAS WONDERING WHAT YOU LIKE ABOUT HER...
WELL...

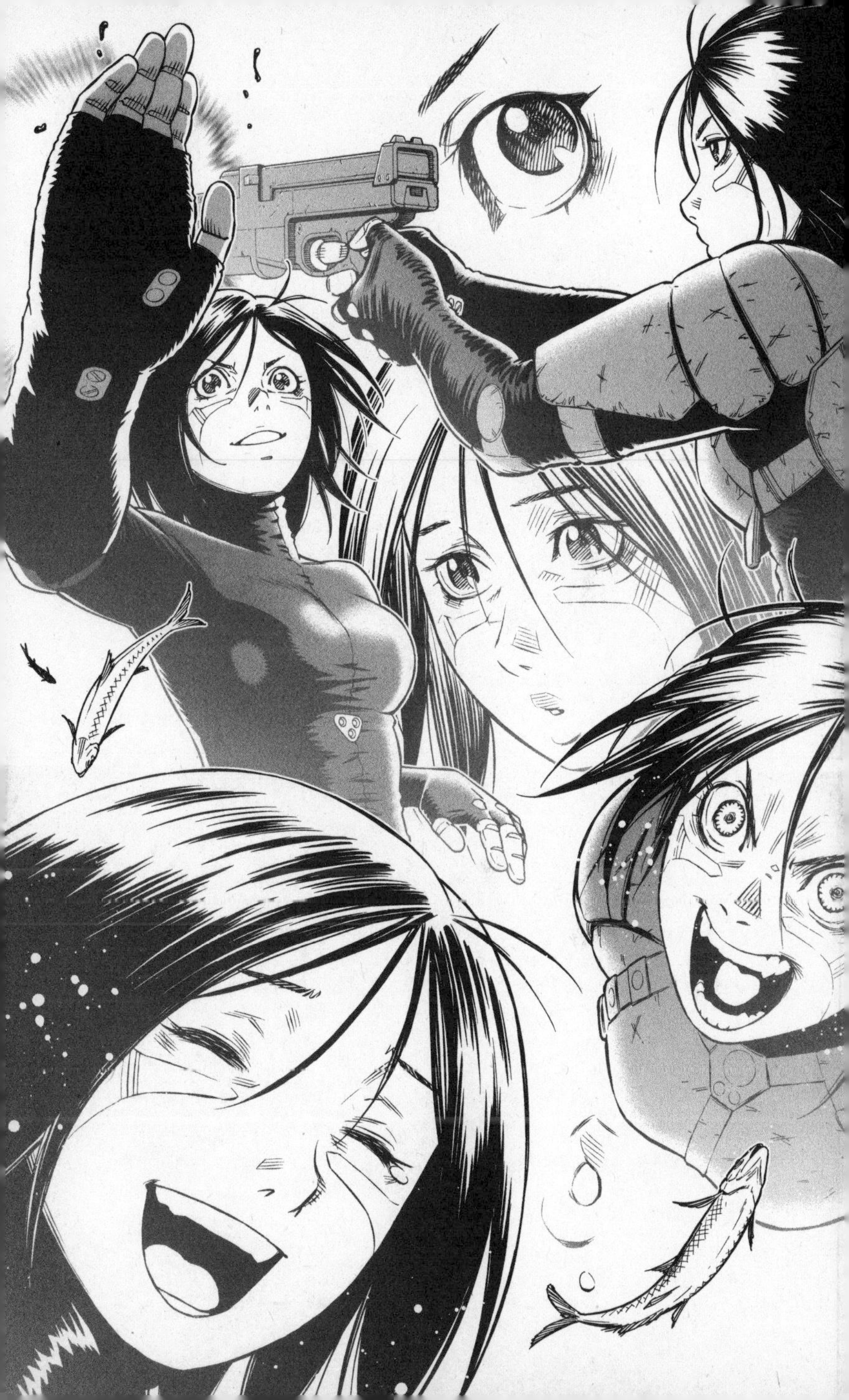

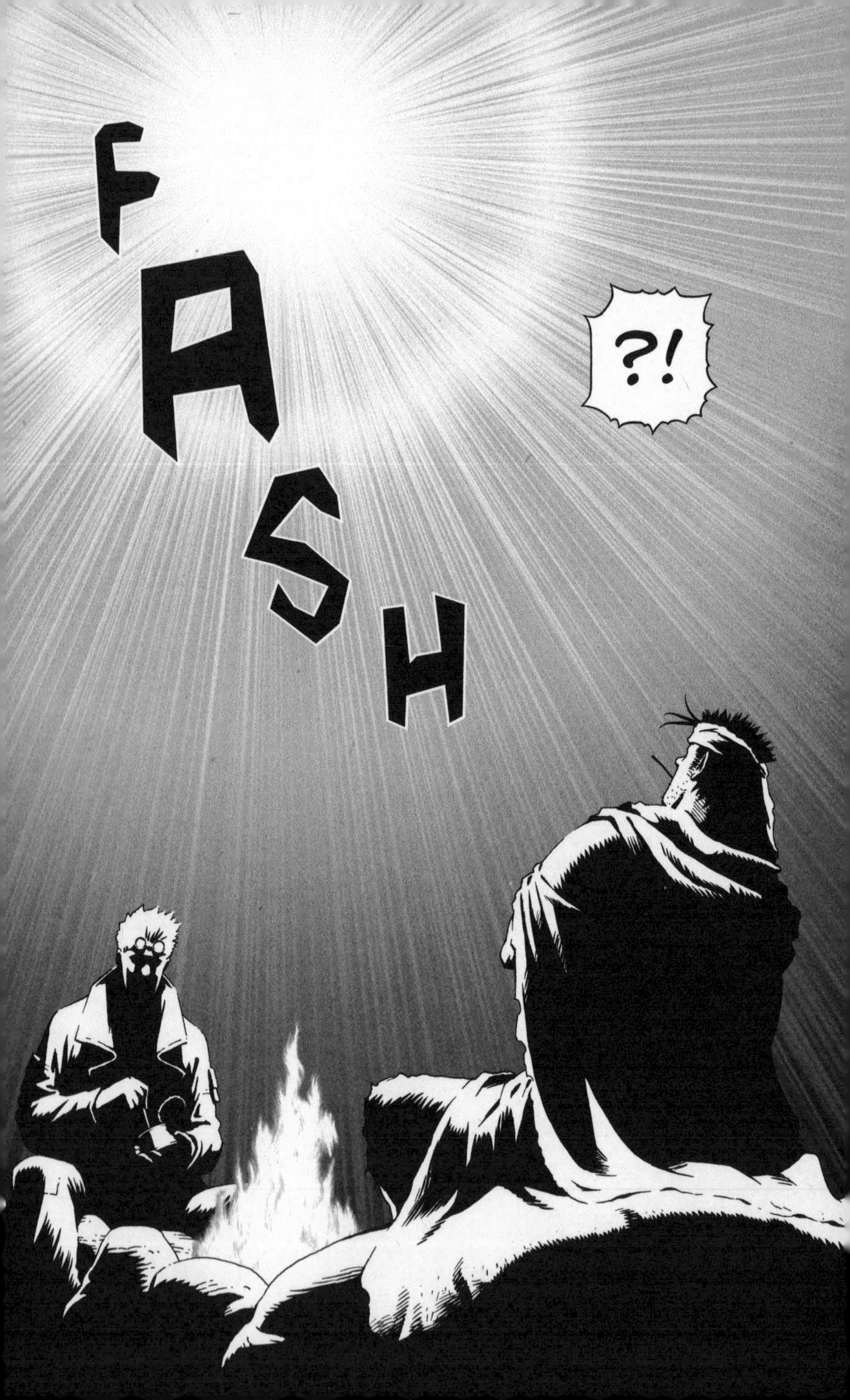
FASH
?!

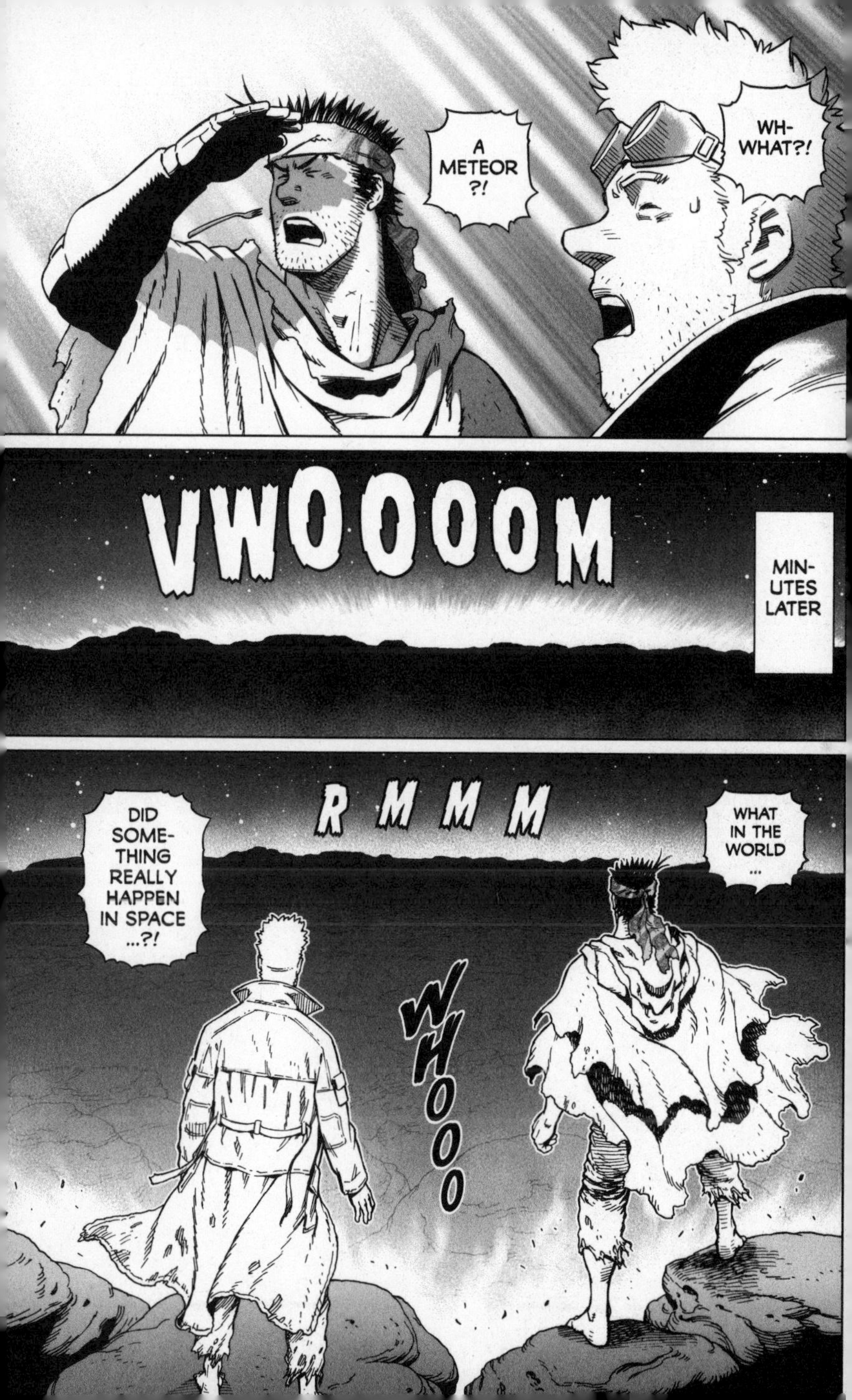
WH- WHAT?!
A METEOR ?!
VWOOOOM
MIN- UTES LATER
WHAT IN THE WORLD ...
R M M M
DID SOME- THING REALLY HAPPEN IN SPACE ...?!
WHOOOO

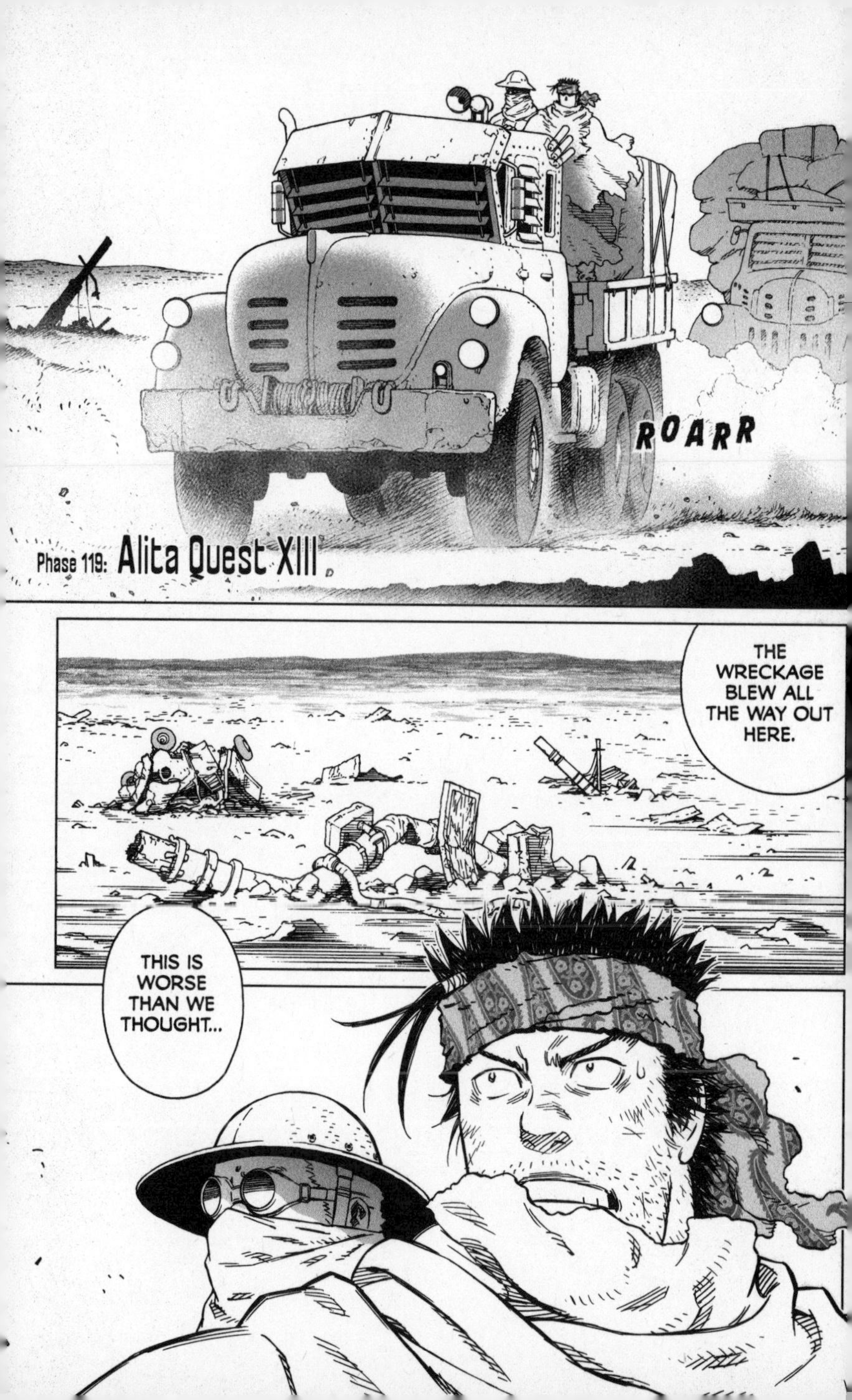
Phase 119: Alita Quest XIII
ROARR
THE WRECKAGE BLEW ALL THE WAY OUT HERE.
THIS IS WORSE THAN WE THOUGHT...

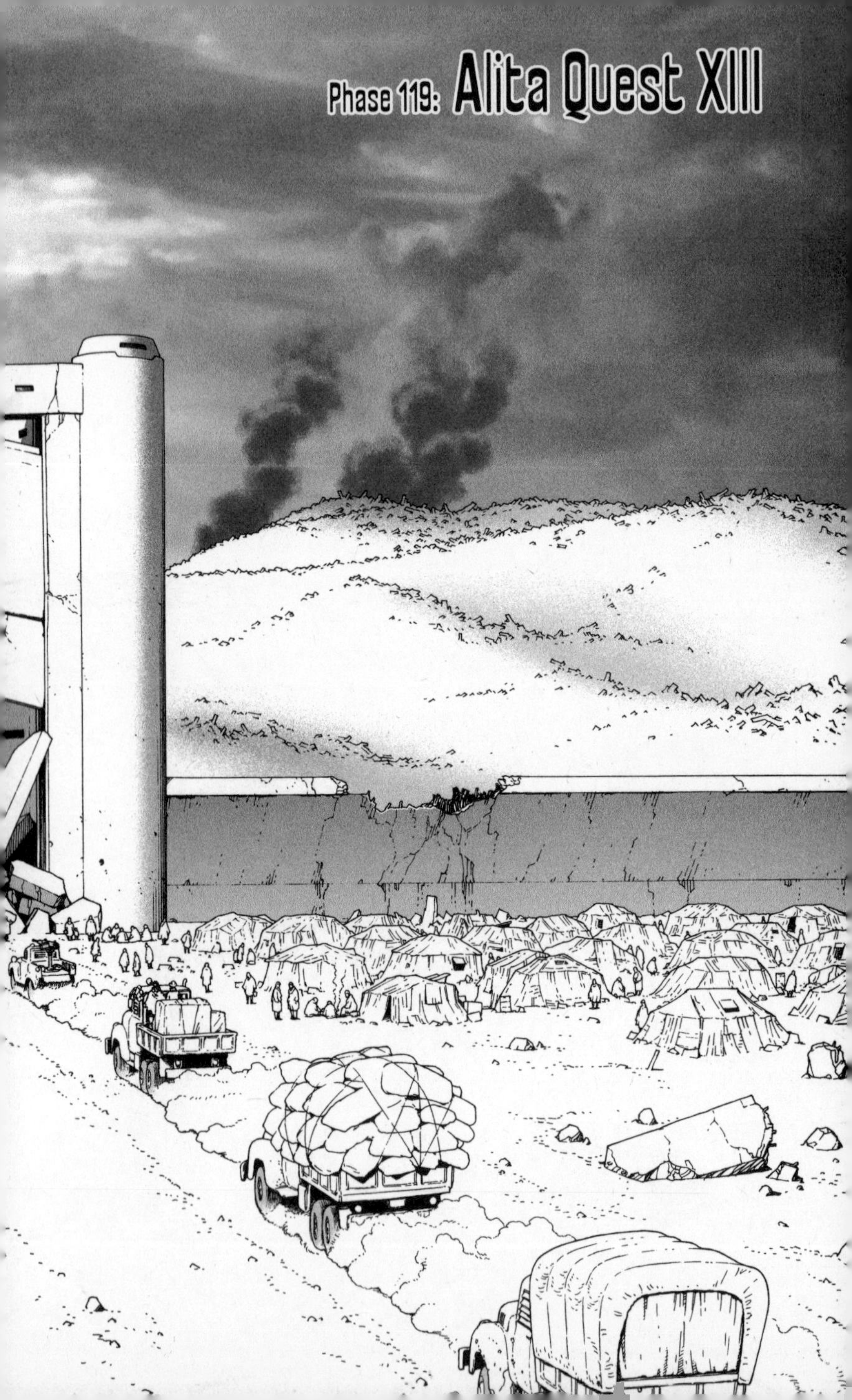
Phase 119: Alita Quest XIII

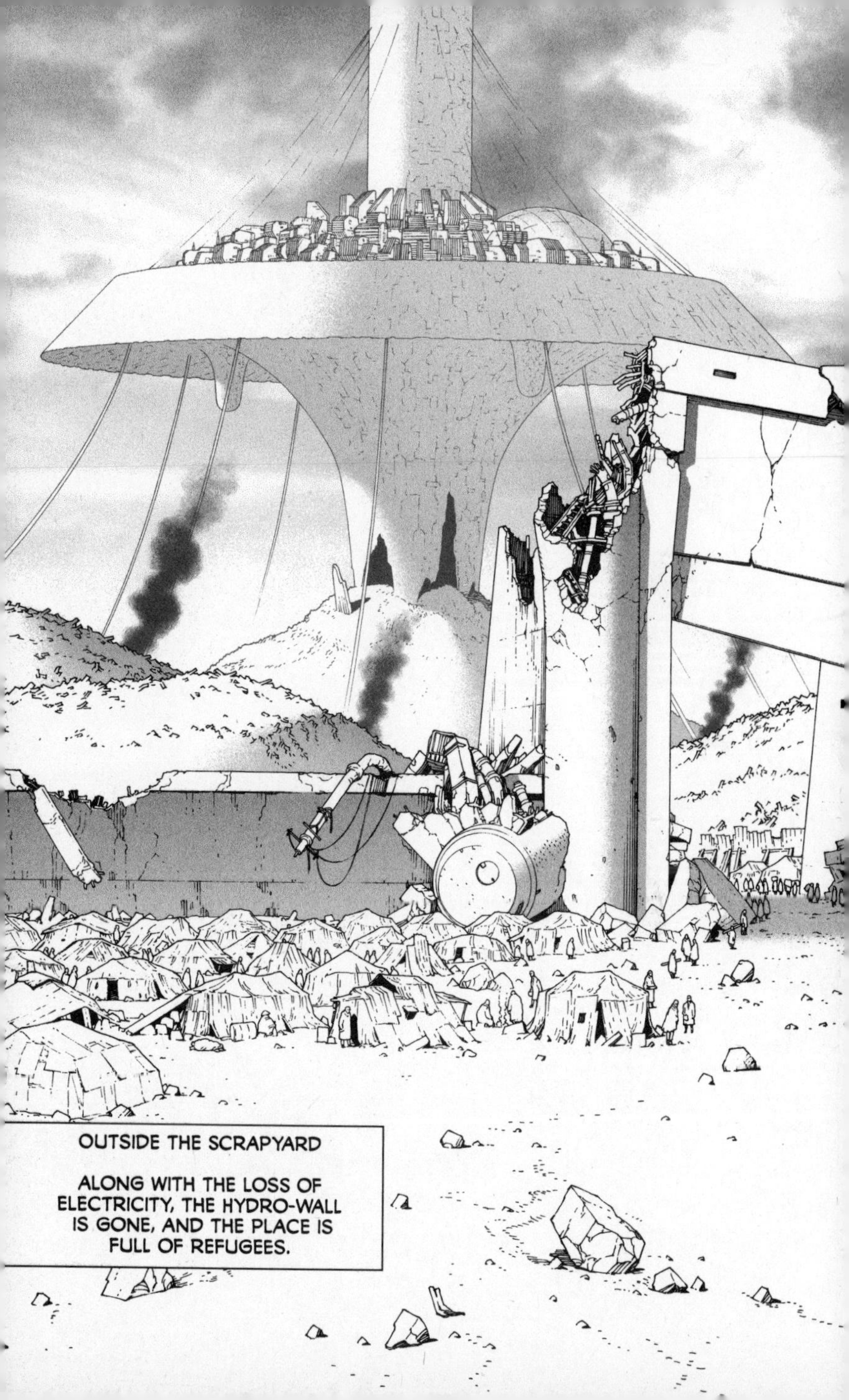
OUTSIDE THE SCRAPYARD
ALONG WITH THE LOSS OF ELECTRICITY, THE HYDRO-WALL IS GONE, AND THE PLACE IS FULL OF REFUGEES.

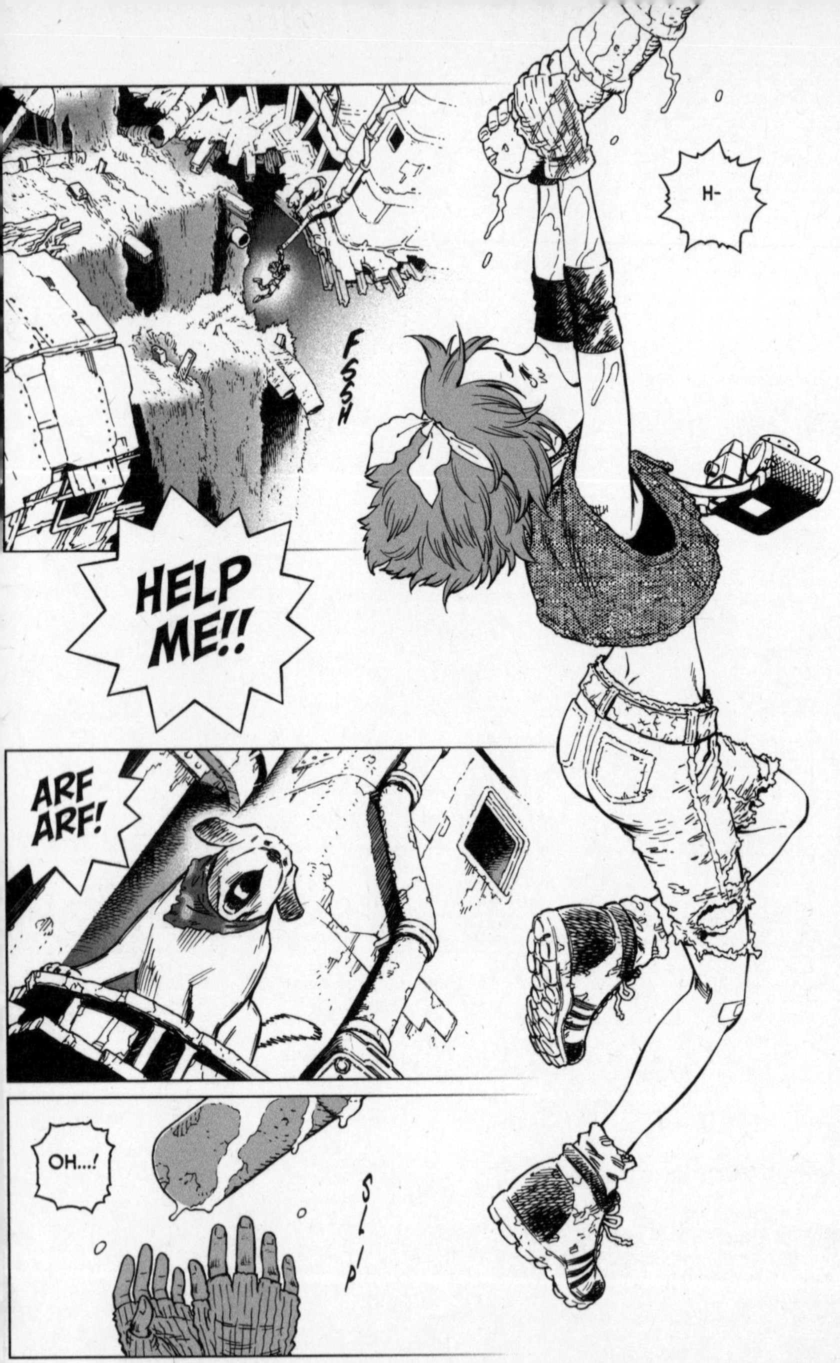
H-
FSSH
HELP ME!!
ARF ARF!
OH...!
SLIP

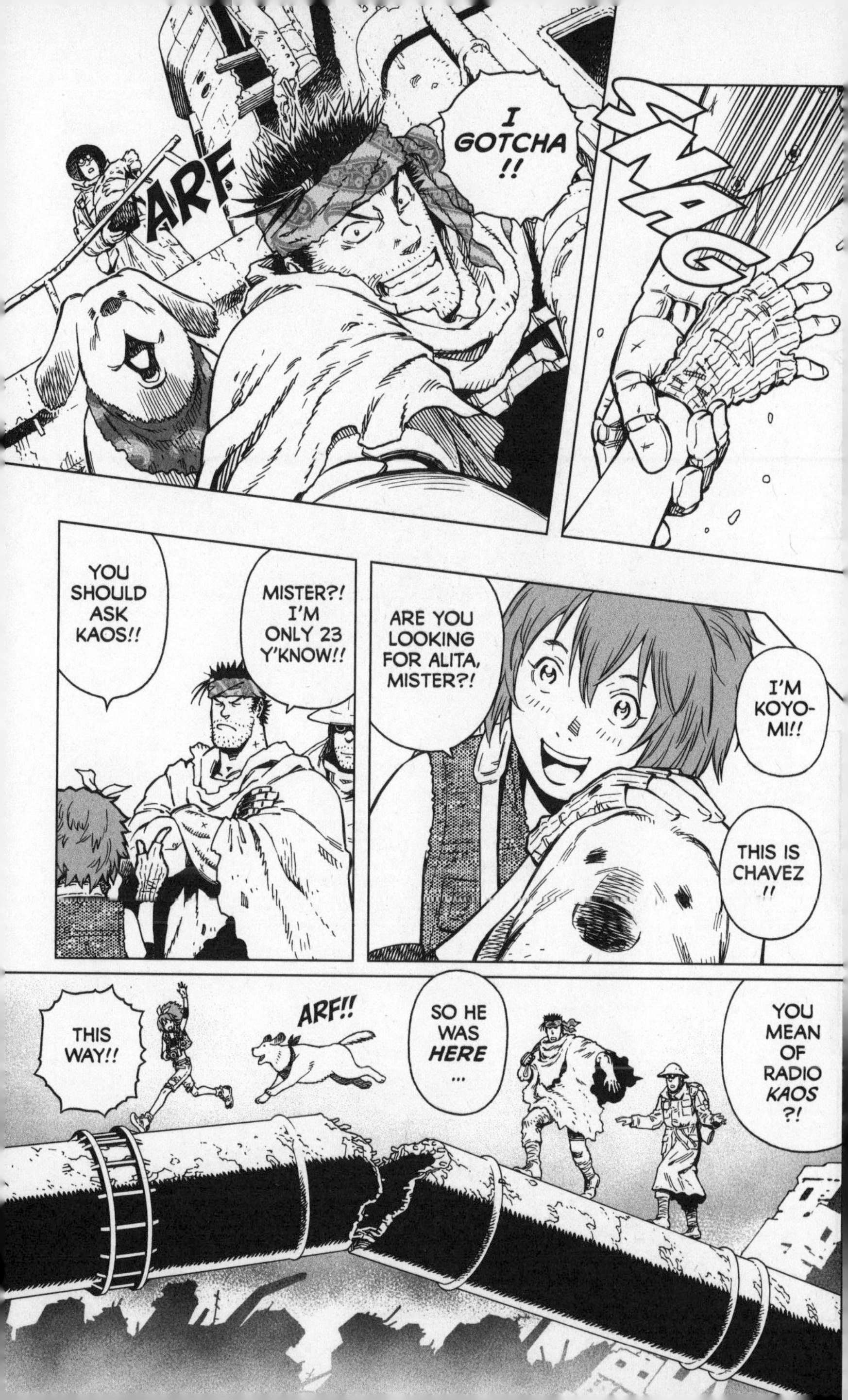
SNAG
I GOTCHA !!
ARF
I'M KOYOMI!!
THIS IS CHAVEZ !!
ARE YOU LOOKING FOR ALITA, MISTER?!
MISTER?! I'M ONLY 23 Y'KNOW!!
YOU SHOULD ASK KAOS!!
YOU MEAN OF RADIO KAOS ?!
SO HE WAS HERE ...
ARF!!
THIS WAY!!

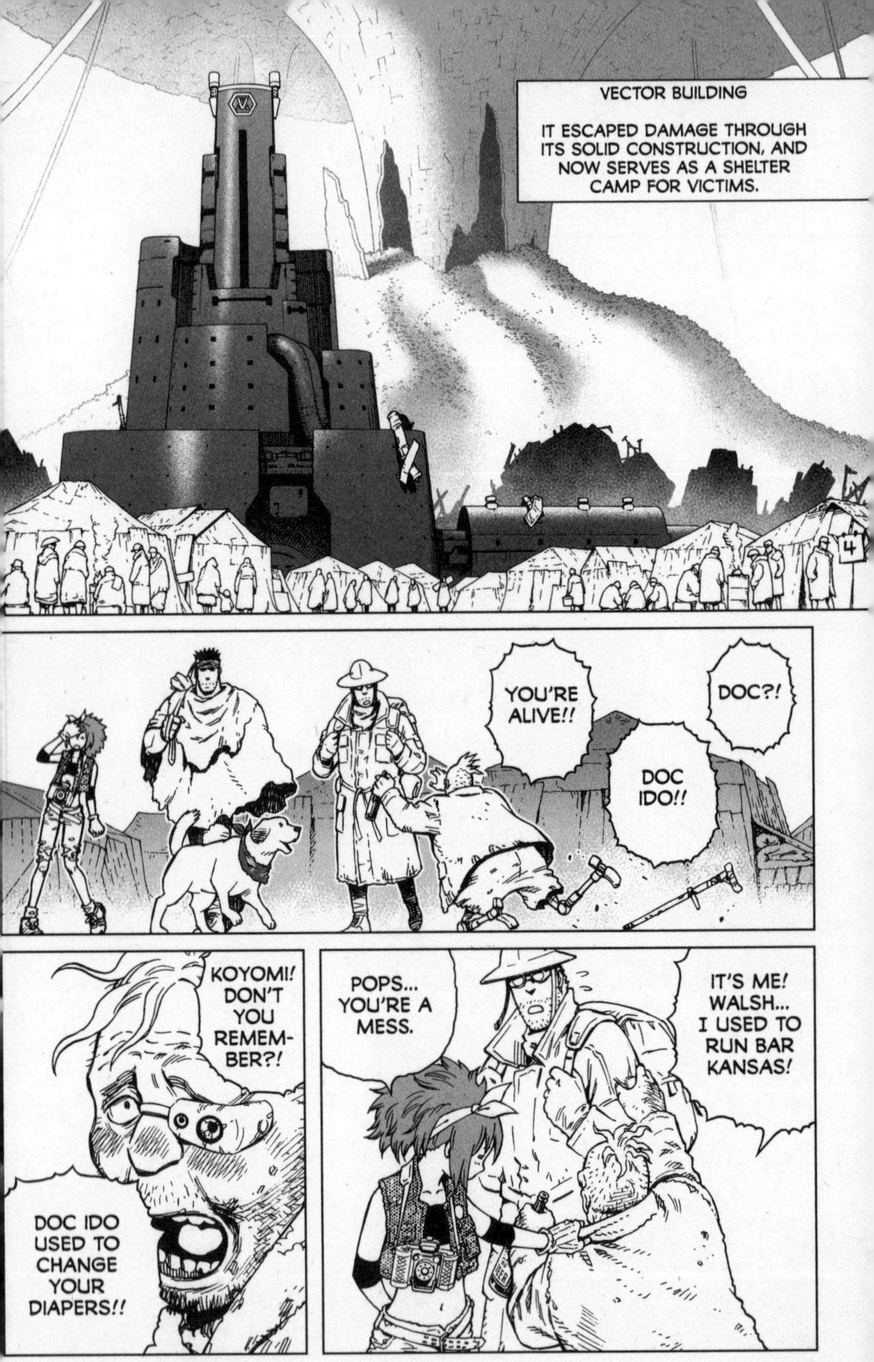
VECTOR BUILDING
IT ESCAPED DAMAGE THROUGH ITS SOLID CONSTRUCTION, AND NOW SERVES AS A SHELTER CAMP FOR VICTIMS.
DOC?!
YOU'RE ALIVE!!
DOC IDO!!
IT'S ME! WALSH... I USED TO RUN BAR KANSAS!
POPS... YOU'RE A MESS.
KOYOMI! DON'T YOU REMEMBER?!
DOC IDO USED TO CHANGE YOUR DIAPERS!!

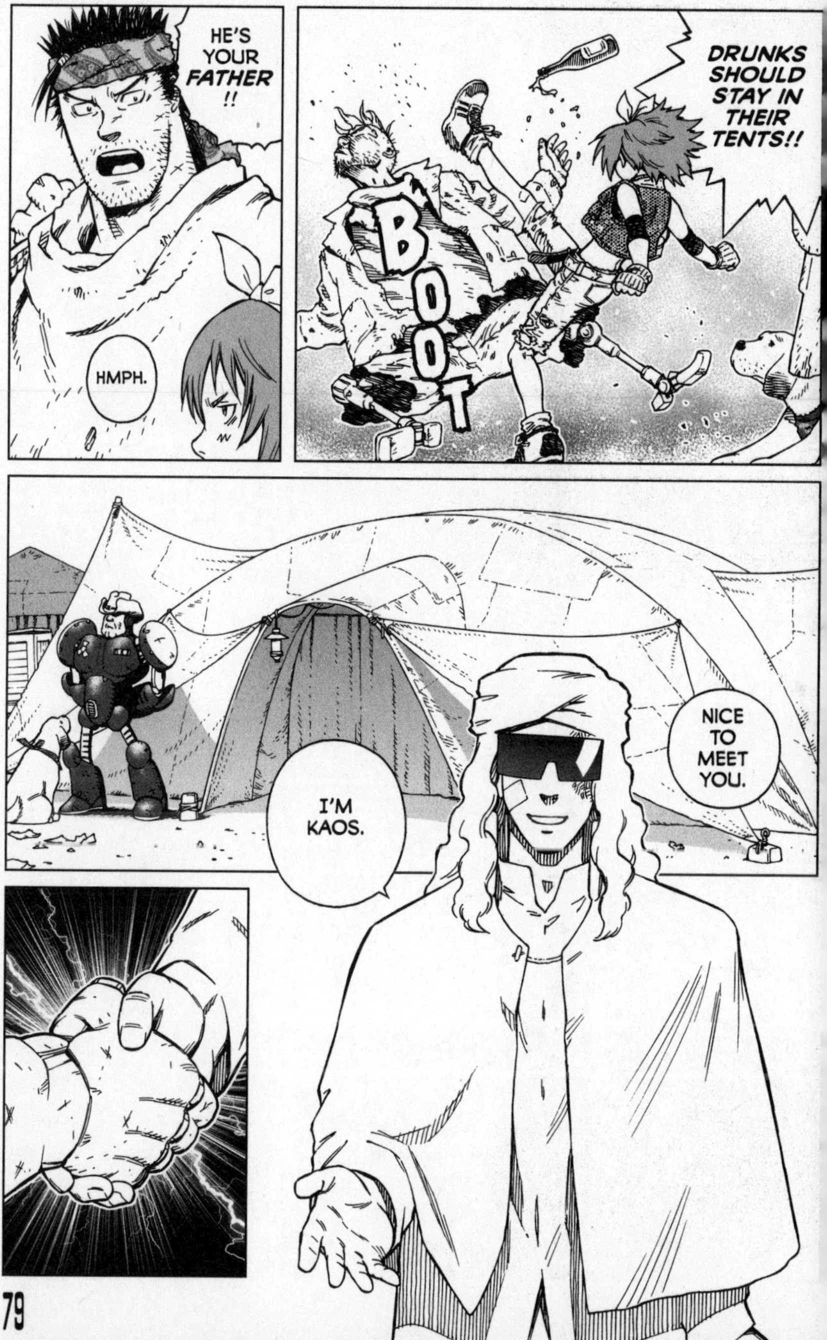
DRUNKS SHOULD STAY IN THEIR TENTS!!
BOOT
HE'S YOUR FATHER!!
HMPH.
NICE TO MEET YOU.
I'M KAOS.

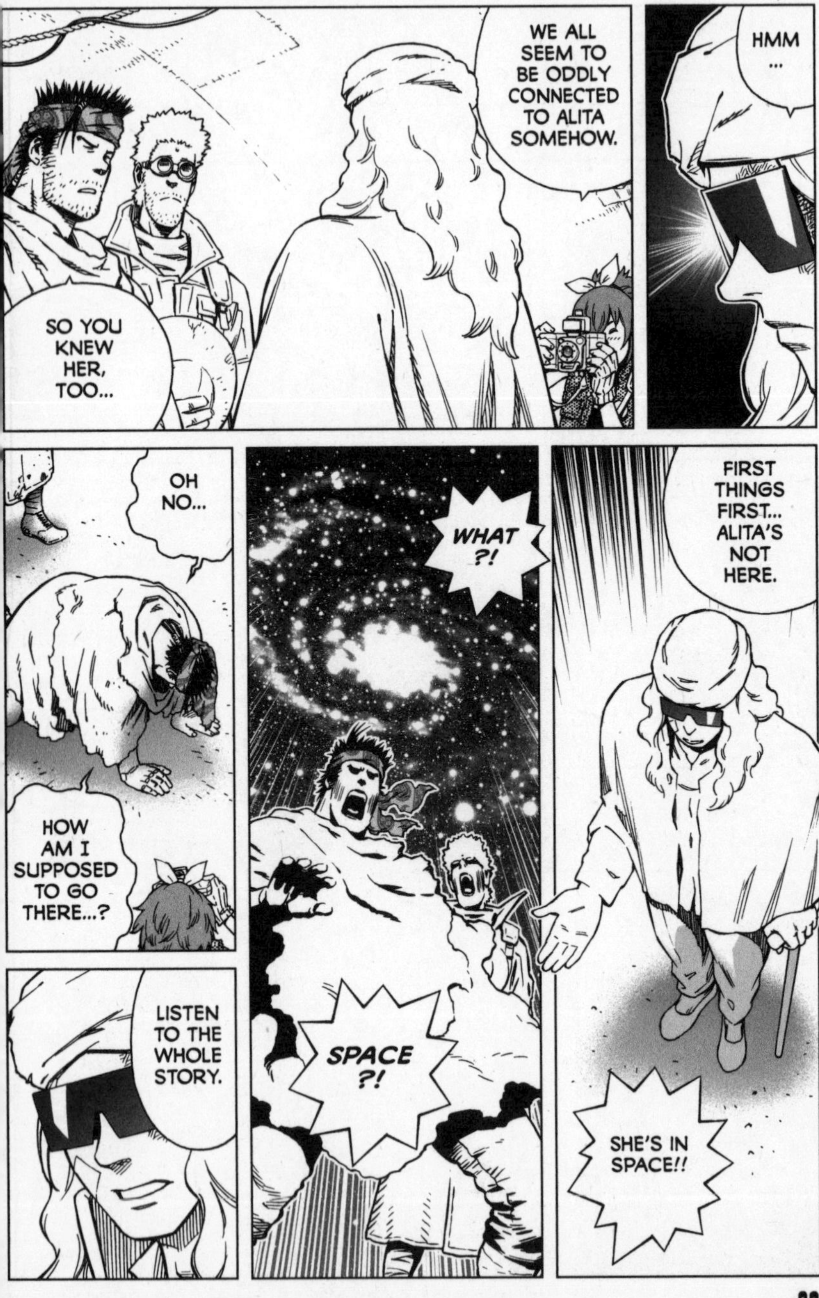
HMM ...
WE ALL SEEM TO BE ODDLY CONNECTED TO ALITA SOMEHOW.
SO YOU KNEW HER, TOO...
FIRST THINGS FIRST... ALITA'S NOT HERE.
SHE'S IN SPACE!!
WHAT ?!
SPACE ?!
OH NO...
HOW AM I SUPPOSED TO GO THERE...?
LISTEN TO THE WHOLE STORY.

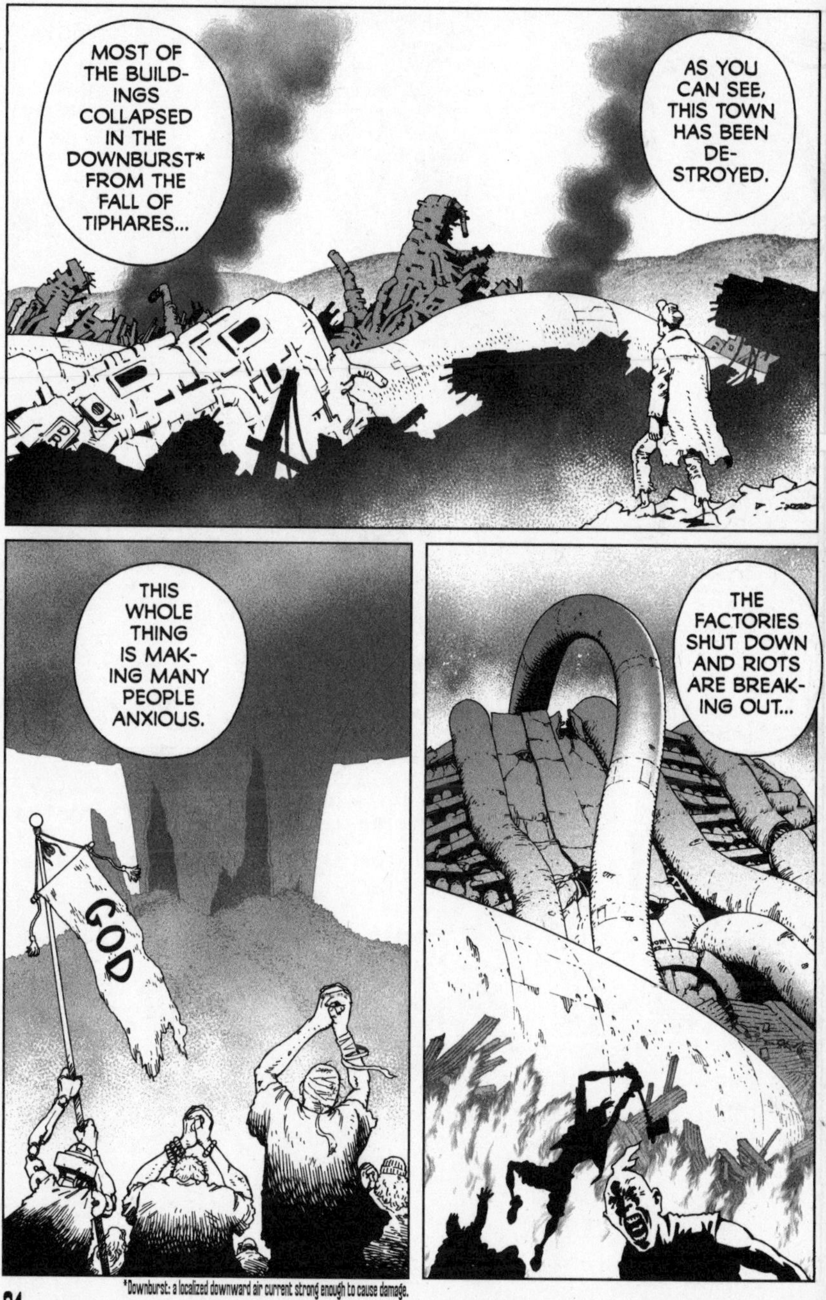
AS YOU CAN SEE, THIS TOWN HAS BEEN DE-STROYED.
MOST OF THE BUILD-INGS COLLAPSED IN THE DOWNBURST* FROM THE FALL OF TIPHARES...
THE FACTORIES SHUT DOWN AND RIOTS ARE BREAK-ING OUT...
THIS WHOLE THING IS MAK-ING MANY PEOPLE ANXIOUS.
GOD

*Downburst: a localized downward air current strong enough to cause damage.

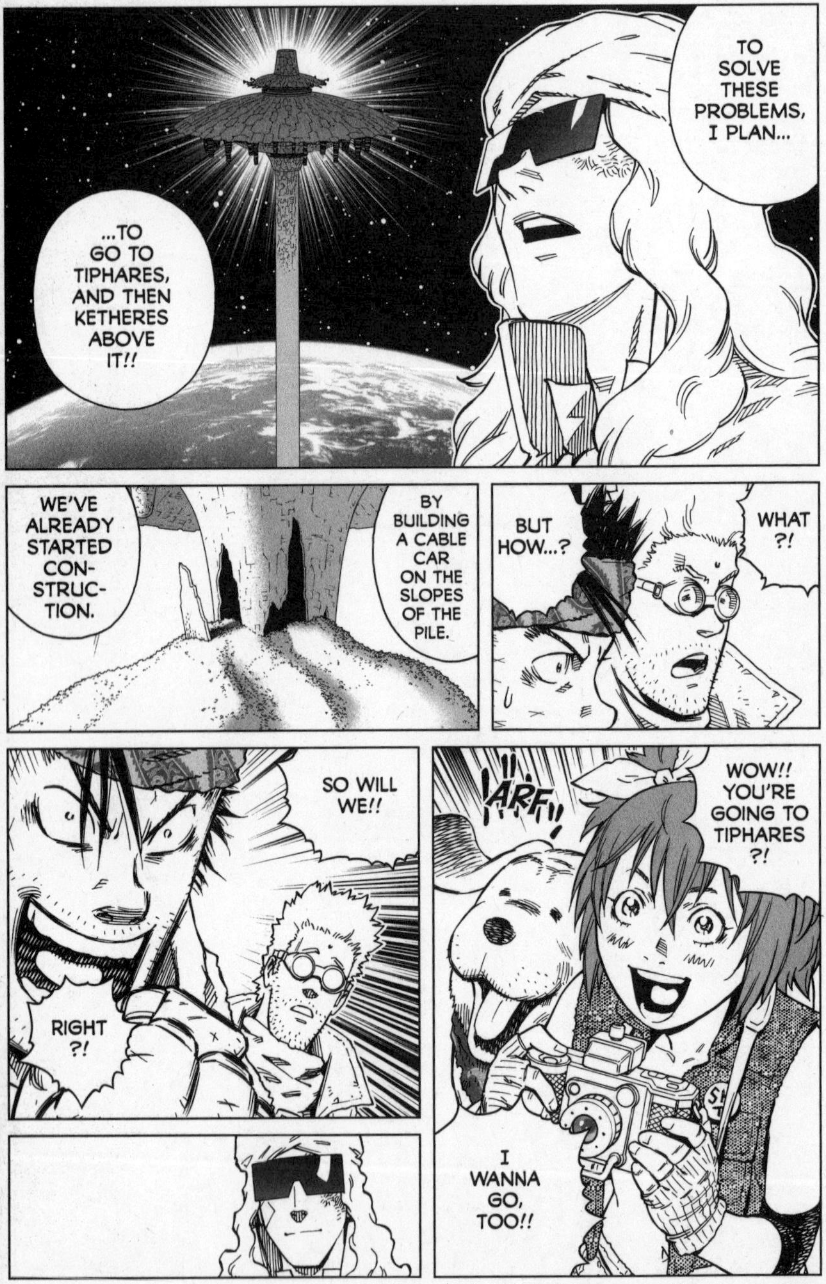
TO SOLVE THESE PROBLEMS, I PLAN...
...TO GO TO TIPHARES, AND THEN KETHERES ABOVE IT!!
WHAT?!
BUT HOW...?
BY BUILDING A CABLE CAR ON THE SLOPES OF THE PILE.
WE'VE ALREADY STARTED CON-STRUC-TION.
ARF!!
WOW!! YOU'RE GOING TO TIPHARES?!
I WANNA GO, TOO!!
SO WILL WE!!
RIGHT?!

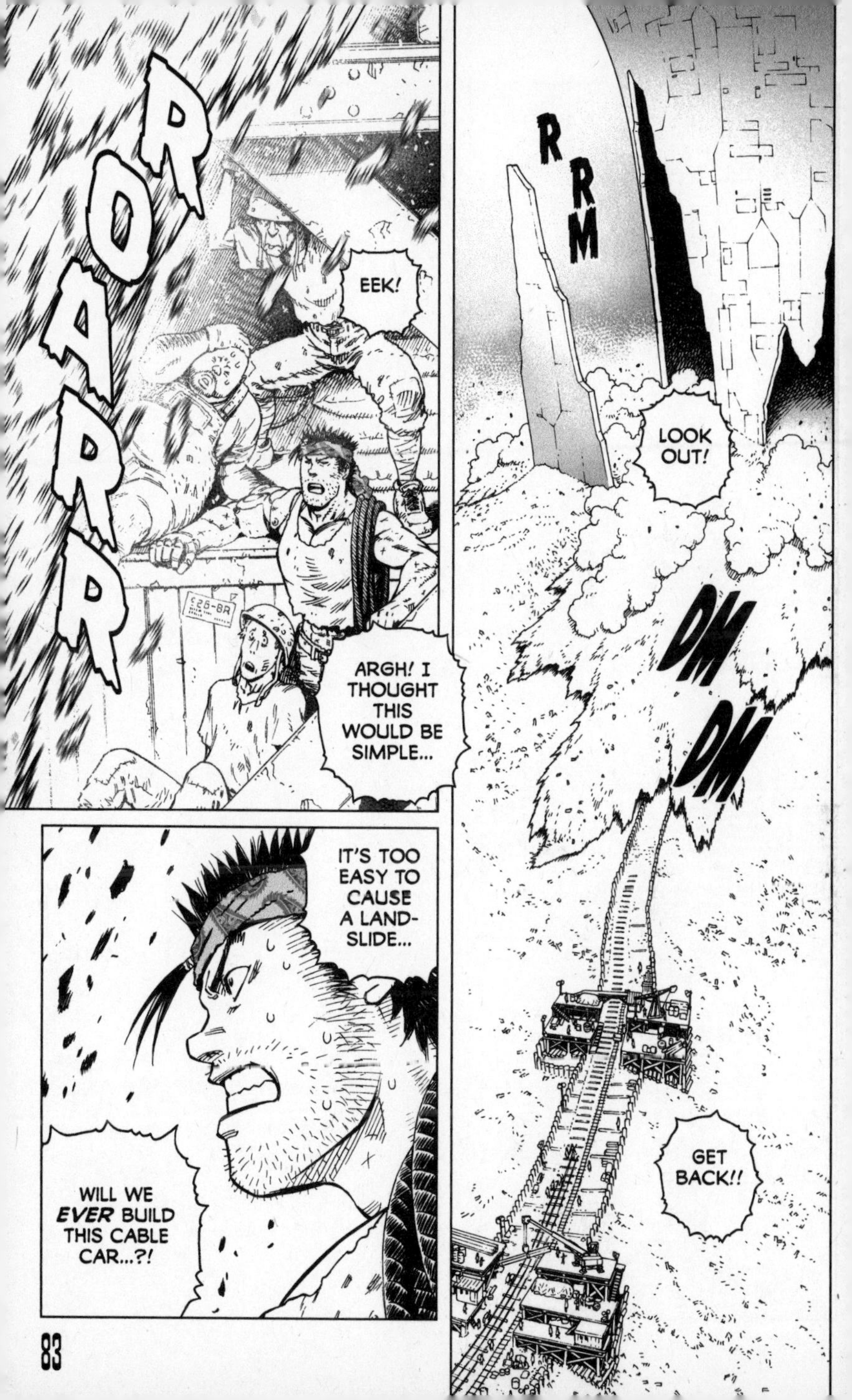
RRM
LOOK OUT!
DM DM
GET BACK!!
ROARR
EEK!
ARGH! I THOUGHT THIS WOULD BE SIMPLE...
IT'S TOO EASY TO CAUSE A LAND-SLIDE...
WILL WE ***EVER*** BUILD THIS CABLE CAR...?!

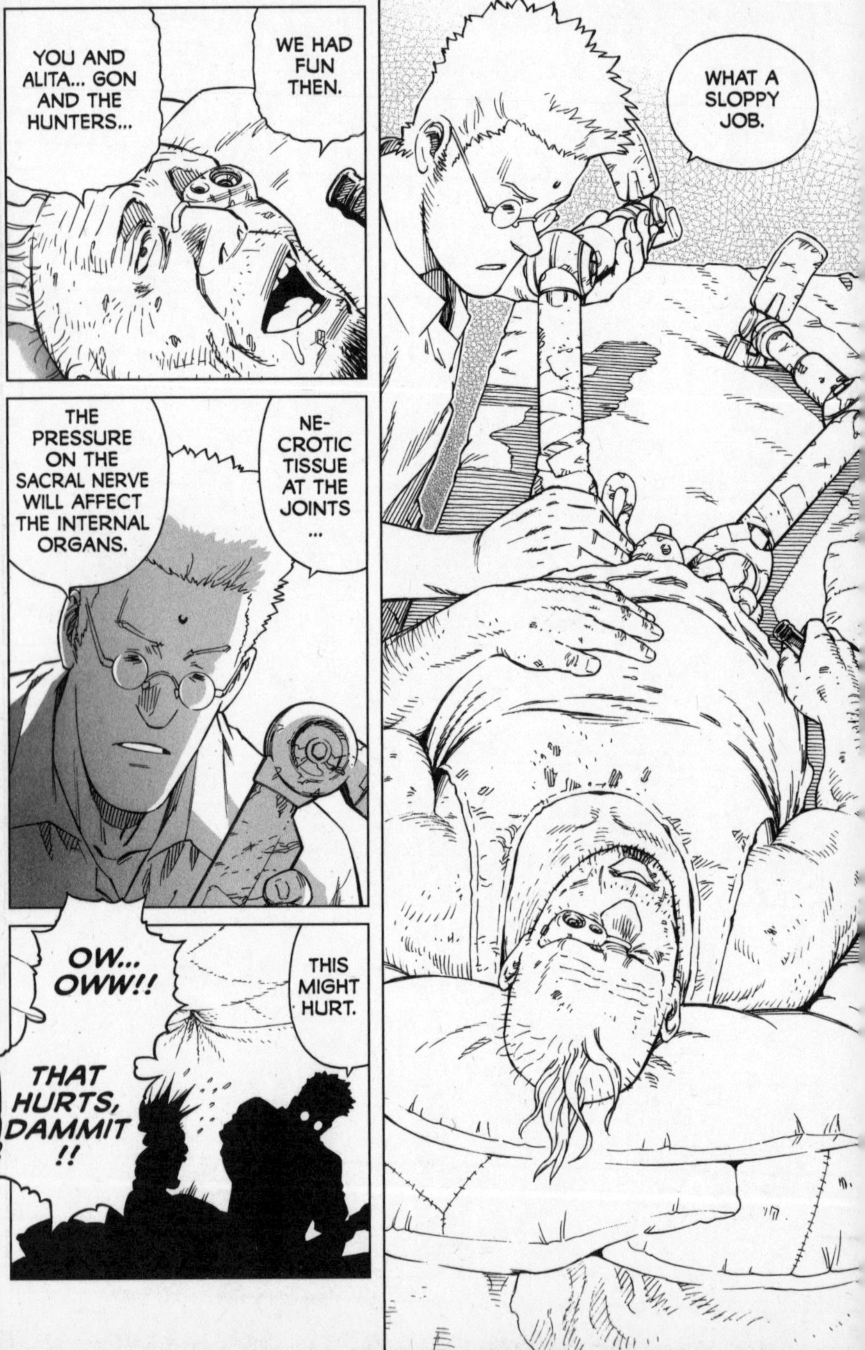
WHAT A SLOPPY JOB.
WE HAD FUN THEN.
YOU AND ALITA... GON AND THE HUNTERS...
NE-CROTIC TISSUE AT THE JOINTS ...
THE PRESSURE ON THE SACRAL NERVE WILL AFFECT THE INTERNAL ORGANS.
THIS MIGHT HURT.
OW... OWW!!
THAT HURTS, DAMMIT !!

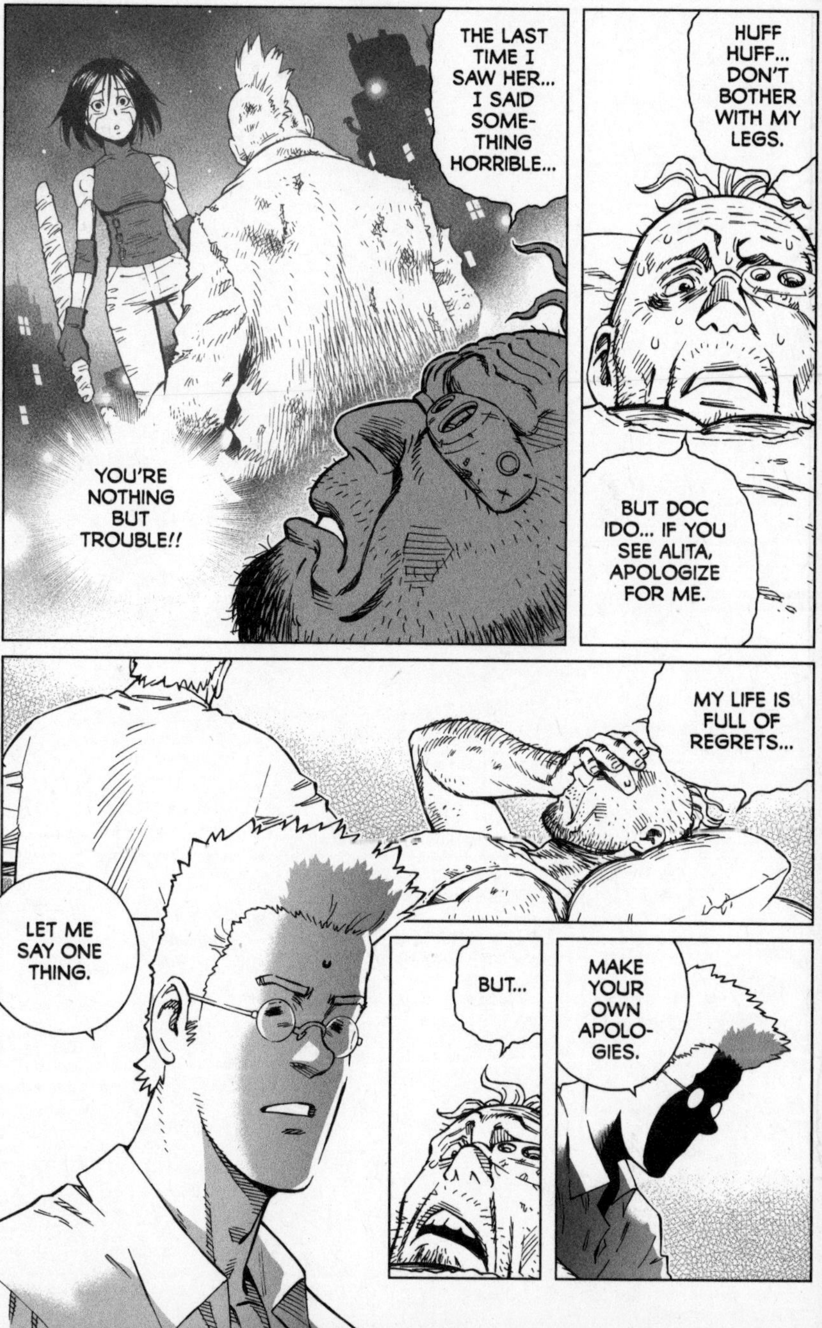
HUFF HUFF... DON'T BOTHER WITH MY LEGS.
BUT DOC IDO... IF YOU SEE ALITA, APOLOGIZE FOR ME.
THE LAST TIME I SAW HER... I SAID SOME-THING HORRIBLE...
YOU'RE NOTHING BUT TROUBLE!!
MY LIFE IS FULL OF REGRETS...
MAKE YOUR OWN APOLO-GIES.
BUT...
LET ME SAY ONE THING.

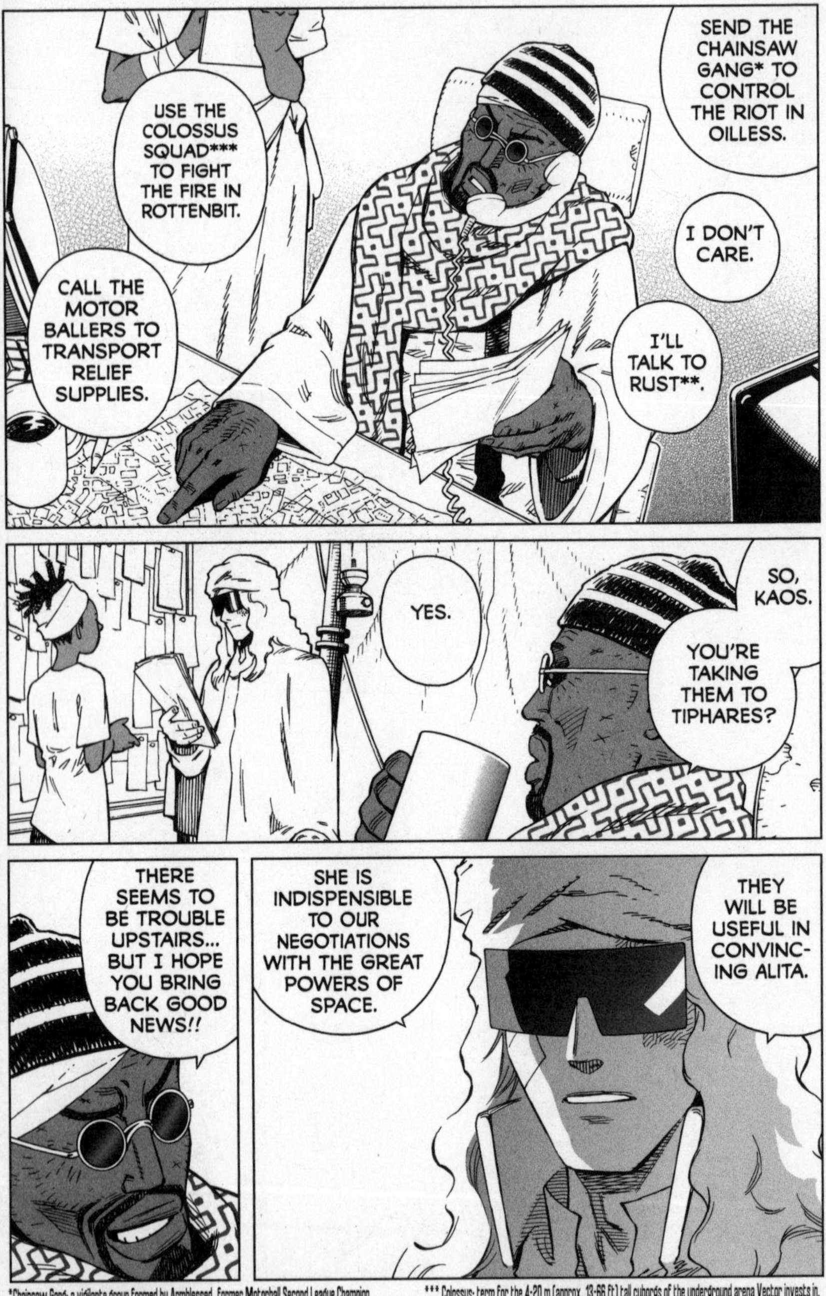
SEND THE CHAINSAW GANG* TO CONTROL THE RIOT IN OILLESS.
I DON'T CARE.
I'LL TALK TO RUST**.
USE THE COLOSSUS SQUAD*** TO FIGHT THE FIRE IN ROTTENBIT.
CALL THE MOTOR BALLERS TO TRANSPORT RELIEF SUPPLIES.
SO, KAOS.
YOU'RE TAKING THEM TO TIPHARES?
YES.
THEY WILL BE USEFUL IN CONVINC-ING ALITA.
SHE IS INDISPENSIBLE TO OUR NEGOTIATIONS WITH THE GREAT POWERS OF SPACE.
THERE SEEMS TO BE TROUBLE UPSTAIRS... BUT I HOPE YOU BRING BACK GOOD NEWS!!

*Chainsaw Gang: a vigilante group formed by Armblessed, former Motorball Second League Champion.

**Rust: the Scrapyard's gangster organization.

*** Colossus: term for the 4-20 m (approx. 13-66 ft) tall cyborgs of the underground arena Vector invests in.

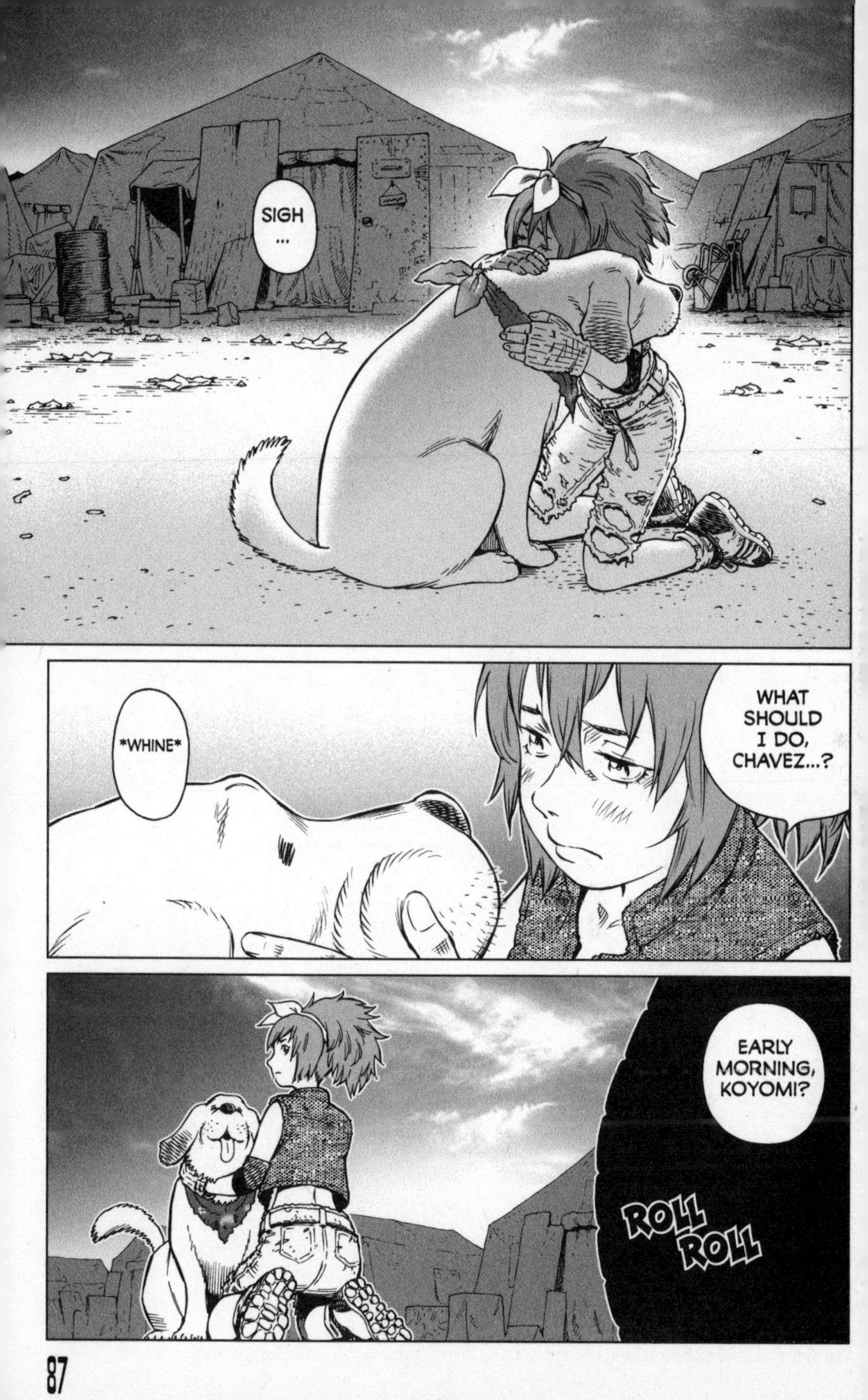
SIGH ...
WHAT SHOULD I DO, CHAVEZ...?
WHINE
EARLY MORNING, KOYOMI?
ROLL ROLL

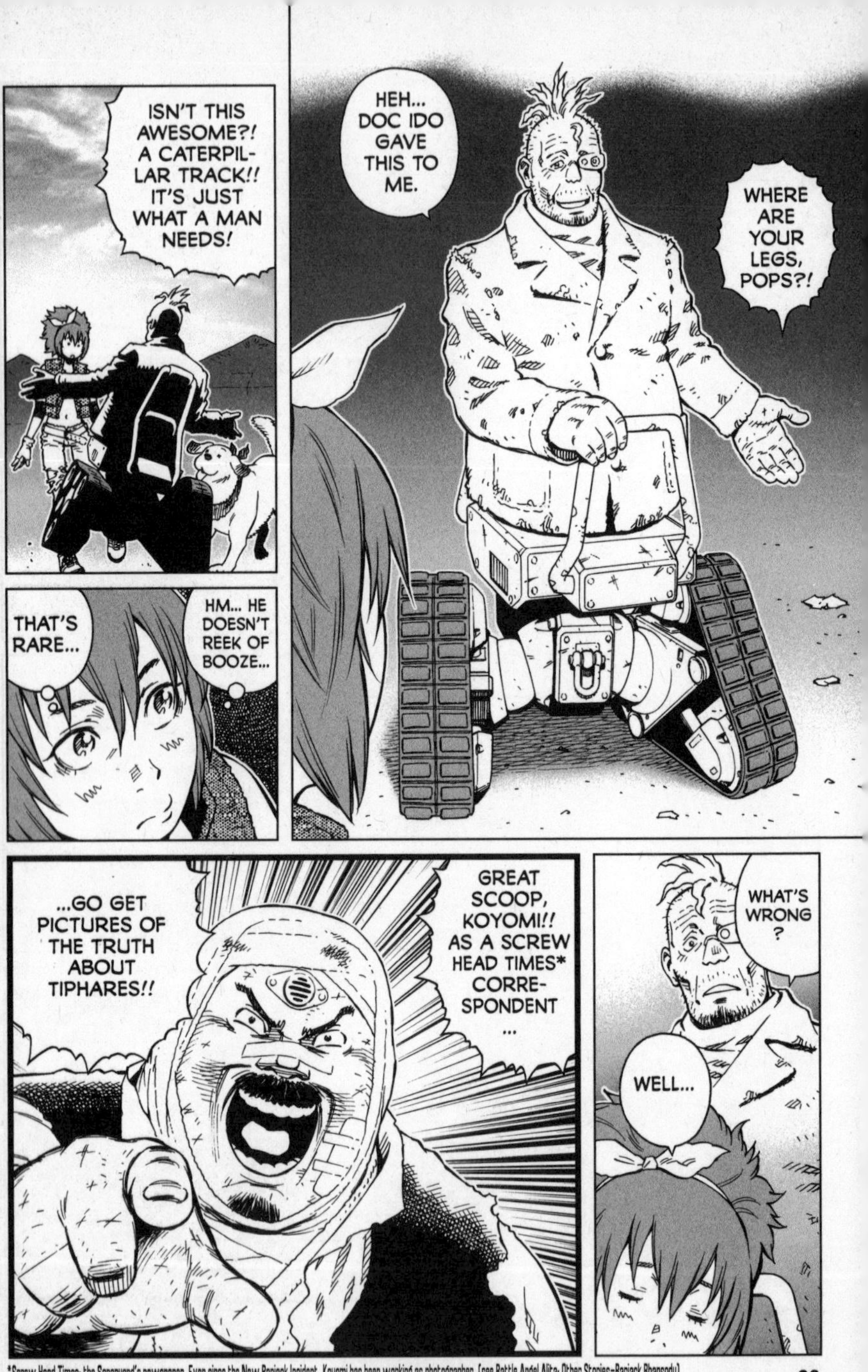
WHERE ARE YOUR LEGS, POPS?!
HEH... DOC IDO GAVE THIS TO ME.
ISN'T THIS AWESOME?! A CATERPIL-LAR TRACK!! IT'S JUST WHAT A MAN NEEDS!
HM... HE DOESN'T REEK OF BOOZE...
THAT'S RARE...
WHAT'S WRONG ?
WELL...
GREAT SCOOP, KOYOMI!! AS A SCREW HEAD TIMES* CORRE-SPONDENT ...
...GO GET PICTURES OF THE TRUTH ABOUT TIPHARES!!

*Screw Head Times: the Scrapyard's newspaper. Ever since the New Barjack Incident, Koyomi has been working as photographer. (see Battle Angel Alita: Other Stories–Barjack Rhapsody)

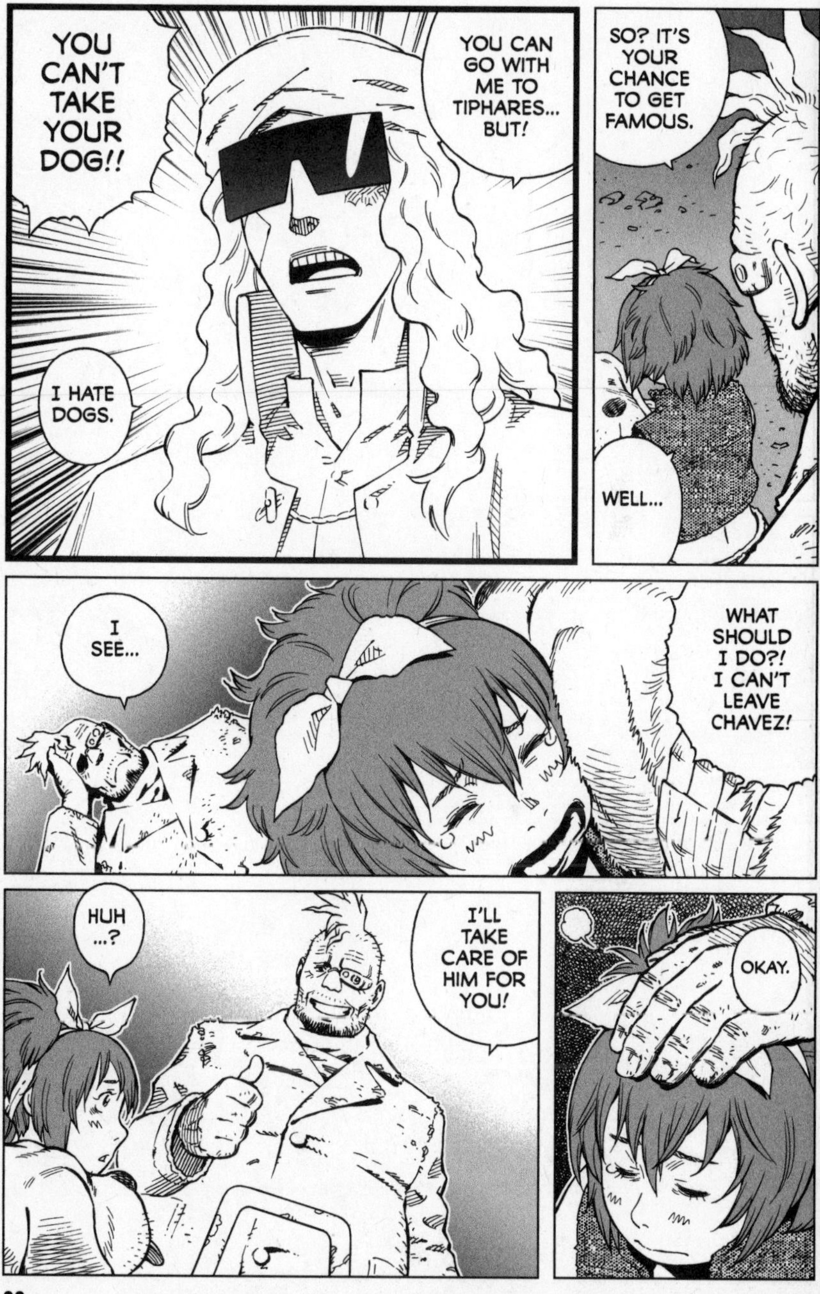
SO? IT'S YOUR CHANCE TO GET FAMOUS.
WELL...
YOU CAN GO WITH ME TO TIPHARES... BUT!
YOU CAN'T TAKE YOUR DOG!!
I HATE DOGS.
WHAT SHOULD I DO?! I CAN'T LEAVE CHAVEZ!
I SEE...
OKAY.
I'LL TAKE CARE OF HIM FOR YOU!
HUH ...?

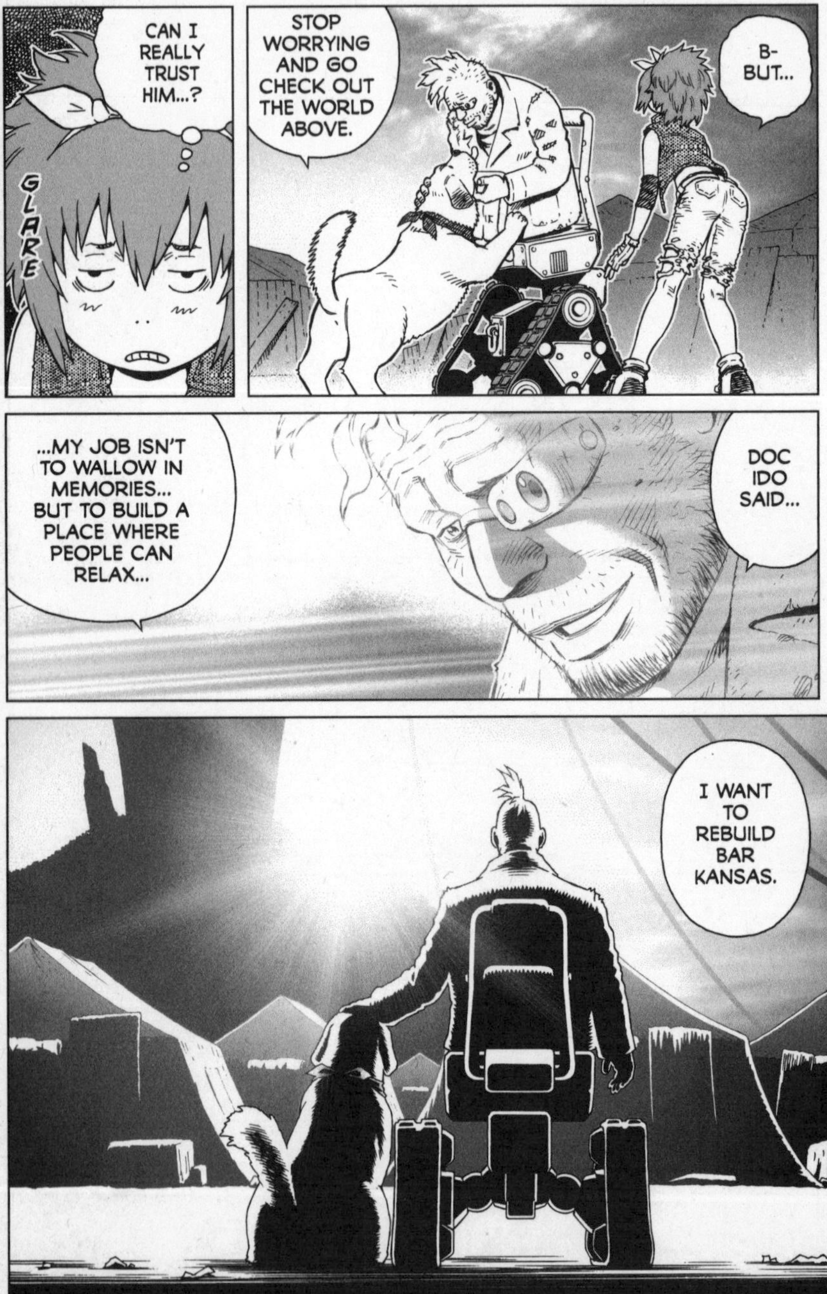
B-BUT...
STOP WORRYING AND GO CHECK OUT THE WORLD ABOVE.
CAN I REALLY TRUST HIM...?
GLARE
DOC IDO SAID...
...MY JOB ISN'T TO WALLOW IN MEMORIES... BUT TO BUILD A PLACE WHERE PEOPLE CAN RELAX...
I WANT TO REBUILD BAR KANSAS.

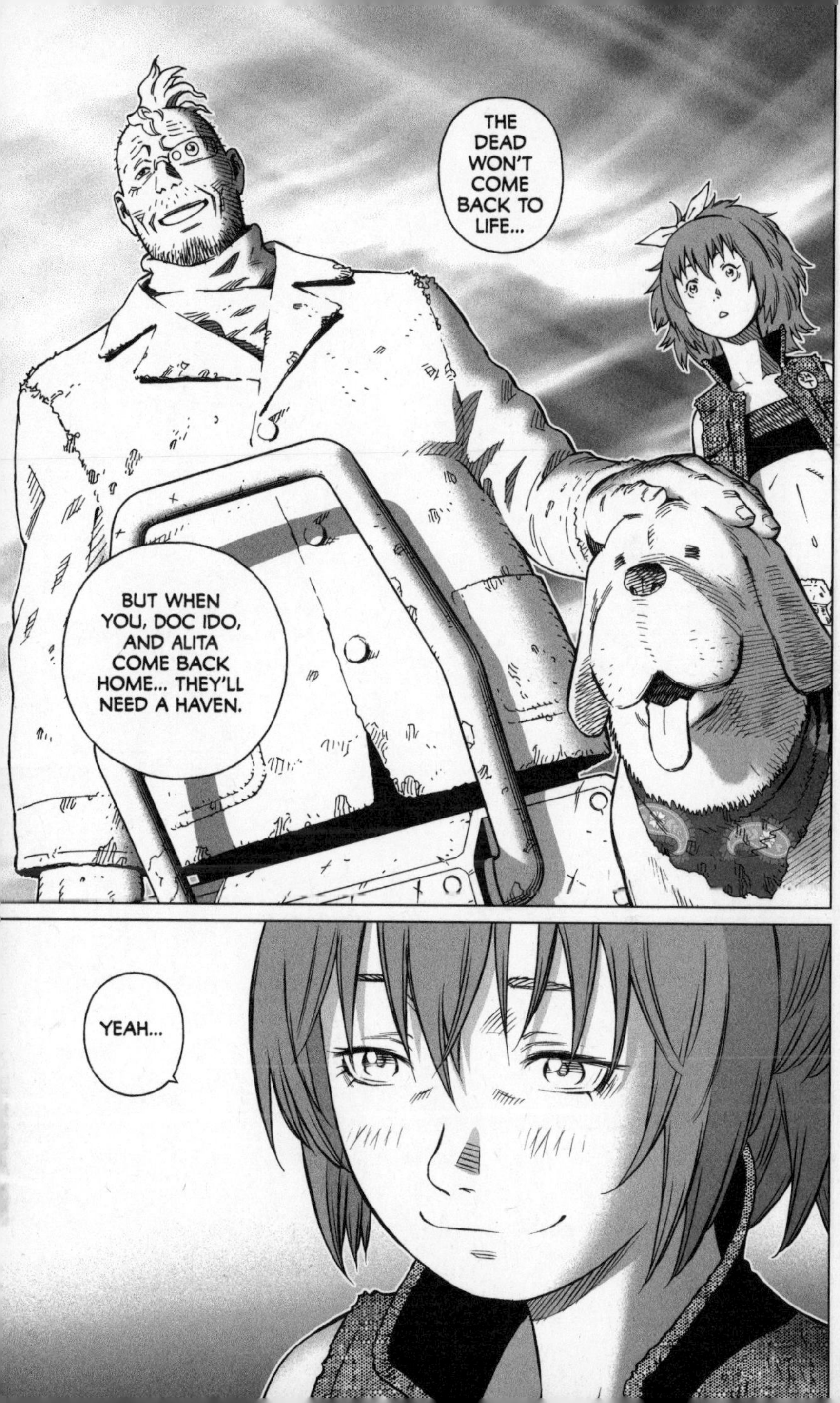
THE DEAD WON'T COME BACK TO LIFE...
BUT WHEN YOU, DOC IDO, AND ALITA COME BACK HOME... THEY'LL NEED A HAVEN.
YEAH...

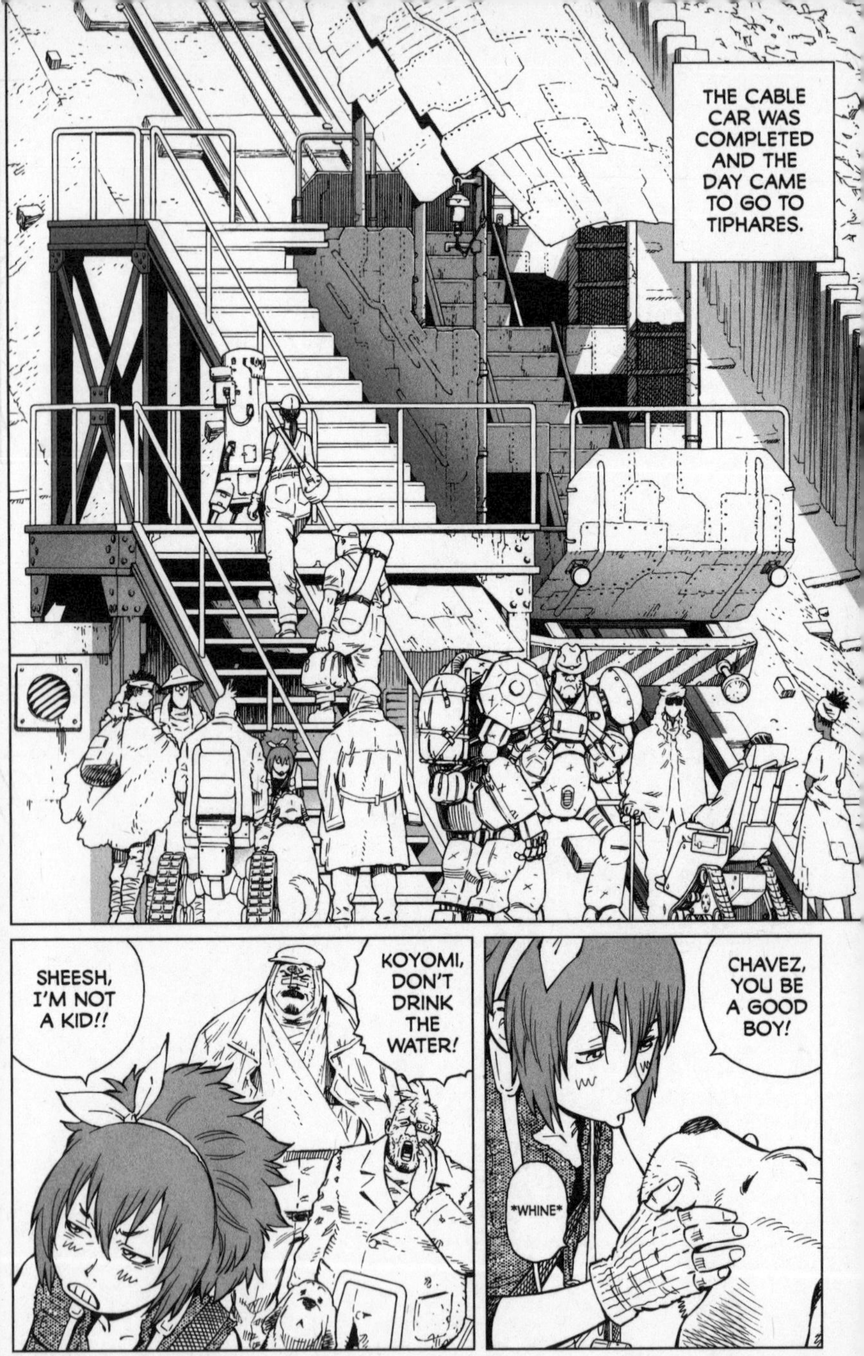
THE CABLE CAR WAS COMPLETED AND THE DAY CAME TO GO TO TIPHARES.
CHAVEZ, YOU BE A GOOD BOY!
WHINE
KOYOMI, DON'T DRINK THE WATER!
SHEESH, I'M NOT A KID!!

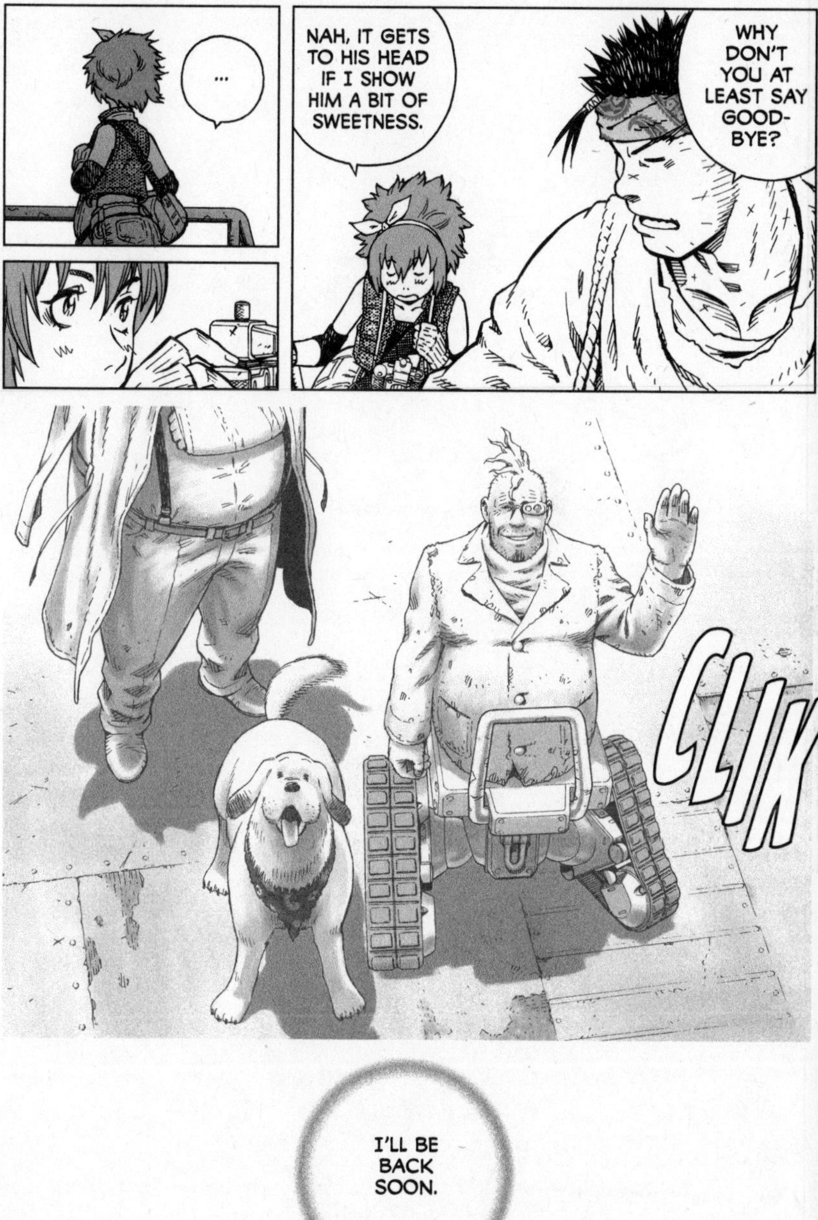
WHY DON'T YOU AT LEAST SAY GOOD-BYE?
NAH, IT GETS TO HIS HEAD IF I SHOW HIM A BIT OF SWEETNESS.
...
CLIK
I'LL BE BACK SOON.

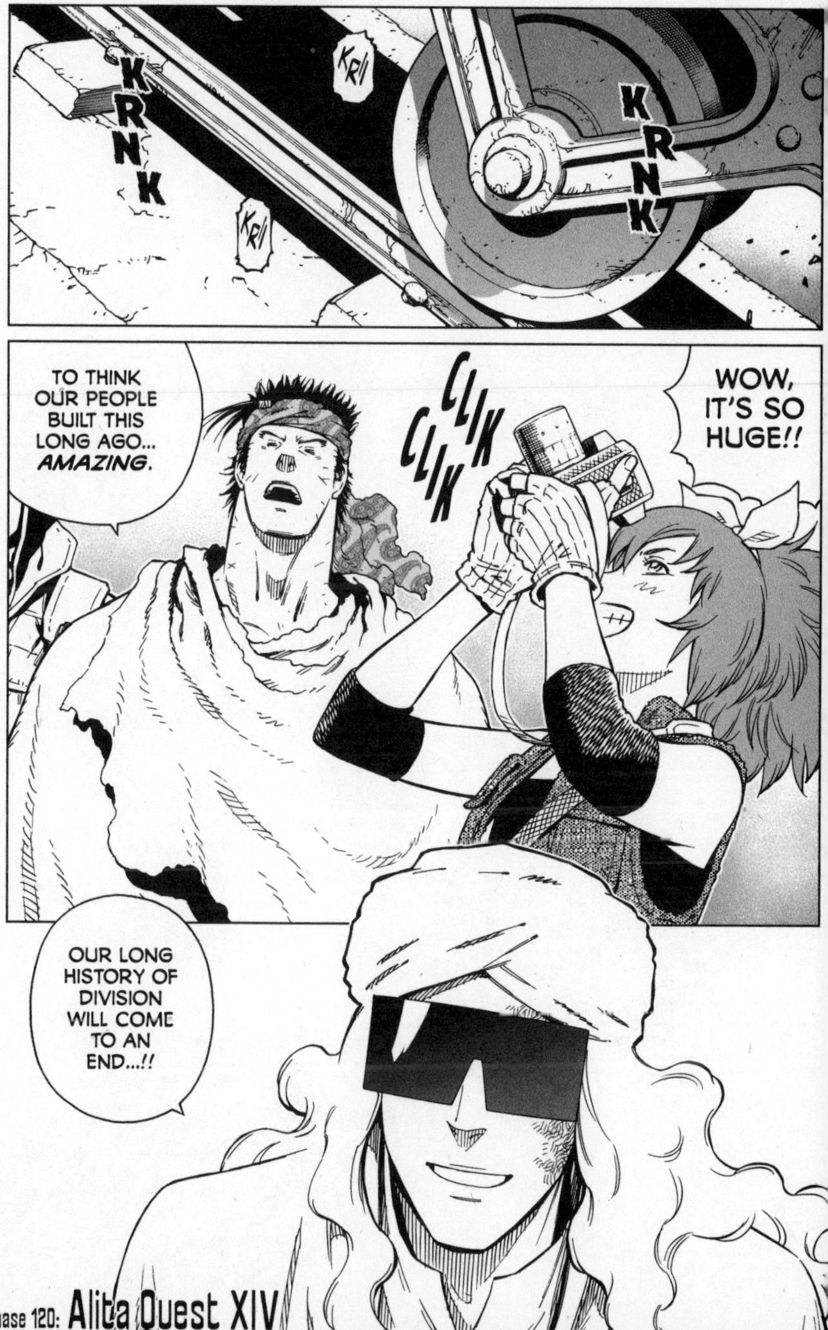
KRNK
KRII
KRNK
KRII
WOW, IT'S SO HUGE!!
CLIK CLIK
TO THINK OUR PEOPLE BUILT THIS LONG AGO... *AMAZING*.
OUR LONG HISTORY OF DIVISION WILL COME TO AN END...!!

Phase 120: Alita Quest XIV

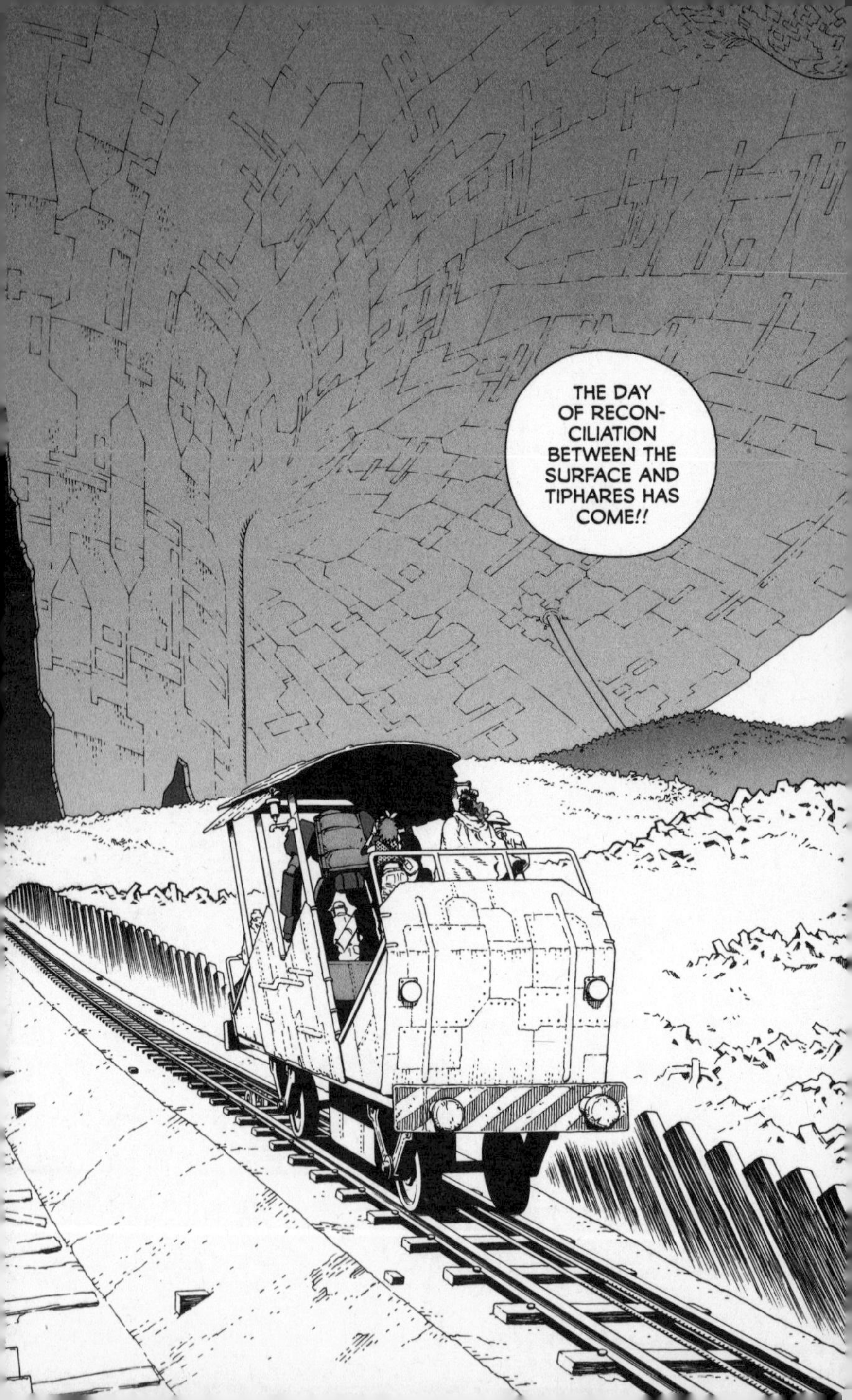
THE DAY OF RECON-CILIATION BETWEEN THE SURFACE AND TIPHARES HAS COME!!

Phase 120: Alita Quest XIV

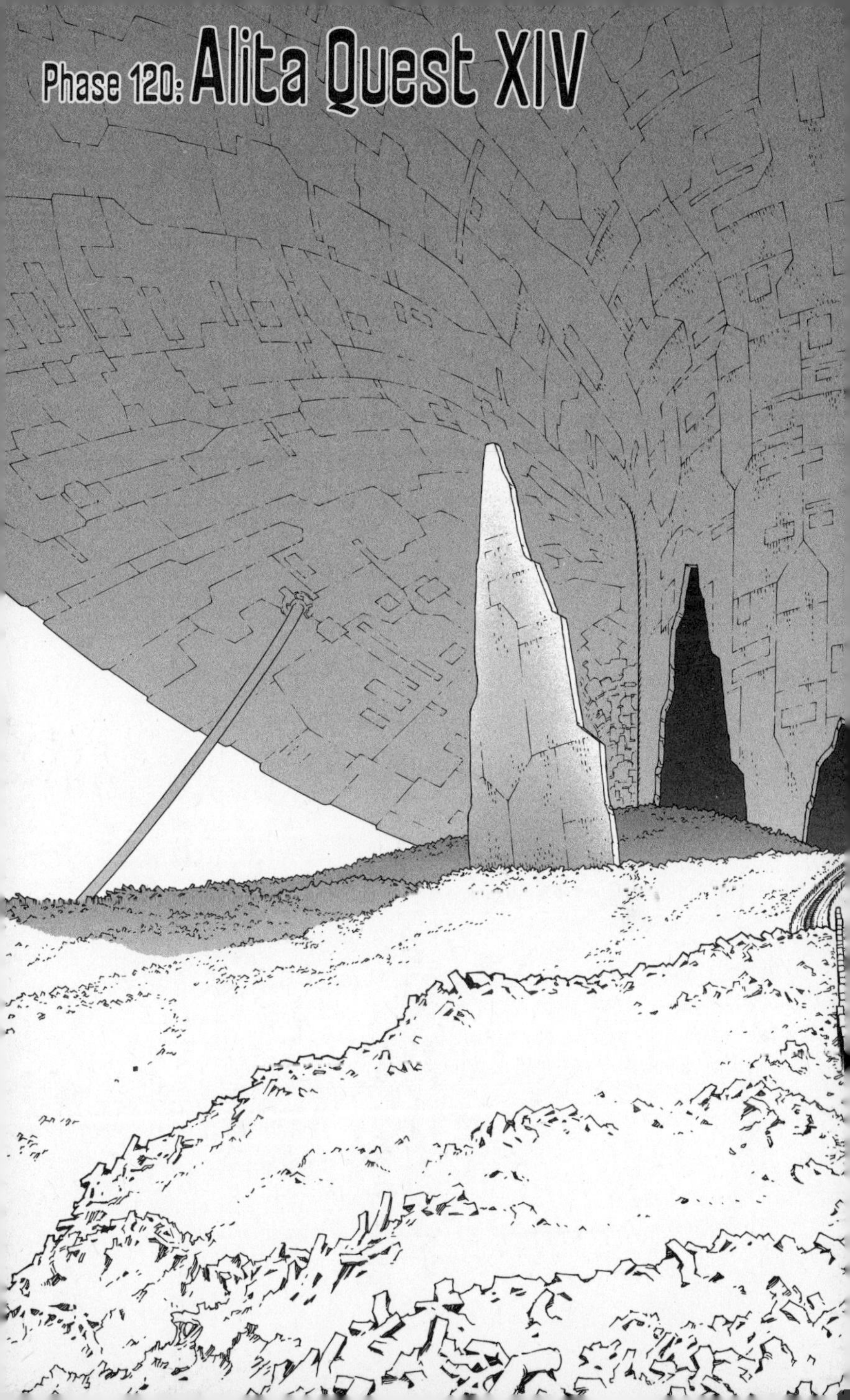

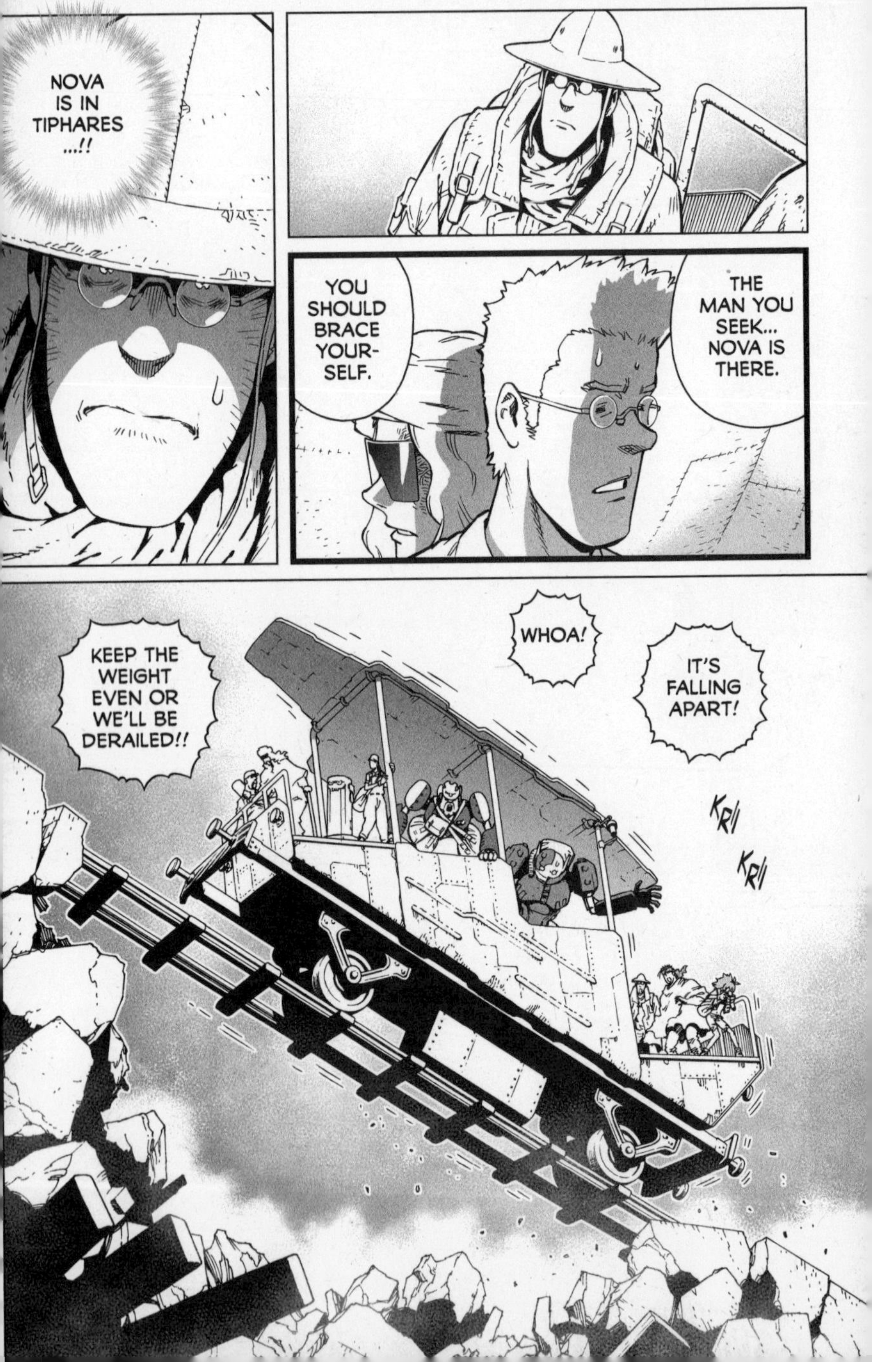
THE MAN YOU SEEK... NOVA IS THERE.
YOU SHOULD BRACE YOUR-SELF.
NOVA IS IN TIPHARES ...!!
IT'S FALLING APART!
WHOA!
KEEP THE WEIGHT EVEN OR WE'LL BE DERAILED!!
KRII
KRII

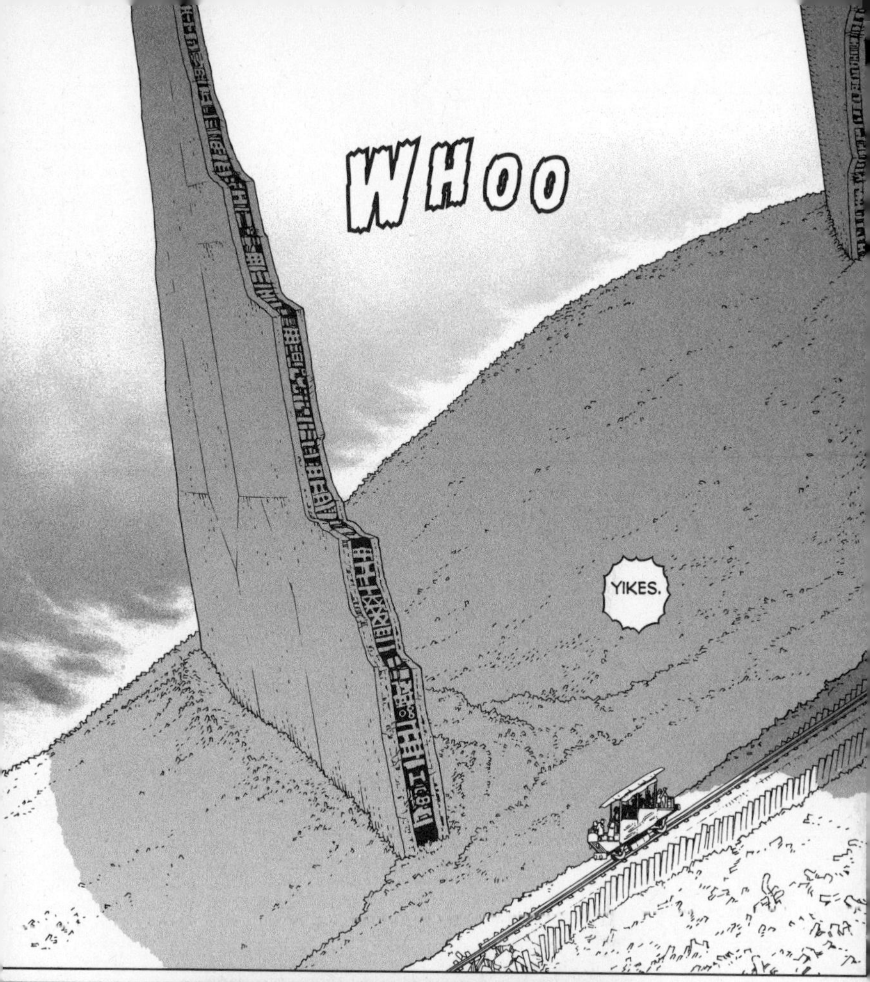
WHOO
YIKES.
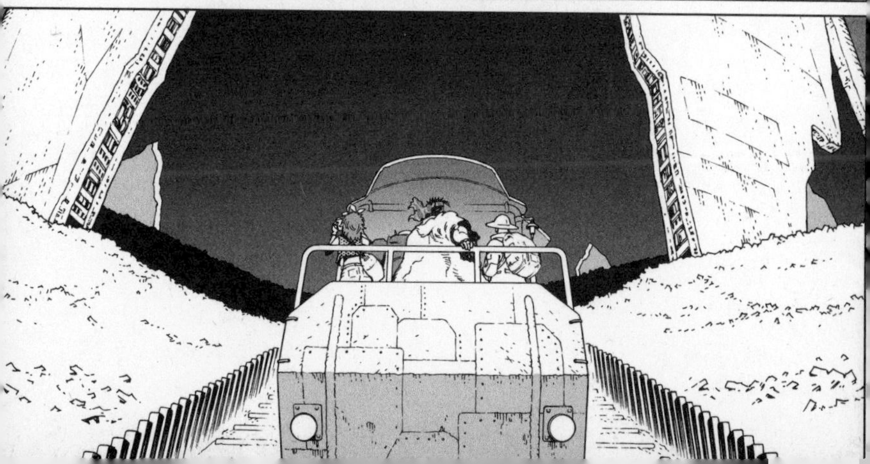

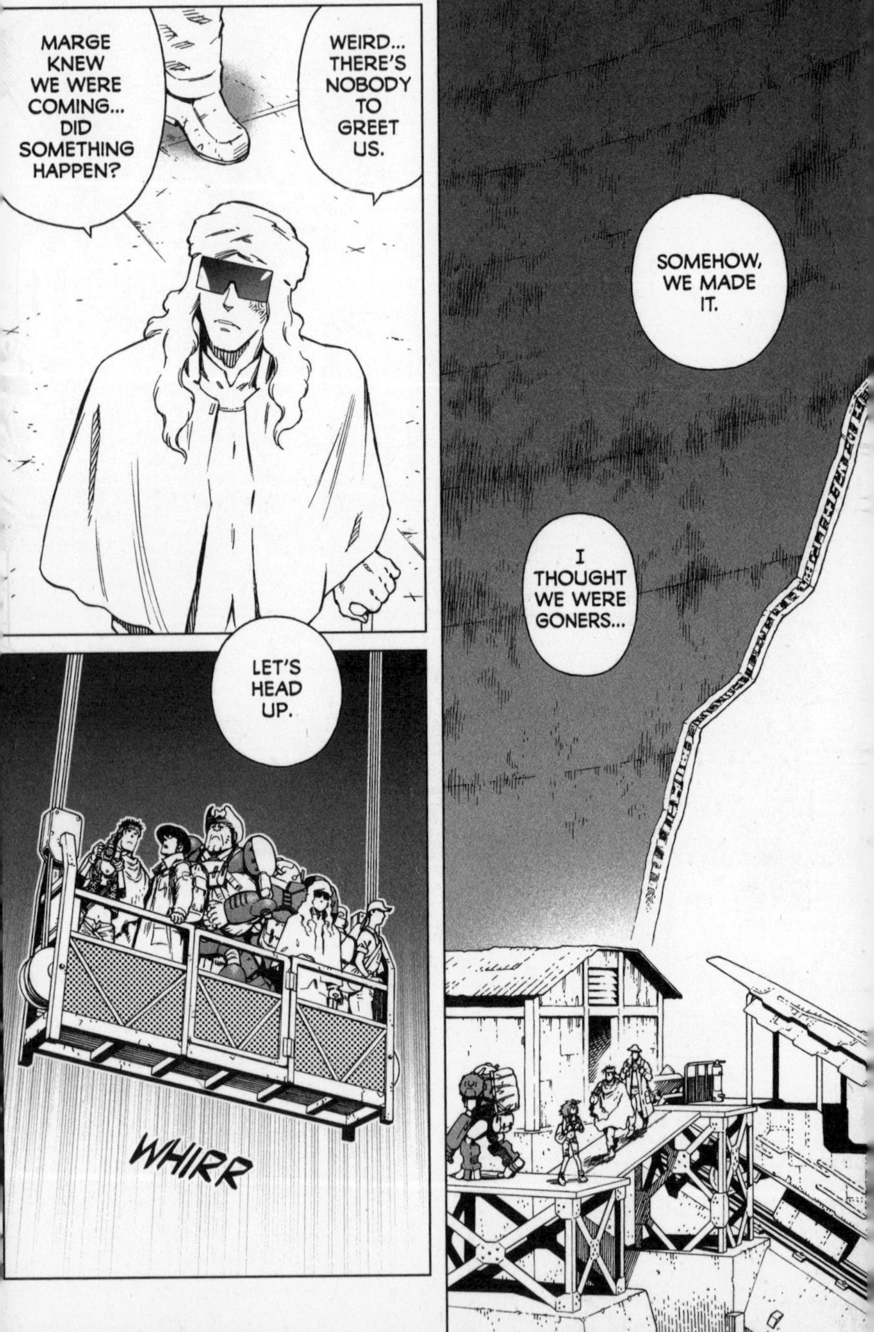
SOMEHOW, WE MADE IT.
I THOUGHT WE WERE GONERS...
WEIRD... THERE'S NOBODY TO GREET US.
MARGE KNEW WE WERE COMING... DID SOMETHING HAPPEN?
LET'S HEAD UP.
WHIRR

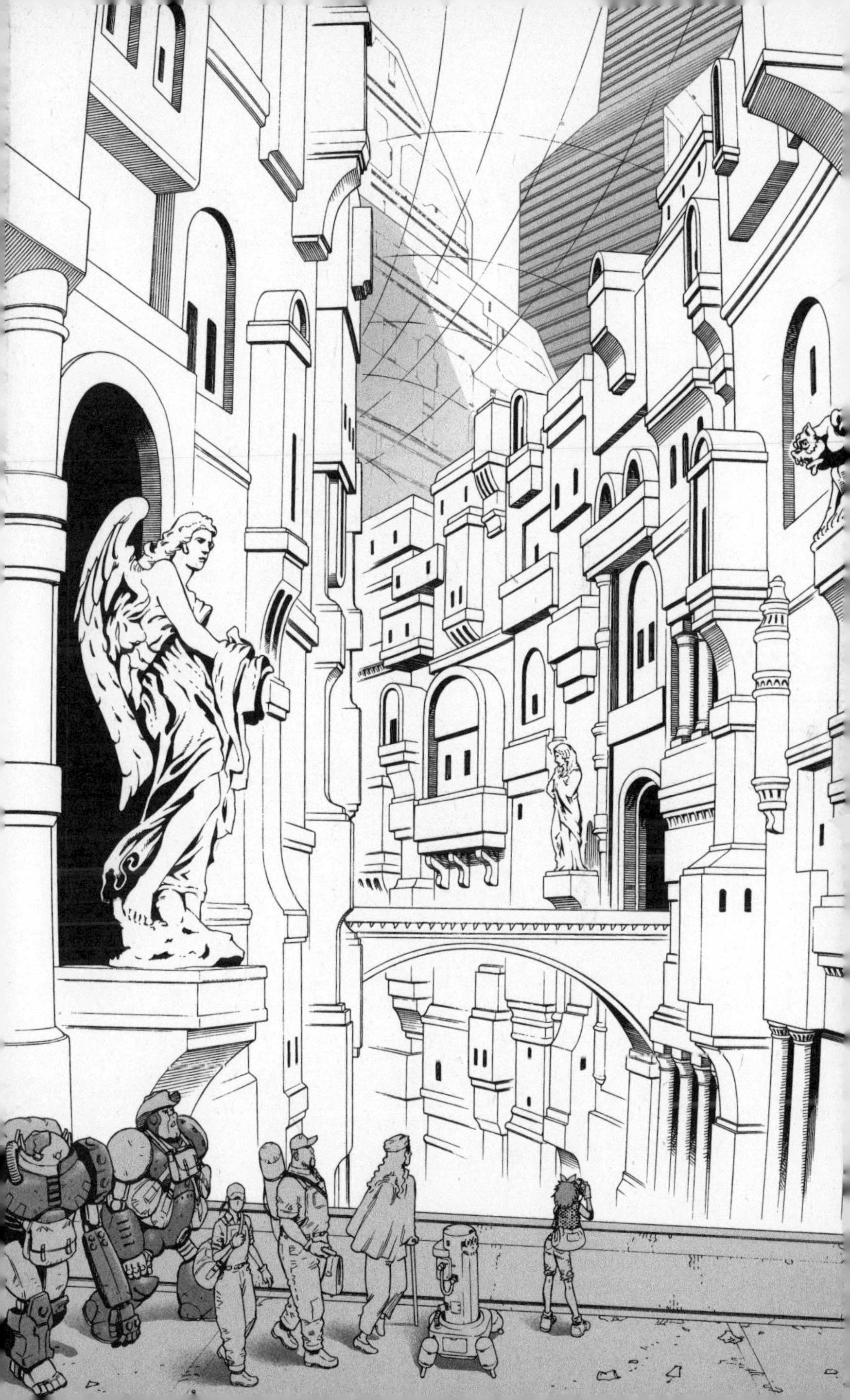

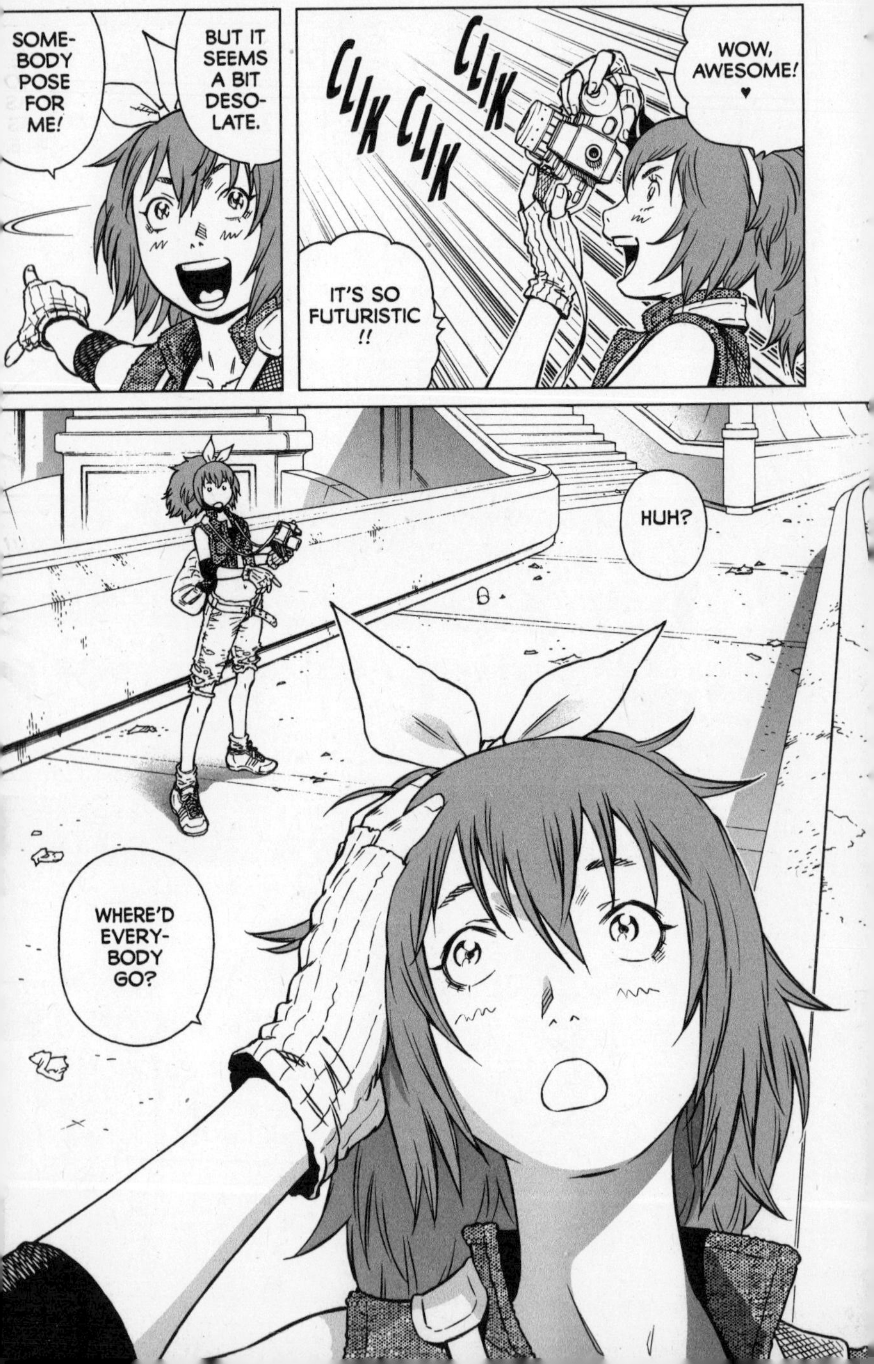
WOW, AWESOME! ♥
CLIK
CLIK CLIK
IT'S SO FUTURISTIC!!
BUT IT SEEMS A BIT DESOLATE.
SOMEBODY POSE FOR ME!
HUH?
WHERE'D EVERYBODY GO?

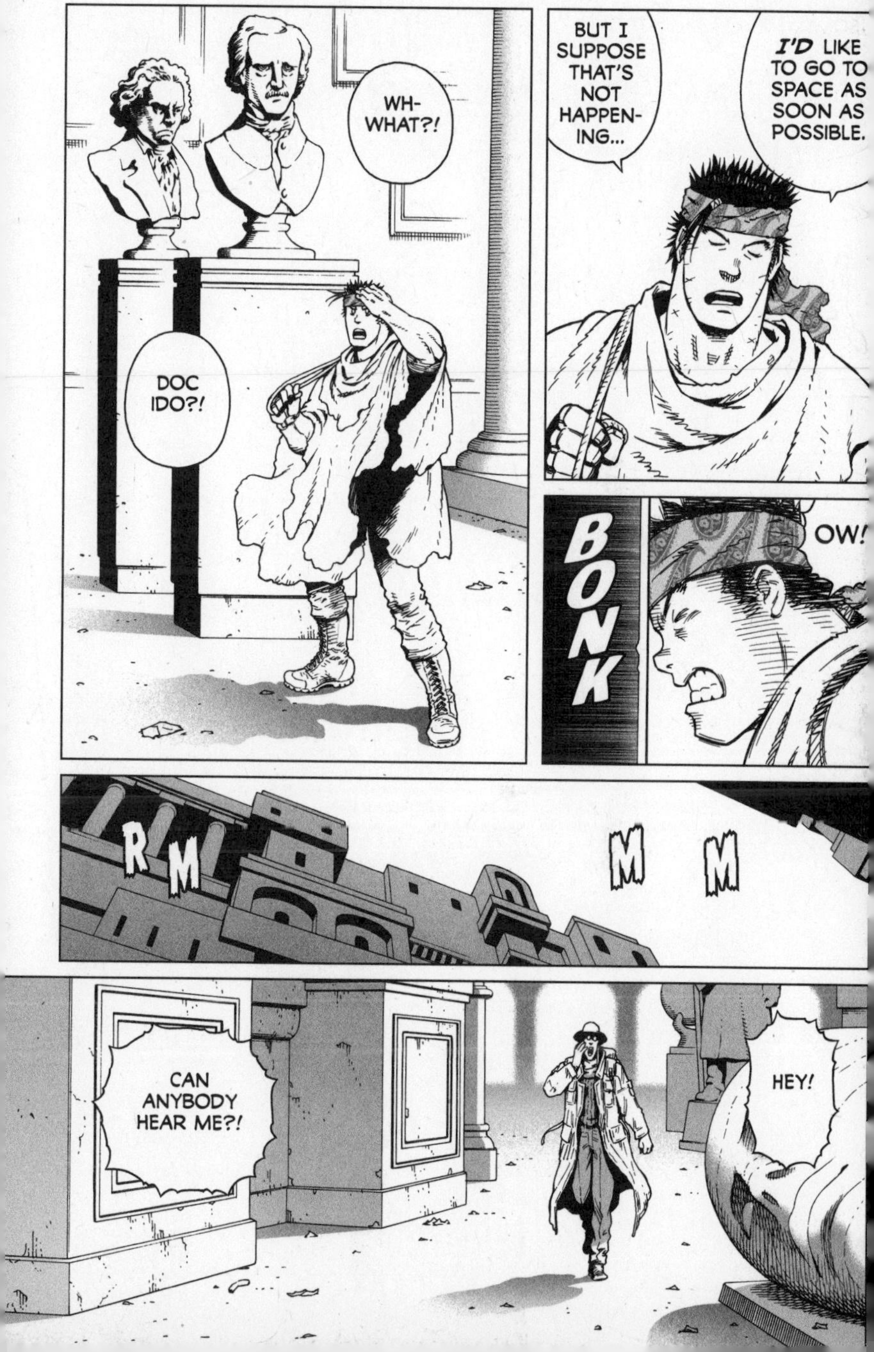
I'D LIKE TO GO TO SPACE AS SOON AS POSSIBLE.
BUT I SUPPOSE THAT'S NOT HAPPENING...
OW!
BONK
WH-WHAT?!
DOC IDO?!
RM M M
HEY!
CAN ANYBODY HEAR ME?!

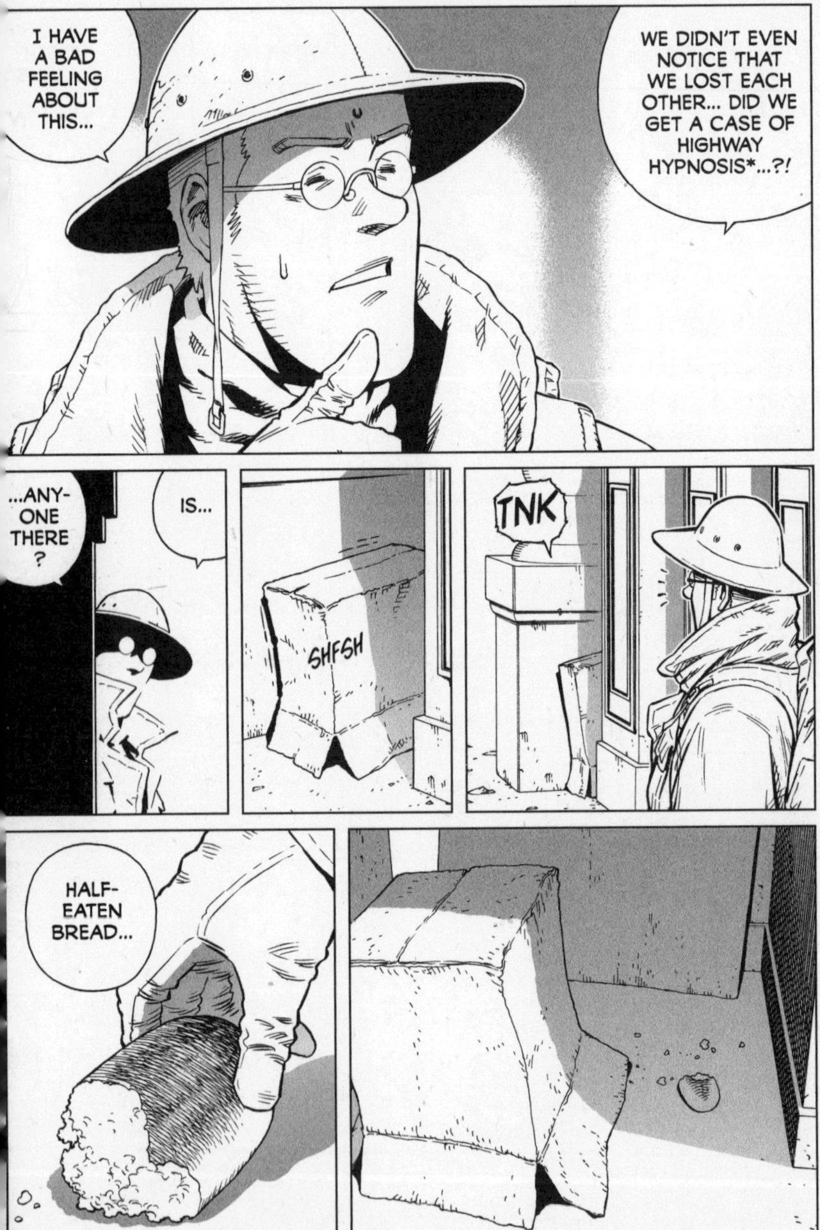
WE DIDN'T EVEN NOTICE THAT WE LOST EACH OTHER... DID WE GET A CASE OF HIGHWAY HYPNOSIS*...?!
I HAVE A BAD FEELING ABOUT THIS...
TNK
SHFSH
IS...
...ANY-ONE THERE?
HALF-EATEN BREAD...

*Highway hypnosis: a state of decreased consciousness that occurs while driving through a monotonous landscape. The difference between this and falling asleep is that the person has no awareness doing so.

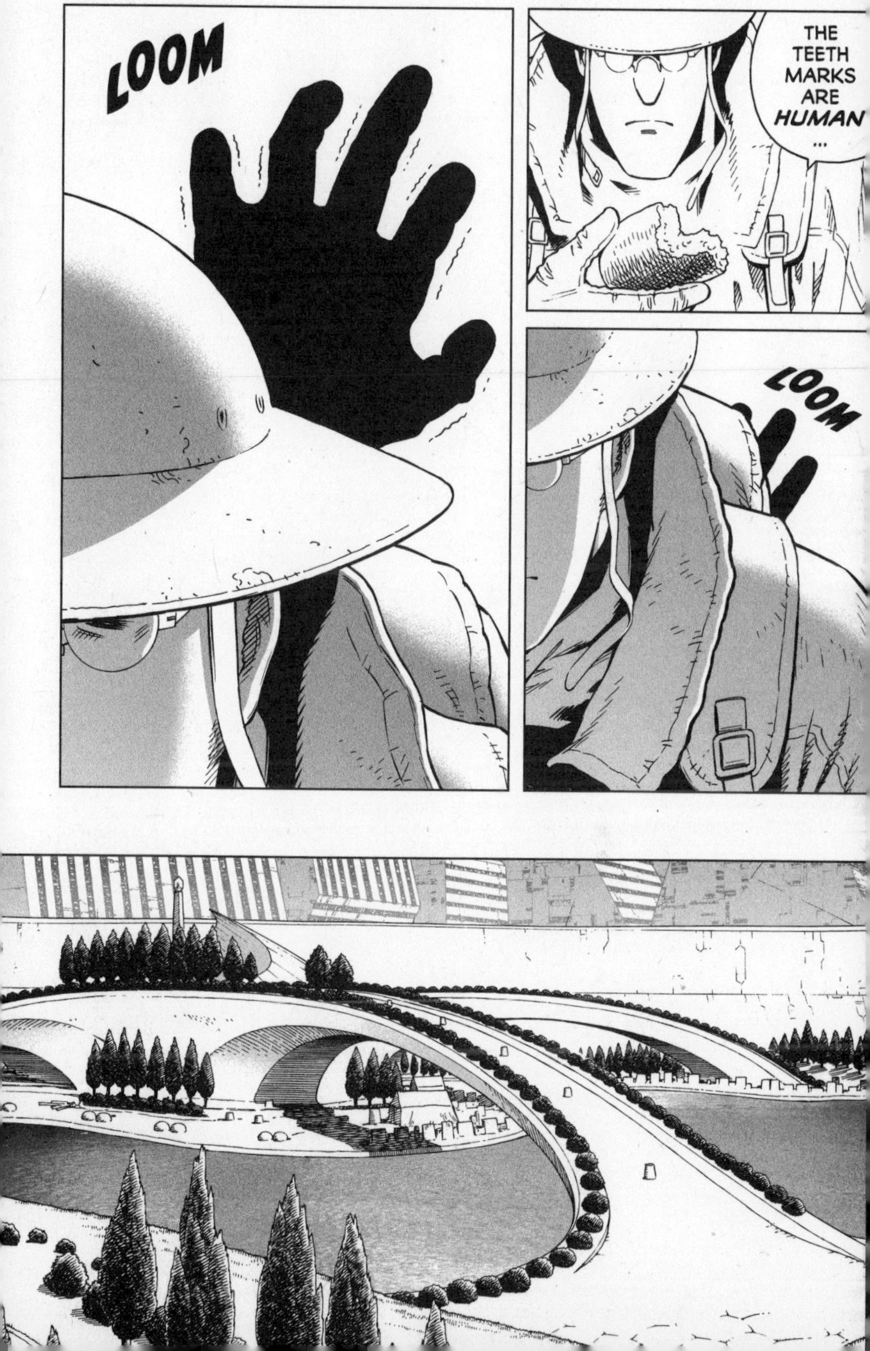
THE TEETH MARKS ARE *HUMAN* ...
LOOM
LOOM

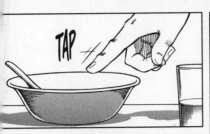

SOUP LEFT UN-EATEN...
REMINDS ME OF THE MARY CELESTE*...
TAP
ODD...
I CAN'T READ ANYTHING THROUGH PSYCHOM-ETRY**...
WE SHOULD REST A BIT AND GO LOOK FOR MARGE...
?!
WH-WHERE IS EVERY-ONE...?!

Mary Celeste: a ship found drifting abandoned in 1872. One of the greatest mysteries in maritime history. A novel by Arthur Conan Doyle based on this case contributed to it becoming an urban legend.

*Psychometry: Kaos's ability to read past incidents from objects.

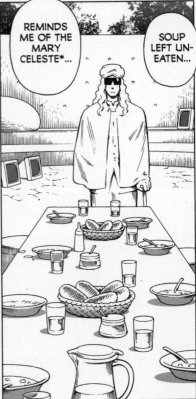

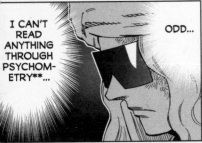

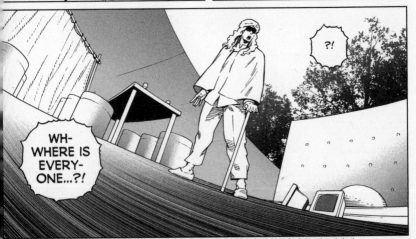

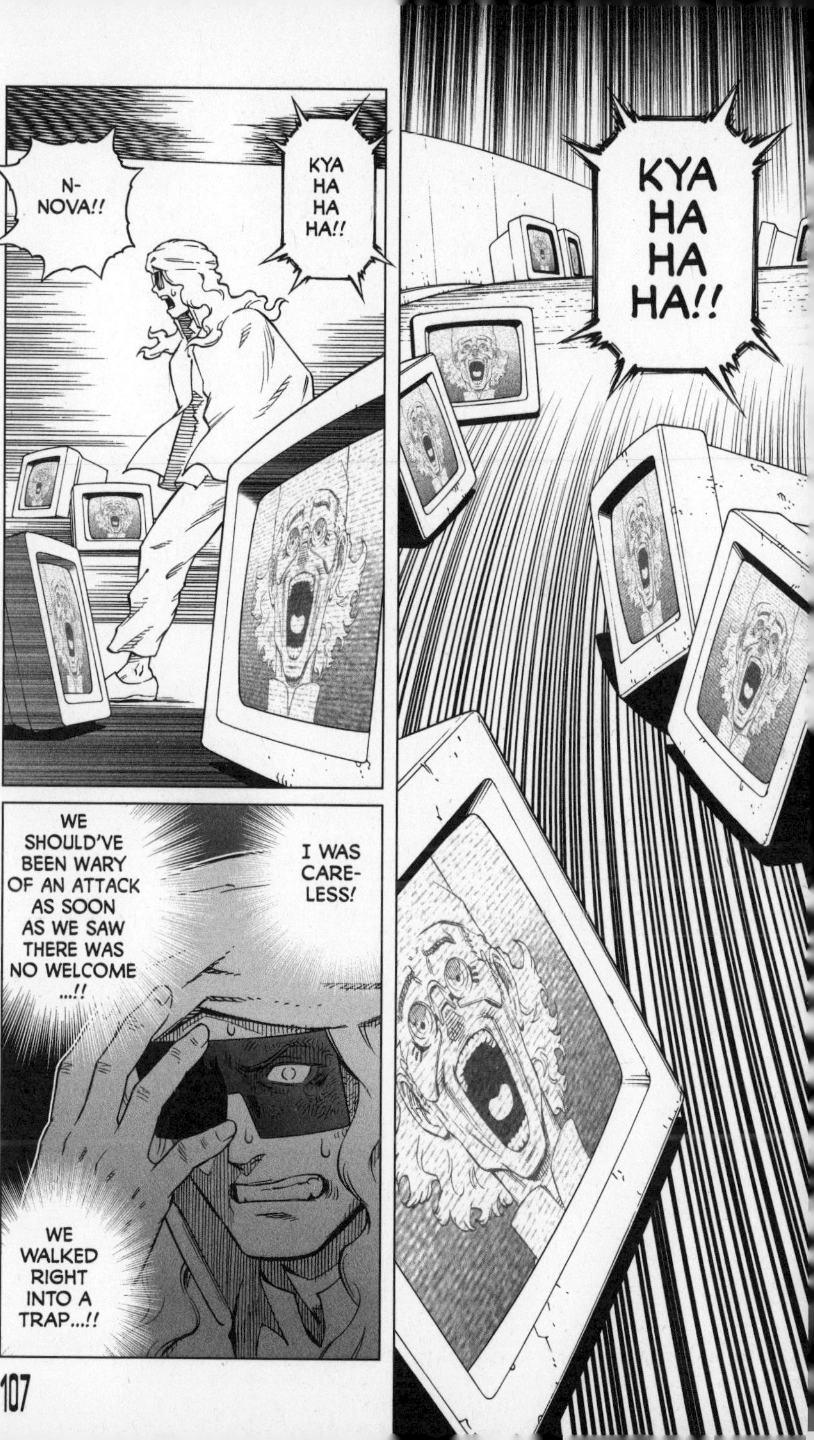
KYA HA HA HA HA!!
KYA HA HA HA!!
N-NOVA!!
I WAS CARE-LESS!
WE SHOULD'VE BEEN WARY OF AN ATTACK AS SOON AS WE SAW THERE WAS NO WELCOME ...!!
WE WALKED RIGHT INTO A TRAP...!!

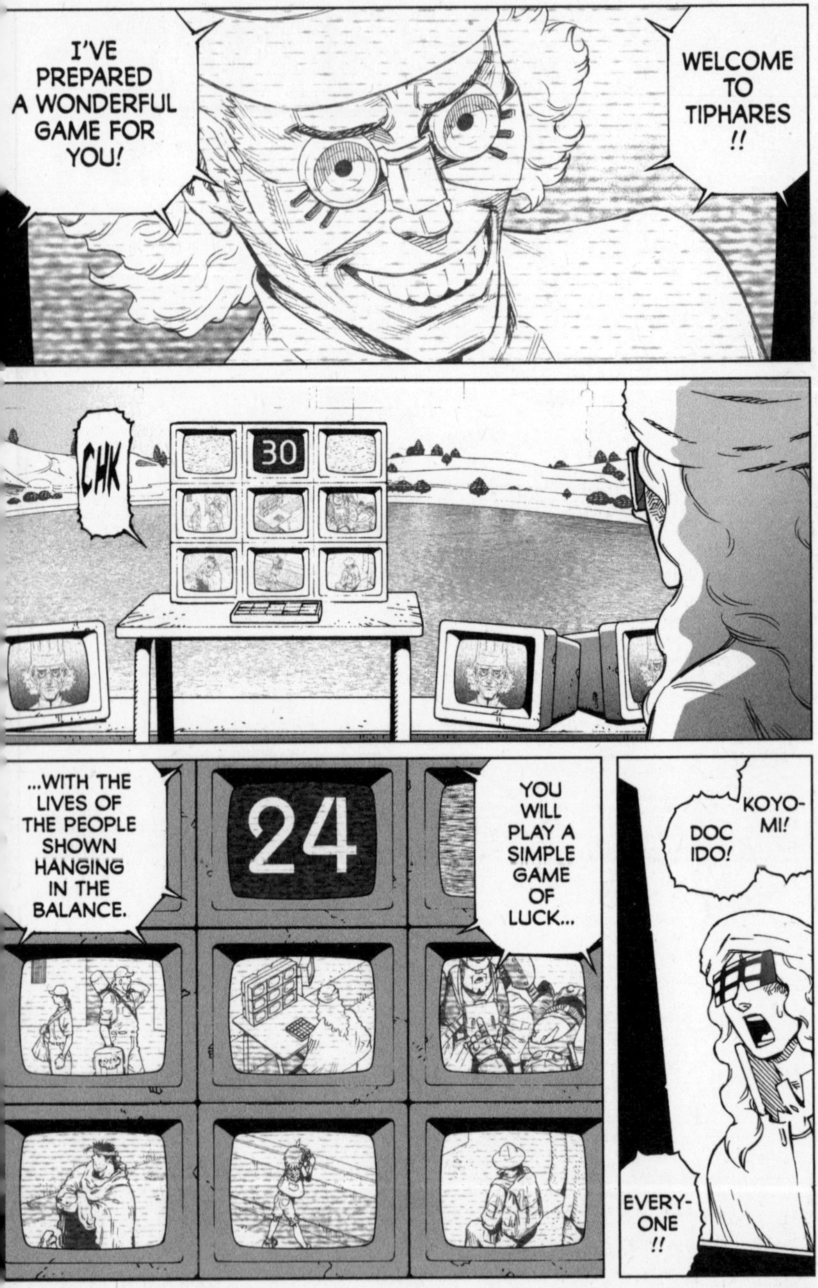
WELCOME TO TIPHARES!!
I'VE PREPARED A WONDERFUL GAME FOR YOU!
CHK
30
KOYO-MI!
DOC IDO!
EVERY-ONE!!
YOU WILL PLAY A SIMPLE GAME OF LUCK...
24
...WITH THE LIVES OF THE PEOPLE SHOWN HANGING IN THE BALANCE.

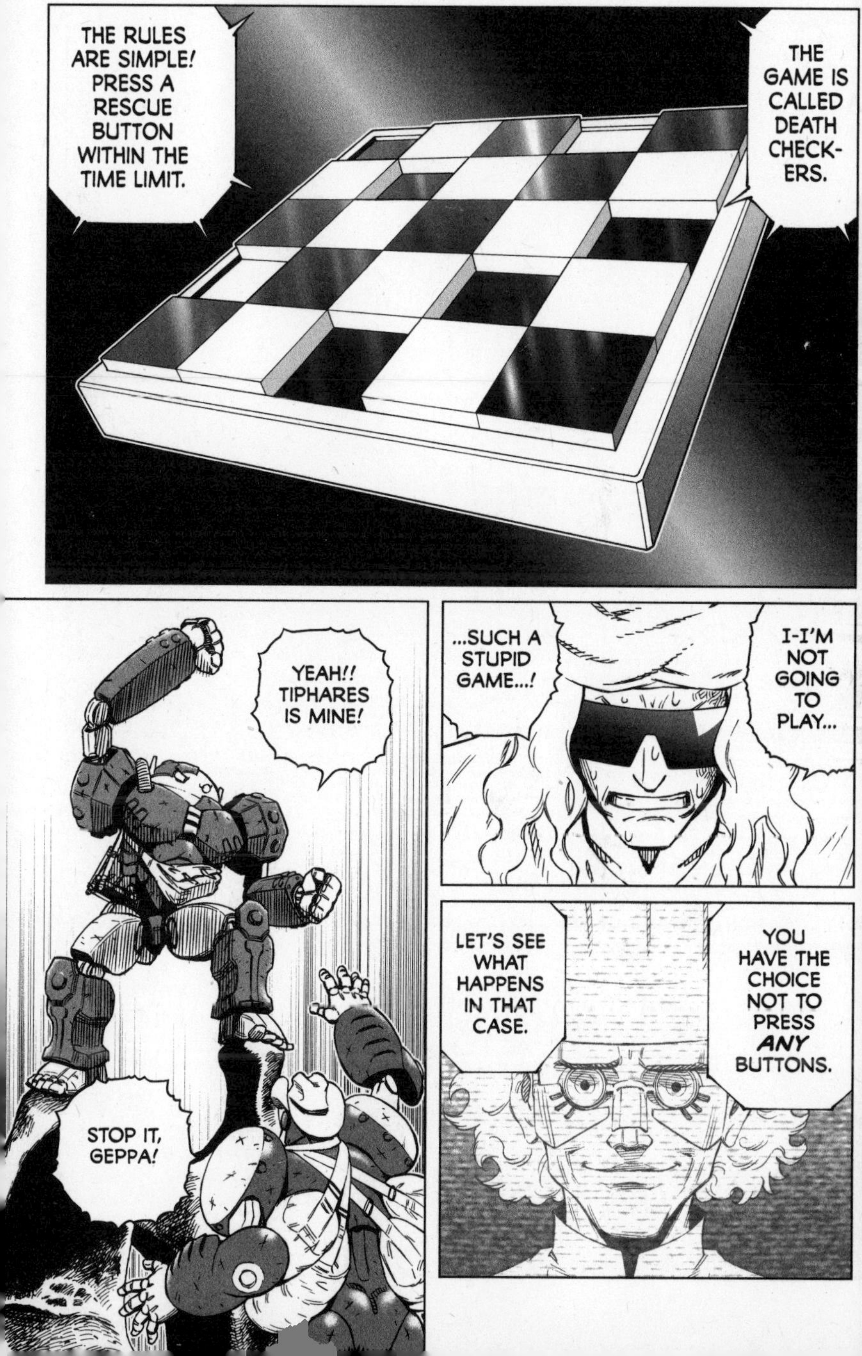
THE GAME IS CALLED DEATH CHECK-ERS.
THE RULES ARE SIMPLE! PRESS A RESCUE BUTTON WITHIN THE TIME LIMIT.
I-I'M NOT GOING TO PLAY...
...SUCH A STUPID GAME...!
YOU HAVE THE CHOICE NOT TO PRESS *ANY* BUTTONS.
LET'S SEE WHAT HAPPENS IN THAT CASE.
YEAH!! TIPHARES IS MINE!
STOP IT, GEPPA!

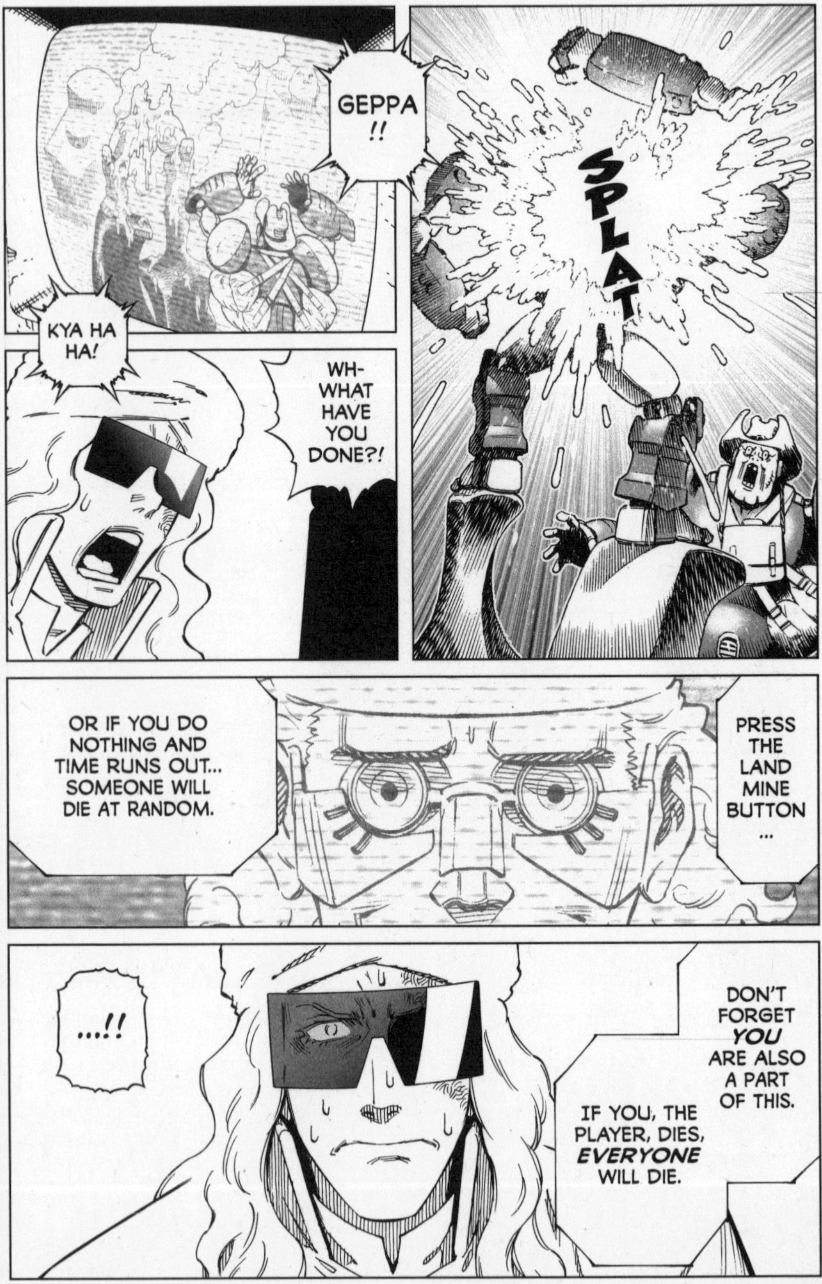
SPLAT
GEPPA!!
KYA HA HA!
WH- WHAT HAVE YOU DONE?!
PRESS THE LAND MINE BUTTON...
OR IF YOU DO NOTHING AND TIME RUNS OUT... SOMEONE WILL DIE AT RANDOM.
DON'T FORGET *YOU* ARE ALSO A PART OF THIS.
IF YOU, THE PLAYER, DIES, *EVERYONE* WILL DIE.
...!!

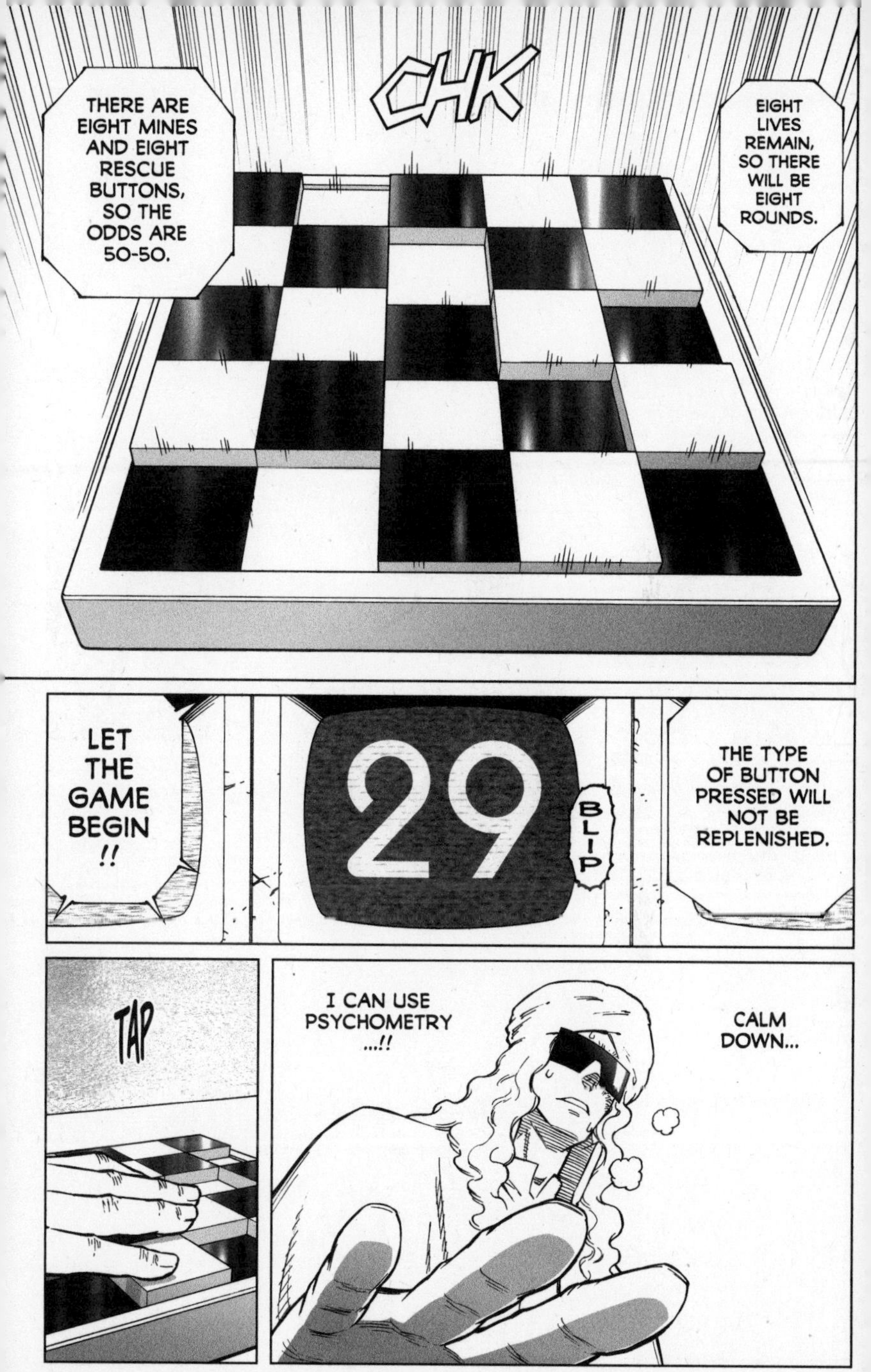
CHK
EIGHT LIVES REMAIN, SO THERE WILL BE EIGHT ROUNDS.
THERE ARE EIGHT MINES AND EIGHT RESCUE BUTTONS, SO THE ODDS ARE 50-50.
THE TYPE OF BUTTON PRESSED WILL NOT BE REPLENISHED.
BLIP
29
LET THE GAME BEGIN!!
CALM DOWN...
I CAN USE PSYCHOMETRY ...!!
TAP

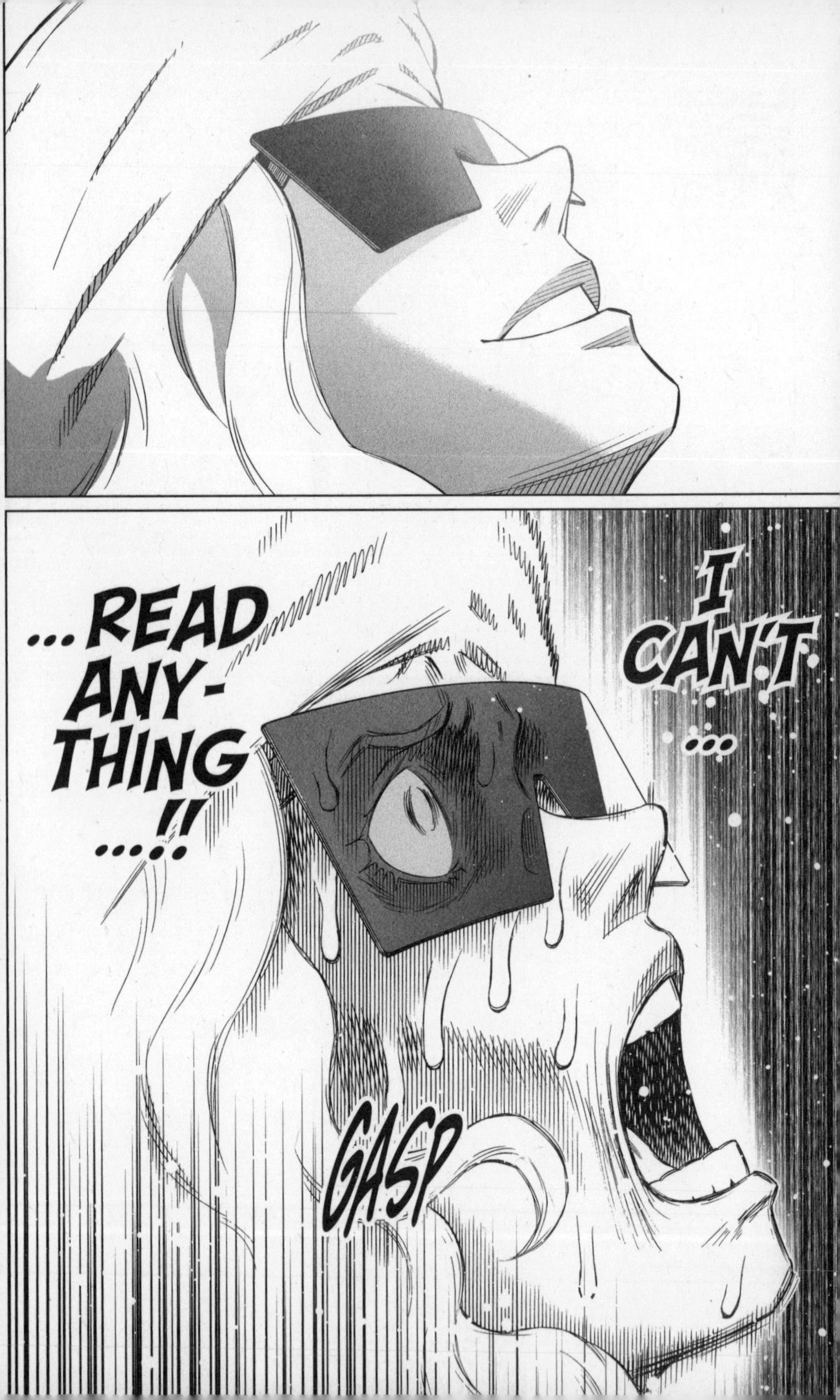
I CAN'T...
...READ ANY-THING...!!
GASP

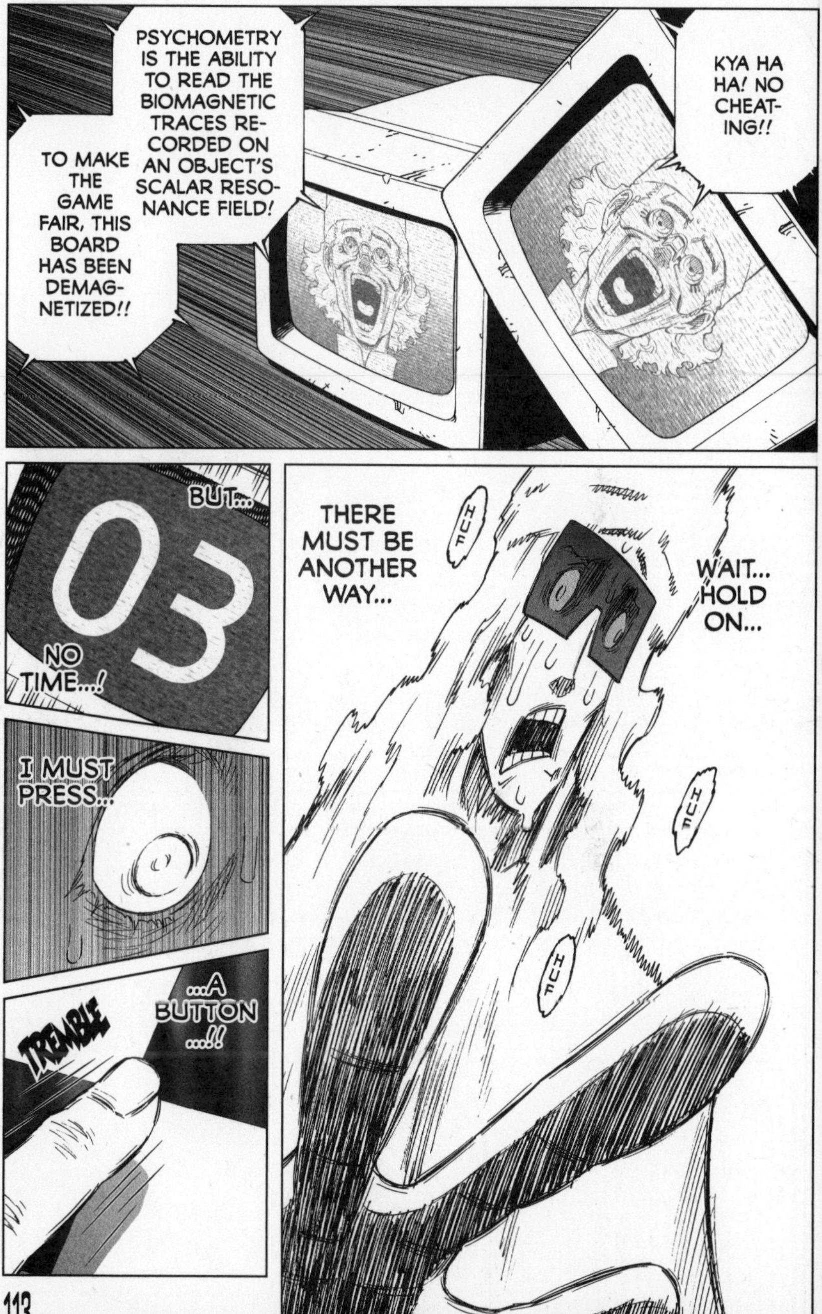
KYA HA HA! NO CHEAT-ING!!
PSYCHOMETRY IS THE ABILITY TO READ THE BIOMAGNETIC TRACES RE-CORDED ON AN OBJECT'S SCALAR RESO-NANCE FIELD!
TO MAKE THE GAME FAIR, THIS BOARD HAS BEEN DEMAG-NETIZED!!
HUF
WAIT... HOLD ON...
THERE MUST BE ANOTHER WAY...
HUF
HUF
BUT...
03
NO TIME...!
I MUST PRESS...
...A BUTTON ...!!
TREMBLE

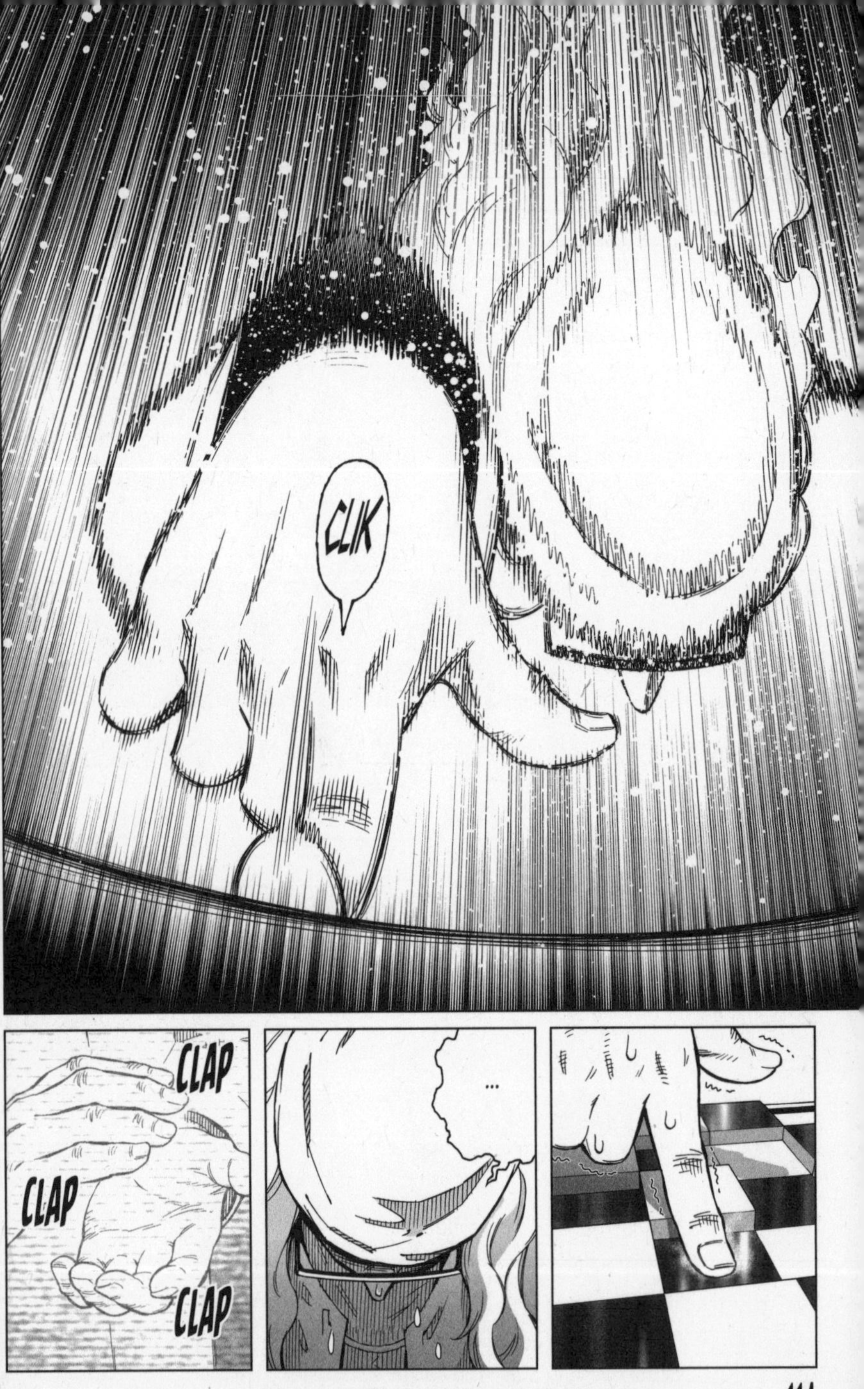
CLIK
...
CLAP
CLAP
CLAP

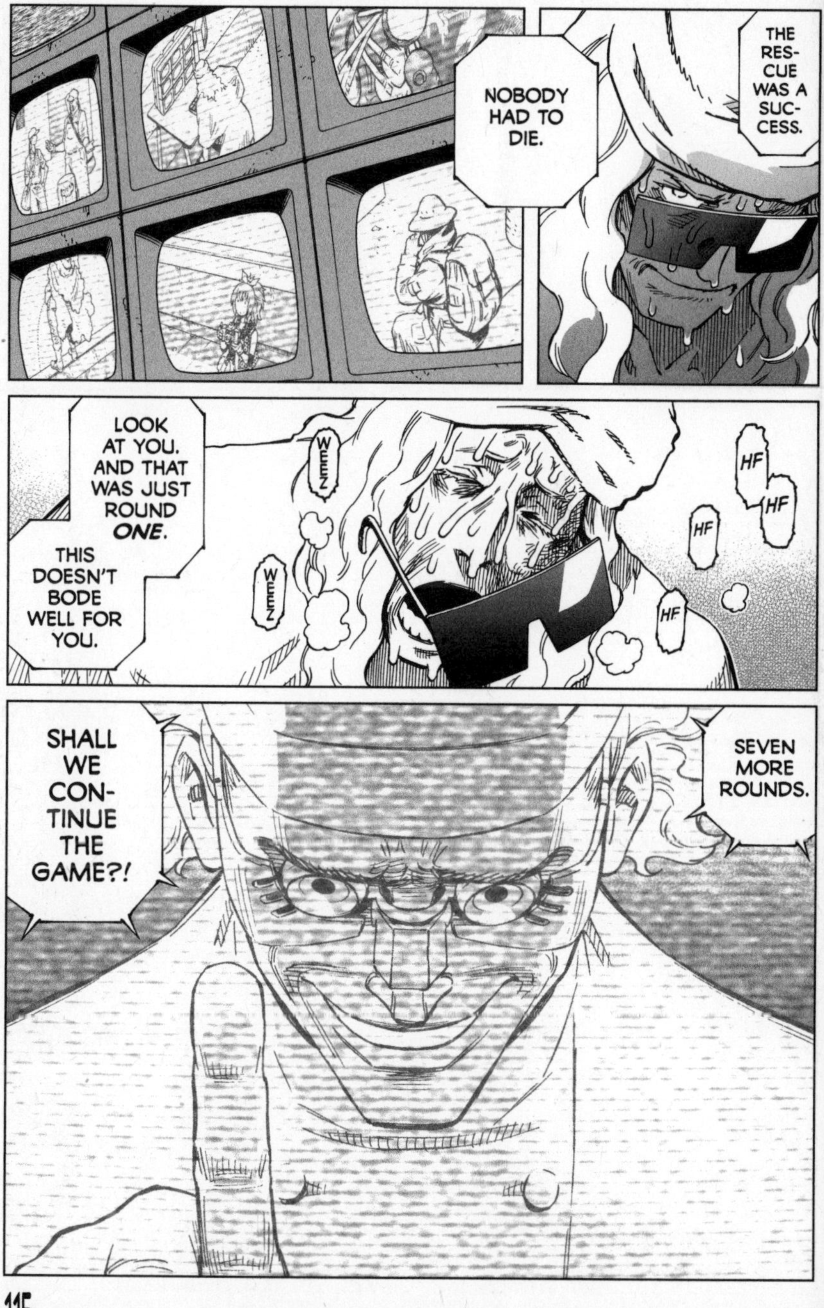
THE RESCUE WAS A SUCCESS.
NOBODY HAD TO DIE.
HF
HF
HF
HF
WEEZ
WEEZ
LOOK AT YOU. AND THAT WAS JUST ROUND ONE.
THIS DOESN'T BODE WELL FOR YOU.
SEVEN MORE ROUNDS.
SHALL WE CONTINUE THE GAME?!

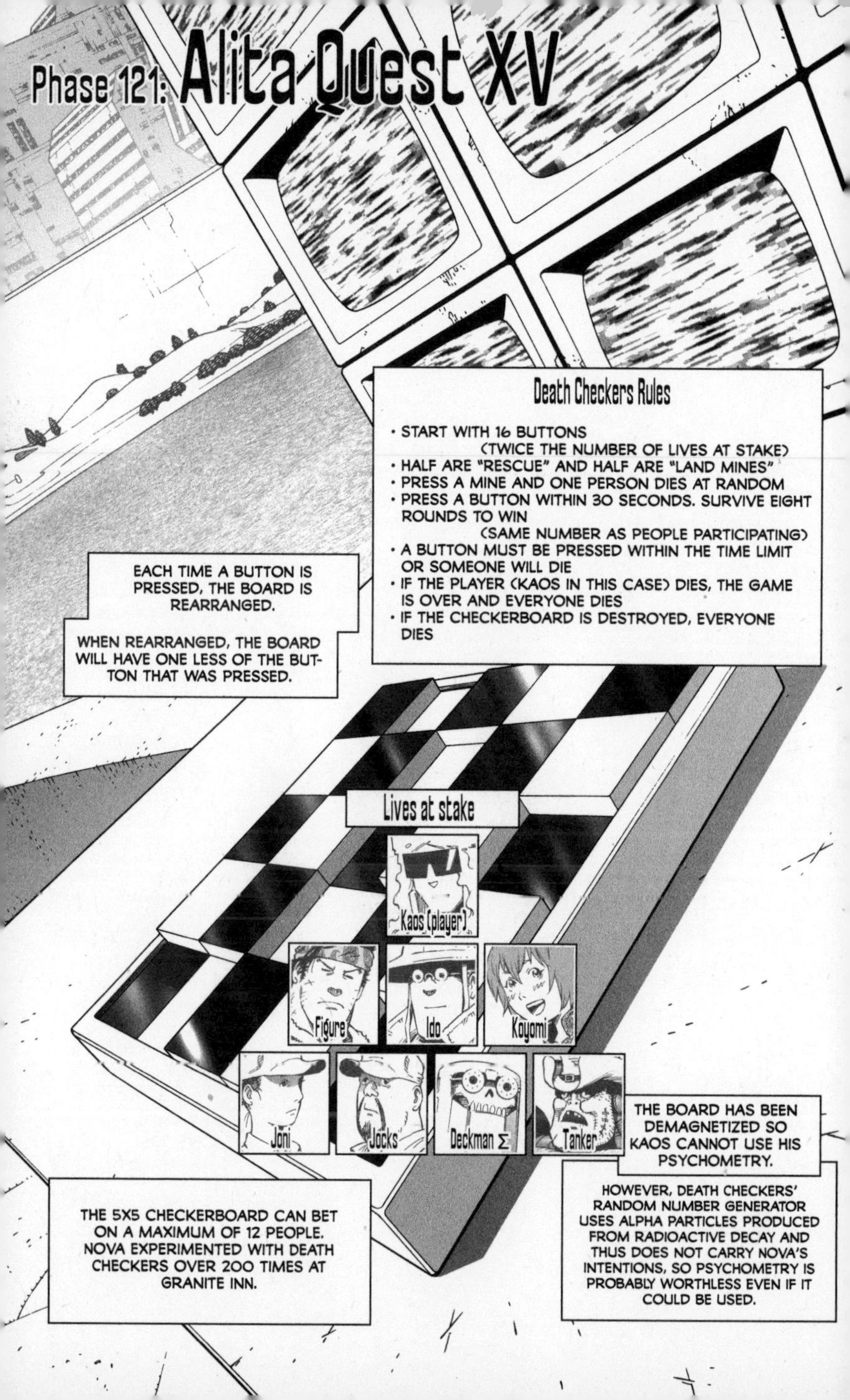
Phase 121: Alita Quest XV
Death Checkers Rules
• START WITH 16 BUTTONS (TWICE THE NUMBER OF LIVES AT STAKE)
• HALF ARE "RESCUE" AND HALF ARE "LAND MINES"
• PRESS A MINE AND ONE PERSON DIES AT RANDOM
• PRESS A BUTTON WITHIN 30 SECONDS. SURVIVE EIGHT ROUNDS TO WIN (SAME NUMBER AS PEOPLE PARTICIPATING)
• A BUTTON MUST BE PRESSED WITHIN THE TIME LIMIT OR SOMEONE WILL DIE
• IF THE PLAYER (KAOS IN THIS CASE) DIES, THE GAME IS OVER AND EVERYONE DIES
• IF THE CHECKERBOARD IS DESTROYED, EVERYONE DIES
EACH TIME A BUTTON IS PRESSED, THE BOARD IS REARRANGED.
WHEN REARRANGED, THE BOARD WILL HAVE ONE LESS OF THE BUTTON THAT WAS PRESSED.
Lives at stake
Kaos (player)
Koyomi
Ido
Figure
Tanker
Deckman Σ
Jocks
Joni
THE BOARD HAS BEEN DEMAGNETIZED SO KAOS CANNOT USE HIS PSYCHOMETRY.
HOWEVER, DEATH CHECKERS' RANDOM NUMBER GENERATOR USES ALPHA PARTICLES PRODUCED FROM RADIOACTIVE DECAY AND THUS DOES NOT CARRY NOVA'S INTENTIONS, SO PSYCHOMETRY IS PROBABLY WORTHLESS EVEN IF IT COULD BE USED.
THE 5X5 CHECKERBOARD CAN BET ON A MAXIMUM OF 12 PEOPLE. NOVA EXPERIMENTED WITH DEATH CHECKERS OVER 200 TIMES AT GRANITE INN.

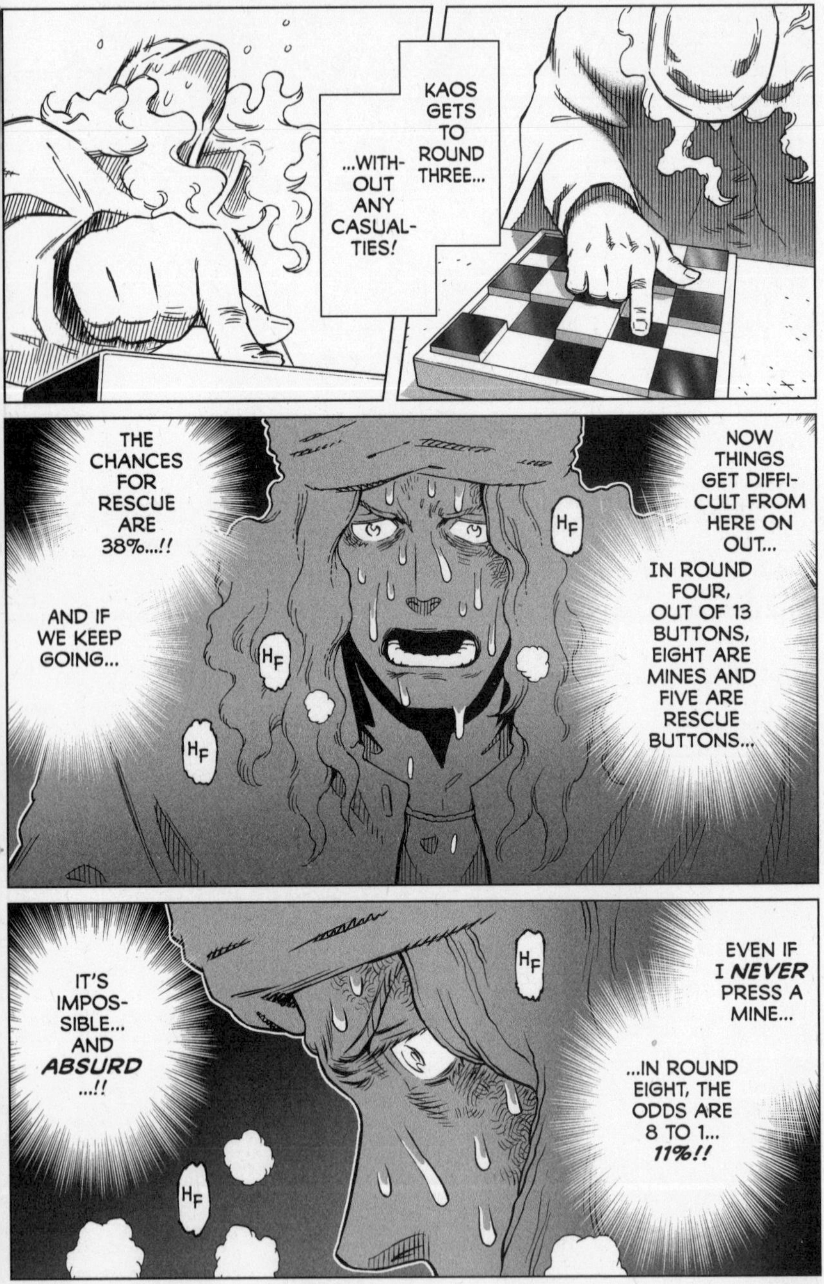
KAOS GETS TO ROUND THREE...
...WITHOUT ANY CASUALTIES!
NOW THINGS GET DIFFICULT FROM HERE ON OUT...
IN ROUND FOUR, OUT OF 13 BUTTONS, EIGHT ARE MINES AND FIVE ARE RESCUE BUTTONS...
HF
THE CHANCES FOR RESCUE ARE 38%...!!
HF
AND IF WE KEEP GOING...
HF
EVEN IF I NEVER PRESS A MINE...
...IN ROUND EIGHT, THE ODDS ARE 8 TO 1... 11%!!
HF
IT'S IMPOSSIBLE... AND ABSURD ...!!
HF

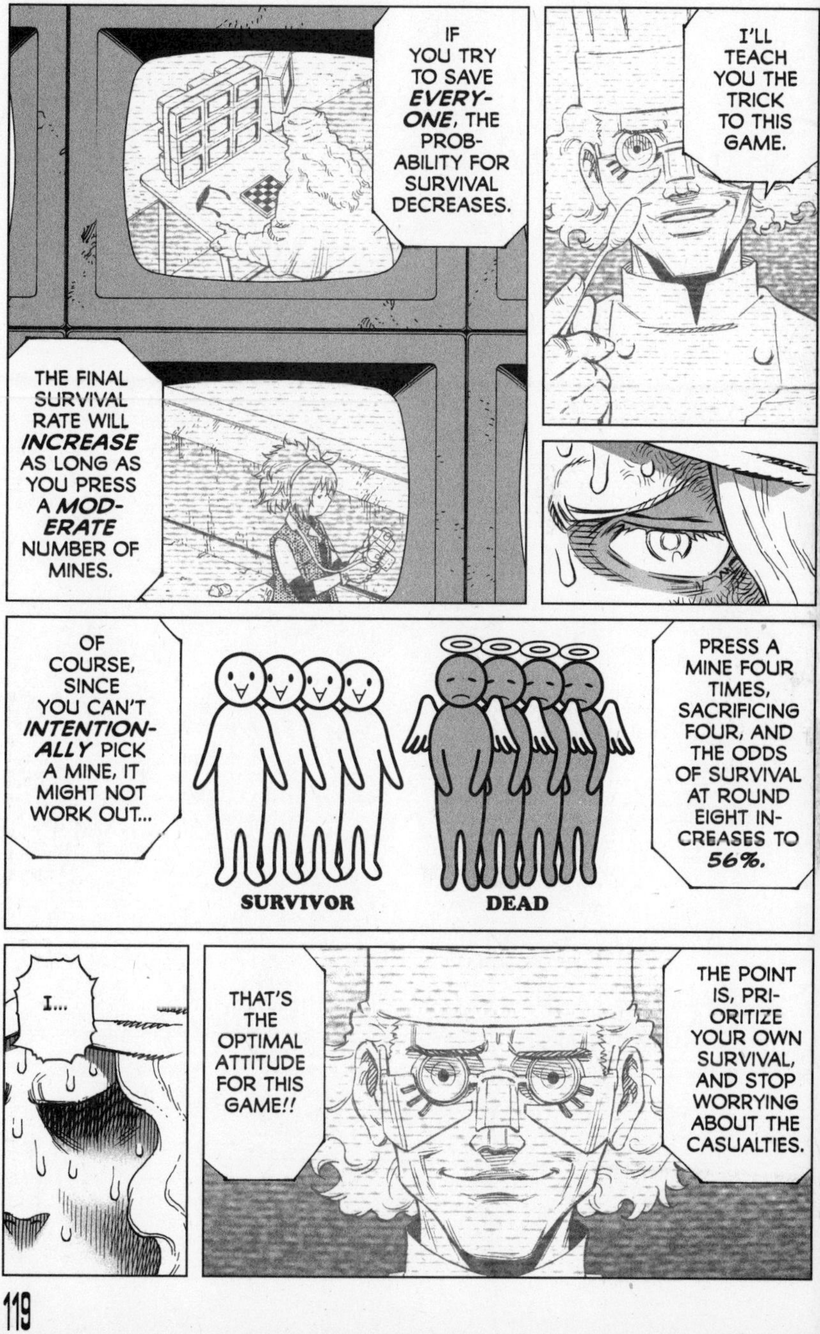
I'LL TEACH YOU THE TRICK TO THIS GAME.
IF YOU TRY TO SAVE EVERYONE, THE PROBABILITY FOR SURVIVAL DECREASES.
THE FINAL SURVIVAL RATE WILL INCREASE AS LONG AS YOU PRESS A MODERATE NUMBER OF MINES.
PRESS A MINE FOUR TIMES, SACRIFICING FOUR, AND THE ODDS OF SURVIVAL AT ROUND EIGHT INCREASES TO 56%.
DEAD
SURVIVOR
OF COURSE, SINCE YOU CAN'T INTENTIONALLY PICK A MINE, IT MIGHT NOT WORK OUT...
THE POINT IS, PRIORITIZE YOUR OWN SURVIVAL, AND STOP WORRYING ABOUT THE CASUALTIES.
THAT'S THE OPTIMAL ATTITUDE FOR THIS GAME!!
I...

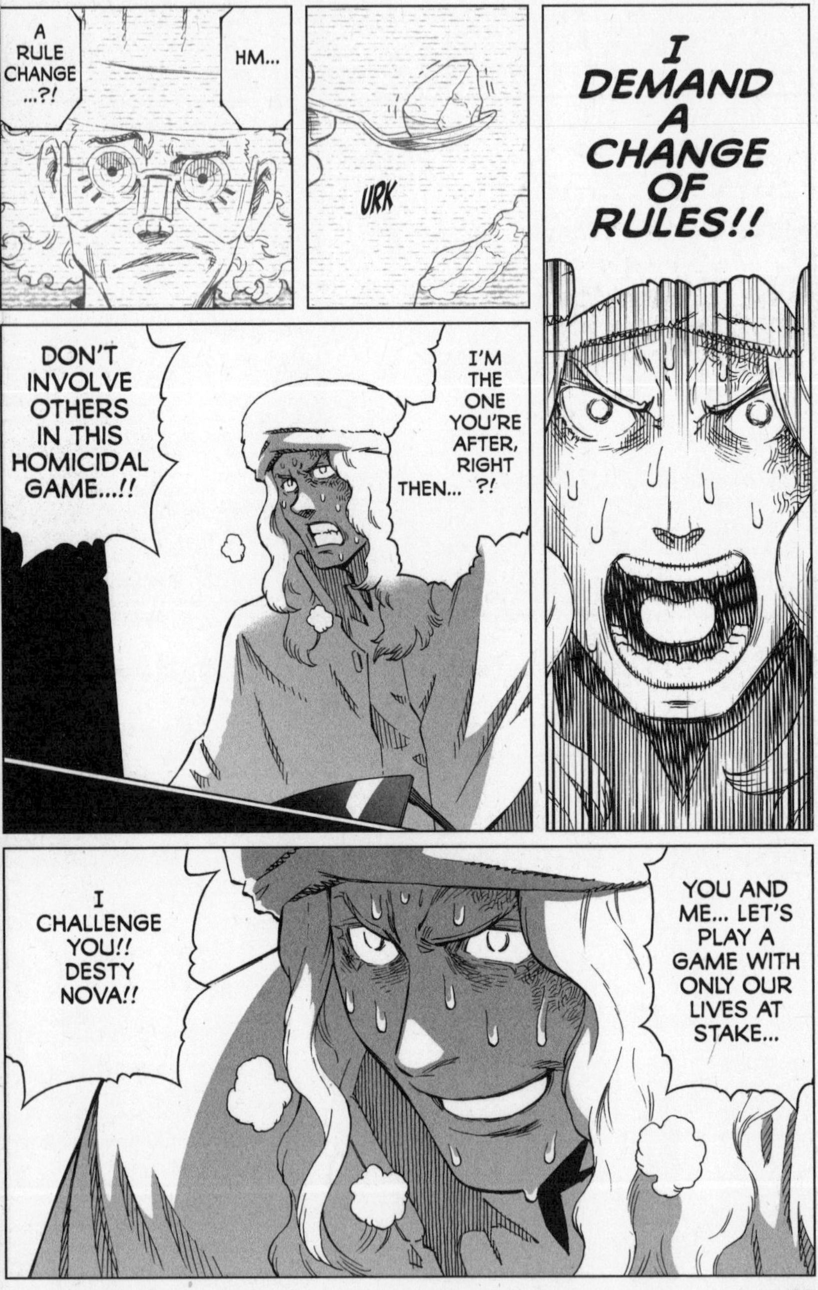
I DEMAND A CHANGE OF RULES!!
URK
HM...
A RULE CHANGE ...?!
I'M THE ONE YOU'RE AFTER, RIGHT ?!
DON'T INVOLVE OTHERS IN THIS HOMICIDAL GAME...!!
THEN...
YOU AND ME... LET'S PLAY A GAME WITH ONLY OUR LIVES AT STAKE...
I CHALLENGE YOU!! DESTY NOVA!!

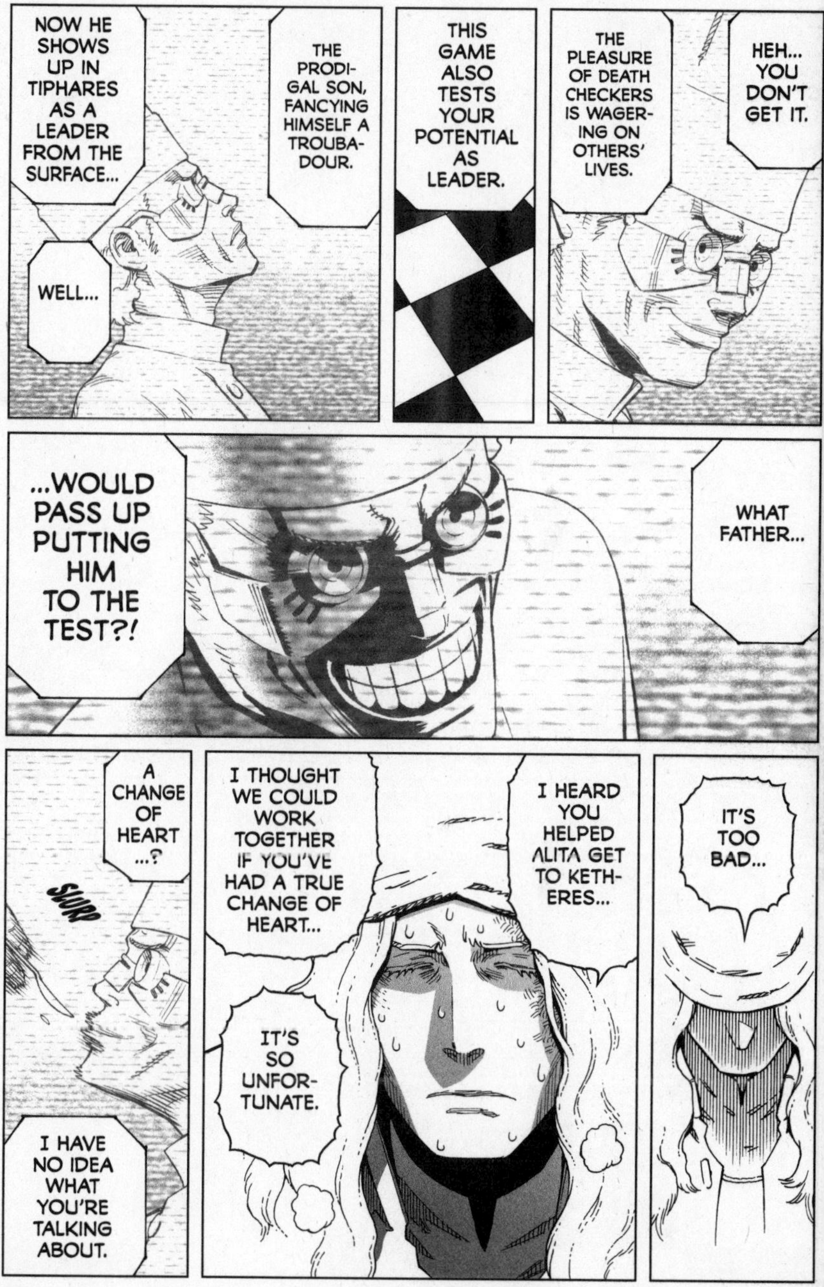
HEH... YOU DON'T GET IT.
THE PLEASURE OF DEATH CHECKERS IS WAGERING ON OTHERS' LIVES.
THIS GAME ALSO TESTS YOUR POTENTIAL AS LEADER.
THE PRODIGAL SON, FANCYING HIMSELF A TROUBADOUR.
NOW HE SHOWS UP IN TIPHARES AS A LEADER FROM THE SURFACE...
WELL...
WHAT FATHER...
...WOULD PASS UP PUTTING HIM TO THE TEST?!
IT'S TOO BAD...
I HEARD YOU HELPED ALITA GET TO KETHERES...
I THOUGHT WE COULD WORK TOGETHER IF YOU'VE HAD A TRUE CHANGE OF HEART...
IT'S SO UNFORTUNATE.
A CHANGE OF HEART...?
SLURP
I HAVE NO IDEA WHAT YOU'RE TALKING ABOUT.

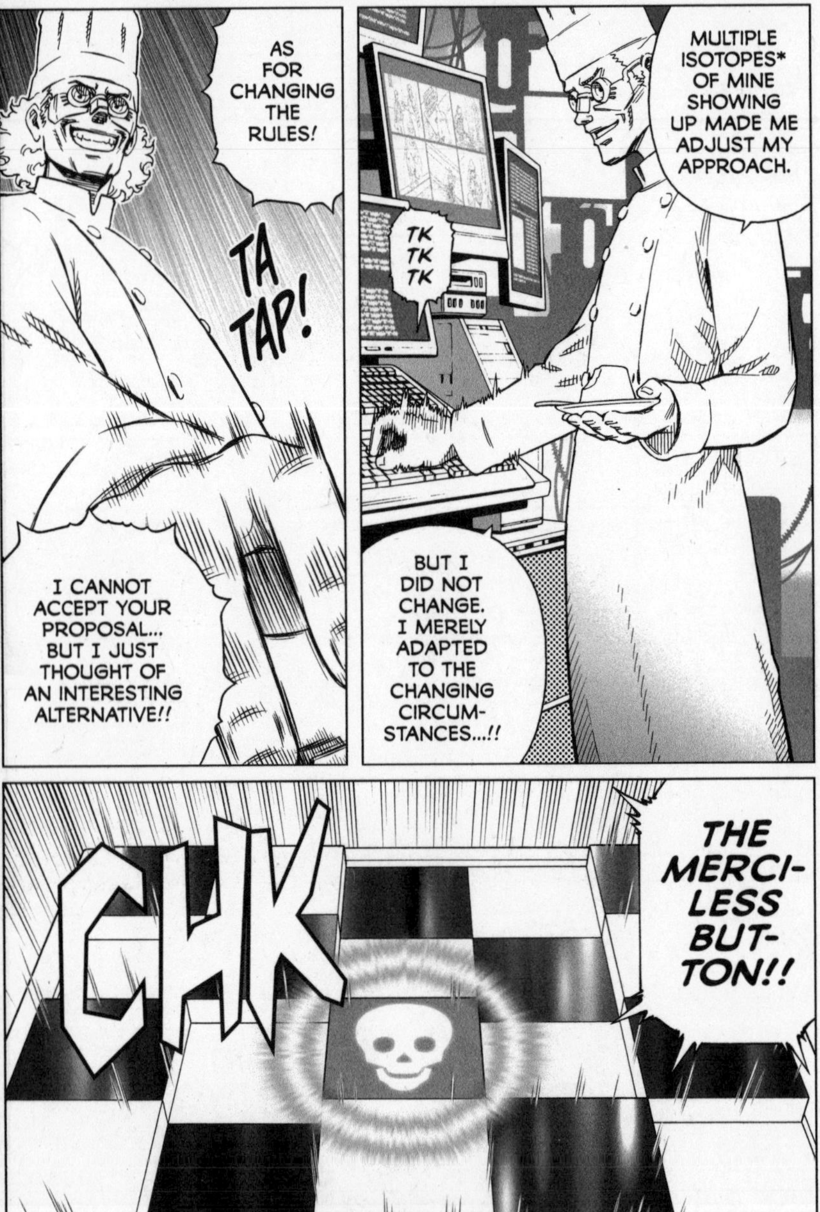
MULTIPLE ISOTOPES* OF MINE SHOWING UP MADE ME ADJUST MY APPROACH.
TK TK TK
BUT I DID NOT CHANGE. I MERELY ADAPTED TO THE CHANGING CIRCUM-STANCES...!!
AS FOR CHANGING THE RULES!
TA TAP!
I CANNOT ACCEPT YOUR PROPOSAL... BUT I JUST THOUGHT OF AN INTERESTING ALTERNATIVE!!
THE MERCI-LESS BUT-TON!!
CHK

*Isotopes: the isotopes here are not the chemical variety but Nova's different versions—Portable Nova and Super Nova. See Battle Angel Alita: Last Order ep. 61

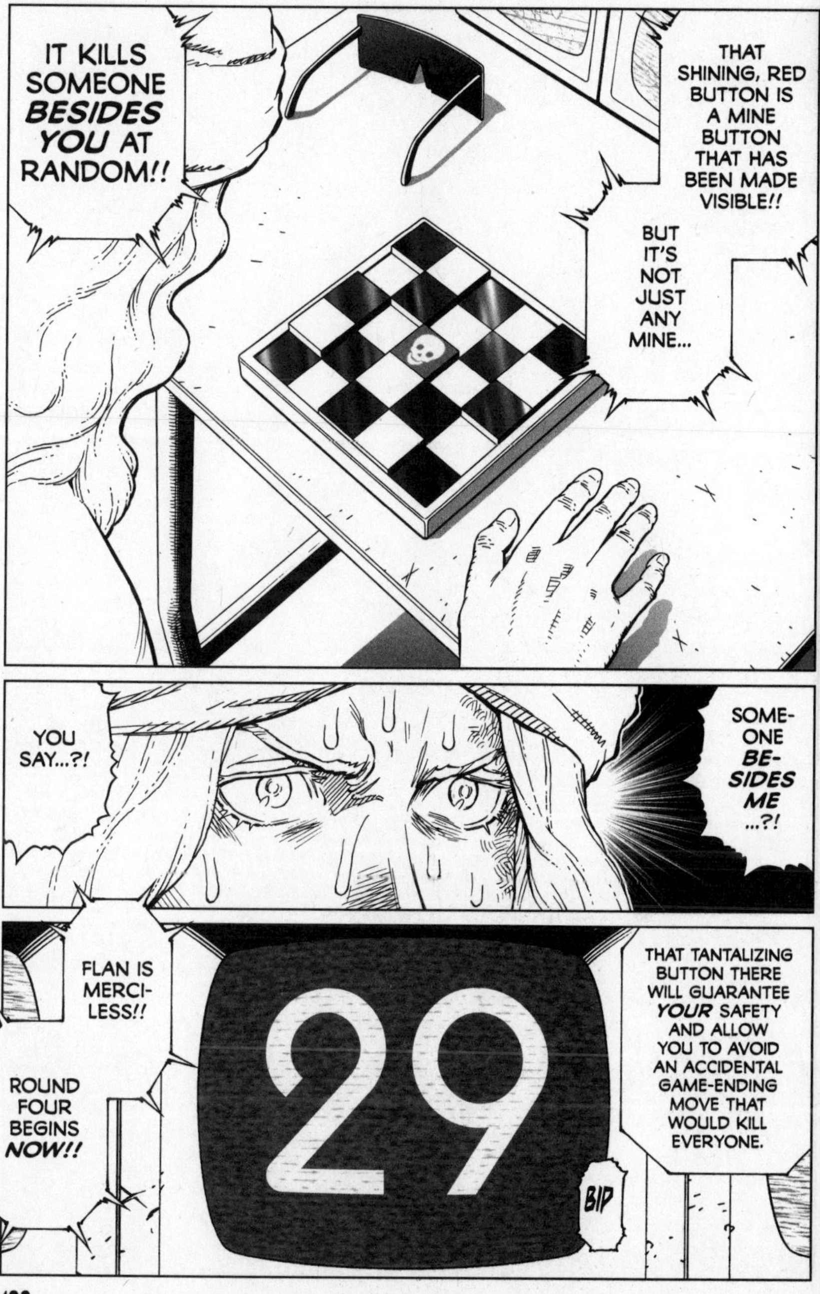
THAT SHINING, RED BUTTON IS A MINE BUTTON THAT HAS BEEN MADE VISIBLE!!
BUT IT'S NOT JUST ANY MINE...
IT KILLS SOMEONE BESIDES YOU AT RANDOM!!
SOME-ONE BE-SIDES ME ...?!
YOU SAY...?!
THAT TANTALIZING BUTTON THERE WILL GUARANTEE YOUR SAFETY AND ALLOW YOU TO AVOID AN ACCIDENTAL GAME-ENDING MOVE THAT WOULD KILL EVERYONE.
BIP
29
FLAN IS MERCI-LESS!!
ROUND FOUR BEGINS NOW!!

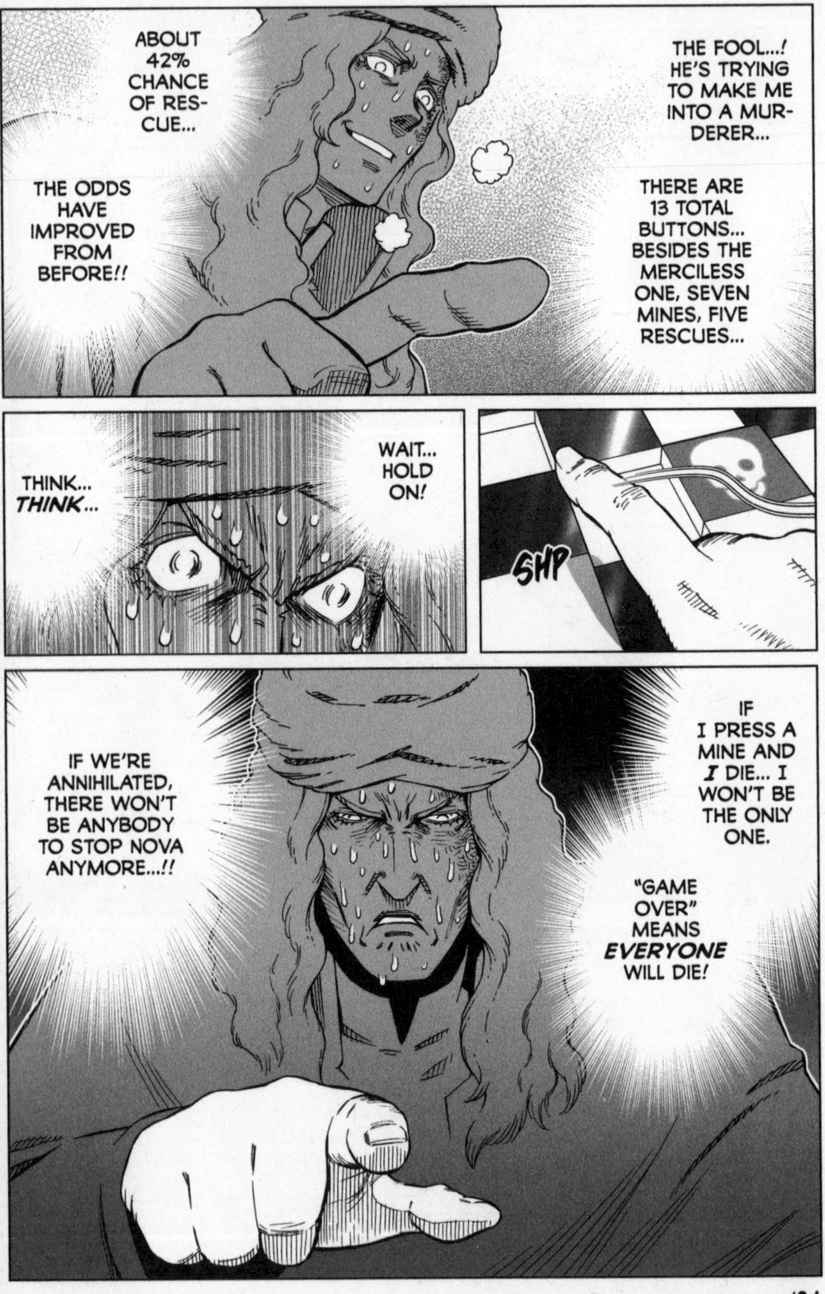
THE FOOL...! HE'S TRYING TO MAKE ME INTO A MURDERER...
THERE ARE 13 TOTAL BUTTONS... BESIDES THE MERCILESS ONE, SEVEN MINES, FIVE RESCUES...
ABOUT 42% CHANCE OF RESCUE...
THE ODDS HAVE IMPROVED FROM BEFORE!!
SHP
WAIT... HOLD ON!
THINK... *THINK*...
IF *I* PRESS A MINE AND *I* DIE... I WON'T BE THE ONLY ONE.
"GAME OVER" MEANS *EVERYONE* WILL DIE!
IF WE'RE ANNIHILATED, THERE WON'T BE ANYBODY TO STOP NOVA ANYMORE...!!

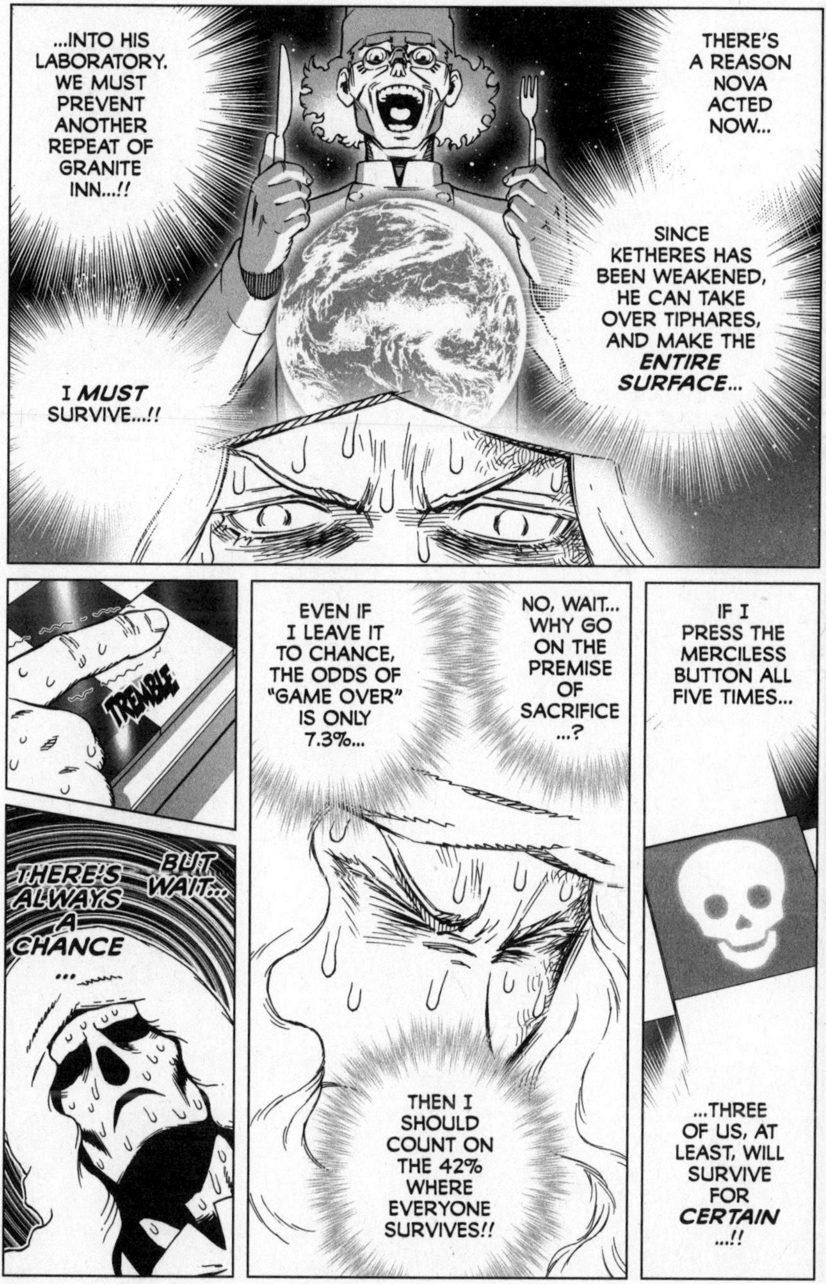
THERE'S A REASON NOVA ACTED NOW...
SINCE KETHERES HAS BEEN WEAKENED, HE CAN TAKE OVER TIPHARES, AND MAKE THE *ENTIRE SURFACE*...
...INTO HIS LABORATORY. WE MUST PREVENT ANOTHER REPEAT OF GRANITE INN...!!
I *MUST* SURVIVE...!!
IF I PRESS THE MERCILESS BUTTON ALL FIVE TIMES...
...THREE OF US, AT LEAST, WILL SURVIVE FOR *CERTAIN*...!!
NO, WAIT... WHY GO ON THE PREMISE OF SACRIFICE...?
EVEN IF I LEAVE IT TO CHANCE, THE ODDS OF "GAME OVER" IS ONLY 7.3%...
THEN I SHOULD COUNT ON THE 42% WHERE EVERYONE SURVIVES!!
TREMBLE
BUT WAIT...
THERE'S ALWAYS A CHANCE...

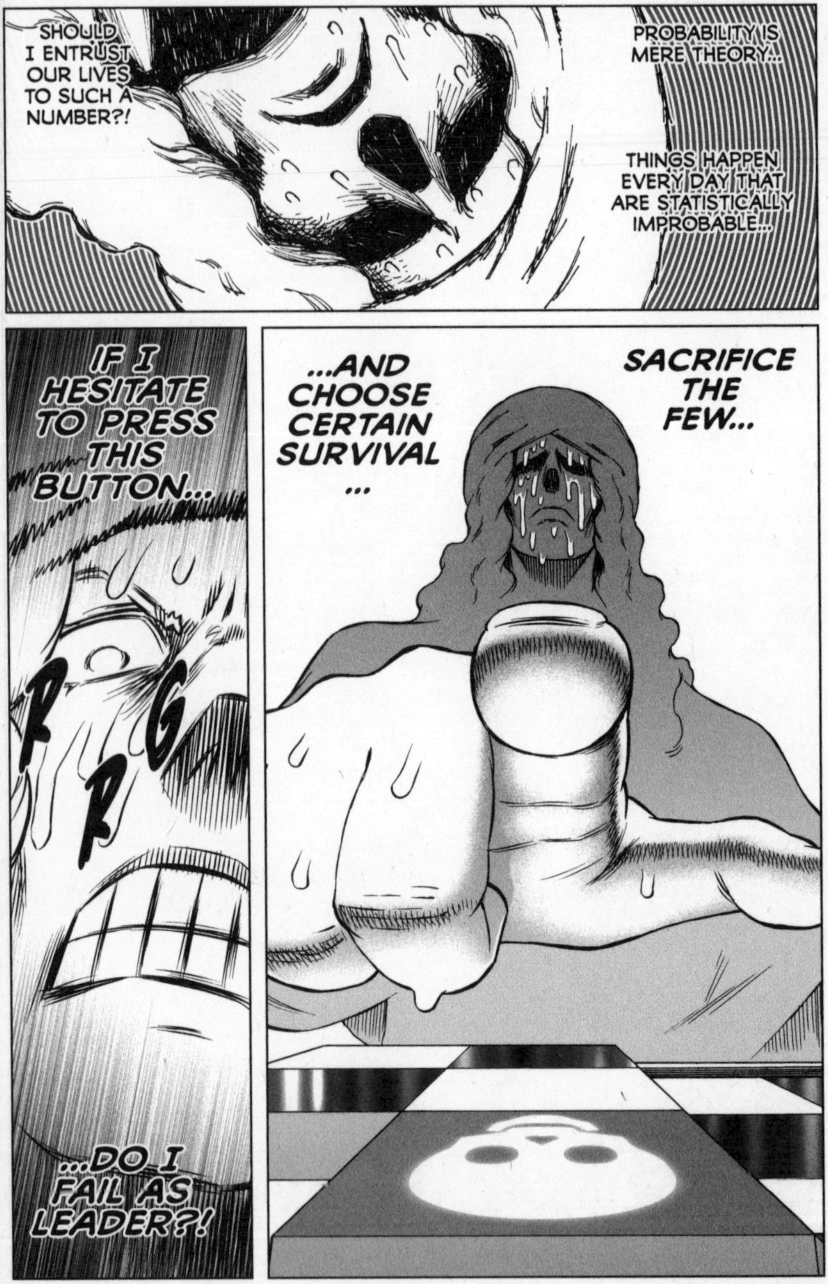

PROBABILITY IS MERE THEORY...
THINGS HAPPEN EVERY DAY THAT ARE STATISTICALLY IMPROBABLE...
SHOULD I ENTRUST OUR LIVES TO SUCH A NUMBER?!
SACRIFICE THE FEW...
...AND CHOOSE CERTAIN SURVIVAL ...
IF I HESITATE TO PRESS THIS BUTTON...
RRG
...DO I FAIL AS LEADER?!

YOU ALWAYS DISAPPOINT ME.

KAOS... MY SON.

...IS A *MINE*.

UNFORTUNATELY, THAT BUTTON...

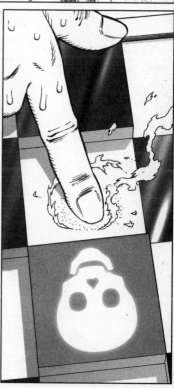

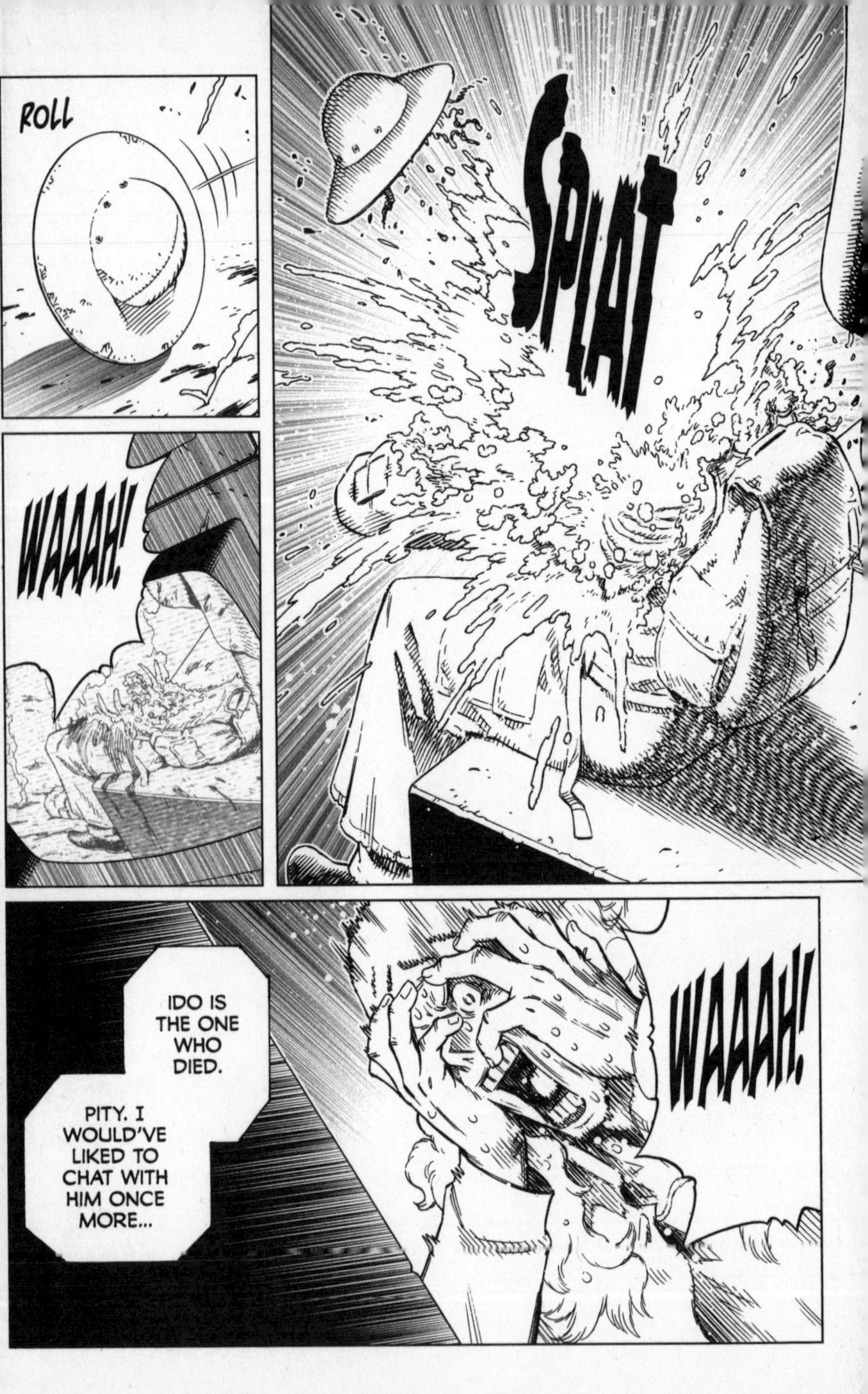
SPLAT
ROLL
WAAAH!
WAAAH!
IDO IS THE ONE WHO DIED.
PITY. I WOULD'VE LIKED TO CHAT WITH HIM ONCE MORE...

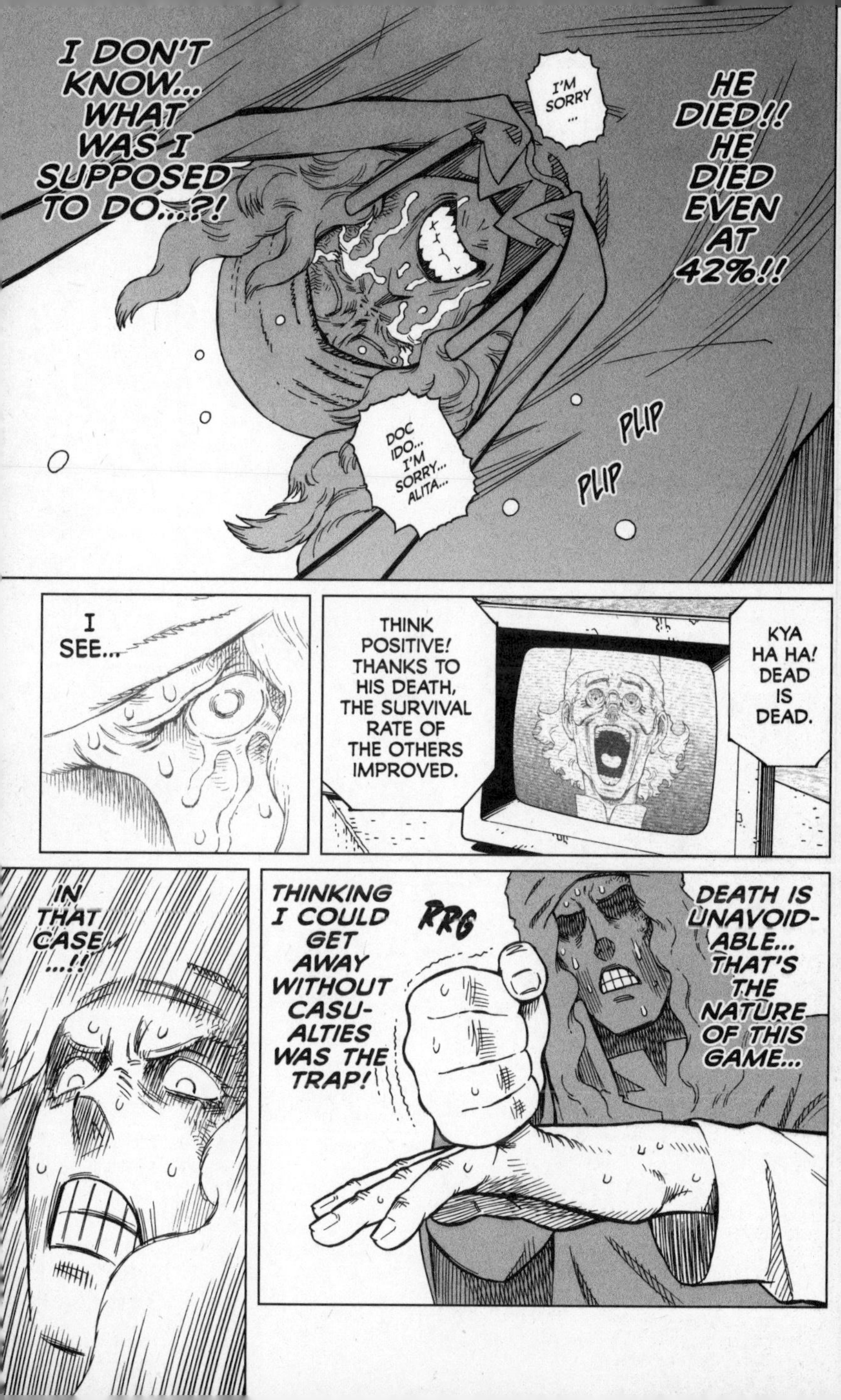
HE DIED!! HE DIED EVEN AT 42%!!
I'M SORRY...
I DON'T KNOW... WHAT WAS I SUPPOSED TO DO...?!
PLIP
PLIP
DOC IDO... I'M SORRY... ALITA...
KYA HA HA! DEAD IS DEAD.
THINK POSITIVE! THANKS TO HIS DEATH, THE SURVIVAL RATE OF THE OTHERS IMPROVED.
I SEE...
DEATH IS UNAVOIDABLE... THAT'S THE NATURE OF THIS GAME...
RRG
THINKING I COULD GET AWAY WITHOUT CASUALTIES WAS THE TRAP!
IN THAT CASE...!!

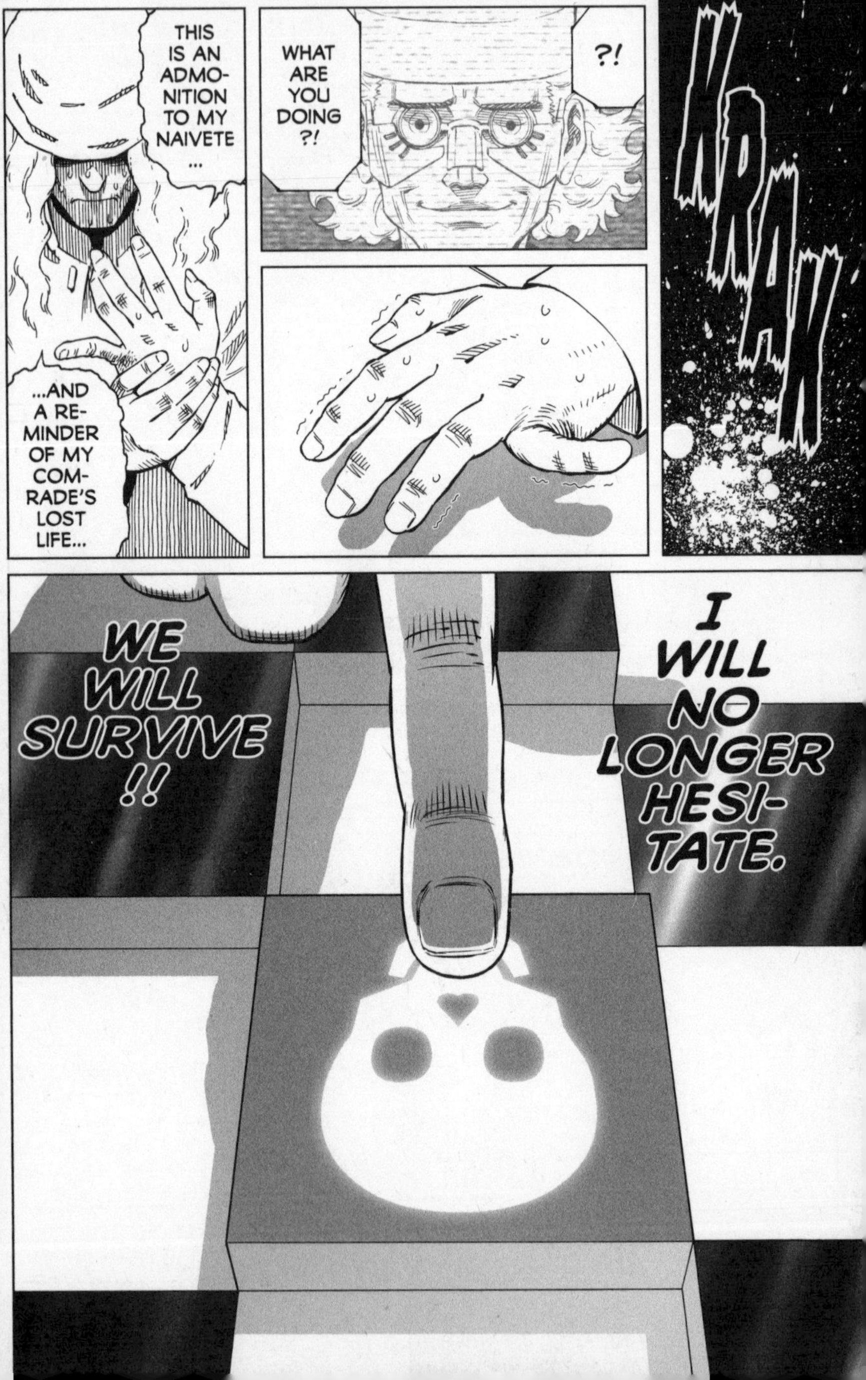
KRAK
?!
WHAT ARE YOU DOING ?!
THIS IS AN ADMONITION TO MY NAIVETE ...
...AND A REMINDER OF MY COMRADE'S LOST LIFE...
I WILL NO LONGER HESITATE.
WE WILL SURVIVE !!

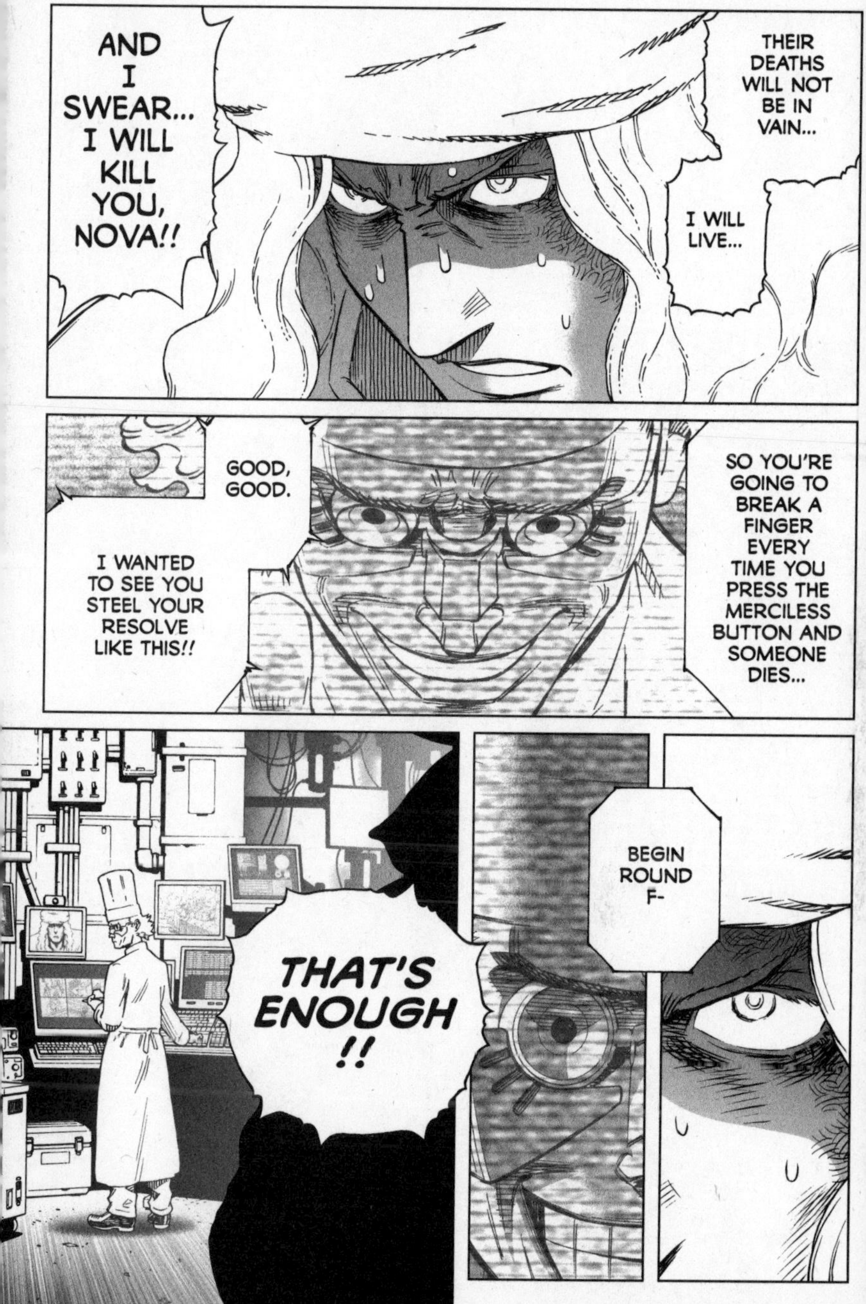
THEIR DEATHS WILL NOT BE IN VAIN...
I WILL LIVE...
AND I SWEAR... I WILL KILL YOU, NOVA!!
SO YOU'RE GOING TO BREAK A FINGER EVERY TIME YOU PRESS THE MERCILESS BUTTON AND SOMEONE DIES...
GOOD, GOOD.
I WANTED TO SEE YOU STEEL YOUR RESOLVE LIKE THIS!!
BEGIN ROUND F-
THAT'S ENOUGH!!

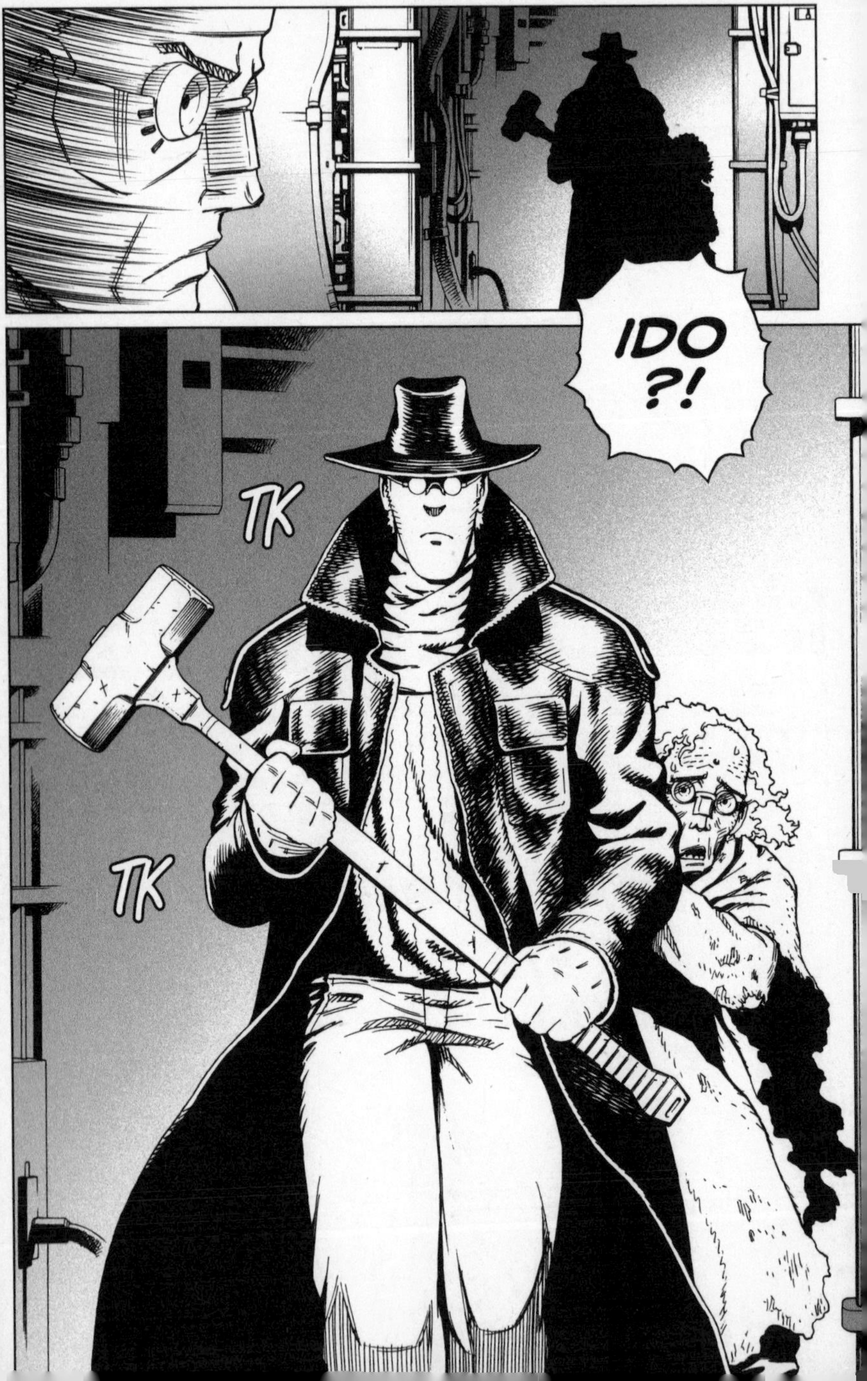
IDO ?!
TK
TK

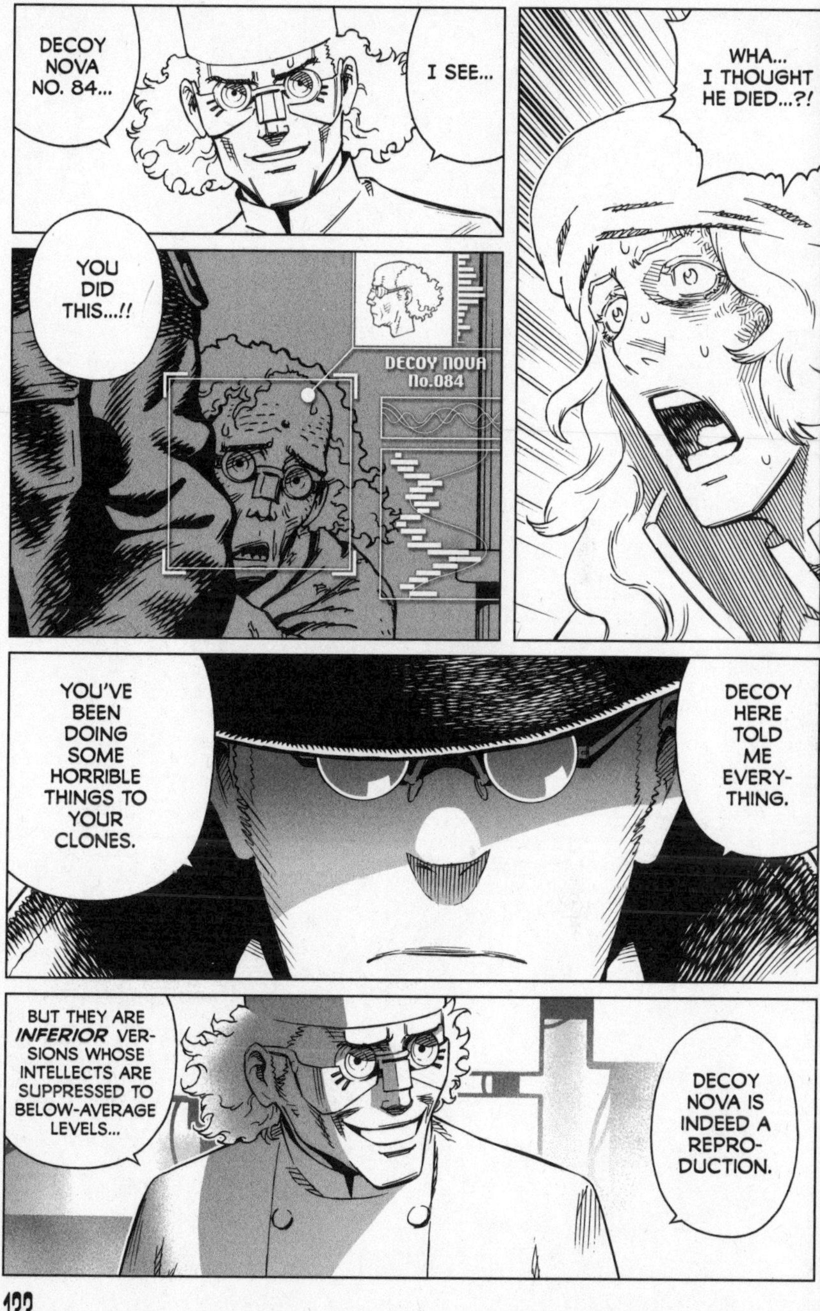
WHA... I THOUGHT HE DIED...?!
DECOY NOVA NO. 84...
I SEE...
YOU DID THIS...!!
DECOY NOVA No.084
DECOY HERE TOLD ME EVERY-THING.
YOU'VE BEEN DOING SOME HORRIBLE THINGS TO YOUR CLONES.
DECOY NOVA IS INDEED A REPRO-DUCTION.
BUT THEY ARE *INFERIOR* VER-SIONS WHOSE INTELLECTS ARE SUPPRESSED TO BELOW-AVERAGE LEVELS...

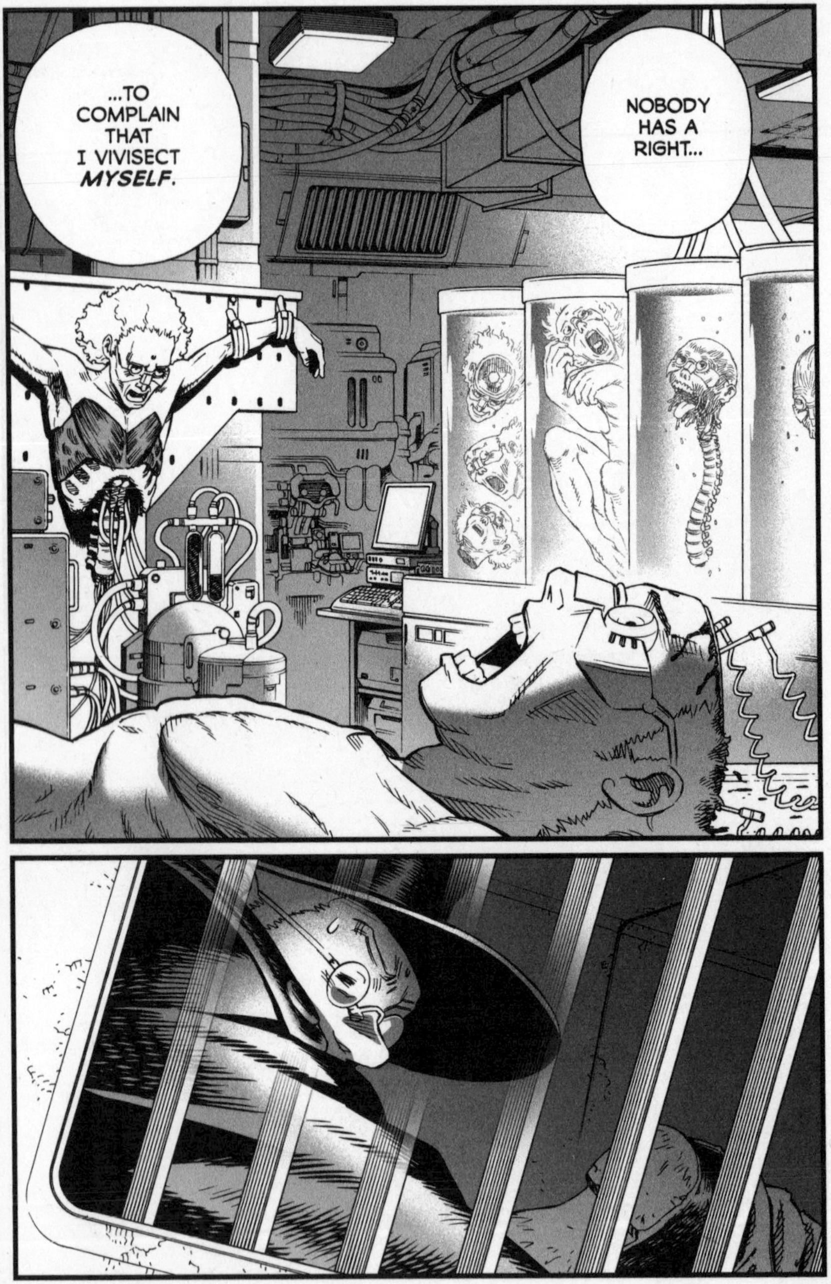
NOBODY HAS A RIGHT...
...TO COMPLAIN THAT I VIVISECT *MYSELF*.

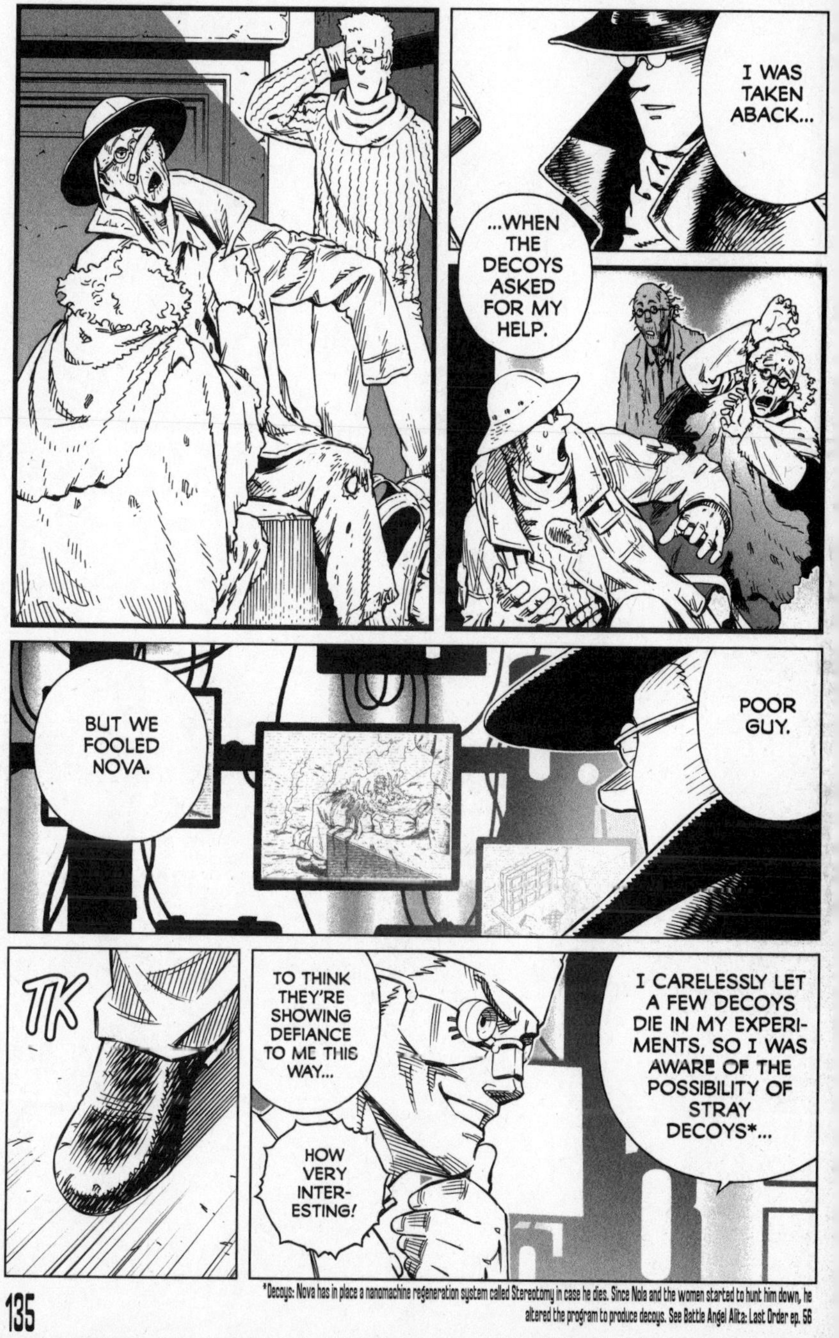
I WAS TAKEN ABACK...
...WHEN THE DECOYS ASKED FOR MY HELP.
POOR GUY.
BUT WE FOOLED NOVA.
I CARELESSLY LET A FEW DECOYS DIE IN MY EXPERIMENTS, SO I WAS AWARE OF THE POSSIBILITY OF STRAY DECOYS*...
TO THINK THEY'RE SHOWING DEFIANCE TO ME THIS WAY...
HOW VERY INTERESTING!
TK

*Decoys: Nova has in place a nanomachine regeneration system called Stereotomy in case he dies. Since Nola and the women started to hunt him down, he altered the program to produce decoys. See Battle Angel Alita: Last Order ep. 56

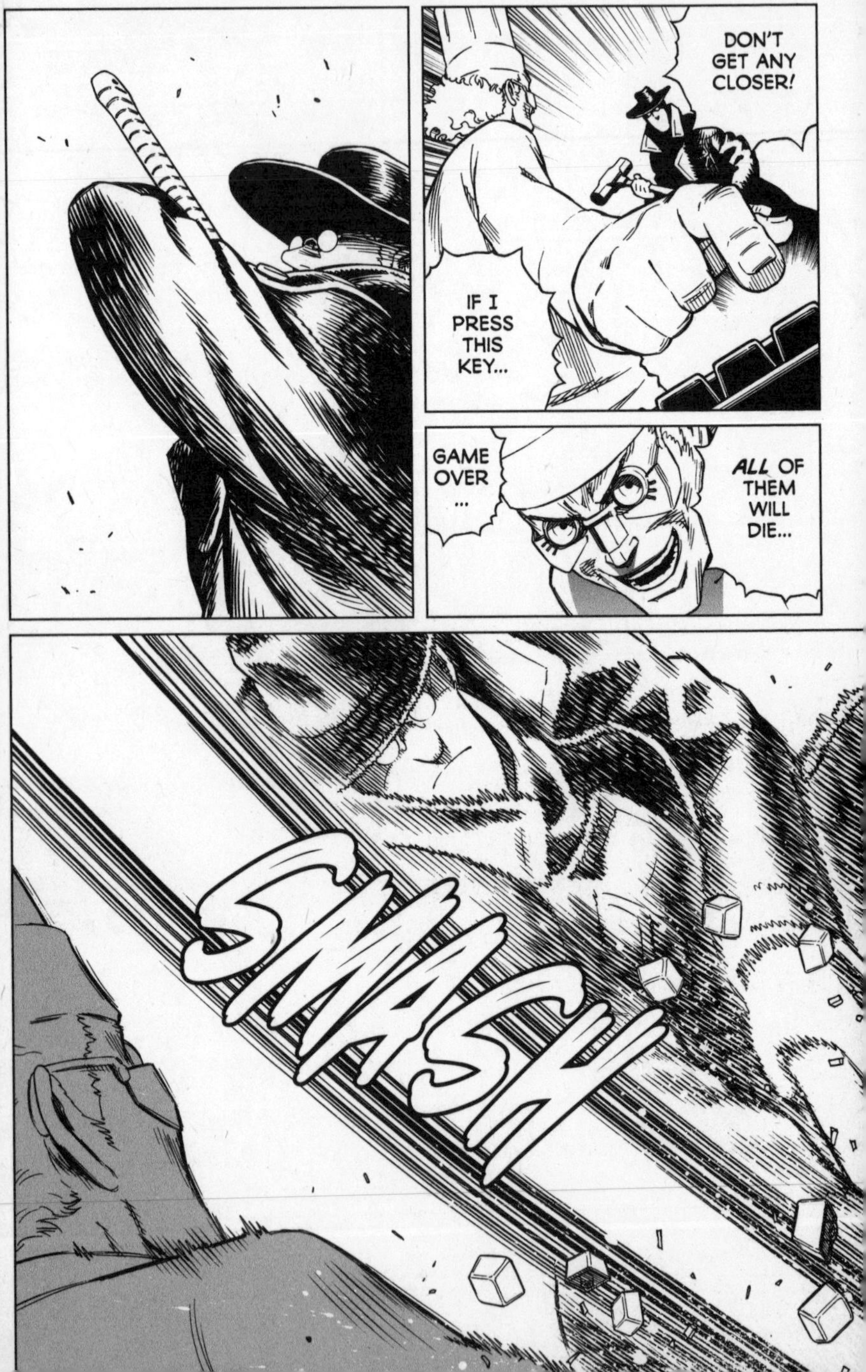
DON'T GET ANY CLOSER!
IF I PRESS THIS KEY...
GAME OVER ...
ALL OF THEM WILL DIE...
SMASH

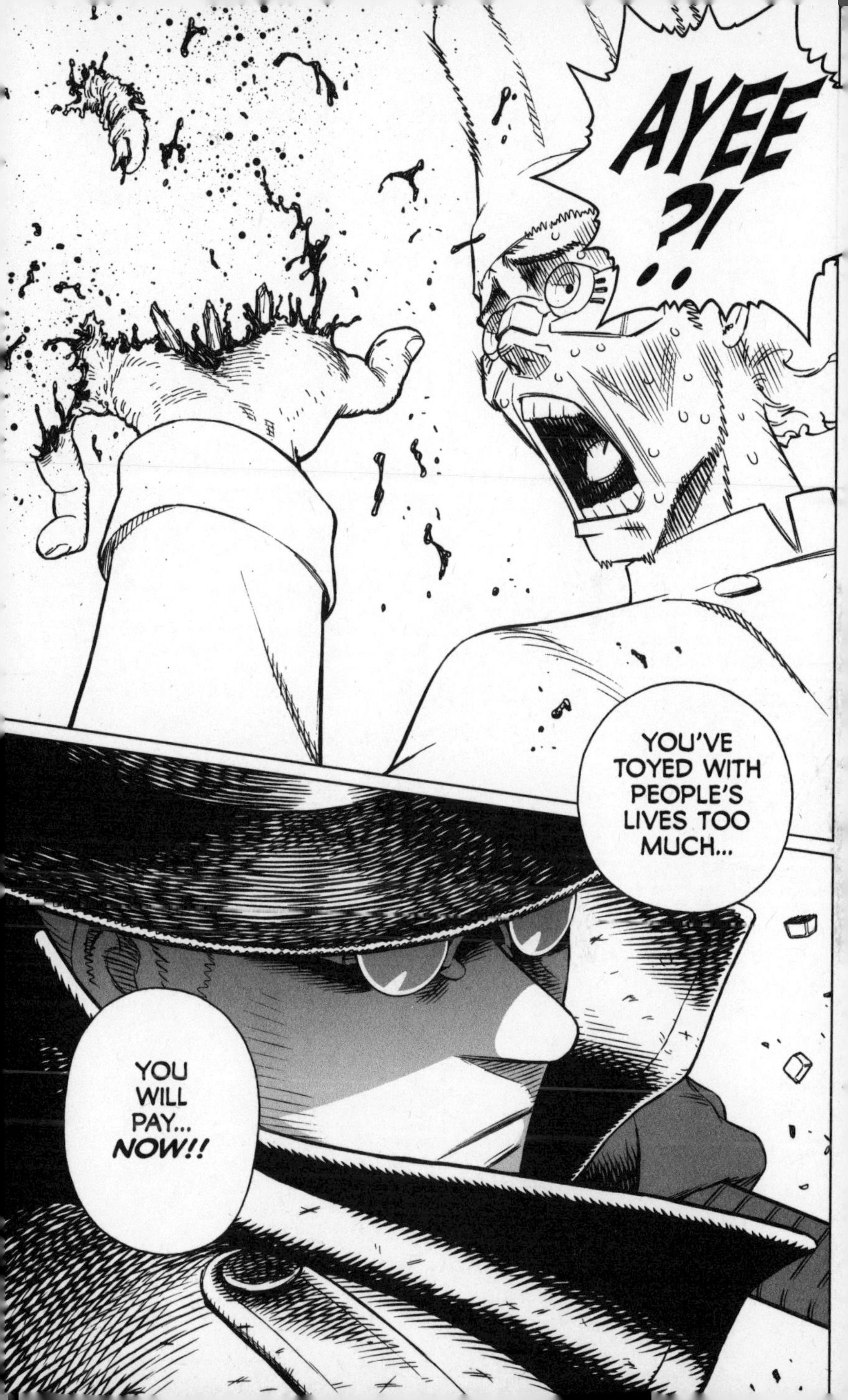
AYEE ?!
YOU'VE TOYED WITH PEOPLE'S LIVES TOO MUCH...
YOU WILL PAY... *NOW!!*

Phase 122: Alita Quest XVI

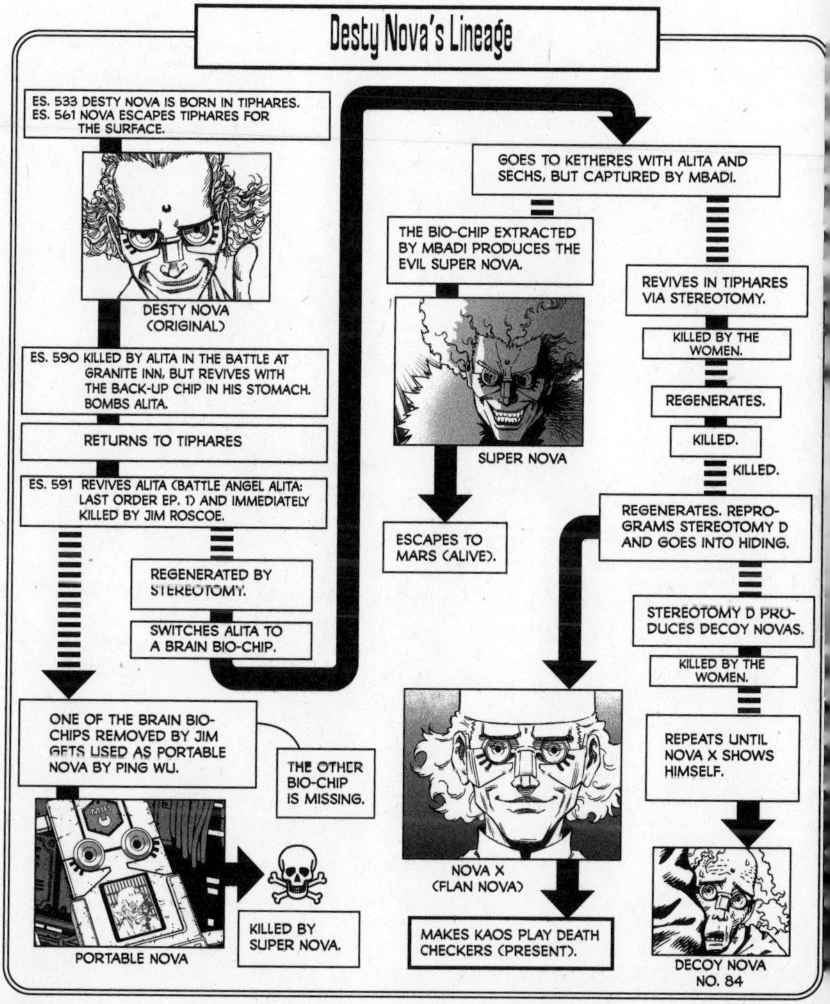
Desty Nova's Lineage
ES. 533 DESTY NOVA IS BORN IN TIPHARES. ES. 561 NOVA ESCAPES TIPHARES FOR THE SURFACE.
DESTY NOVA (ORIGINAL)
ES. 590 KILLED BY ALITA IN THE BATTLE AT GRANITE INN, BUT REVIVES WITH THE BACK-UP CHIP IN HIS STOMACH. BOMBS ALITA.
RETURNS TO TIPHARES
ES. 591 REVIVES ALITA (BATTLE ANGEL ALITA: LAST ORDER EP. 1) AND IMMEDIATELY KILLED BY JIM ROSCOE.
REGENERATED BY STEREOTOMY.
SWITCHES ALITA TO A BRAIN BIO-CHIP.
ONE OF THE BRAIN BIO-CHIPS REMOVED BY JIM GETS USED AS PORTABLE NOVA BY PING WU.
THE OTHER BIO-CHIP IS MISSING.
MIB
PORTABLE NOVA
KILLED BY SUPER NOVA.
GOES TO KETHERES WITH ALITA AND SECHS, BUT CAPTURED BY MBADI.
THE BIO-CHIP EXTRACTED BY MBADI PRODUCES THE EVIL SUPER NOVA.
SUPER NOVA
ESCAPES TO MARS (ALIVE).
REVIVES IN TIPHARES VIA STEREOTOMY.
KILLED BY THE WOMEN.
REGENERATES.
KILLED.
KILLED.
REGENERATES. REPROGRAMS STEREOTOMY D AND GOES INTO HIDING.
NOVA X (FLAN NOVA)
MAKES KAOS PLAY DEATH CHECKERS (PRESENT).
STEREOTOMY D PRODUCES DECOY NOVAS.
KILLED BY THE WOMEN.
REPEATS UNTIL NOVA X SHOWS HIMSELF.
DECOY NOVA NO. 84

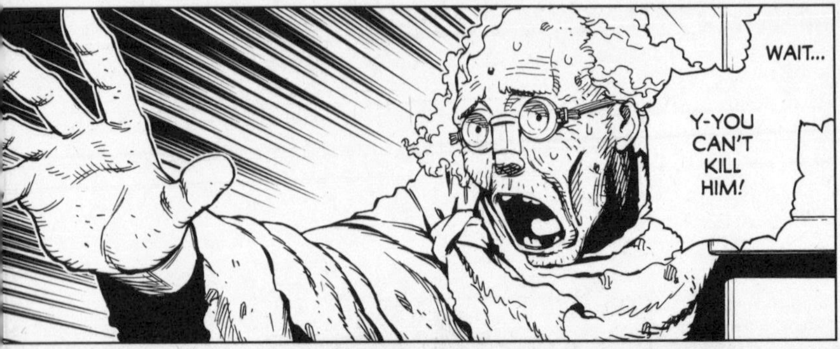
WAIT...
Y-YOU CAN'T KILL HIM!
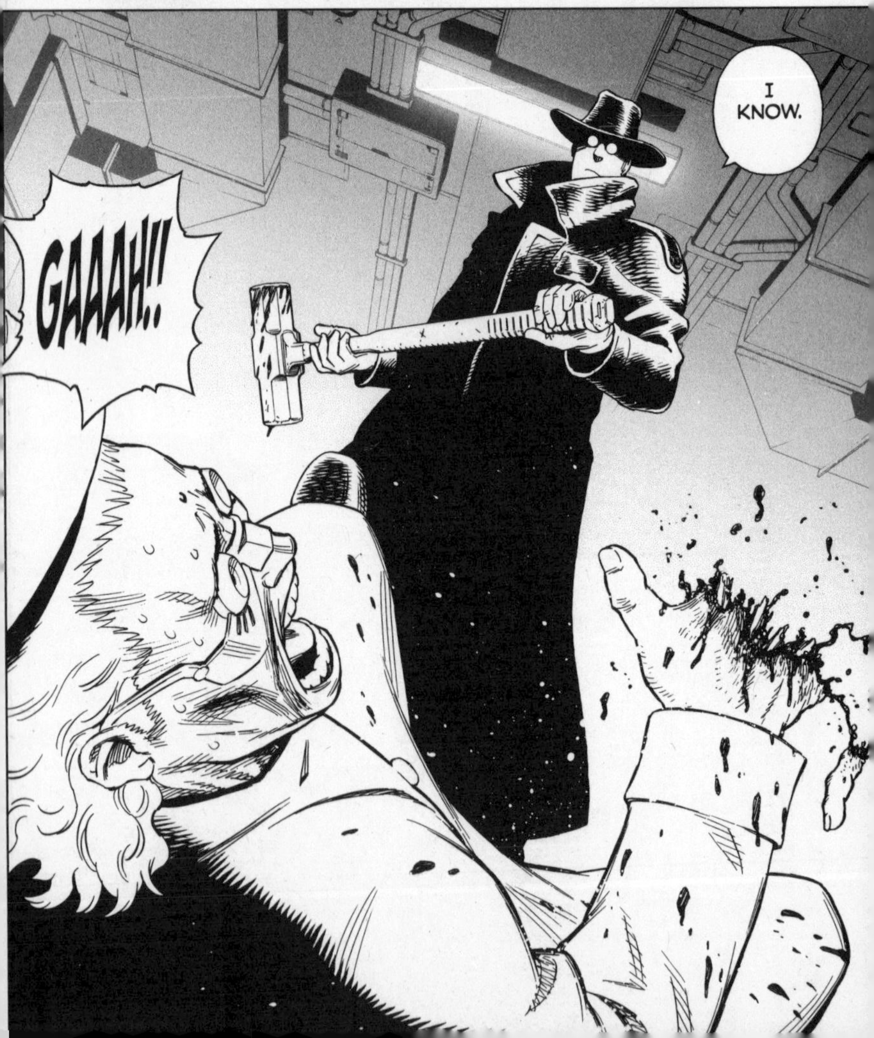
I KNOW.
GAAAH!!

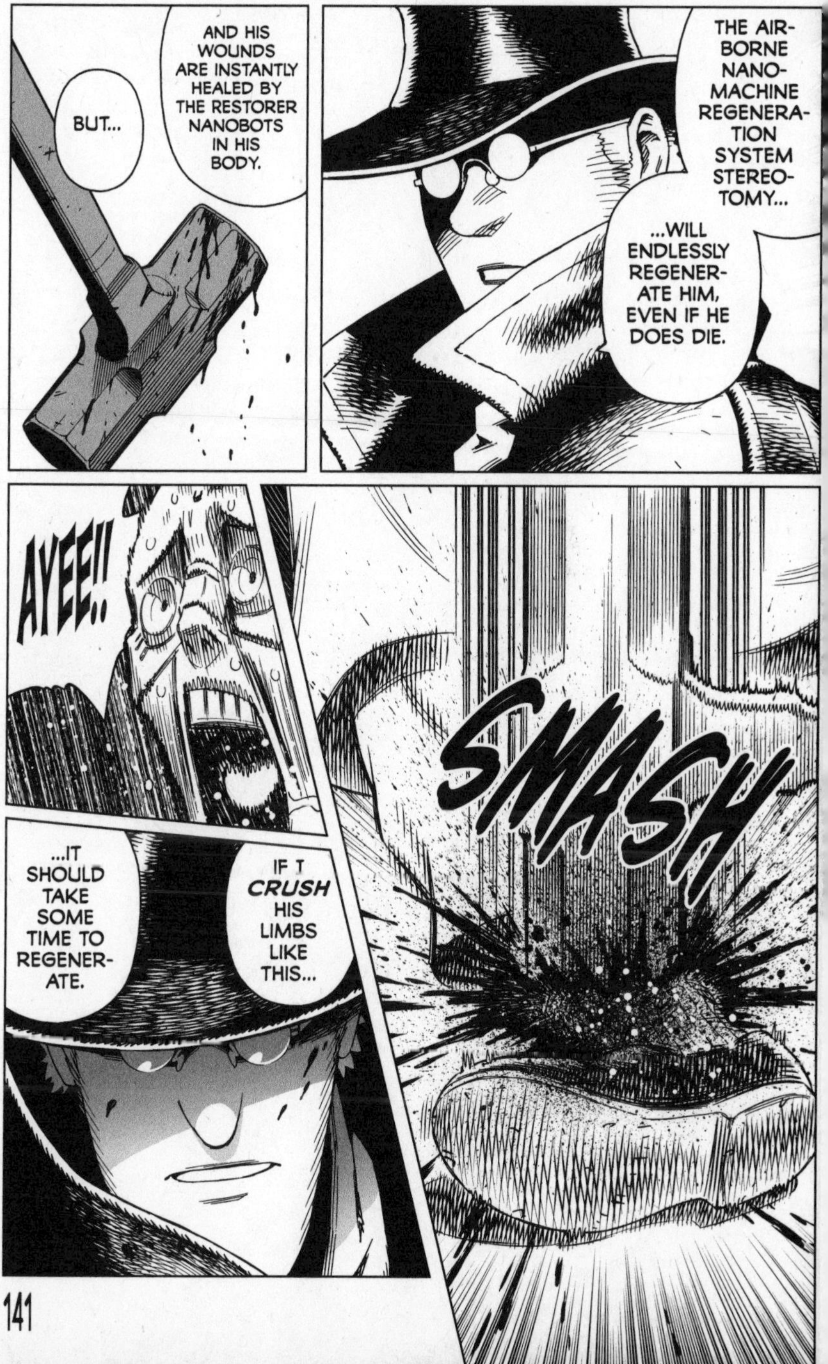
THE AIRBORNE NANOMACHINE REGENERATION SYSTEM STEREOTOMY...
...WILL ENDLESSLY REGENERATE HIM, EVEN IF HE DOES DIE.
AND HIS WOUNDS ARE INSTANTLY HEALED BY THE RESTORER NANOBOTS IN HIS BODY.
BUT...
SMASH
AYEE!!
IF I *CRUSH* HIS LIMBS LIKE THIS...
...IT SHOULD TAKE SOME TIME TO REGENERATE.

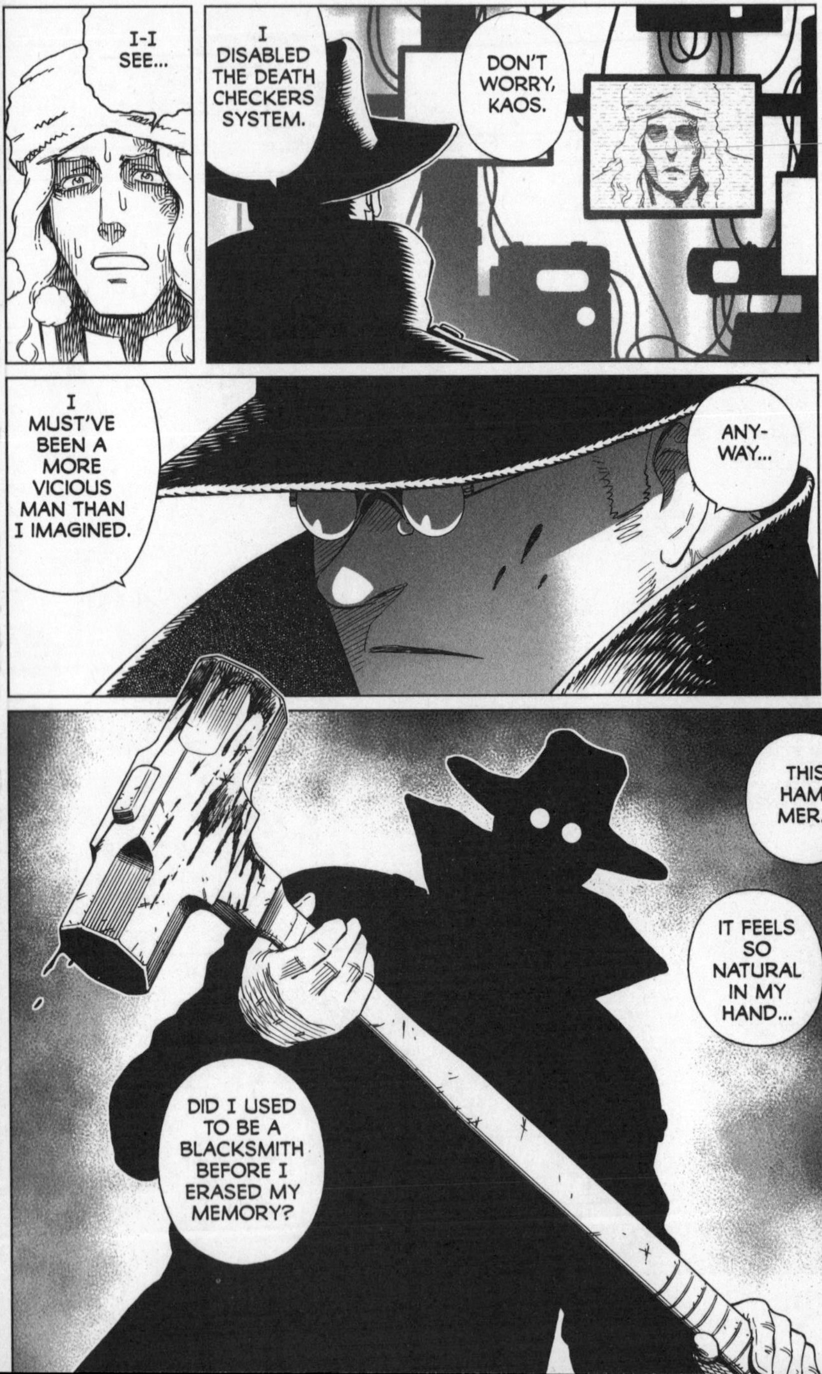
DON'T WORRY, KAOS.
I DISABLED THE DEATH CHECKERS SYSTEM.
I-I SEE...
ANY-WAY...
I MUST'VE BEEN A MORE VICIOUS MAN THAN I IMAGINED.
THIS HAM-MER...
IT FEELS SO NATURAL IN MY HAND...
DID I USED TO BE A BLACKSMITH BEFORE I ERASED MY MEMORY?

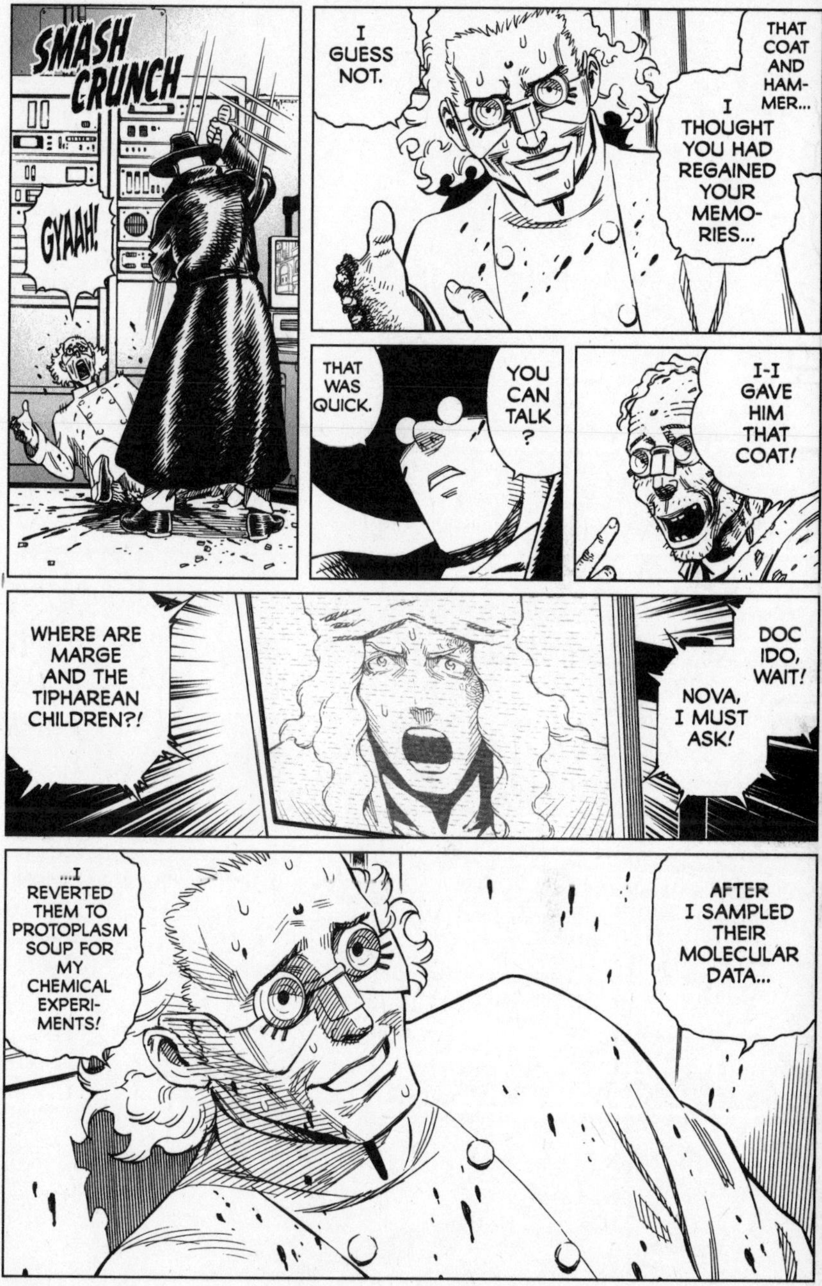
THAT COAT AND HAMMER...
I THOUGHT YOU HAD REGAINED YOUR MEMORIES...
I GUESS NOT.
I-I GAVE HIM THAT COAT!
YOU CAN TALK?
THAT WAS QUICK.
SMASH CRUNCH
GYAAH!
DOC IDO, WAIT!
NOVA, I MUST ASK!
WHERE ARE MARGE AND THE TIPHAREAN CHILDREN?!
AFTER I SAMPLED THEIR MOLECULAR DATA...
...I REVERTED THEM TO PROTOPLASM SOUP FOR MY CHEMICAL EXPERIMENTS!

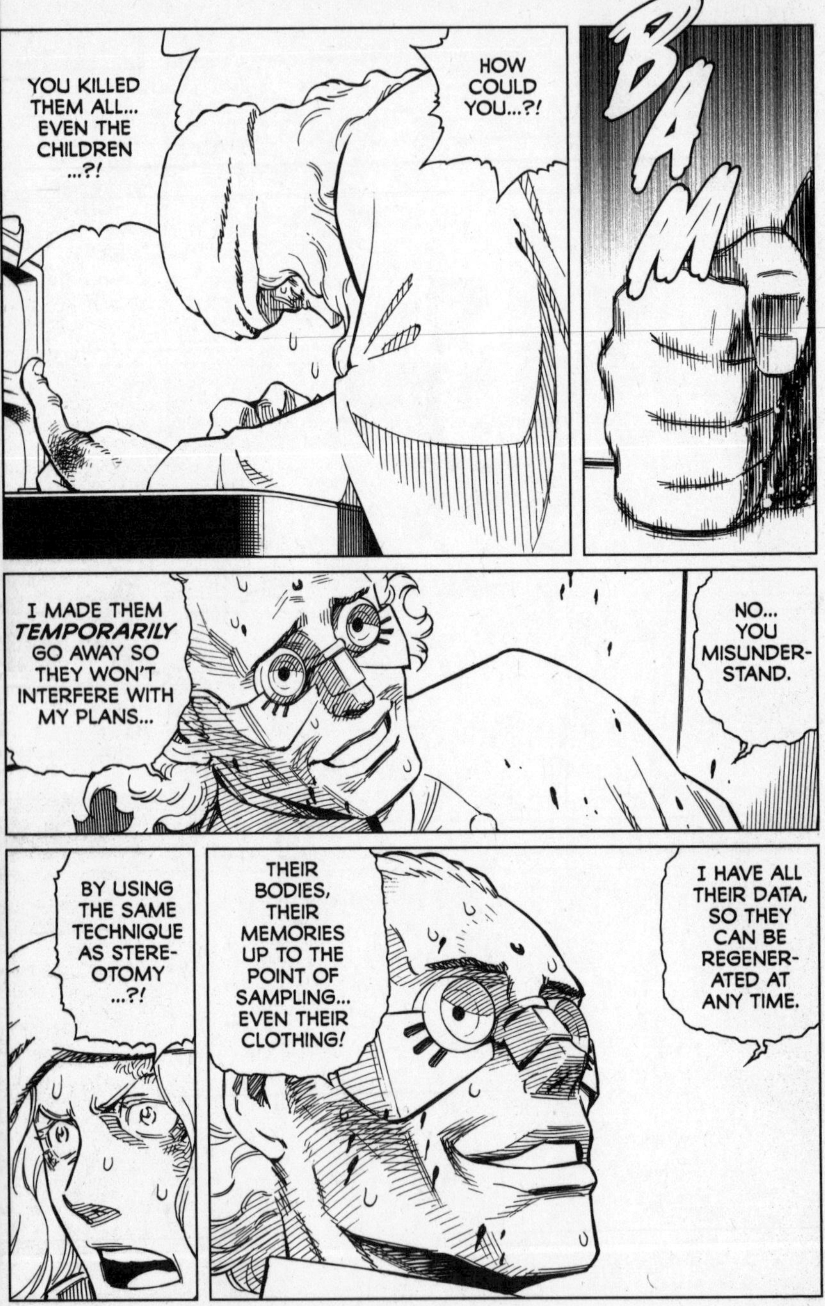
BAM
HOW COULD YOU...?!
YOU KILLED THEM ALL... EVEN THE CHILDREN ...?!
NO... YOU MISUNDERSTAND.
I MADE THEM *TEMPORARILY* GO AWAY SO THEY WON'T INTERFERE WITH MY PLANS...
I HAVE ALL THEIR DATA, SO THEY CAN BE REGENERATED AT ANY TIME.
THEIR BODIES, THEIR MEMORIES UP TO THE POINT OF SAMPLING... EVEN THEIR CLOTHING!
BY USING THE SAME TECHNIQUE AS STEREOTOMY ...?!

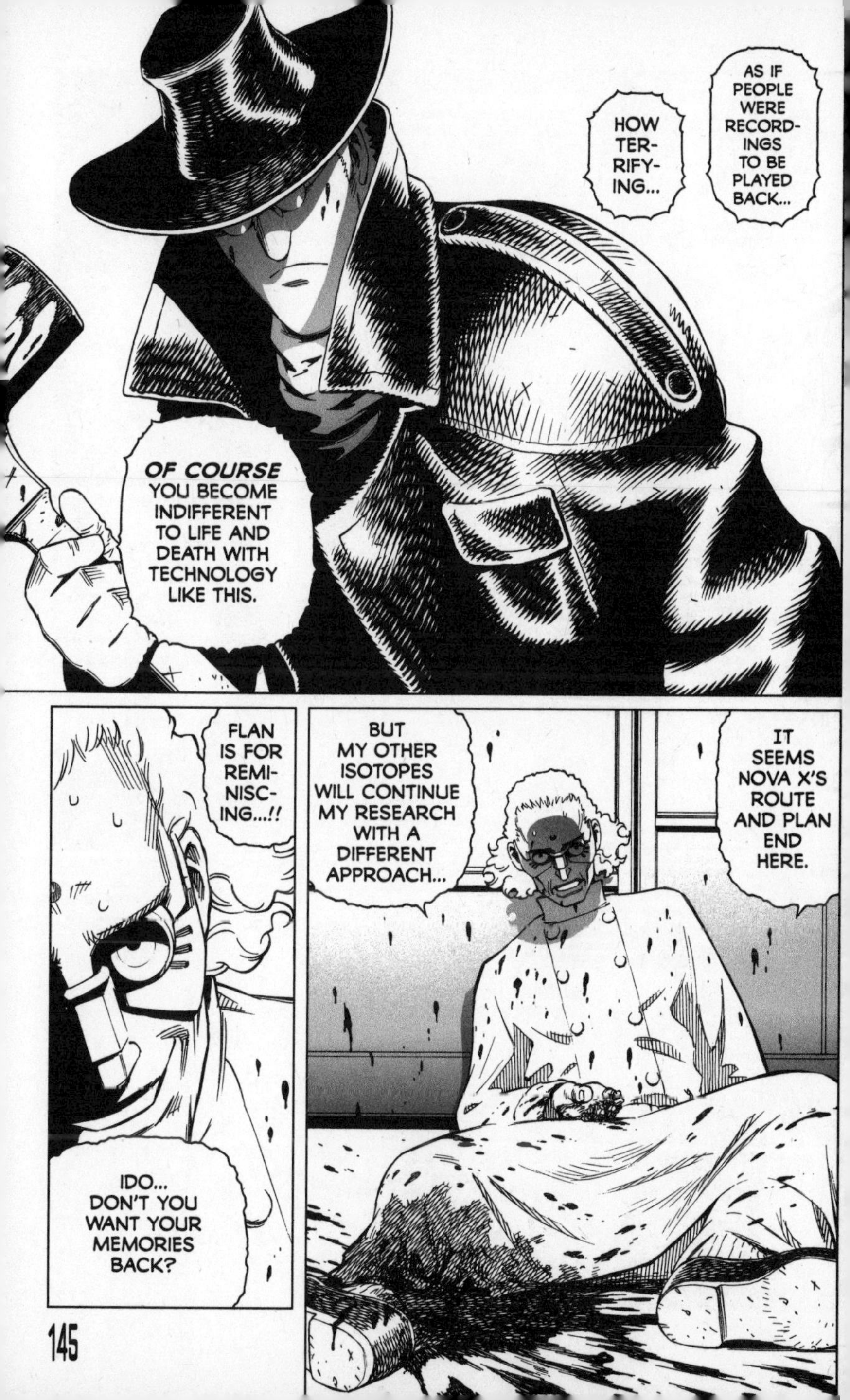
AS IF PEOPLE WERE RECORDINGS TO BE PLAYED BACK...
HOW TERRIFYING...
OF COURSE YOU BECOME INDIFFERENT TO LIFE AND DEATH WITH TECHNOLOGY LIKE THIS.
IT SEEMS NOVA X'S ROUTE AND PLAN END HERE.
BUT MY OTHER ISOTOPES WILL CONTINUE MY RESEARCH WITH A DIFFERENT APPROACH...
FLAN IS FOR REMINISCING...!!
IDO... DON'T YOU WANT YOUR MEMORIES BACK?

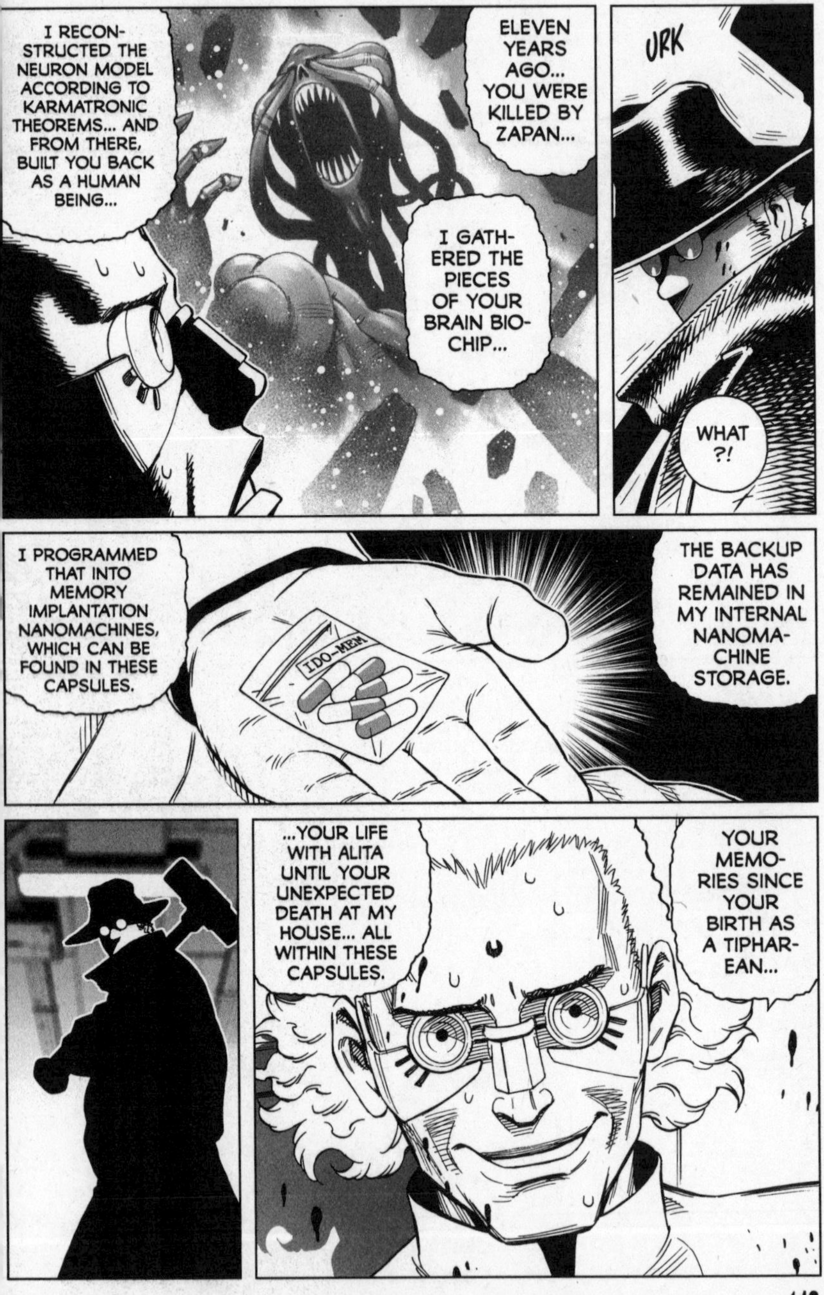
URK
WHAT ?!
ELEVEN YEARS AGO... YOU WERE KILLED BY ZAPAN...
I GATHERED THE PIECES OF YOUR BRAIN BIOCHIP...
I RECONSTRUCTED THE NEURON MODEL ACCORDING TO KARMATRONIC THEOREMS... AND FROM THERE, BUILT YOU BACK AS A HUMAN BEING...
THE BACKUP DATA HAS REMAINED IN MY INTERNAL NANOMACHINE STORAGE.
IDO-MEM
I PROGRAMMED THAT INTO MEMORY IMPLANTATION NANOMACHINES, WHICH CAN BE FOUND IN THESE CAPSULES.
YOUR MEMORIES SINCE YOUR BIRTH AS A TIPHAREAN...
...YOUR LIFE WITH ALITA UNTIL YOUR UNEXPECTED DEATH AT MY HOUSE... ALL WITHIN THESE CAPSULES.

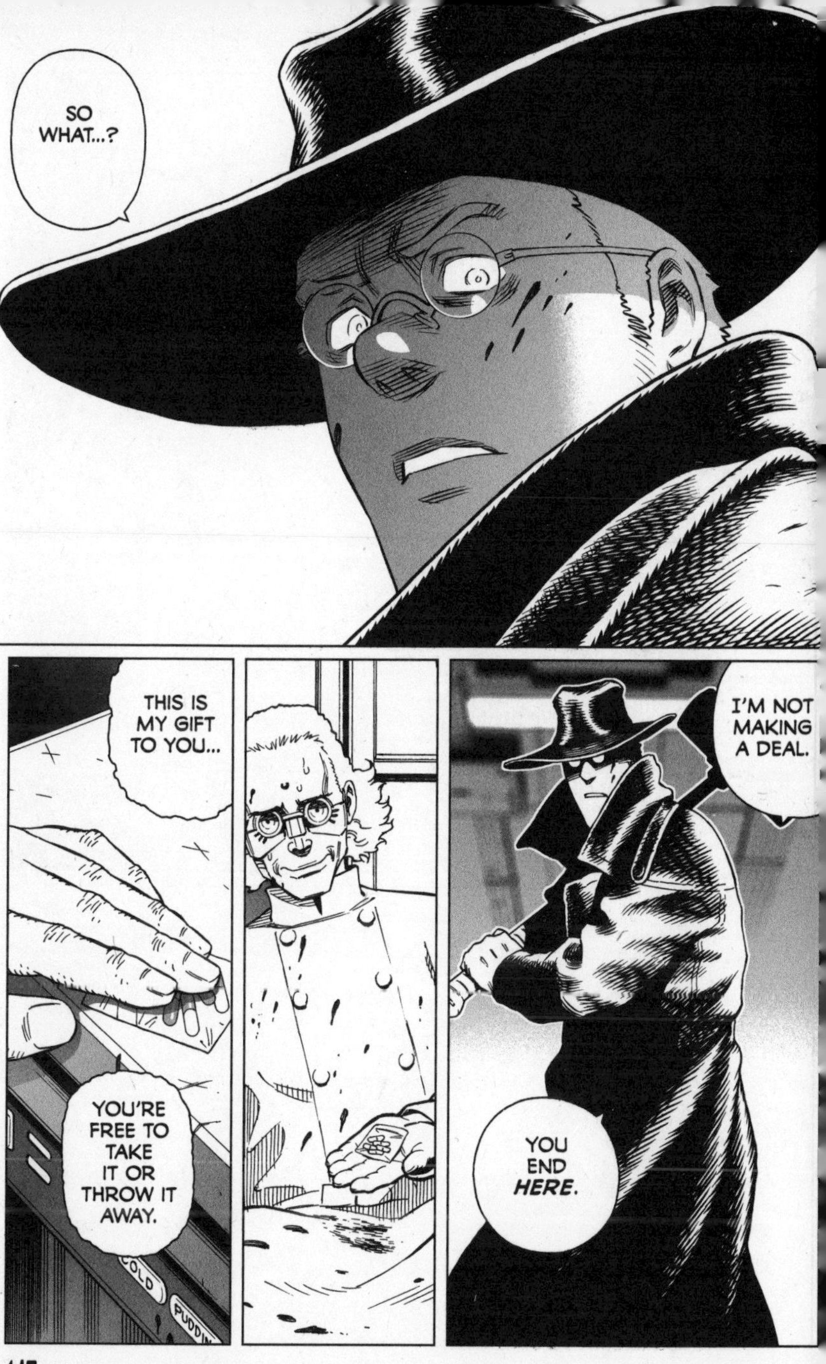
SO WHAT...?
I'M NOT MAKING A DEAL.
YOU END *HERE*.
THIS IS MY GIFT TO YOU...
YOU'RE FREE TO TAKE IT OR THROW IT AWAY.
COLD

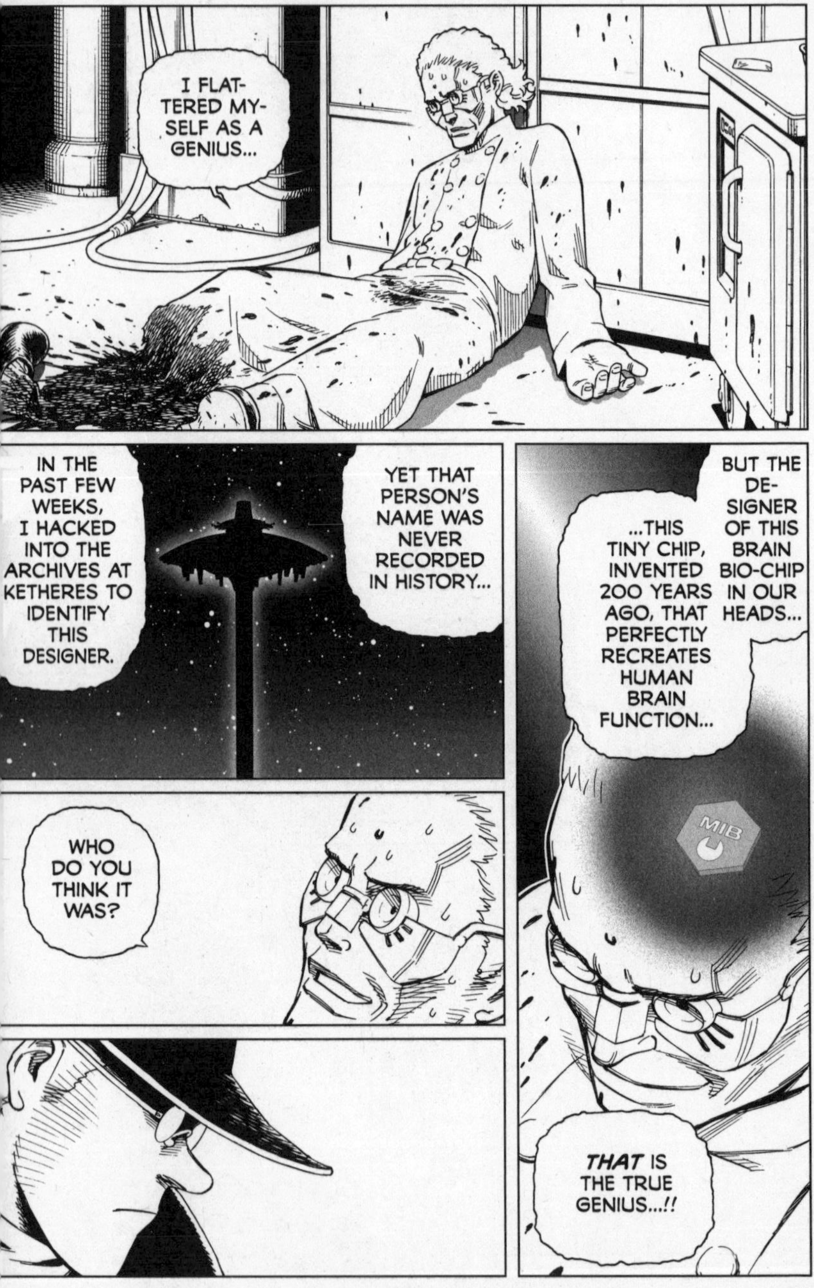
I FLATTERED MYSELF AS A GENIUS...
BUT THE DESIGNER OF THIS BRAIN BIO-CHIP IN OUR HEADS...
...THIS TINY CHIP, INVENTED 200 YEARS AGO, THAT PERFECTLY RECREATES HUMAN BRAIN FUNCTION...
MIB
THAT IS THE TRUE GENIUS...!!
IN THE PAST FEW WEEKS, I HACKED INTO THE ARCHIVES AT KETHERES TO IDENTIFY THIS DESIGNER.
YET THAT PERSON'S NAME WAS NEVER RECORDED IN HISTORY...
WHO DO YOU THINK IT WAS?

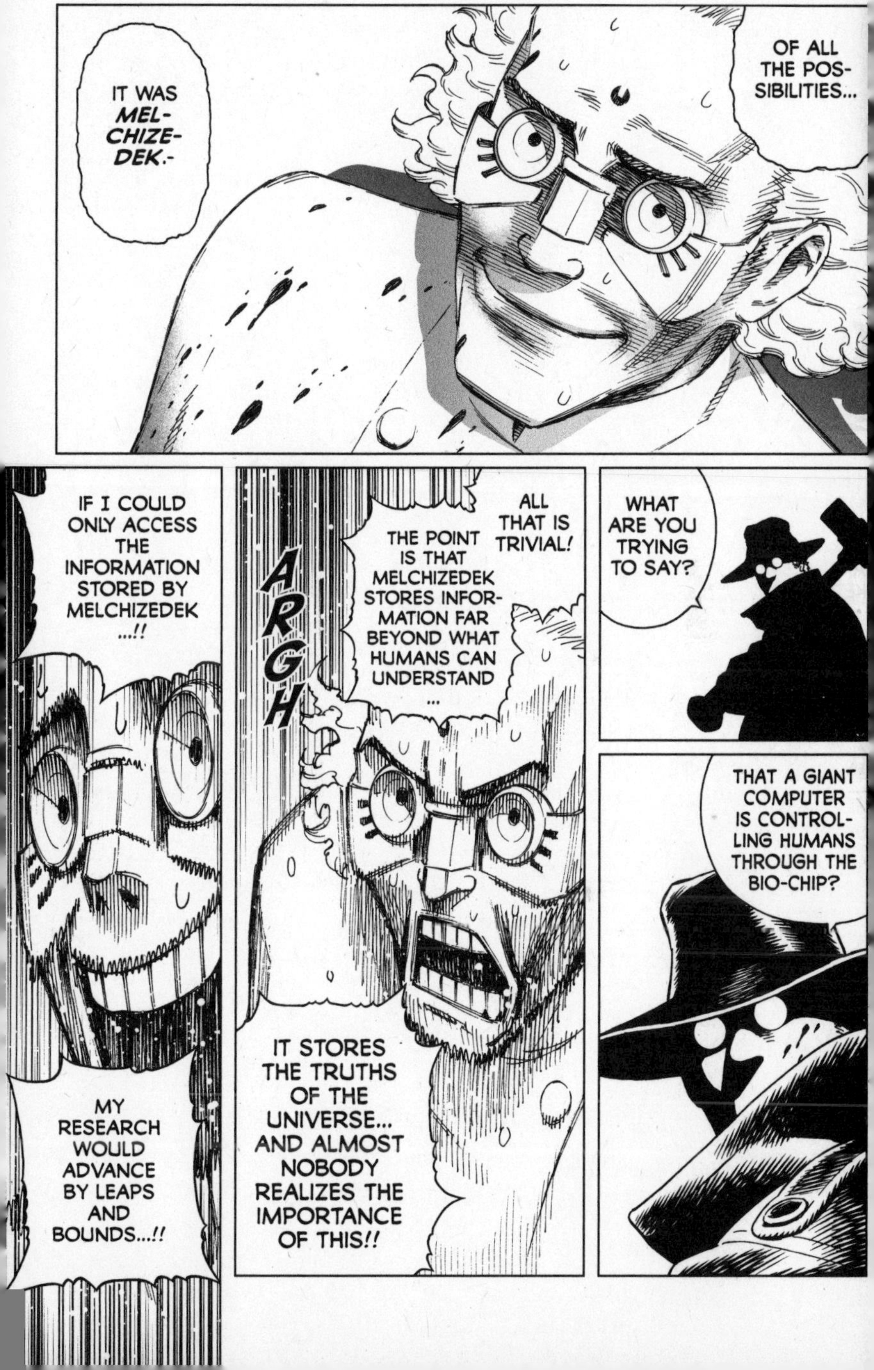
OF ALL THE POSSIBILITIES...
IT WAS *MELCHIZEDEK*.-
WHAT ARE YOU TRYING TO SAY?
THAT A GIANT COMPUTER IS CONTROLLING HUMANS THROUGH THE BIO-CHIP?
ALL THAT IS TRIVIAL!
THE POINT IS THAT MELCHIZEDEK STORES INFORMATION FAR BEYOND WHAT HUMANS CAN UNDERSTAND...
ARGH
IT STORES THE TRUTHS OF THE UNIVERSE... AND ALMOST NOBODY REALIZES THE IMPORTANCE OF THIS!!
IF I COULD ONLY ACCESS THE INFORMATION STORED BY MELCHIZEDEK...!!
MY RESEARCH WOULD ADVANCE BY LEAPS AND BOUNDS...!!

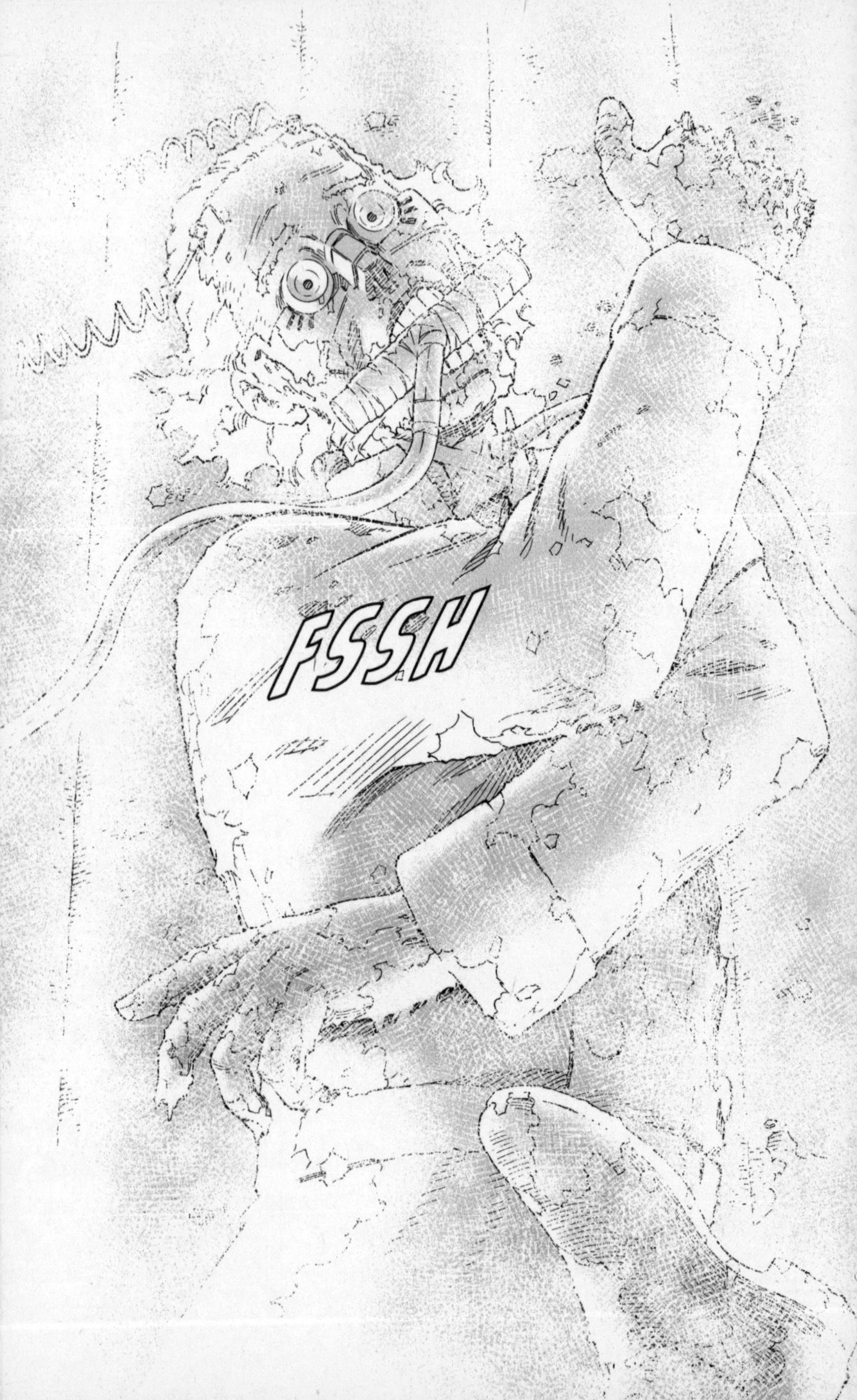
FSSH

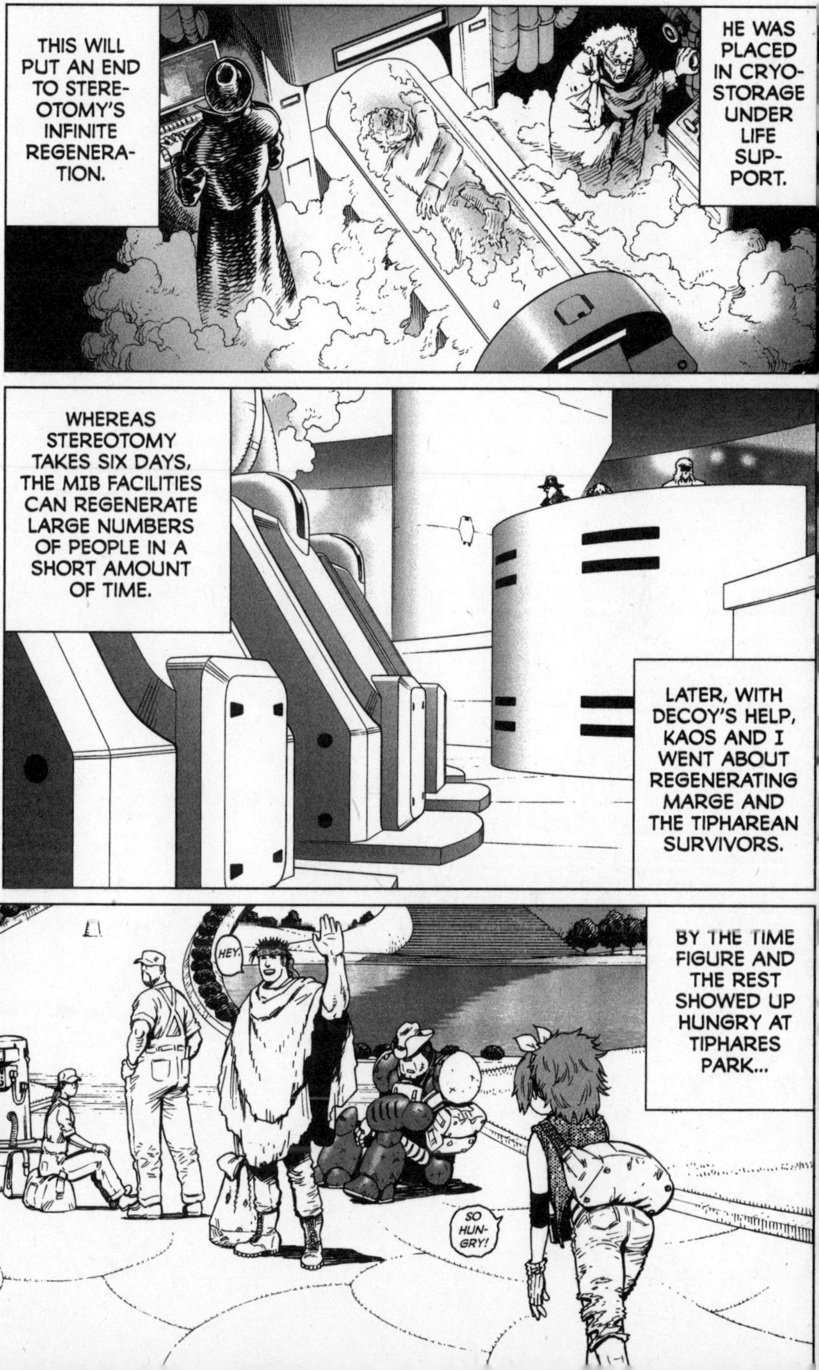
HE WAS PLACED IN CRYO-STORAGE UNDER LIFE SUP-PORT.
THIS WILL PUT AN END TO STERE-OTOMY'S INFINITE REGENERA-TION.
WHEREAS STEREOTOMY TAKES SIX DAYS, THE MIB FACILITIES CAN REGENERATE LARGE NUMBERS OF PEOPLE IN A SHORT AMOUNT OF TIME.
LATER, WITH DECOY'S HELP, KAOS AND I WENT ABOUT REGENERATING MARGE AND THE TIPHAREAN SURVIVORS.
BY THE TIME FIGURE AND THE REST SHOWED UP HUNGRY AT TIPHARES PARK...
HEY.
SO HUN-GRY!

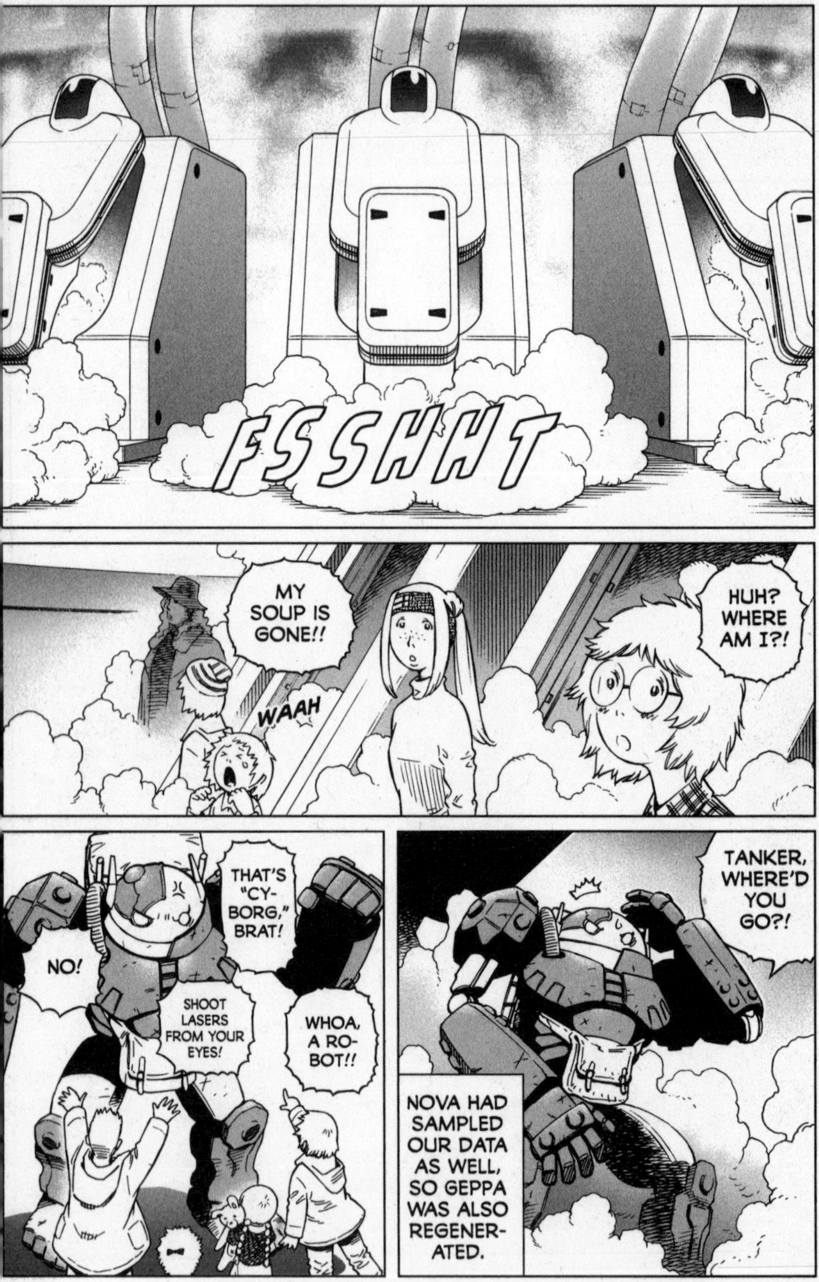
FSSHHT
HUH? WHERE AM I?!
MY SOUP IS GONE!!
WAAH
TANKER, WHERE'D YOU GO?!
NOVA HAD SAMPLED OUR DATA AS WELL, SO GEPPA WAS ALSO REGENERATED.
THAT'S "CYBORG," BRAT!
NO!
WHOA, A ROBOT!!
SHOOT LASERS FROM YOUR EYES!

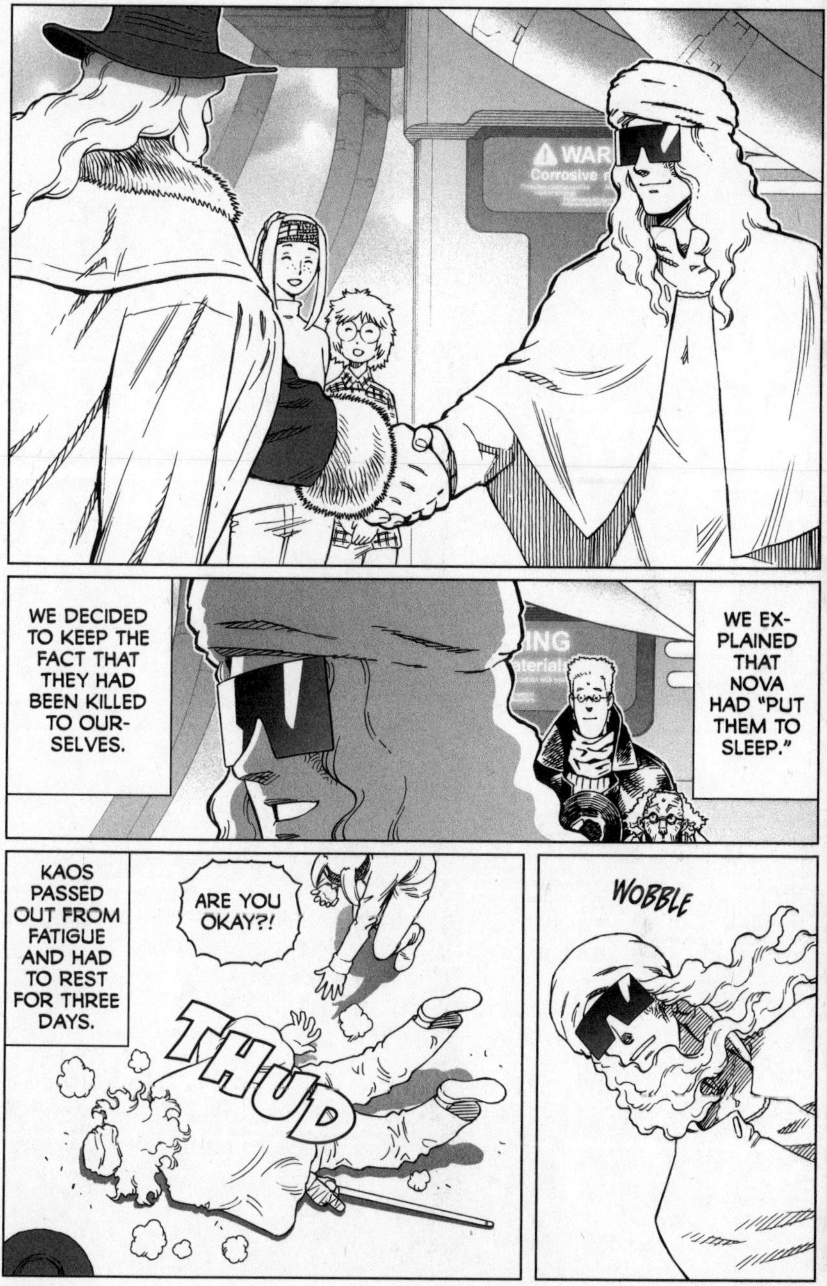
WAR
Corrosive
WE EXPLAINED THAT NOVA HAD "PUT THEM TO SLEEP."
WE DECIDED TO KEEP THE FACT THAT THEY HAD BEEN KILLED TO OURSELVES.
WOBBLE
ARE YOU OKAY?!
KAOS PASSED OUT FROM FATIGUE AND HAD TO REST FOR THREE DAYS.
THUD

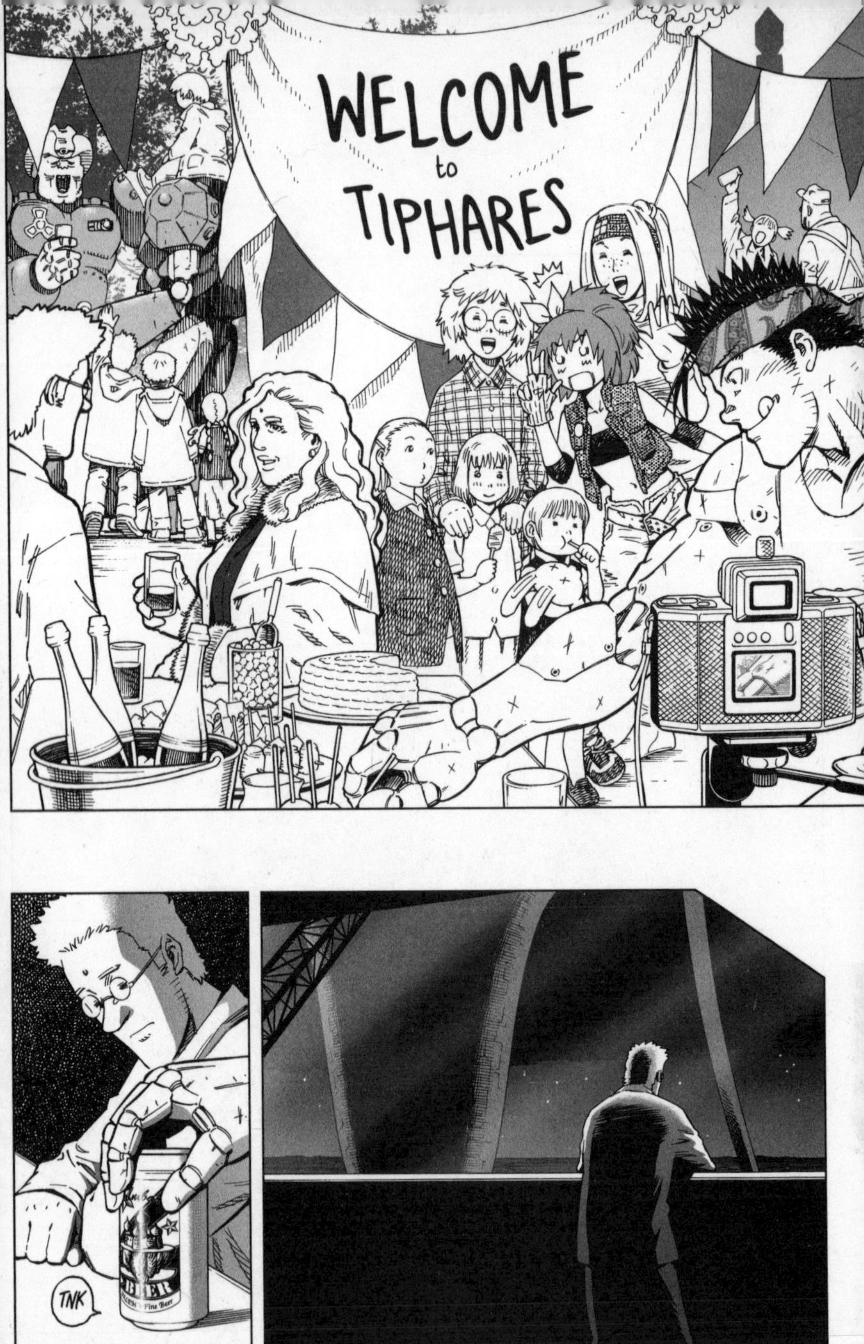
WELCOME to TIPHARES
TNK

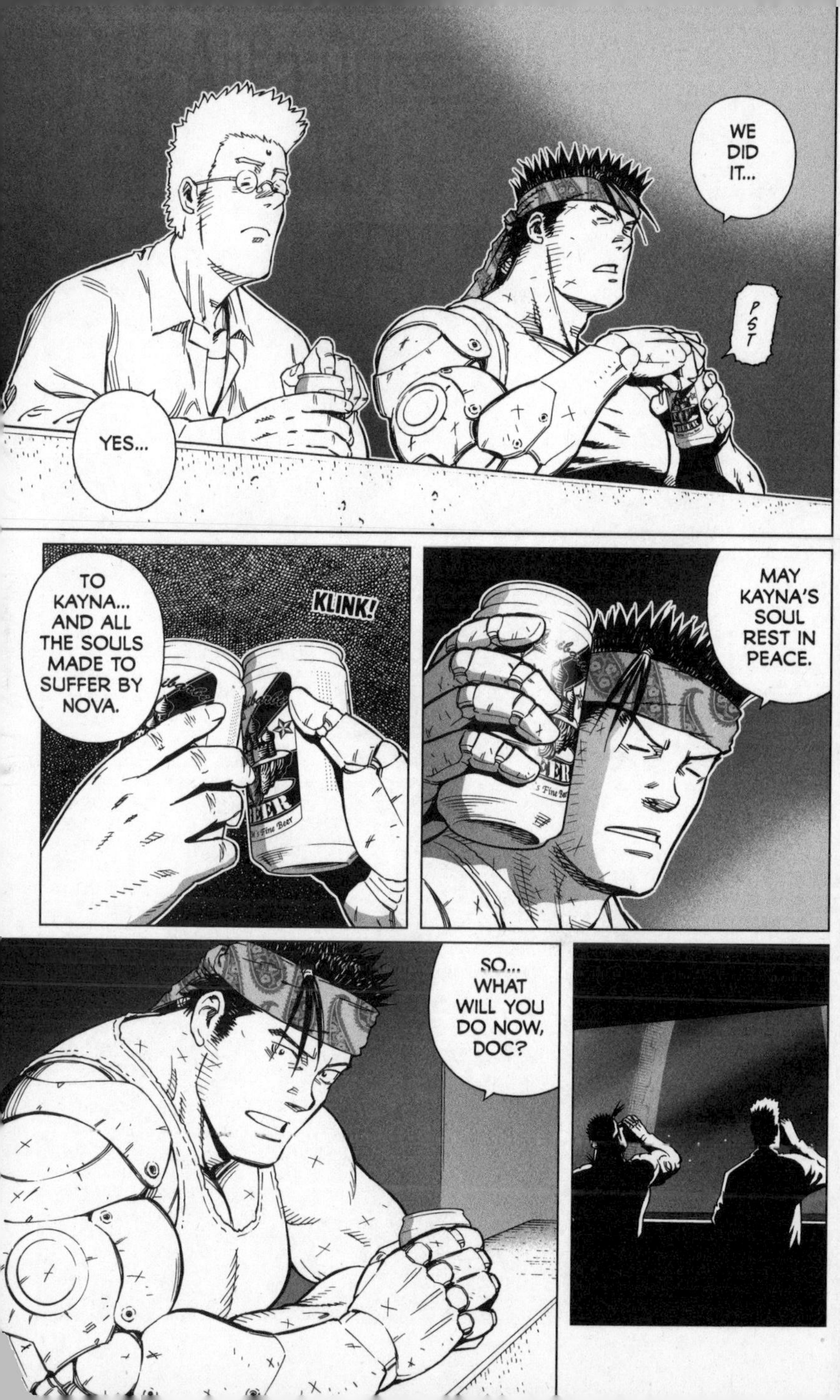
WE DID IT...
PST
YES...
MAY KAYNA'S SOUL REST IN PEACE.
TO KAYNA... AND ALL THE SOULS MADE TO SUFFER BY NOVA.
KLINK!
SO... WHAT WILL YOU DO NOW, DOC?

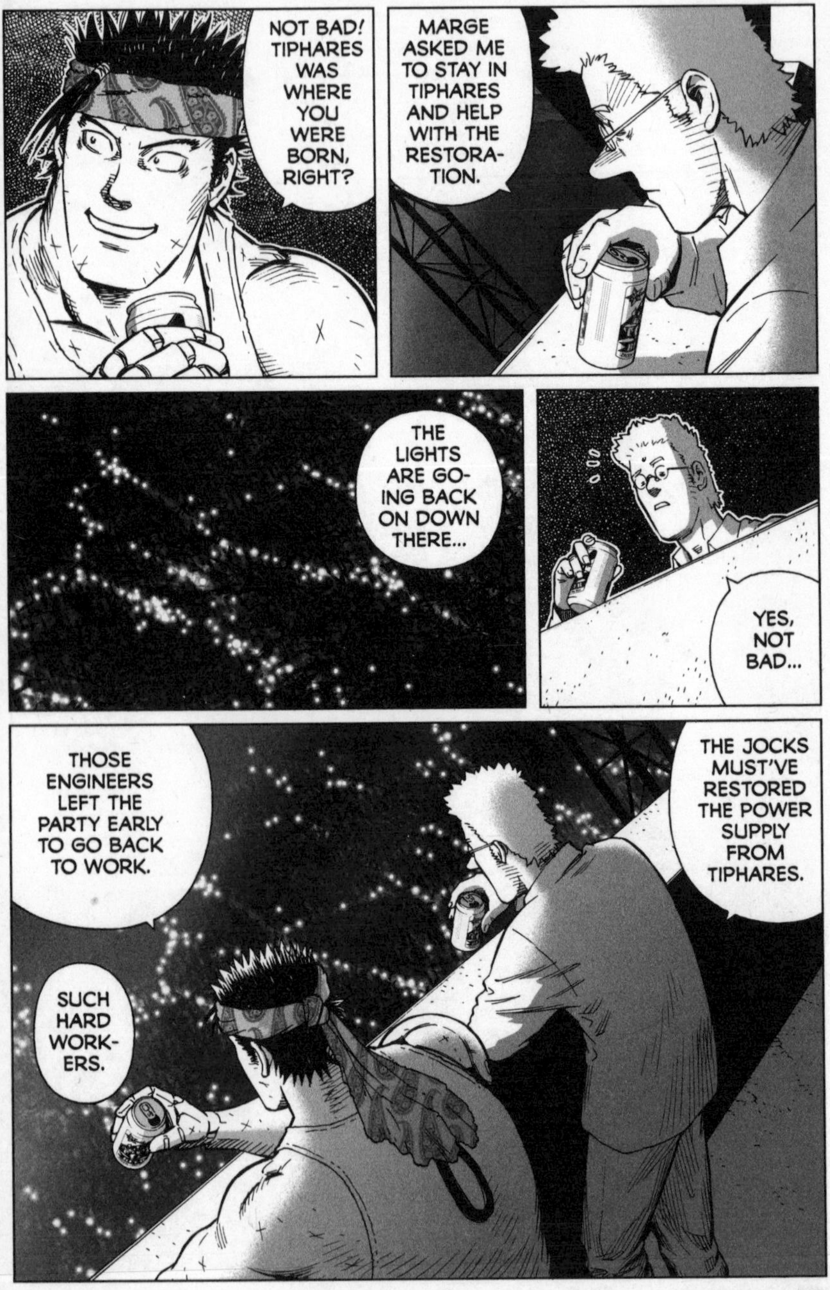
MARGE ASKED ME TO STAY IN TIPHARES AND HELP WITH THE RESTORA-TION.
NOT BAD! TIPHARES WAS WHERE YOU WERE BORN, RIGHT?
YES, NOT BAD...
THE LIGHTS ARE GO-ING BACK ON DOWN THERE...
THE JOCKS MUST'VE RESTORED THE POWER SUPPLY FROM TIPHARES.
THOSE ENGINEERS LEFT THE PARTY EARLY TO GO BACK TO WORK.
SUCH HARD WORK-ERS.

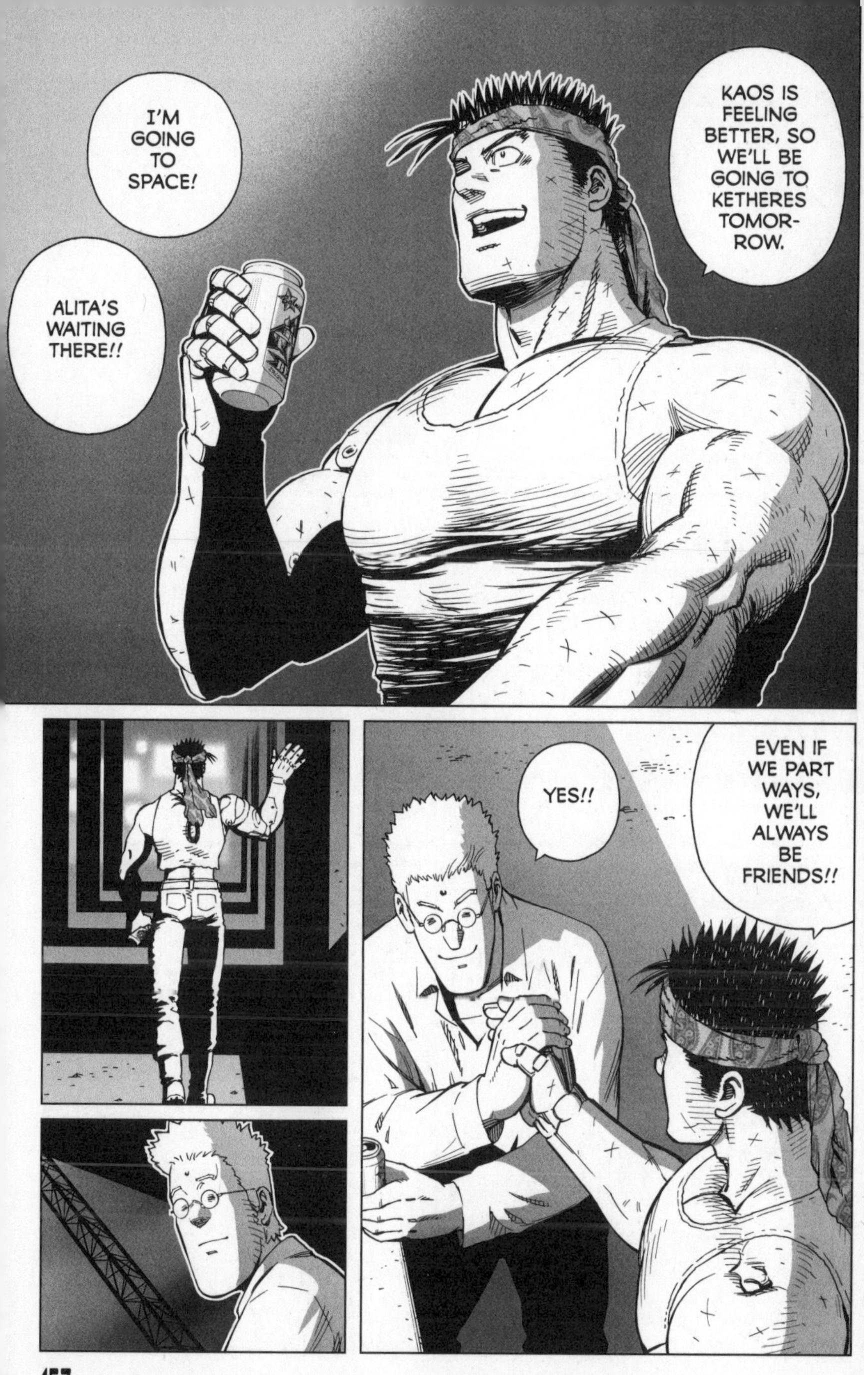
KAOS IS FEELING BETTER, SO WE'LL BE GOING TO KETHERES TOMOR-ROW.
I'M GOING TO SPACE!
ALITA'S WAITING THERE!!
EVEN IF WE PART WAYS, WE'LL ALWAYS BE FRIENDS!!
YES!!

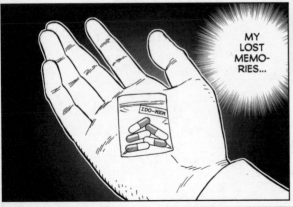

MY LOST MEMO-RIES...
IDO-MEM
...
PSYCHOMETRY DOESN'T REVEAL ANY SUSPICIOUS BEHAVIOR FROM NOVA'S PAST ACTIONS...
IDOMEM-_NM2233
IT'S EXACTLY AS NOVA EX-PLAINED ...
SEEMS TO BE A NANO-MACHINE THAT DIS-SOLVES IN THE BODY.
I SUG-GEST THROW-ING IT AWAY.
WHO KNOWS WHAT KIND OF SIDE EFFECT OR TRAP THERE COULD BE.

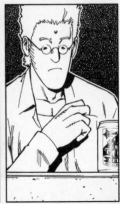

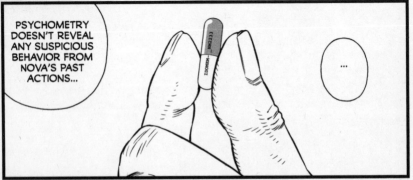

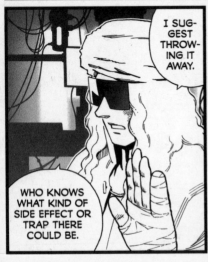

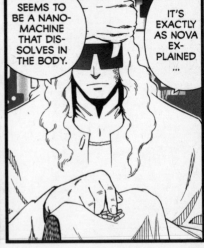

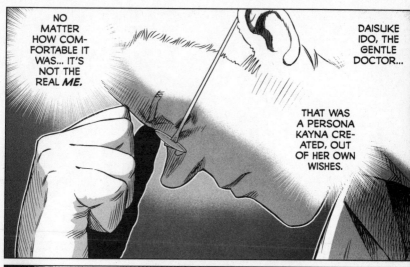

DAISUKE IDO, THE GENTLE DOCTOR...
THAT WAS A PERSONA KAYNA CREATED, OUT OF HER OWN WISHES.
NO MATTER HOW COMFORTABLE IT WAS... IT'S NOT THE REAL *ME.*
I'M MUCH DARKER...
THAT HIDEOUS JOY THAT WELLED UP FROM DEEP WITHIN...
...AS I PUNISHED NOVA...!!
I'M SOMEONE WHO *ENJOYS* THOSE THINGS...!!
NO MATTER WHAT HORRIBLE THINGS YOU MAY FACE...
DON'T LOSE SIGHT OF YOURSELF!!

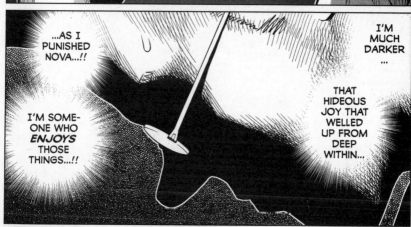

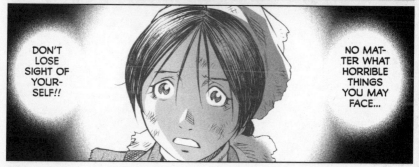

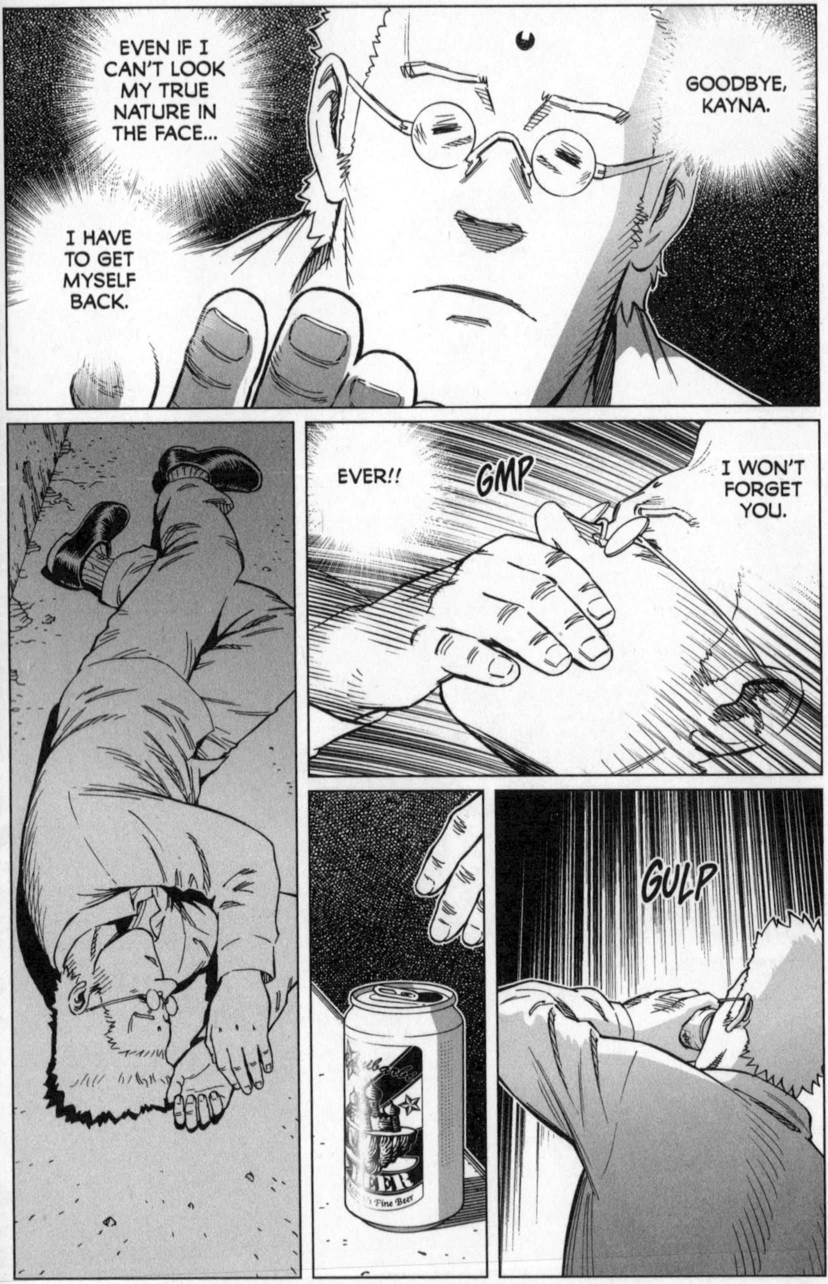
GOODBYE, KAYNA.
EVEN IF I CAN'T LOOK MY TRUE NATURE IN THE FACE...
I HAVE TO GET MYSELF BACK.
I WON'T FORGET YOU.
GMP
EVER!!
GULP

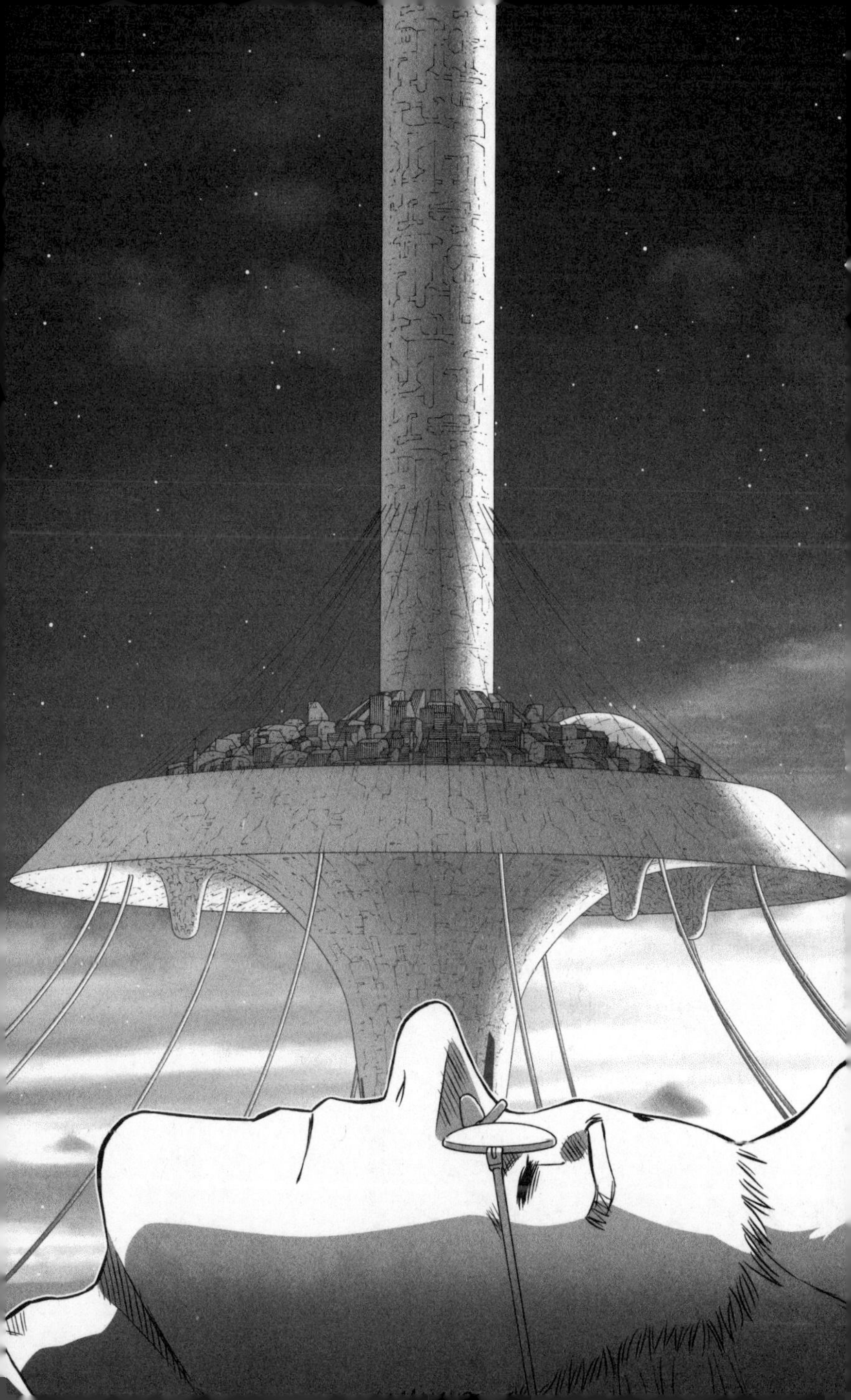

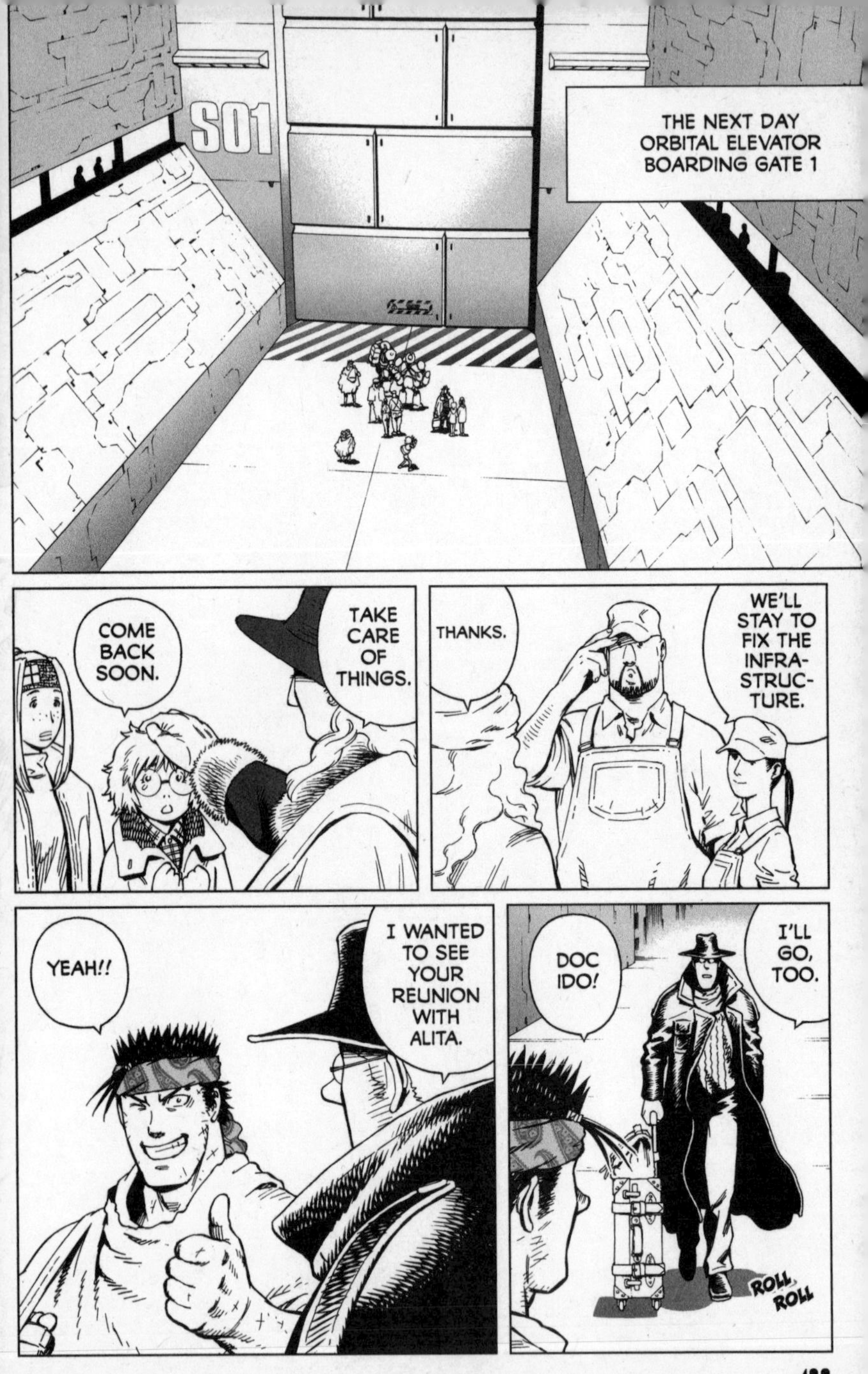
THE NEXT DAY
ORBITAL ELEVATOR
BOARDING GATE 1
S01
WE'LL STAY TO FIX THE INFRA-STRUC-TURE.
THANKS.
TAKE CARE OF THINGS.
COME BACK SOON.
I'LL GO, TOO.
DOC IDO!
ROLL ROLL
I WANTED TO SEE YOUR REUNION WITH ALITA.
YEAH!!

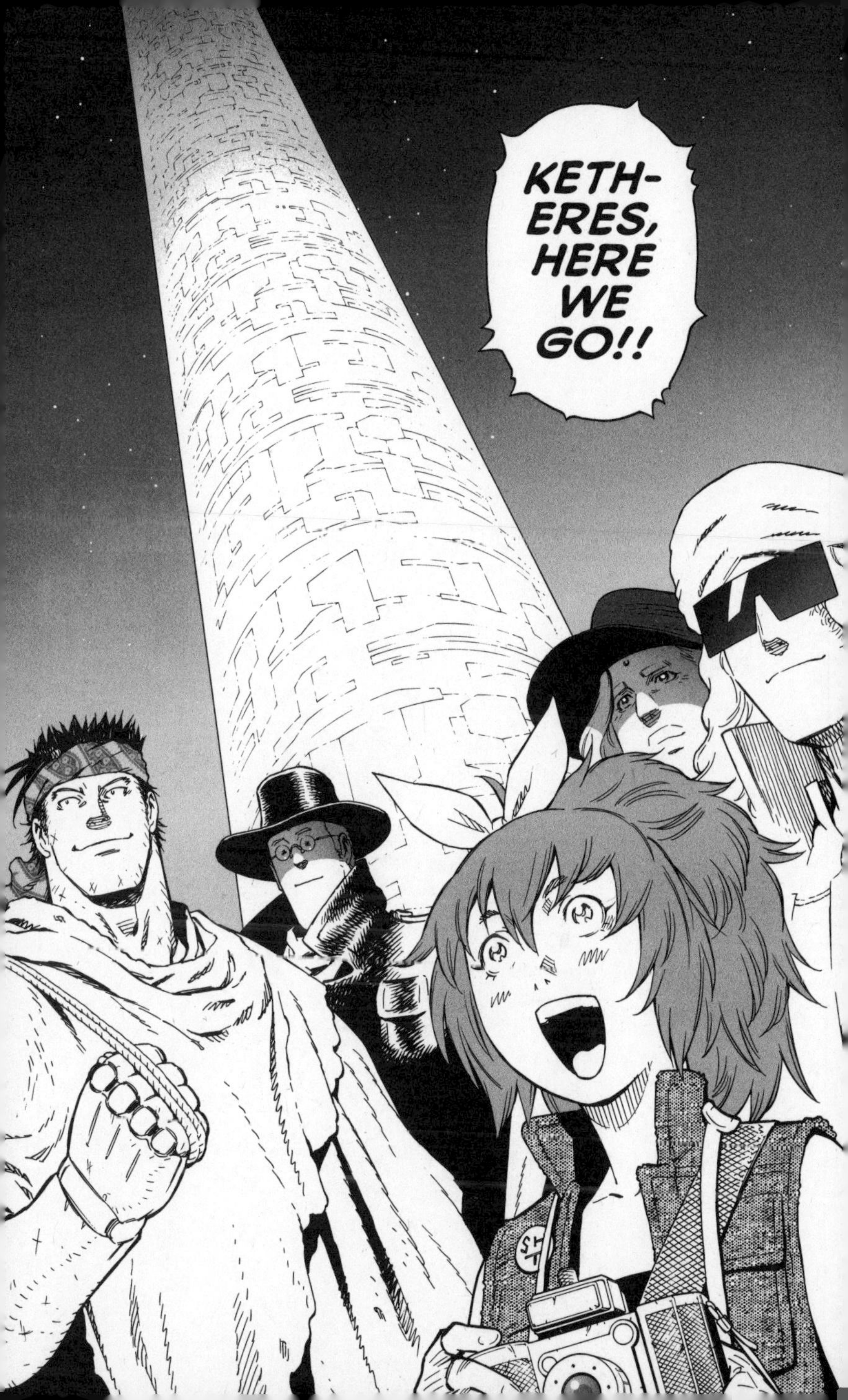
KETH-ERES, HERE WE GO!!

Phase 123: Alita Quest XVII

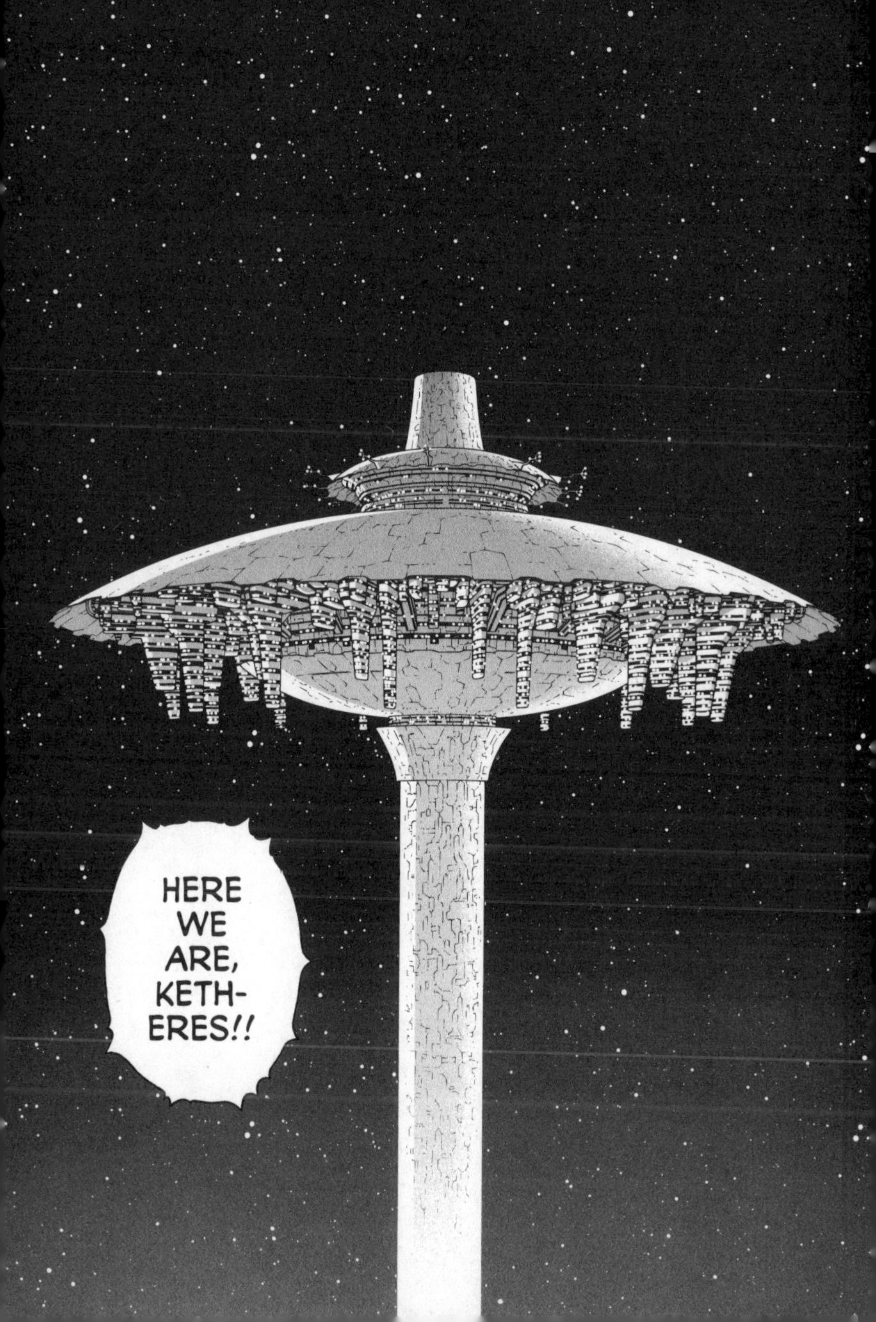
HERE WE ARE, KETH-ERES!!

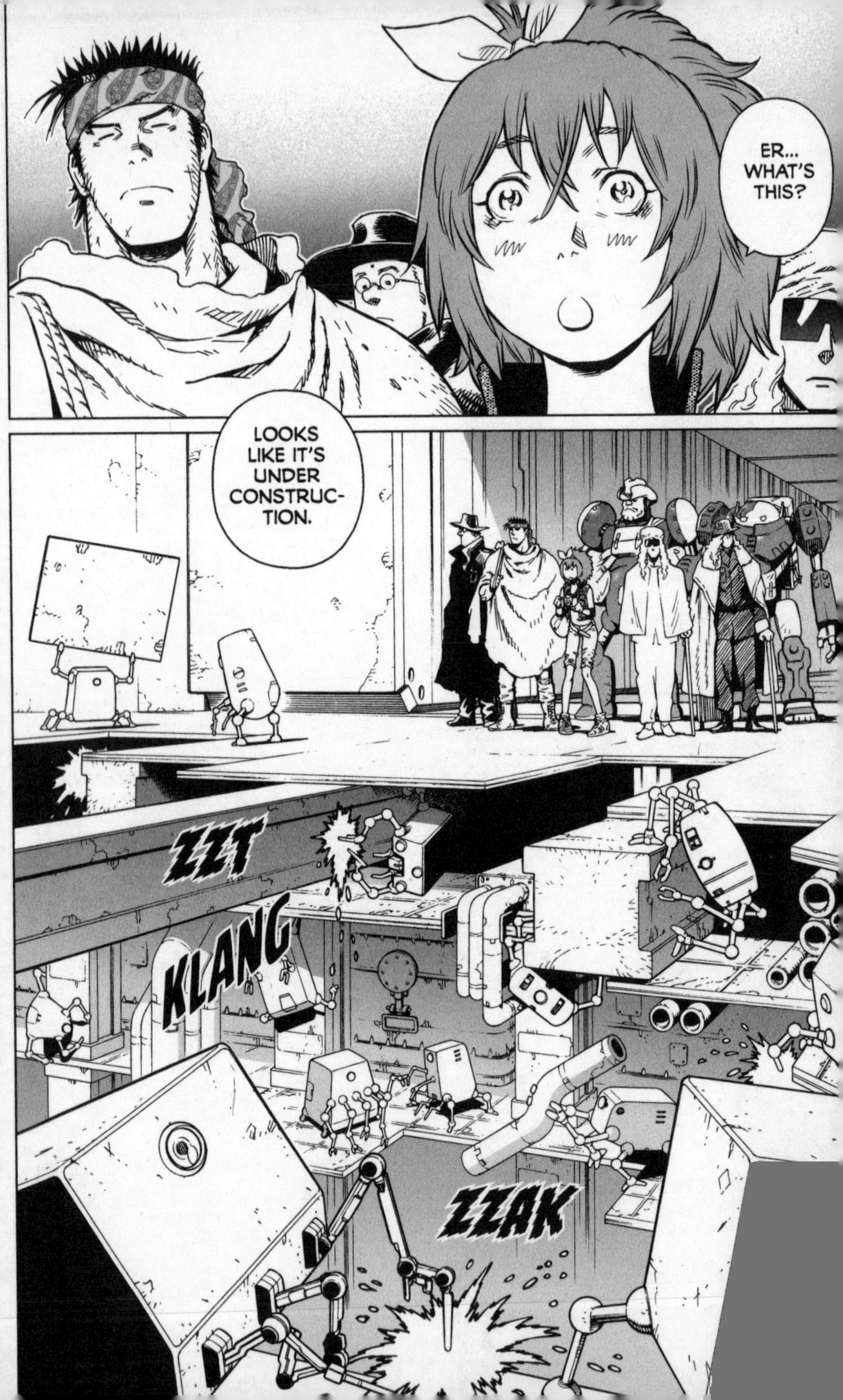
ER... WHAT'S THIS?
LOOKS LIKE IT'S UNDER CONSTRUC-TION.
ZZT
KLANG
ZZAK

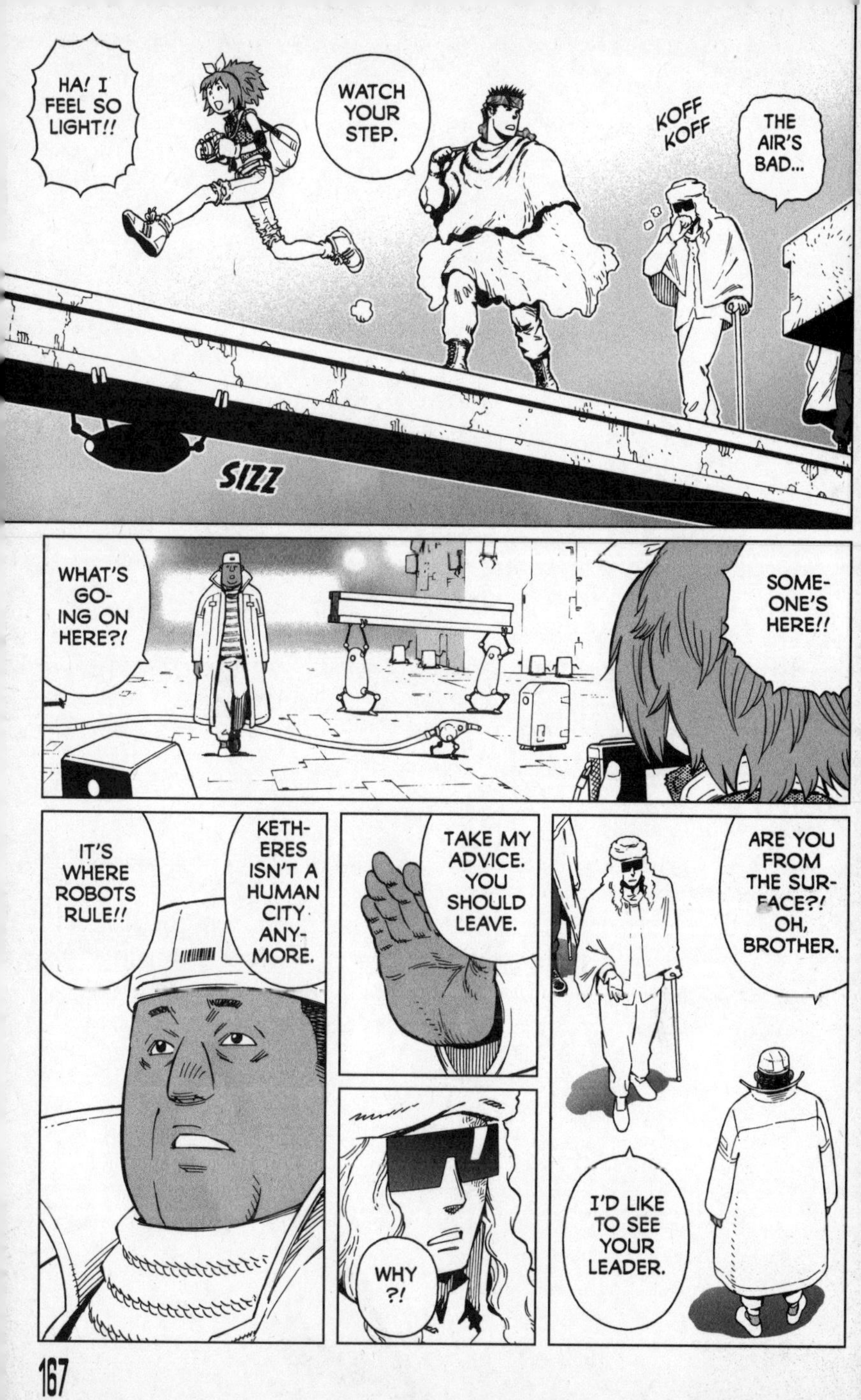
THE AIR'S BAD...
KOFF KOFF
WATCH YOUR STEP.
HA! I FEEL SO LIGHT!!
SIZZ
SOME-ONE'S HERE!!
WHAT'S GO-ING ON HERE?!
ARE YOU FROM THE SUR-FACE?! OH, BROTHER.
I'D LIKE TO SEE YOUR LEADER.
TAKE MY ADVICE. YOU SHOULD LEAVE.
WHY ?!
KETH-ERES ISN'T A HUMAN CITY ANY-MORE.
IT'S WHERE ROBOTS RULE!!

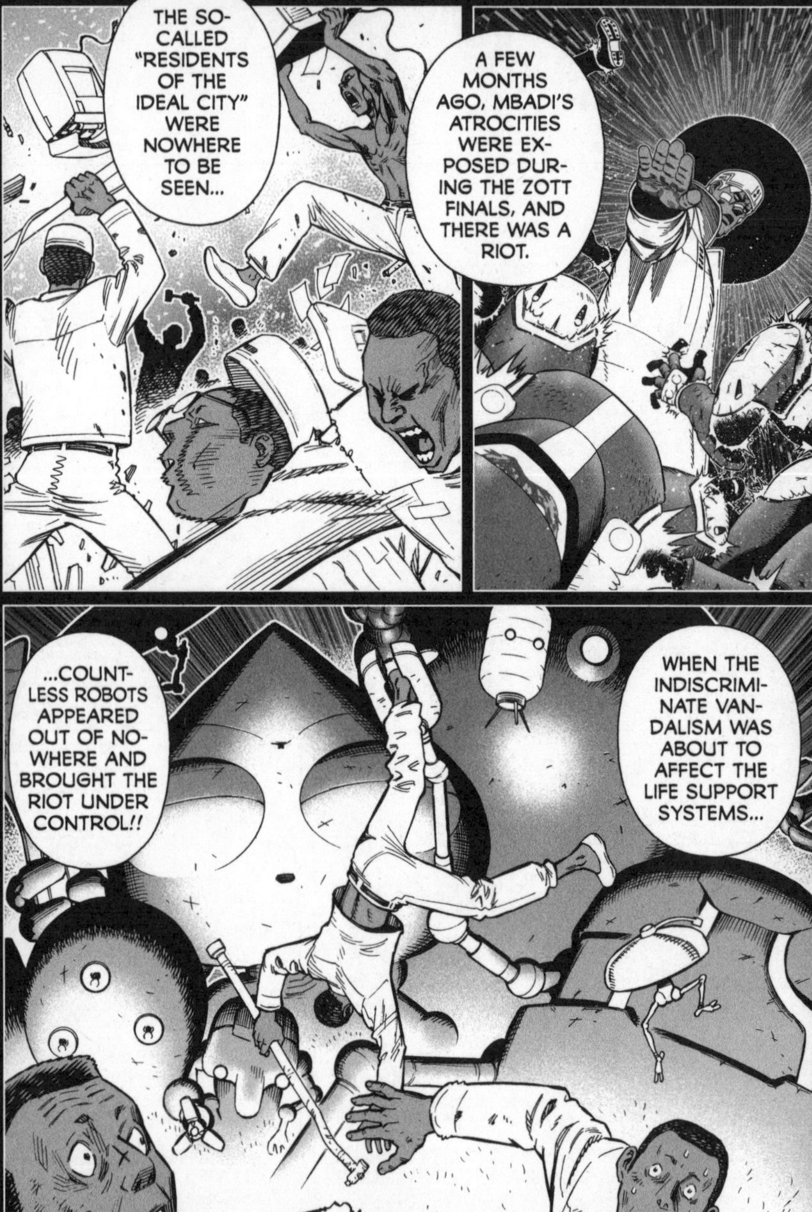
A FEW MONTHS AGO, MBADI'S ATROCITIES WERE EX-POSED DUR-ING THE ZOTT FINALS, AND THERE WAS A RIOT.
THE SO-CALLED "RESIDENTS OF THE IDEAL CITY" WERE NOWHERE TO BE SEEN...
WHEN THE INDISCRIMI-NATE VAN-DALISM WAS ABOUT TO AFFECT THE LIFE SUPPORT SYSTEMS...
...COUNT-LESS ROBOTS APPEARED OUT OF NO-WHERE AND BROUGHT THE RIOT UNDER CONTROL!!

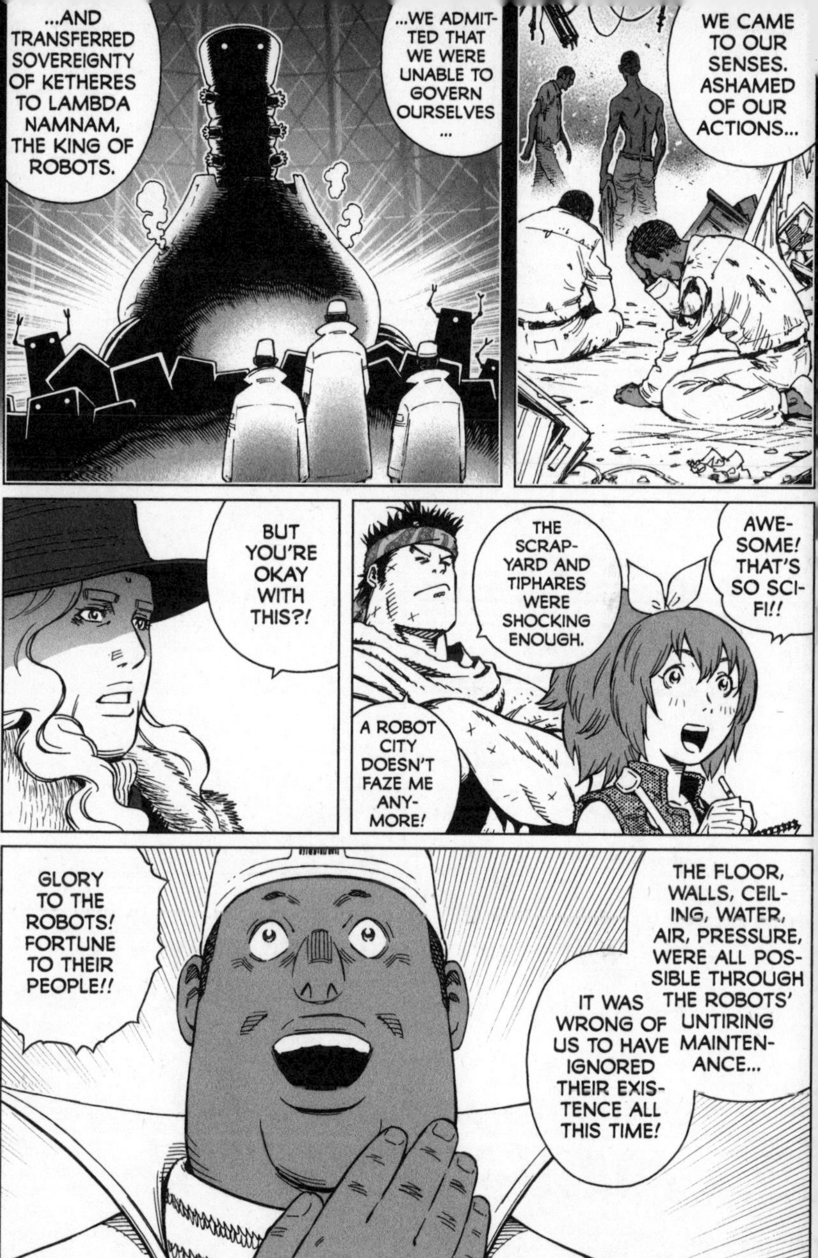

WE CAME TO OUR SENSES. ASHAMED OF OUR ACTIONS...
...WE ADMITTED THAT WE WERE UNABLE TO GOVERN OURSELVES...
...AND TRANSFERRED SOVEREIGNTY OF KETHERES TO LAMBDA NAMNAM, THE KING OF ROBOTS.
AWESOME! THAT'S SO SCI-FI!!
THE SCRAPYARD AND TIPHARES WERE SHOCKING ENOUGH.
A ROBOT CITY DOESN'T FAZE ME ANYMORE!
BUT YOU'RE OKAY WITH THIS?!
THE FLOOR, WALLS, CEILING, WATER, AIR, PRESSURE, WERE ALL POSSIBLE THROUGH THE ROBOTS' UNTIRING MAINTENANCE...
IT WAS WRONG OF US TO HAVE IGNORED THEIR EXISTENCE ALL THIS TIME!
GLORY TO THE ROBOTS! FORTUNE TO THEIR PEOPLE!!

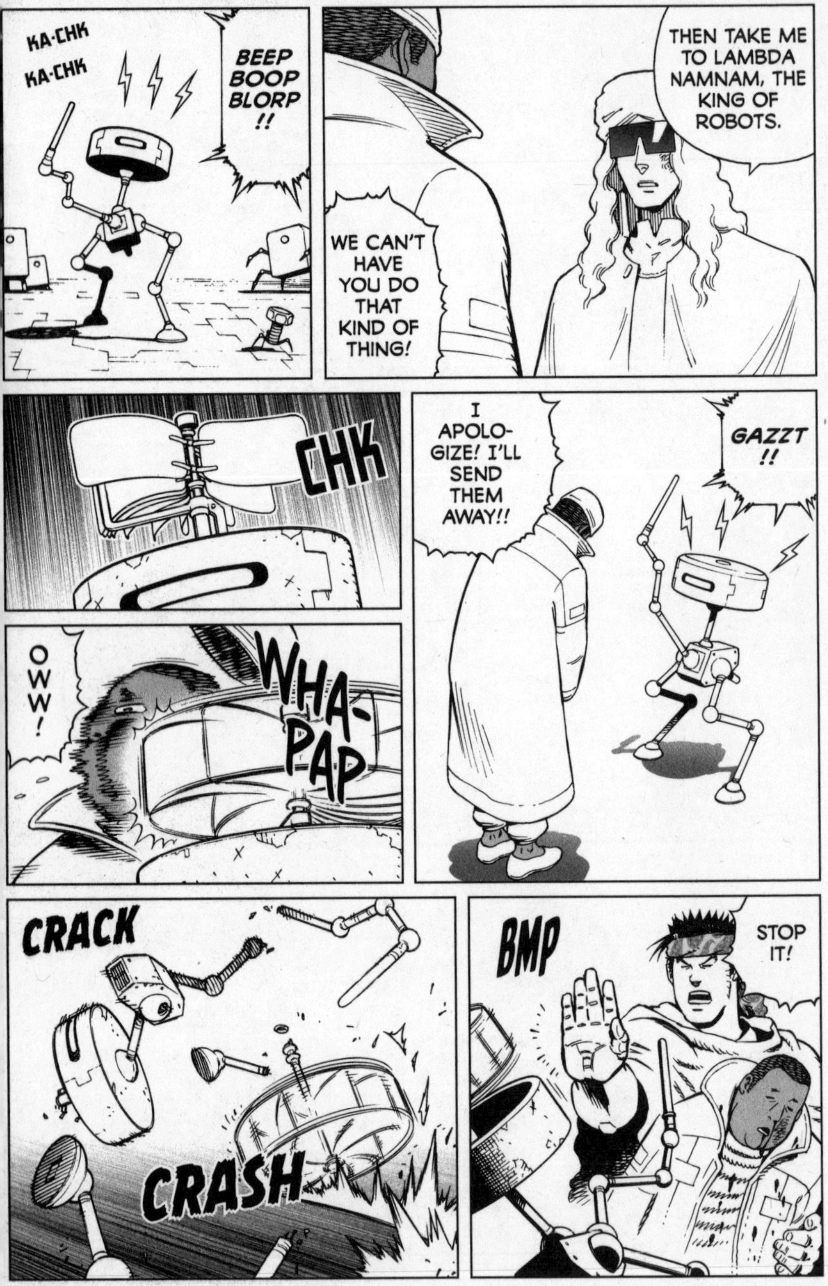

THEN TAKE ME TO LAMBDA NAMNAM, THE KING OF ROBOTS.
WE CAN'T HAVE YOU DO THAT KIND OF THING!
BEEP BOOP BLORP!!
KA-CHK
KA-CHK
GAZZT!!
I APOLOGIZE! I'LL SEND THEM AWAY!!
CHK
WHA-PAP
OWW!
STOP IT!
BMP
CRACK
CRASH

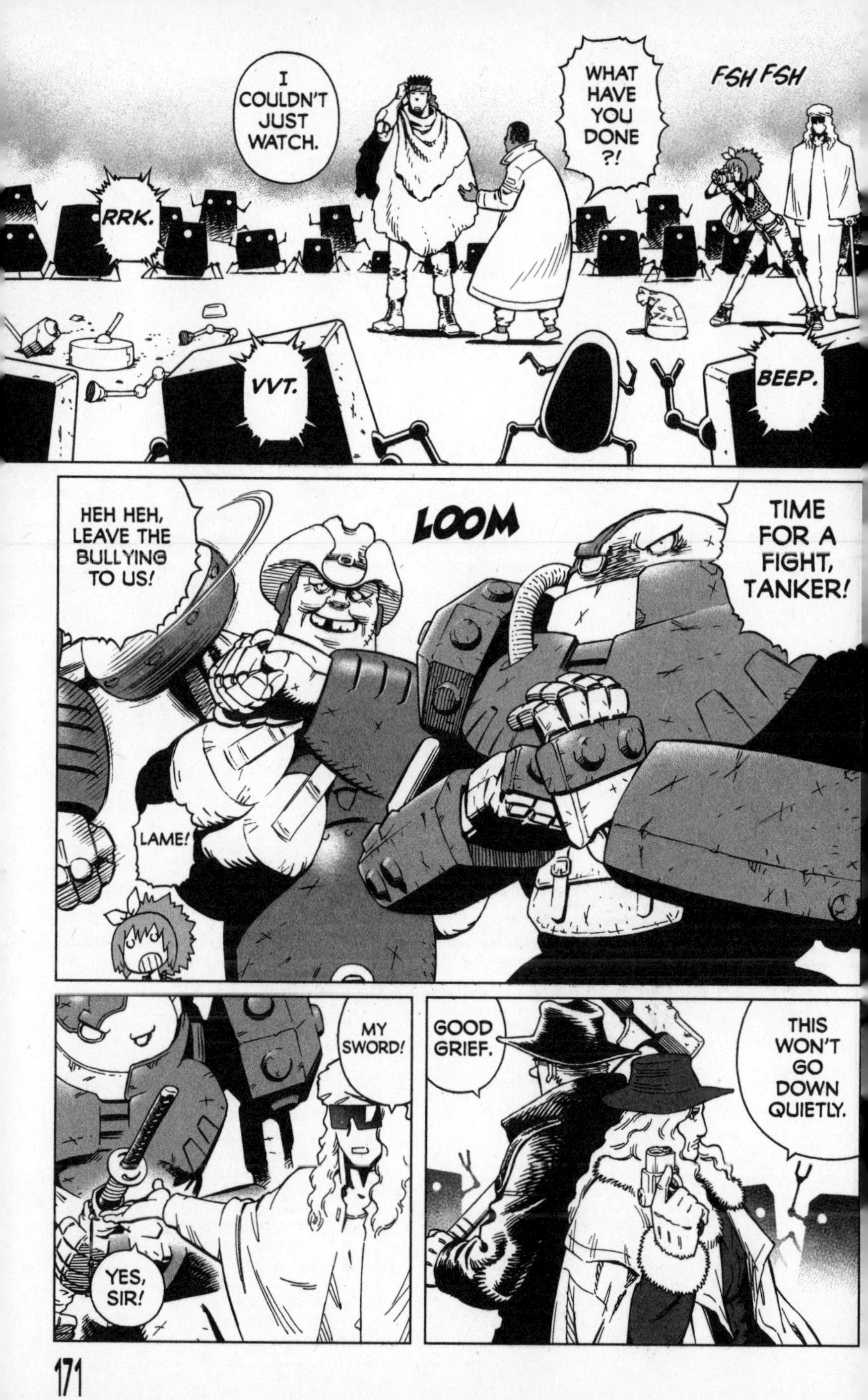
FSH FSH
WHAT HAVE YOU DONE ?!
I COULDN'T JUST WATCH.
RRK.
BEEP.
VVT.
TIME FOR A FIGHT, TANKER!
LOOM
HEH HEH, LEAVE THE BULLYING TO US!
LAME!
THIS WON'T GO DOWN QUIETLY.
GOOD GRIEF.
MY SWORD!
YES, SIR!

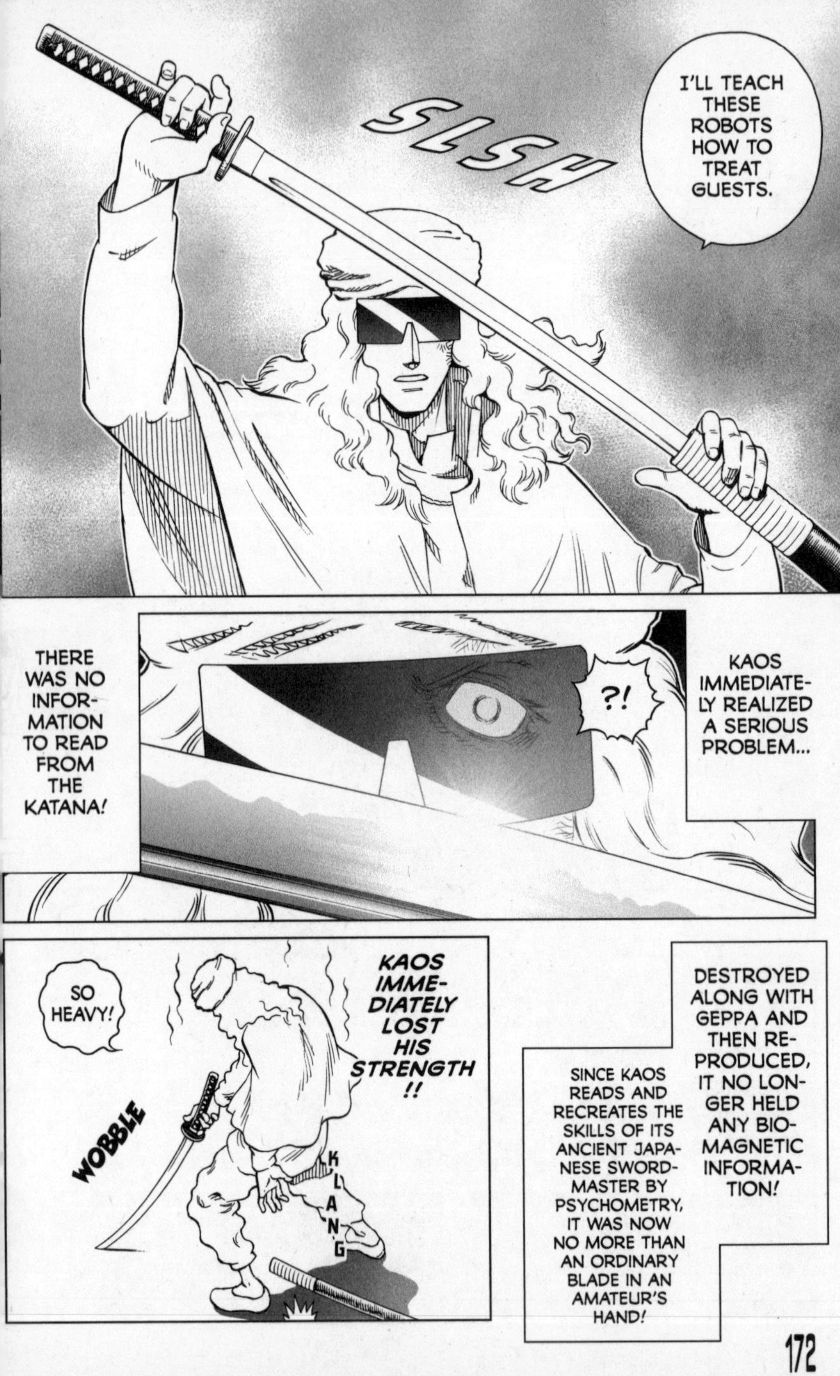

SISH
I'LL TEACH THESE ROBOTS HOW TO TREAT GUESTS.
KAOS IMMEDIATE-LY REALIZED A SERIOUS PROBLEM...
?!
THERE WAS NO INFOR-MATION TO READ FROM THE KATANA!
DESTROYED ALONG WITH GEPPA AND THEN RE-PRODUCED, IT NO LON-GER HELD ANY BIO-MAGNETIC INFORMA-TION!
SINCE KAOS READS AND RECREATES THE SKILLS OF ITS ANCIENT JAPA-NESE SWORD-MASTER BY PSYCHOMETRY, IT WAS NOW NO MORE THAN AN ORDINARY BLADE IN AN AMATEUR'S HAND!
KAOS IMME-DIATELY LOST HIS STRENGTH !!
SO HEAVY!
WOBBLE
KLANG

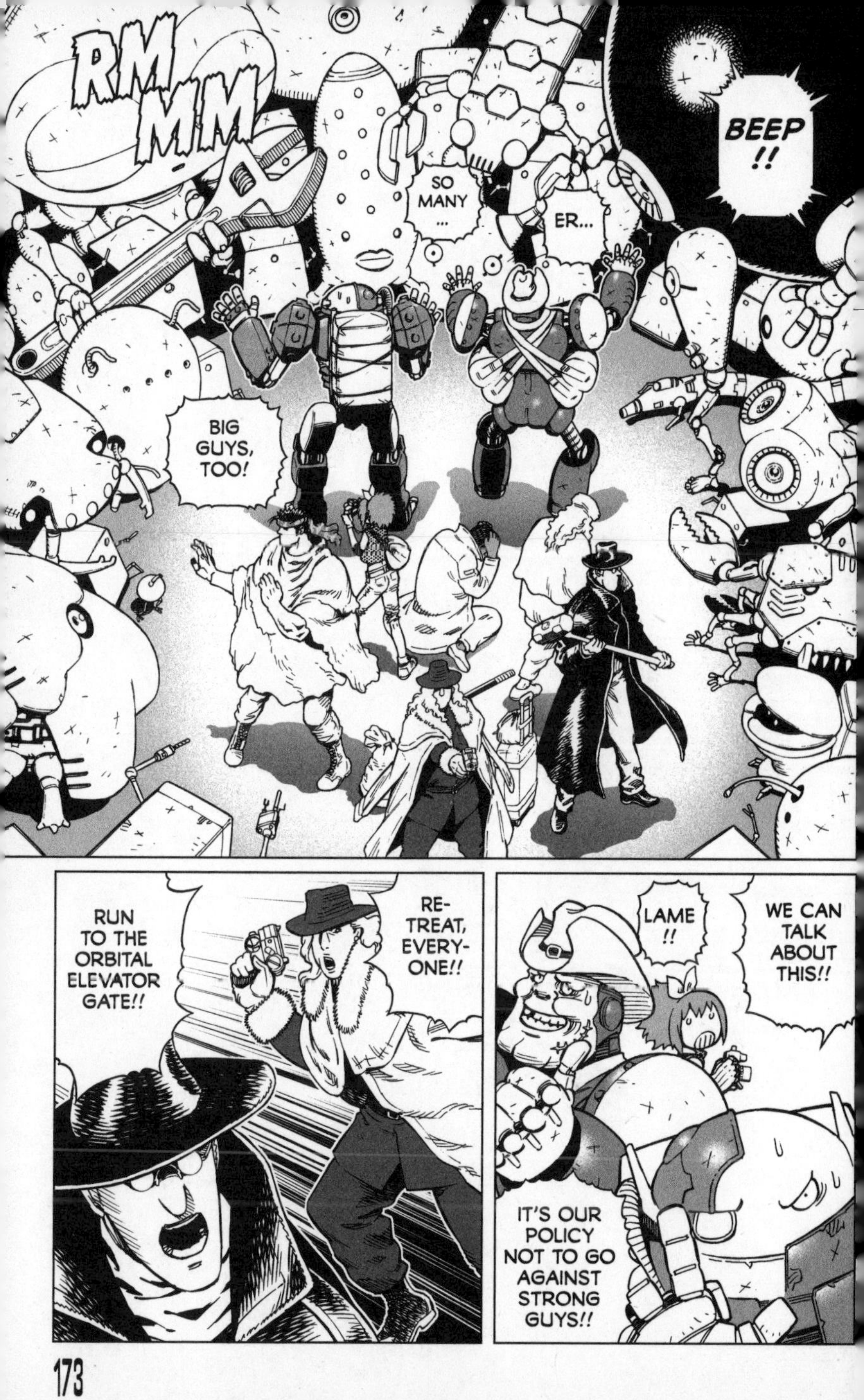
RM MM
BEEP!!
ER...
SO MANY ...
BIG GUYS, TOO!
WE CAN TALK ABOUT THIS!!
LAME!!
IT'S OUR POLICY NOT TO GO AGAINST STRONG GUYS!!
RE-TREAT, EVERY-ONE!!
RUN TO THE ORBITAL ELEVATOR GATE!!

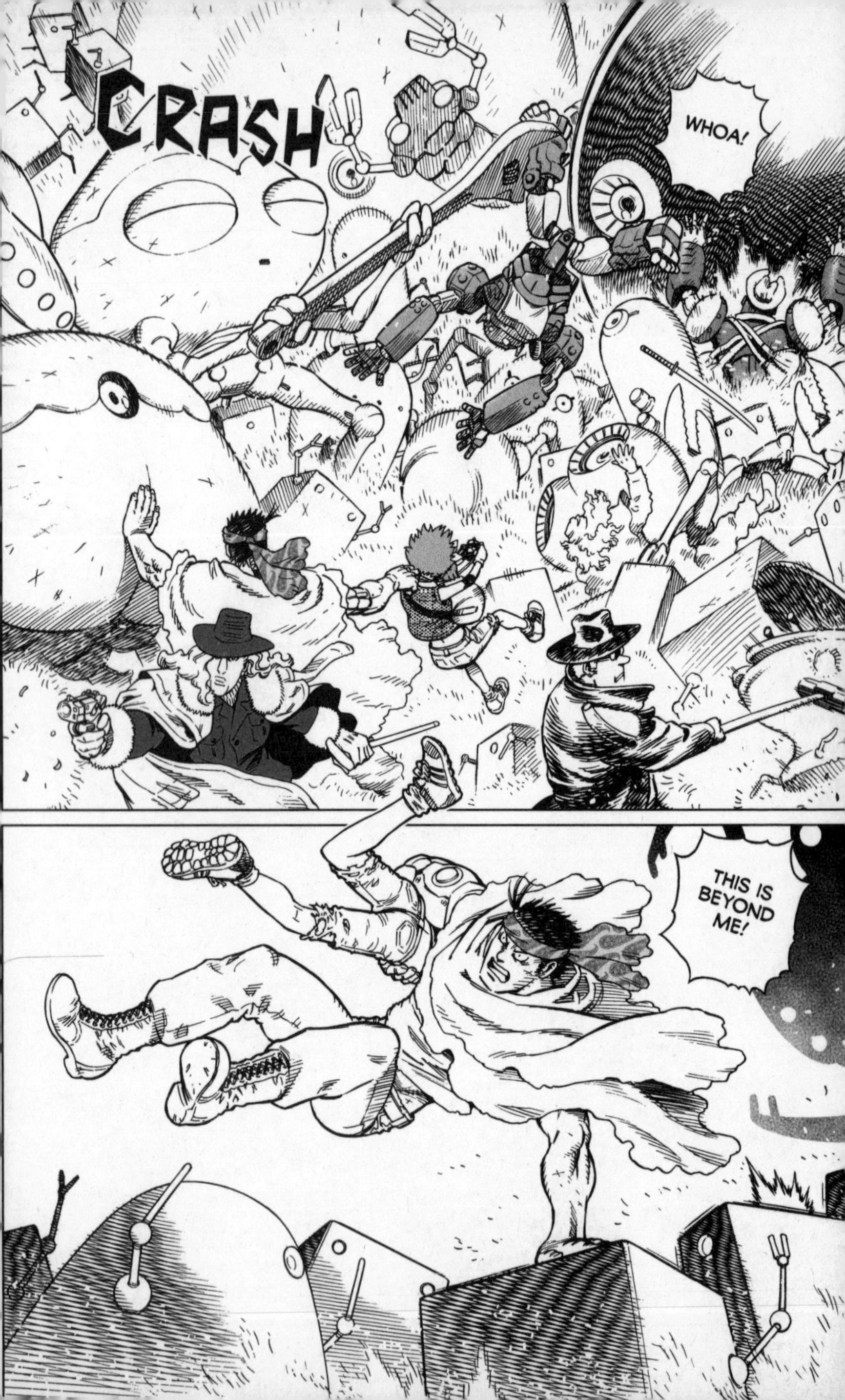
CRASH
WHOA!
THIS IS BEYOND ME!

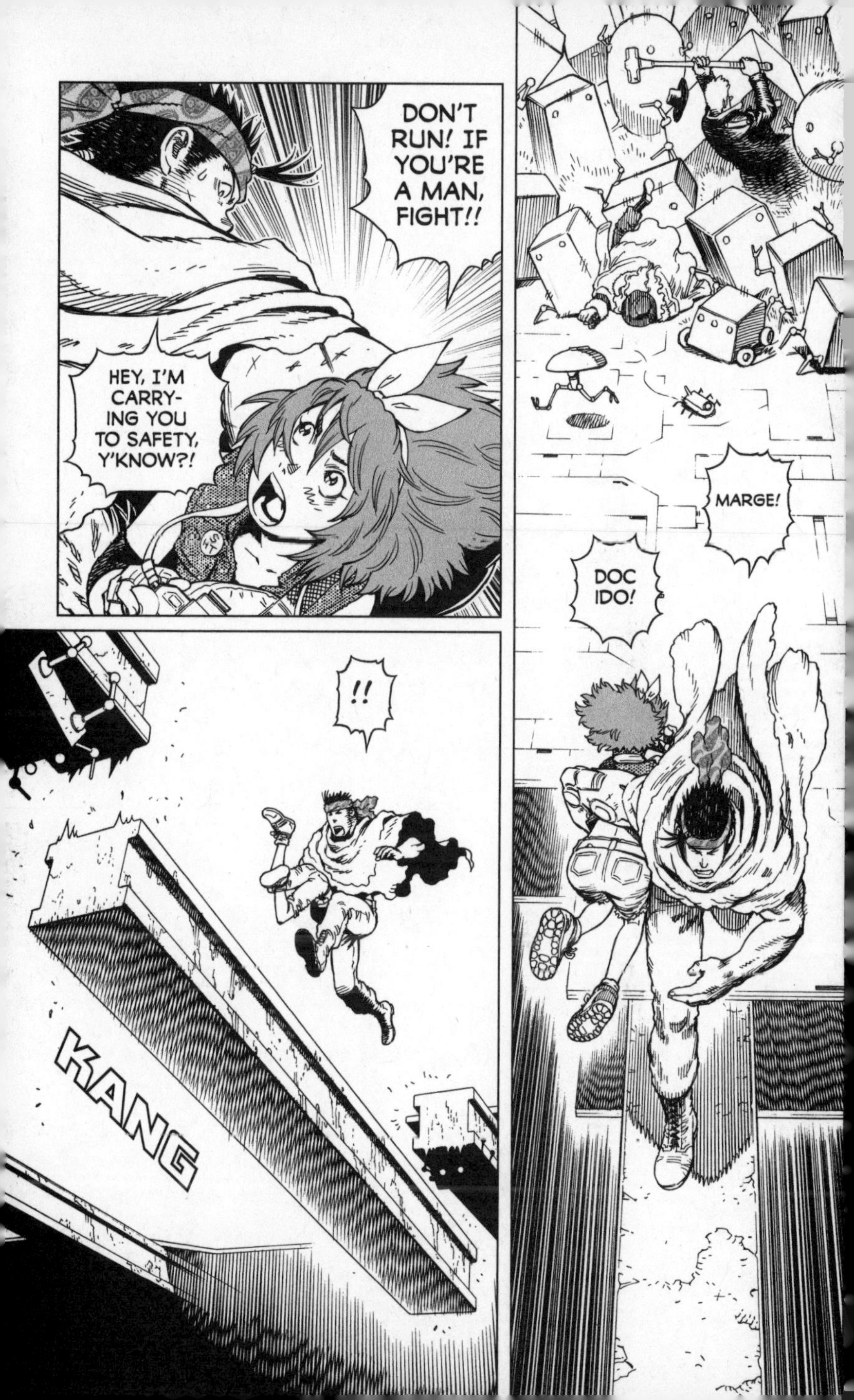
MARGE!
DOC IDO!
DON'T RUN! IF YOU'RE A MAN, FIGHT!!
HEY, I'M CARRYING YOU TO SAFETY, Y'KNOW?!
!!
KANG

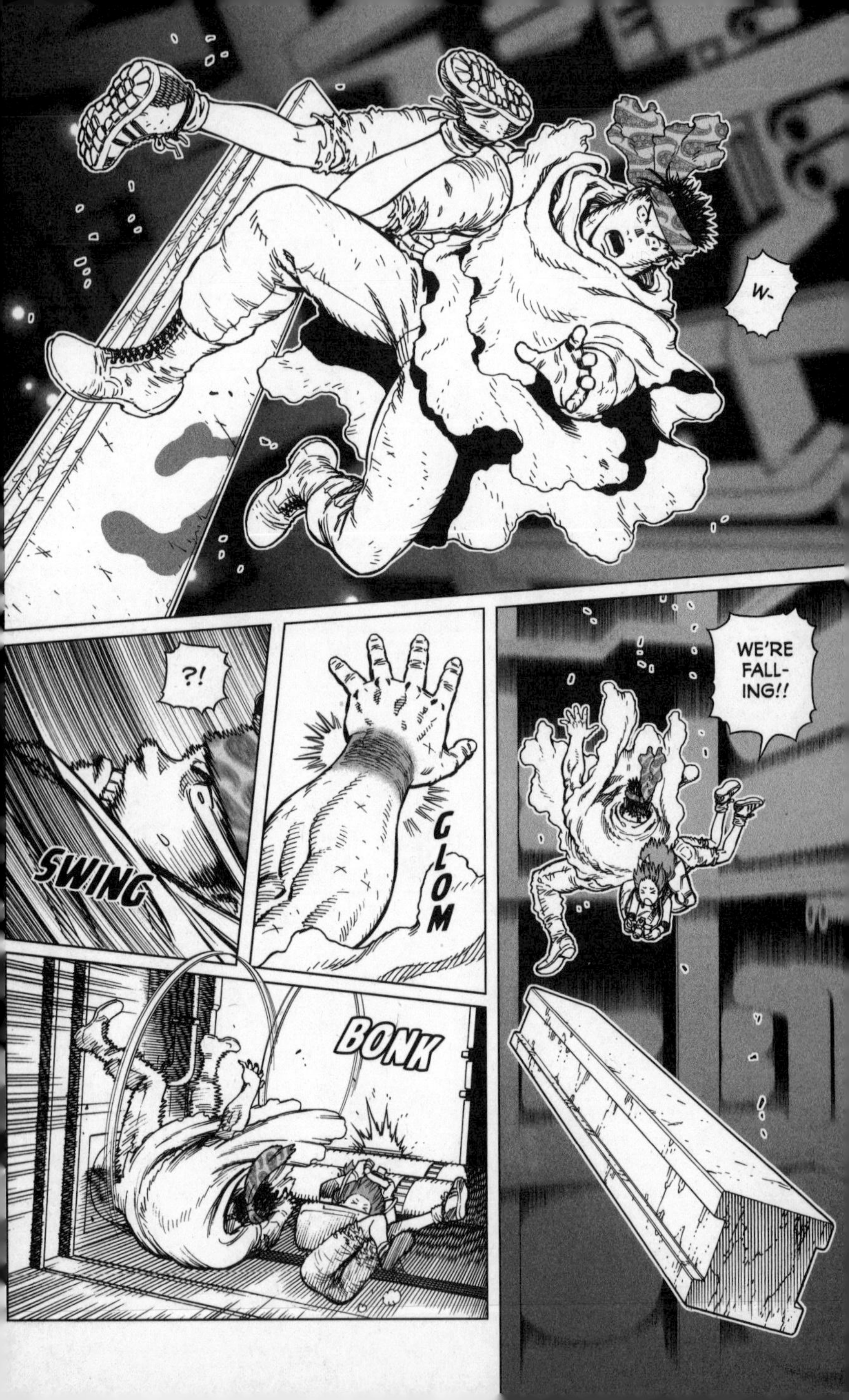
W-
WE'RE FALLING!!
GLOM
?!
SWING
BONK

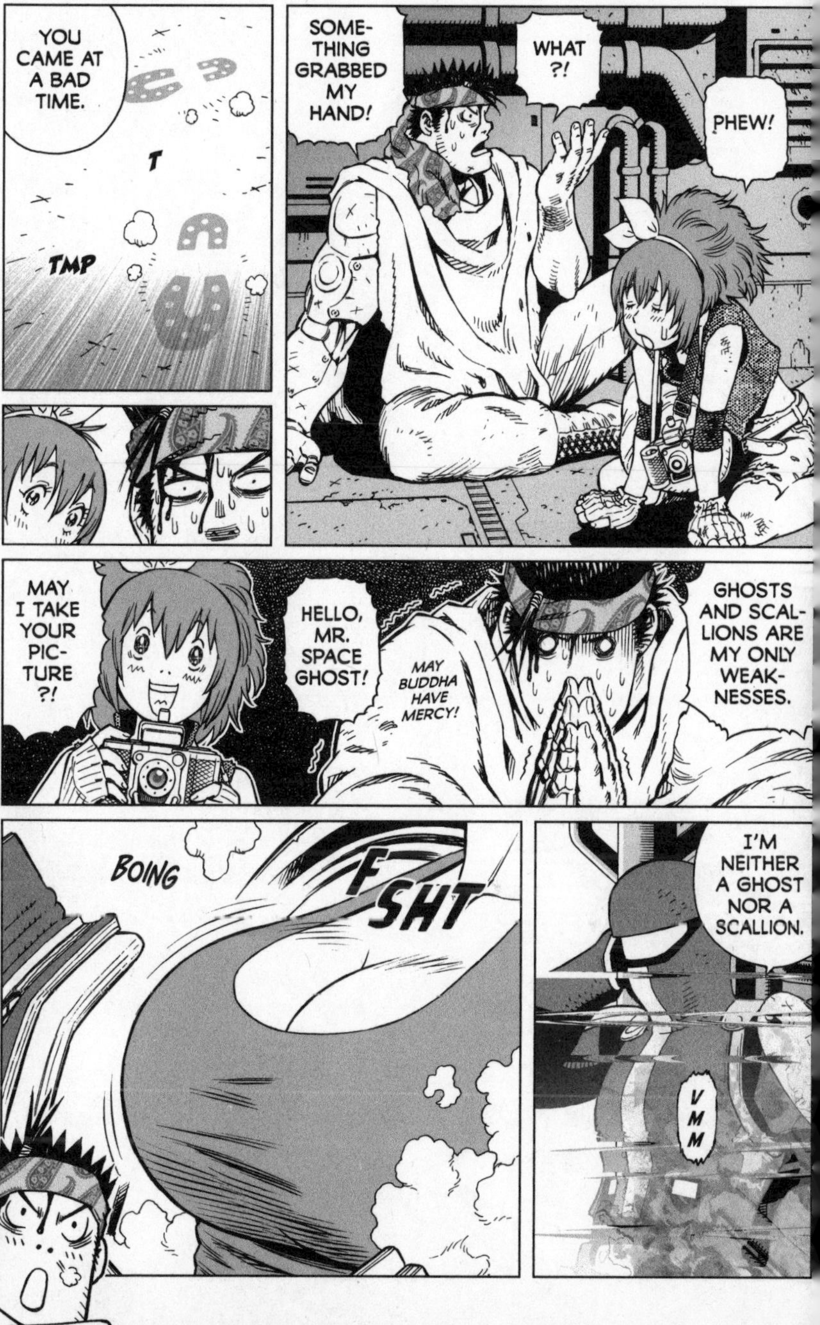
PHEW!
WHAT ?!
SOME-THING GRABBED MY HAND!
YOU CAME AT A BAD TIME.
T
TMP
GHOSTS AND SCAL-LIONS ARE MY ONLY WEAK-NESSES.
MAY BUDDHA HAVE MERCY!
HELLO, MR. SPACE GHOST!
MAY I TAKE YOUR PIC-TURE ?!
I'M NEITHER A GHOST NOR A SCALLION.
VMM
FSHT
BOING

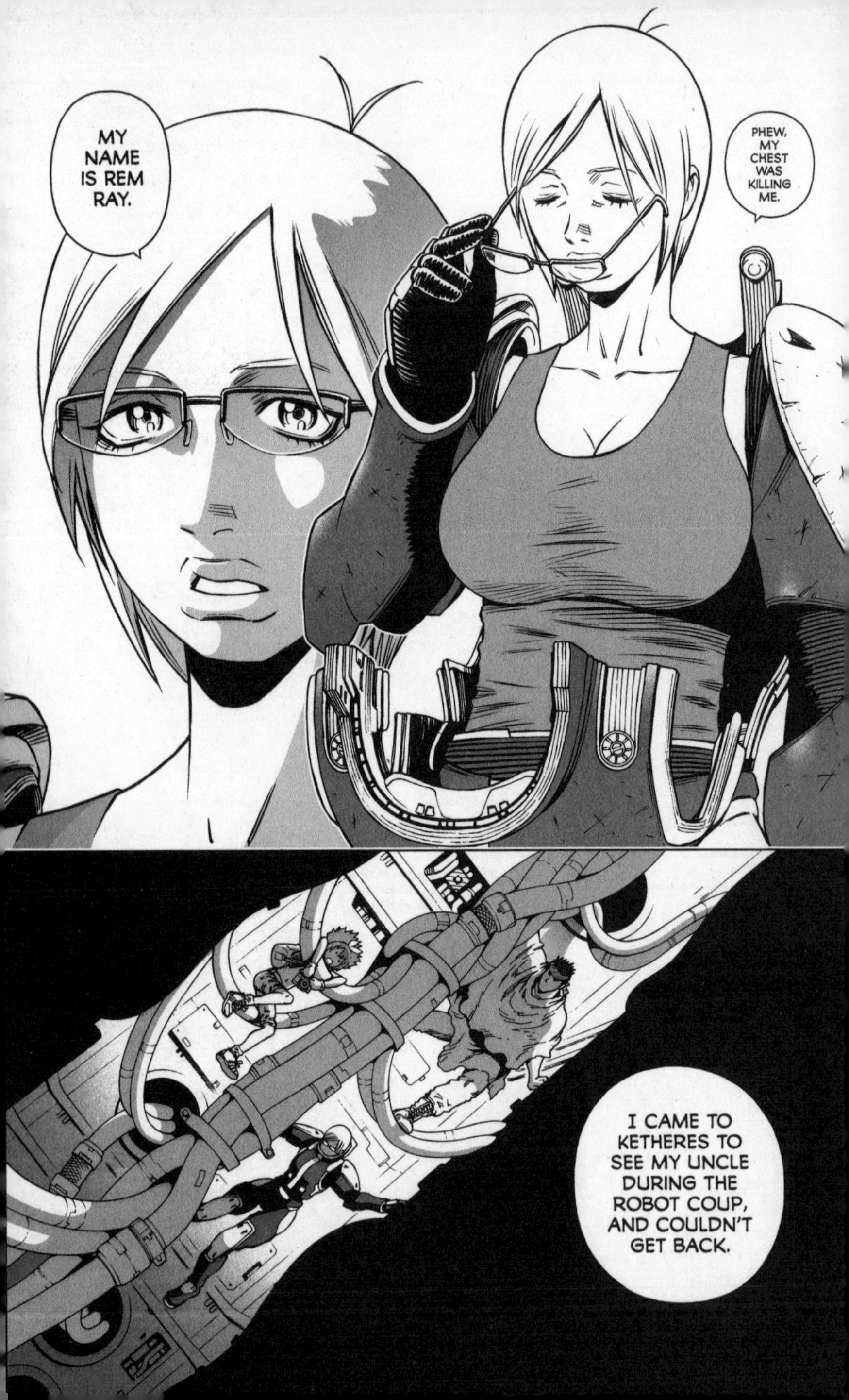
PHEW, MY CHEST WAS KILLING ME.
MY NAME IS REM RAY.
I CAME TO KETHERES TO SEE MY UNCLE DURING THE ROBOT COUP, AND COULDN'T GET BACK.

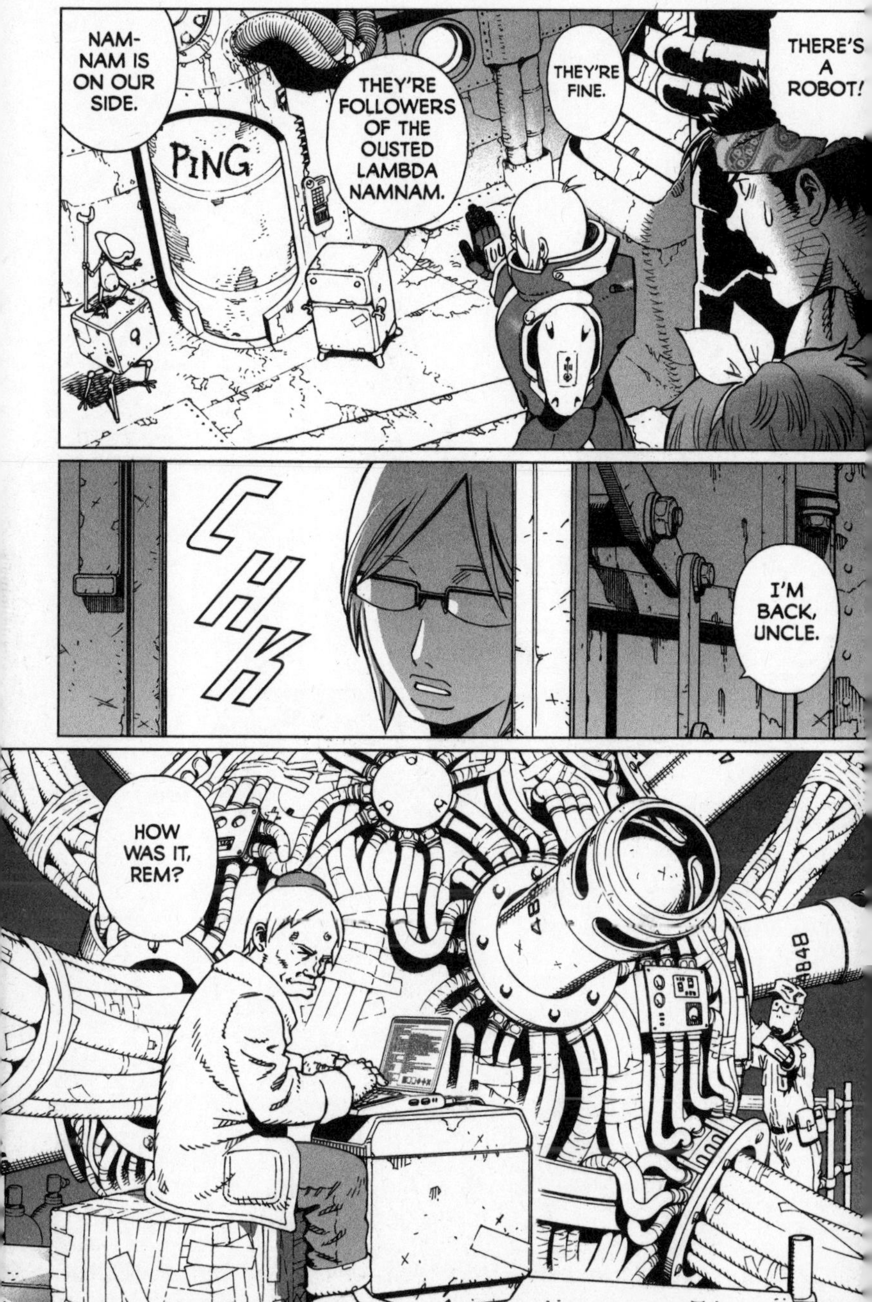
THERE'S A ROBOT!
THEY'RE FINE.
THEY'RE FOLLOWERS OF THE OUSTED LAMBDA NAMNAM.
NAM-NAM IS ON OUR SIDE.
PING
I'M BACK, UNCLE.
CHK
HOW WAS IT, REM?

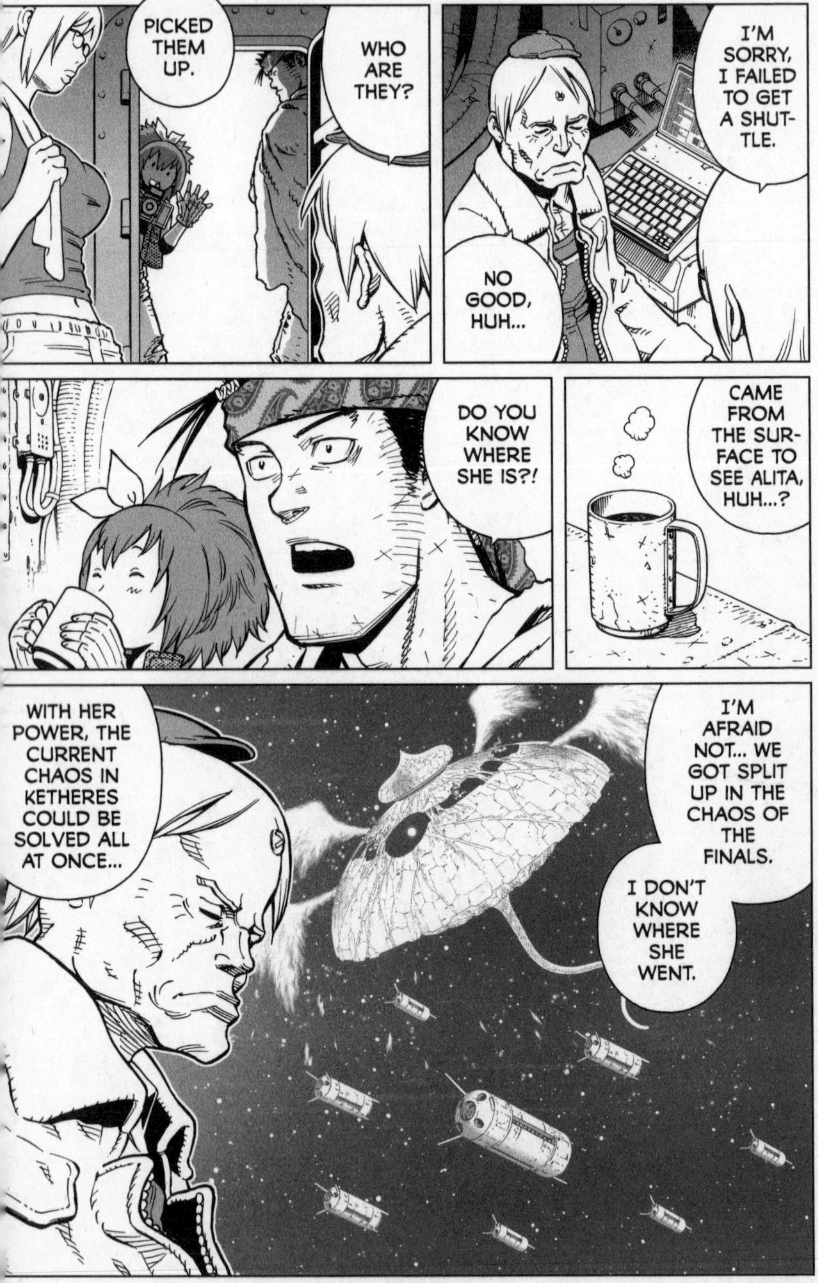
I'M SORRY, I FAILED TO GET A SHUT-TLE.
NO GOOD, HUH...
WHO ARE THEY?
PICKED THEM UP.
CAME FROM THE SUR-FACE TO SEE ALITA, HUH...?
DO YOU KNOW WHERE SHE IS?!
I'M AFRAID NOT... WE GOT SPLIT UP IN THE CHAOS OF THE FINALS.
I DON'T KNOW WHERE SHE WENT.
WITH HER POWER, THE CURRENT CHAOS IN KETHERES COULD BE SOLVED ALL AT ONCE...

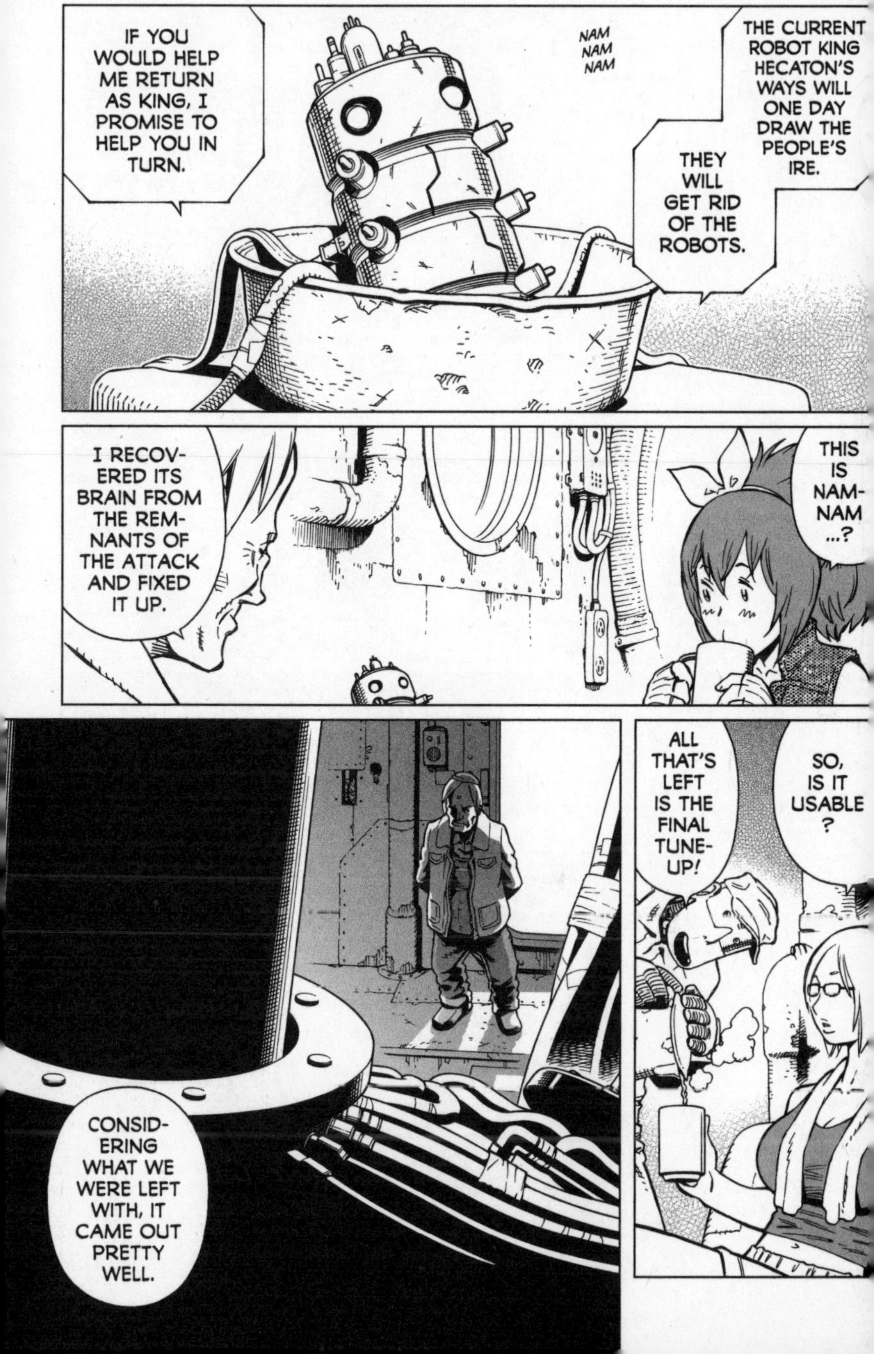

THE CURRENT ROBOT KING HECATON'S WAYS WILL ONE DAY DRAW THE PEOPLE'S IRE.
THEY WILL GET RID OF THE ROBOTS.
NAM NAM NAM
IF YOU WOULD HELP ME RETURN AS KING, I PROMISE TO HELP YOU IN TURN.
THIS IS NAM-NAM ...?
I RECOV-ERED ITS BRAIN FROM THE REM-NANTS OF THE ATTACK AND FIXED IT UP.
SO, IS IT USABLE ?
ALL THAT'S LEFT IS THE FINAL TUNE-UP!
CONSID-ERING WHAT WE WERE LEFT WITH, IT CAME OUT PRETTY WELL.

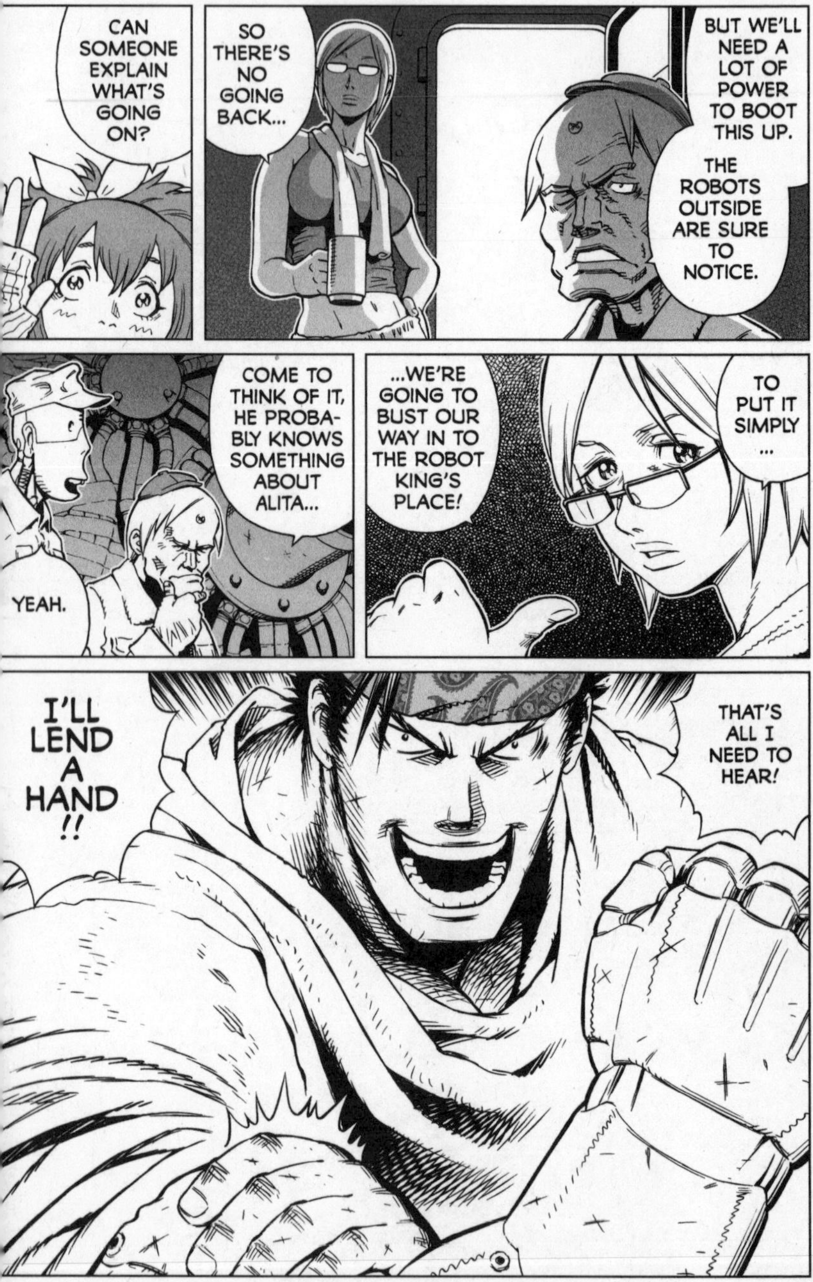
BUT WE'LL NEED A LOT OF POWER TO BOOT THIS UP.
THE ROBOTS OUTSIDE ARE SURE TO NOTICE.
SO THERE'S NO GOING BACK...
CAN SOMEONE EXPLAIN WHAT'S GOING ON?
TO PUT IT SIMPLY ...
...WE'RE GOING TO BUST OUR WAY IN TO THE ROBOT KING'S PLACE!
COME TO THINK OF IT, HE PROBA-BLY KNOWS SOMETHING ABOUT ALITA...
YEAH.
THAT'S ALL I NEED TO HEAR!
I'LL LEND A HAND !!

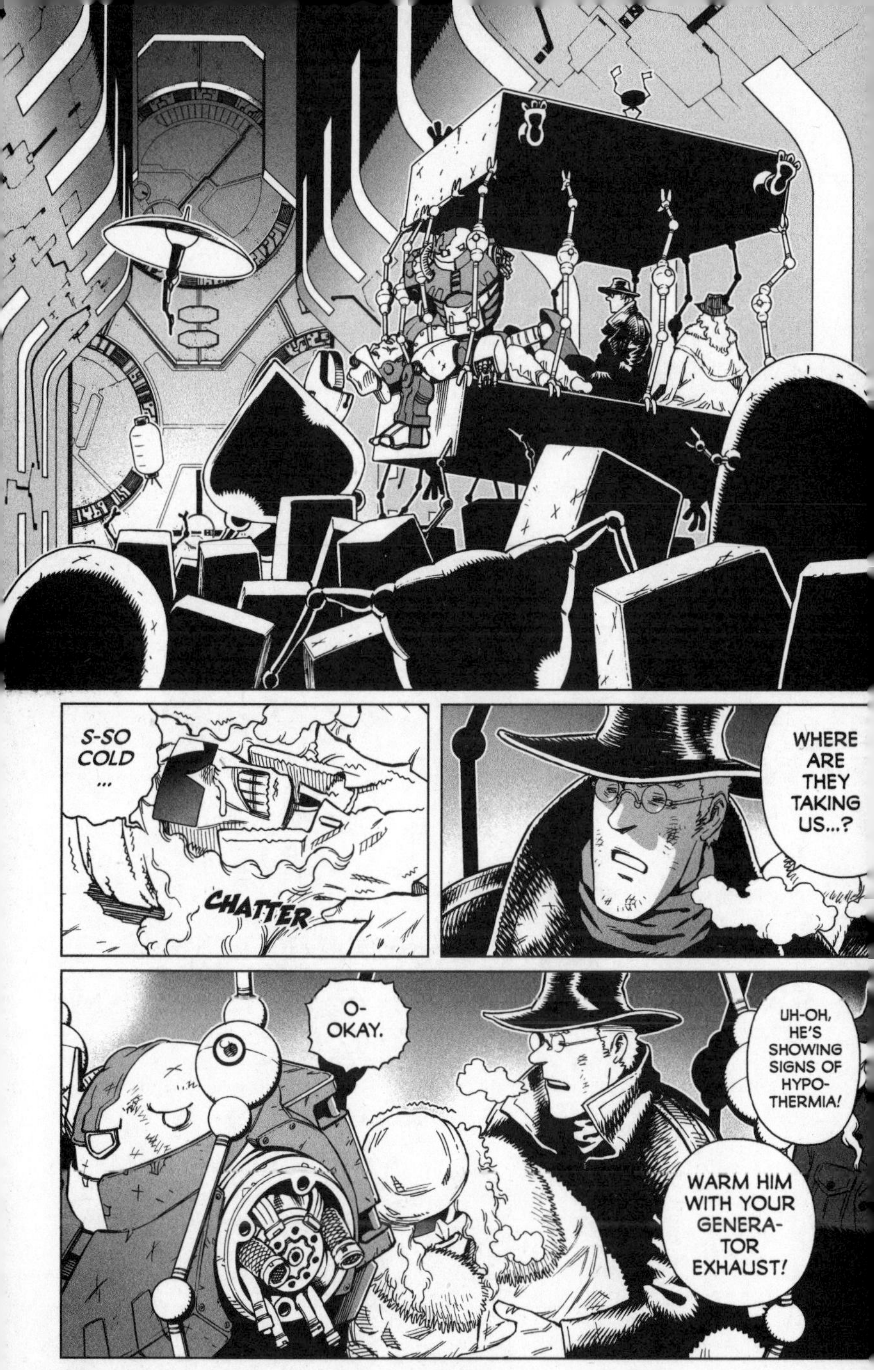
WHERE ARE THEY TAKING US...?
S-SO COLD ...
CHATTER
UH-OH, HE'S SHOWING SIGNS OF HYPOTHERMIA!
WARM HIM WITH YOUR GENERATOR EXHAUST!
O-OKAY.

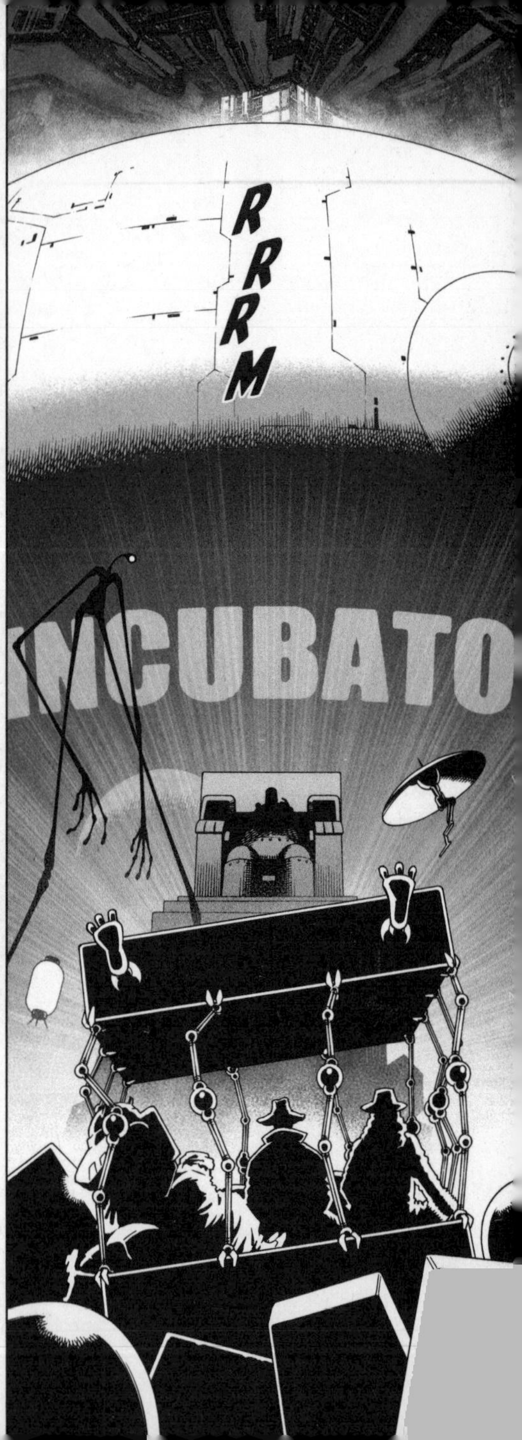
RRRM
INCUBATO

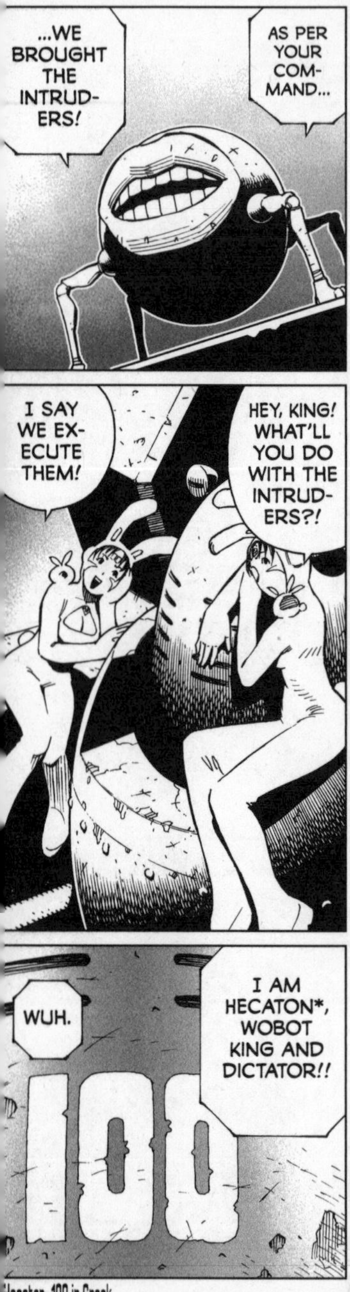
AS PER YOUR COMMAND...
...WE BROUGHT THE INTRUDERS!
HEY, KING! WHAT'LL YOU DO WITH THE INTRUDERS?!
I SAY WE EXECUTE THEM!
I AM HECATON*, WOBOT KING AND DICTATOR!!
WUH.
100

*Hecaton: 100 in Greek.

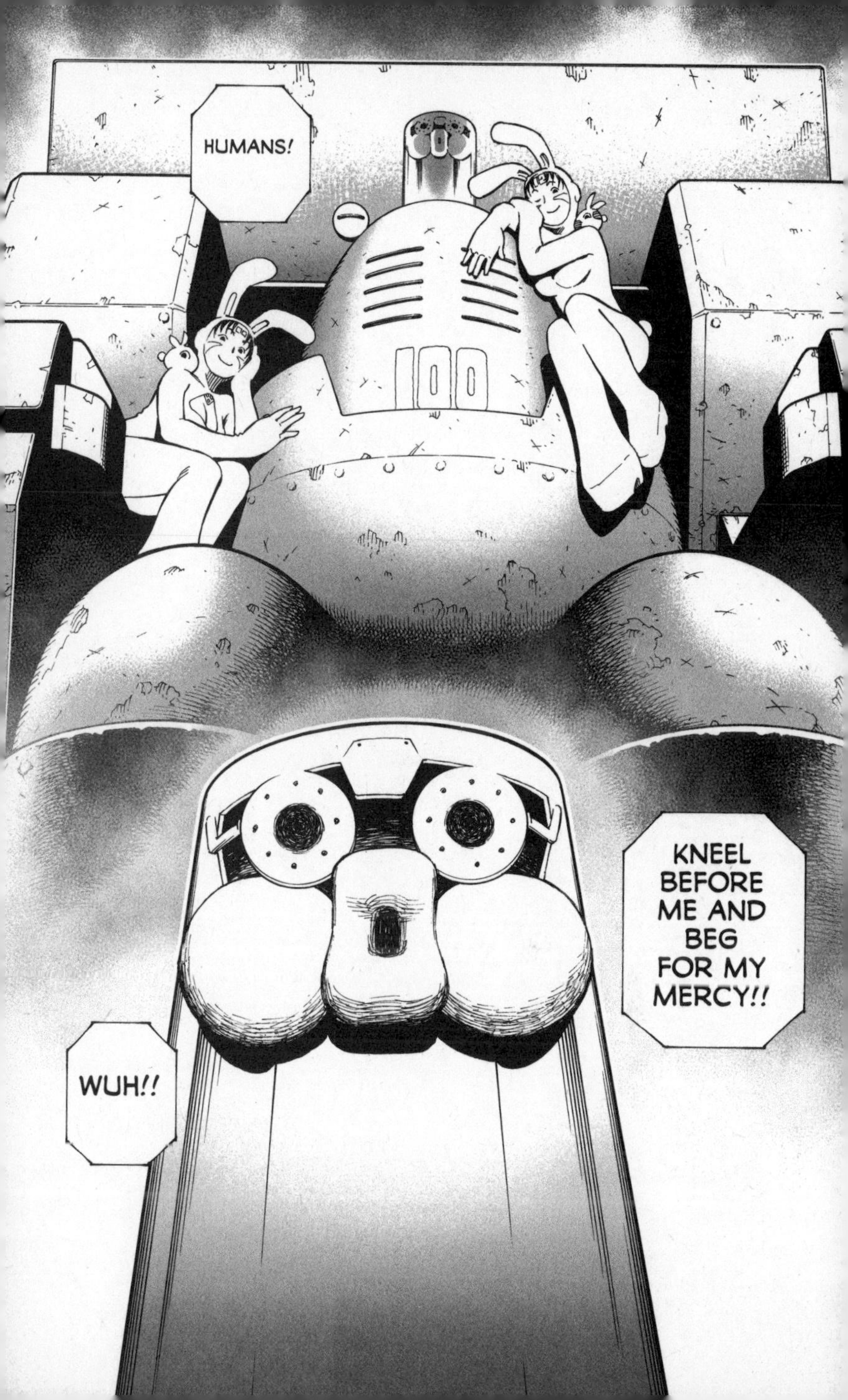
HUMANS!
KNEEL BEFORE ME AND BEG FOR MY MERCY!!
WUH!!

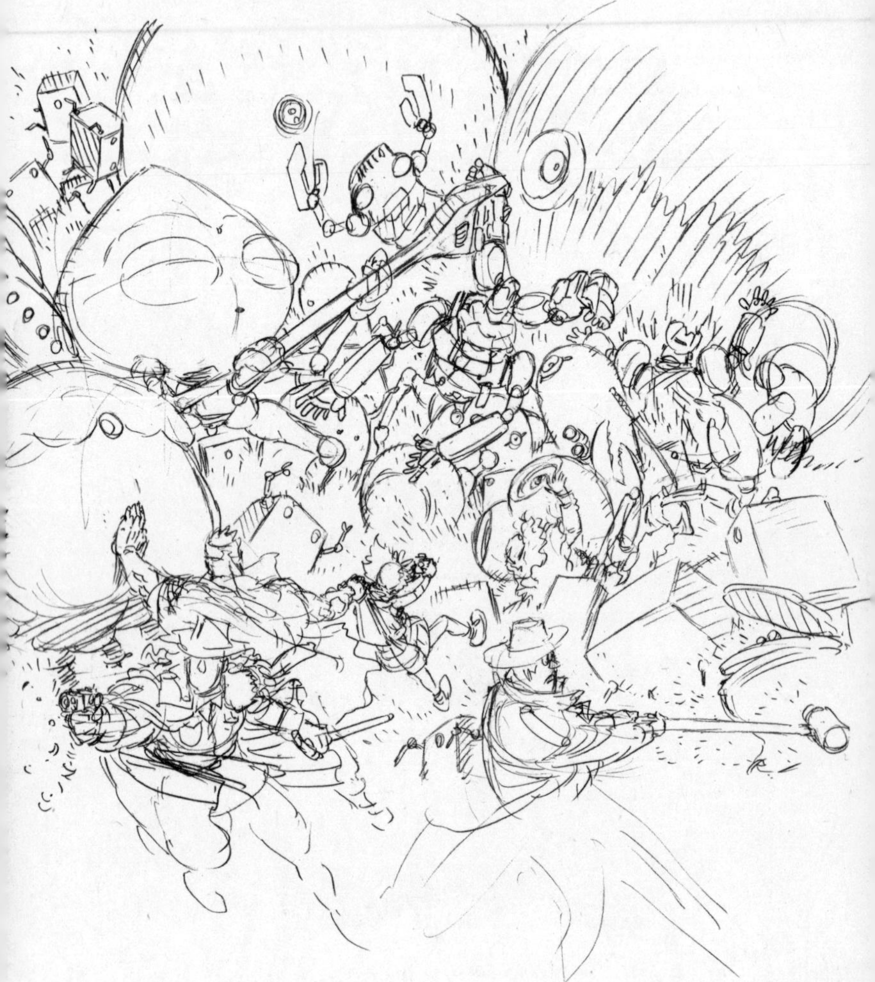

Final Phase: Alita Quest XVIII

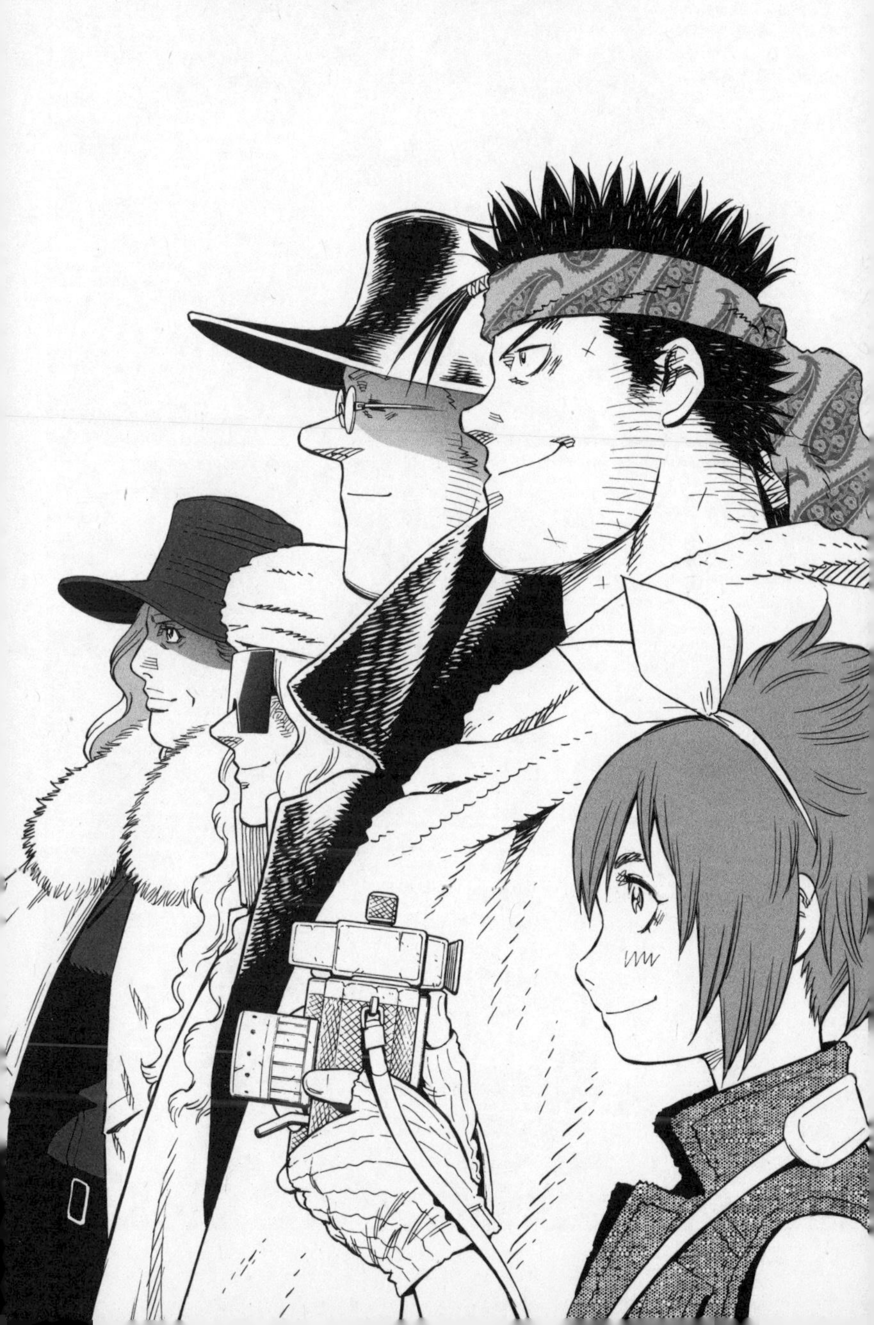

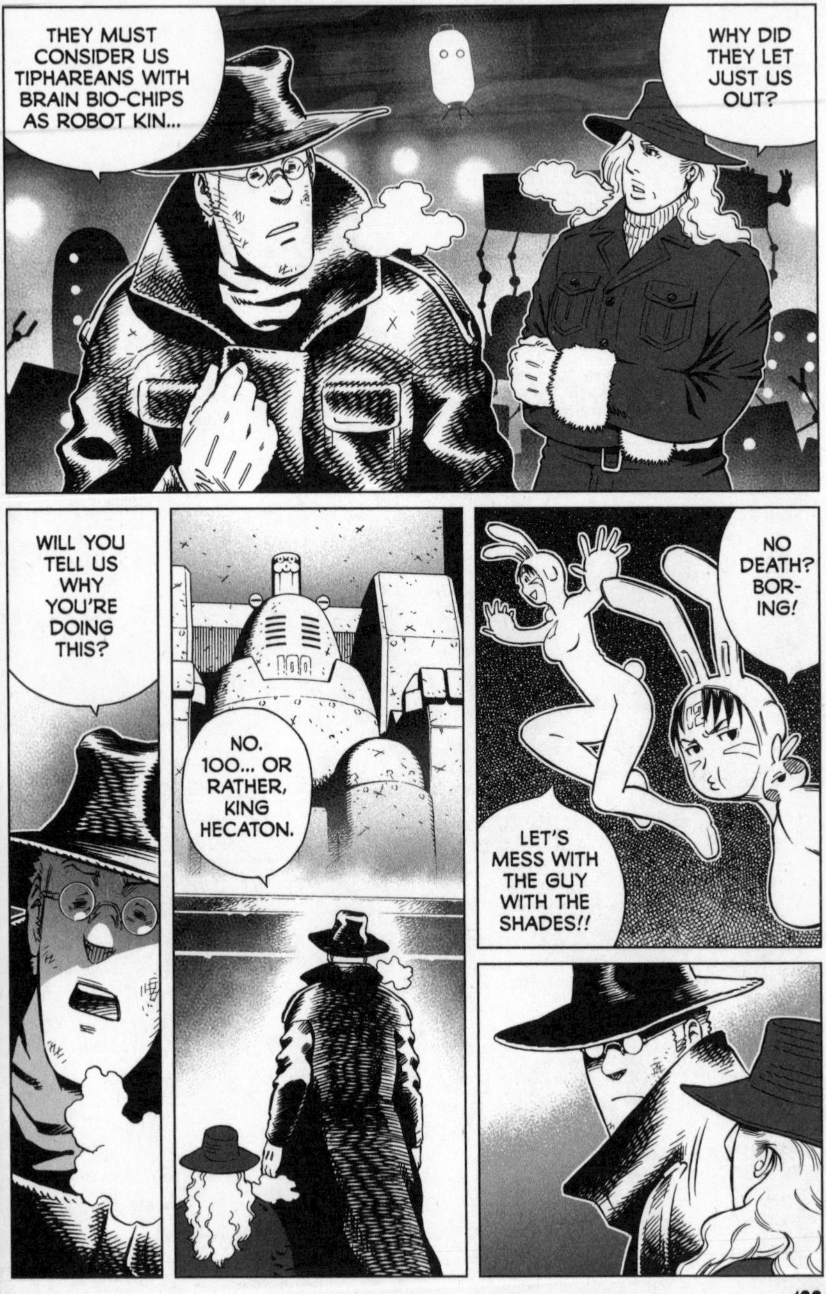
WHY DID THEY LET JUST US OUT?
THEY MUST CONSIDER US TIPHAREANS WITH BRAIN BIO-CHIPS AS ROBOT KIN...
NO DEATH? BOR-ING!
LET'S MESS WITH THE GUY WITH THE SHADES!!
NO. 100... OR RATHER, KING HECATON.
WILL YOU TELL US WHY YOU'RE DOING THIS?

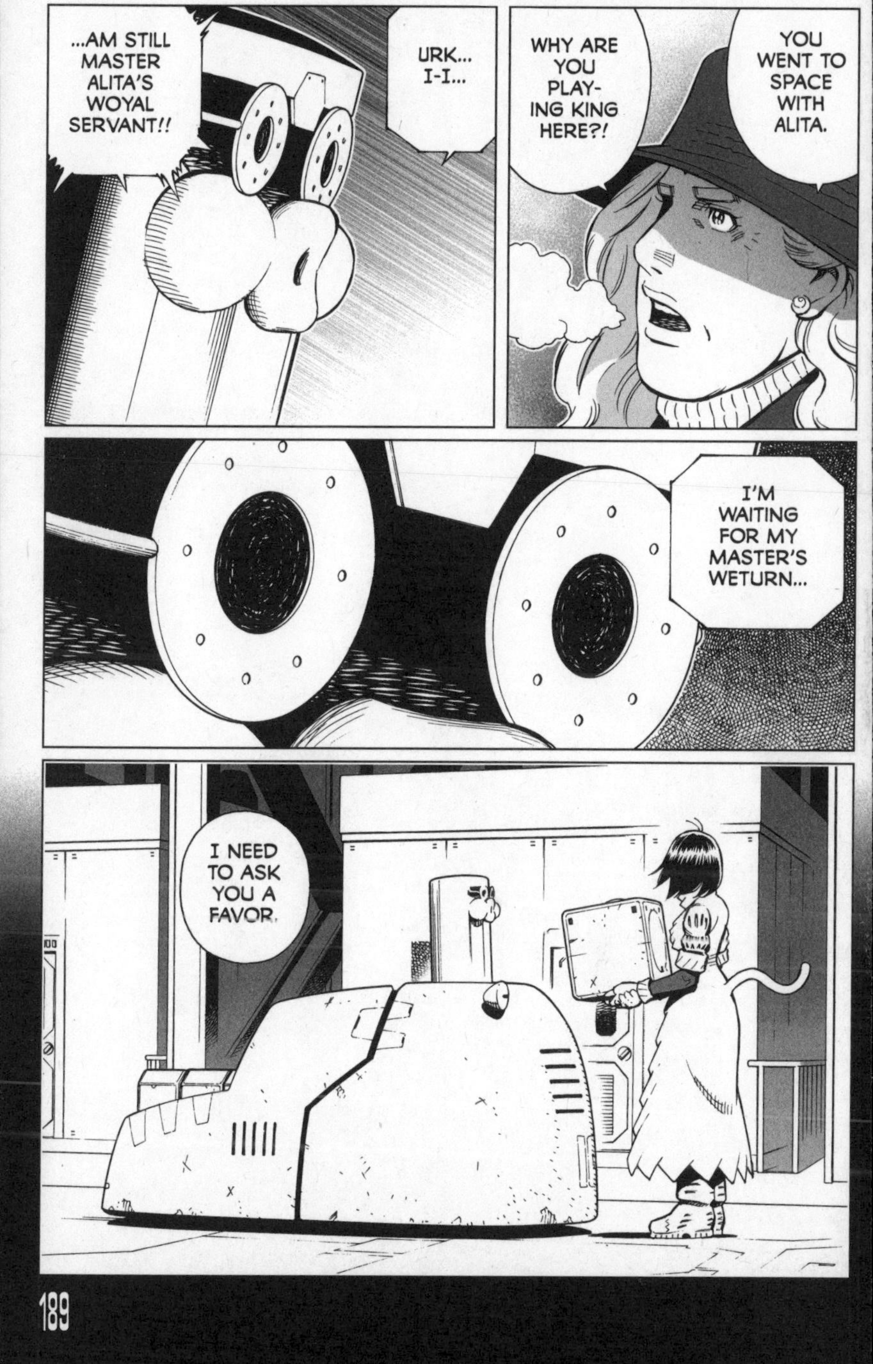
YOU WENT TO SPACE WITH ALITA.
WHY ARE YOU PLAY-ING KING HERE?!
URK... I-I...
...AM STILL MASTER ALITA'S WOYAL SERVANT!!
I'M WAITING FOR MY MASTER'S WETURN...
I NEED TO ASK YOU A FAVOR.

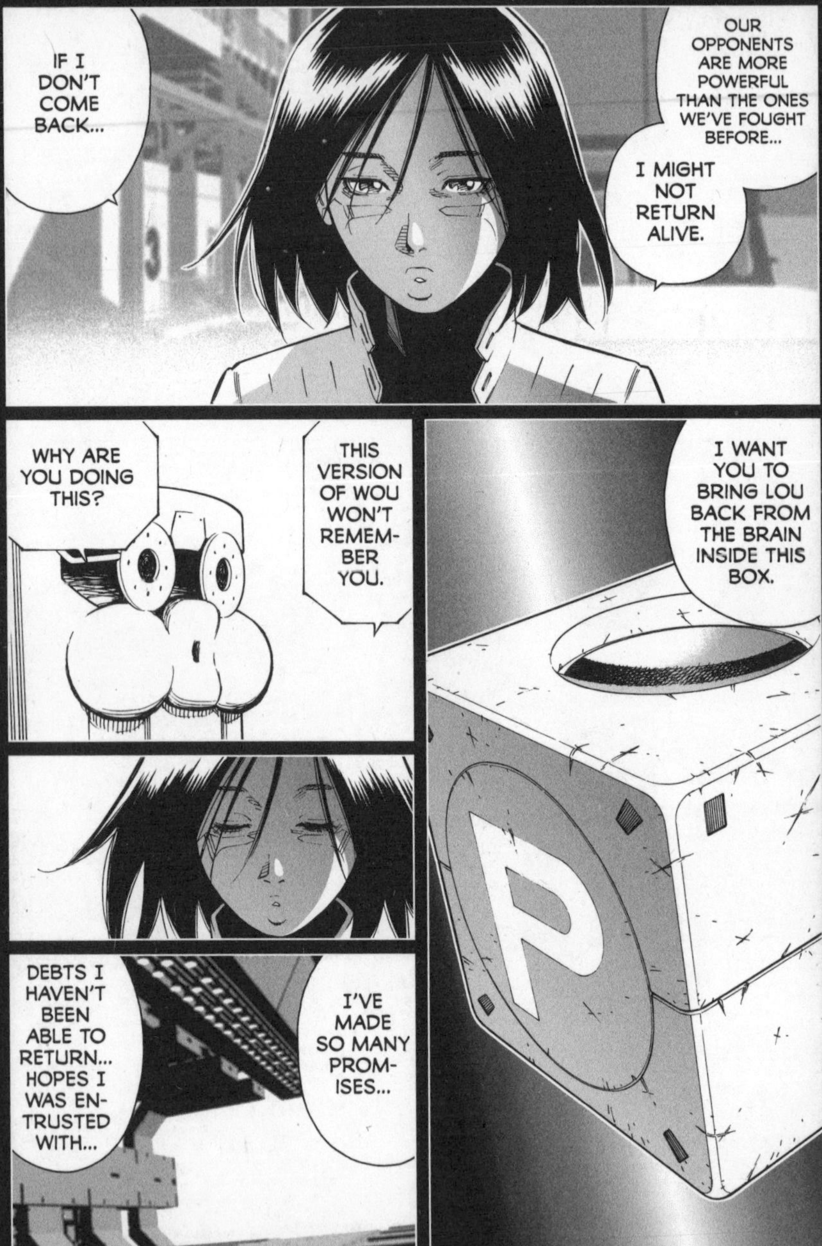
OUR OPPONENTS ARE MORE POWERFUL THAN THE ONES WE'VE FOUGHT BEFORE...
I MIGHT NOT RETURN ALIVE.
IF I DON'T COME BACK...
I WANT YOU TO BRING LOU BACK FROM THE BRAIN INSIDE THIS BOX.
THIS VERSION OF WOU WON'T REMEMBER YOU.
WHY ARE YOU DOING THIS?
I'VE MADE SO MANY PROMISES...
DEBTS I HAVEN'T BEEN ABLE TO RETURN... HOPES I WAS ENTRUSTED WITH...

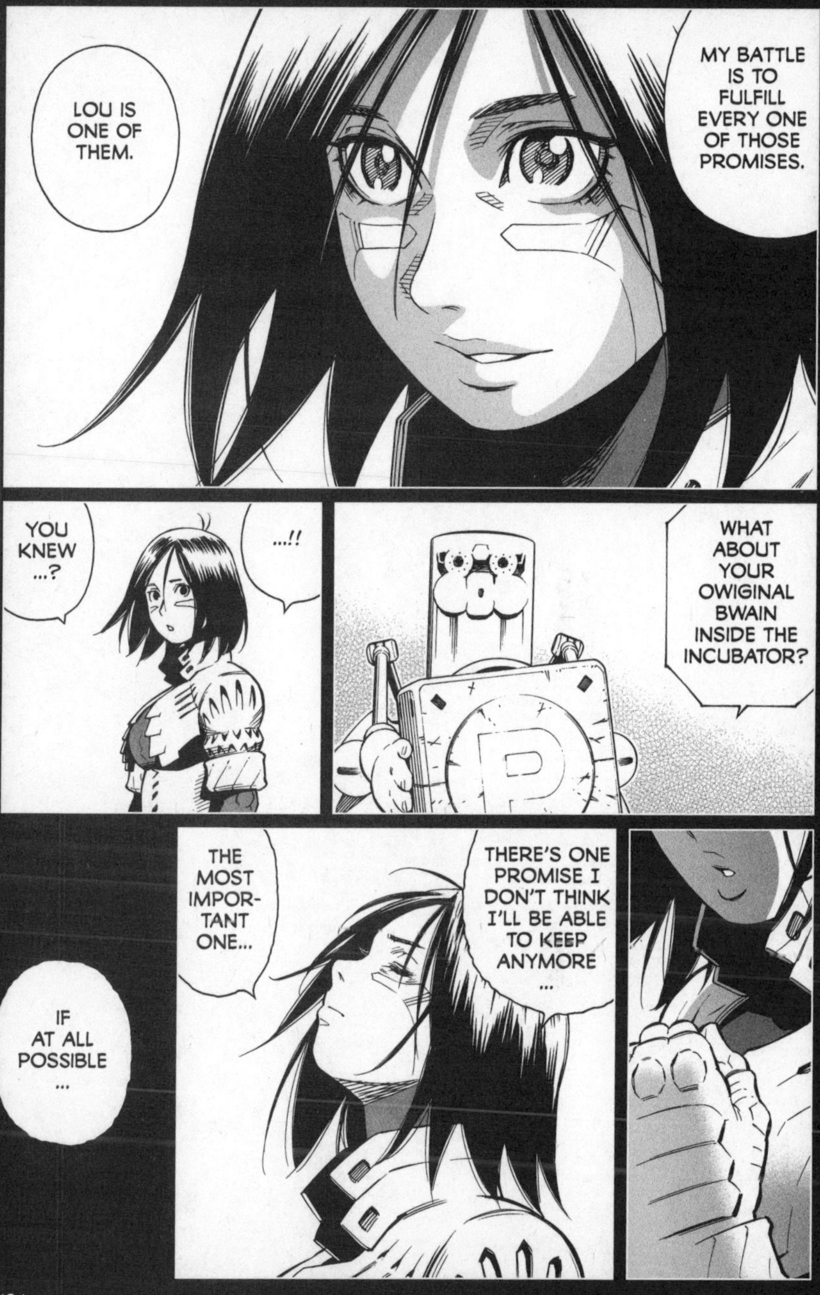
MY BATTLE IS TO FULFILL EVERY ONE OF THOSE PROMISES.
LOU IS ONE OF THEM.
WHAT ABOUT YOUR OWIGINAL BWAIN INSIDE THE INCUBATOR?
...!!
YOU KNEW ...?
THERE'S ONE PROMISE I DON'T THINK I'LL BE ABLE TO KEEP ANYMORE ...
THE MOST IMPOR-TANT ONE...
IF AT ALL POSSIBLE ...

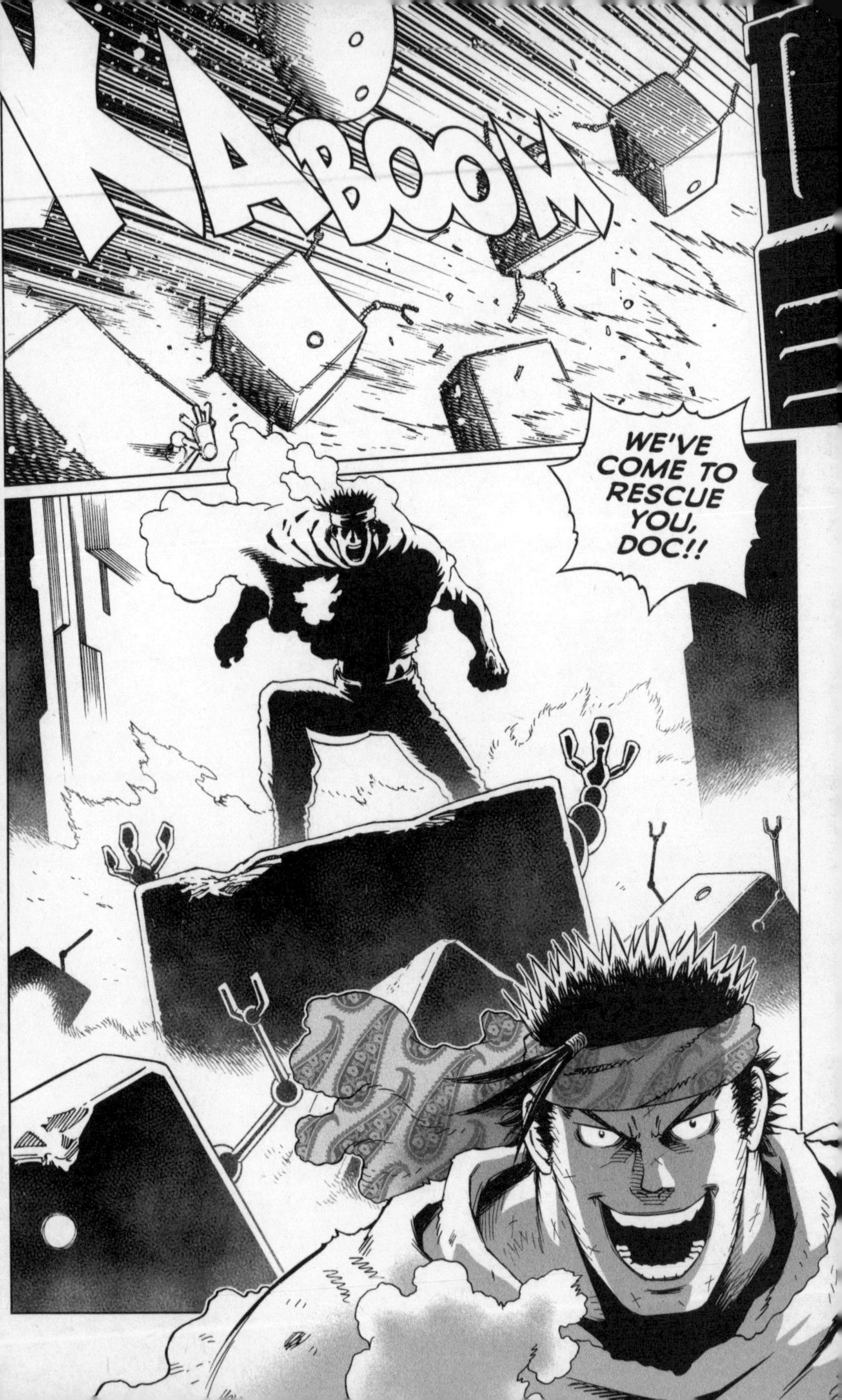
KA-BOOM
WE'VE COME TO RESCUE YOU, DOC!!

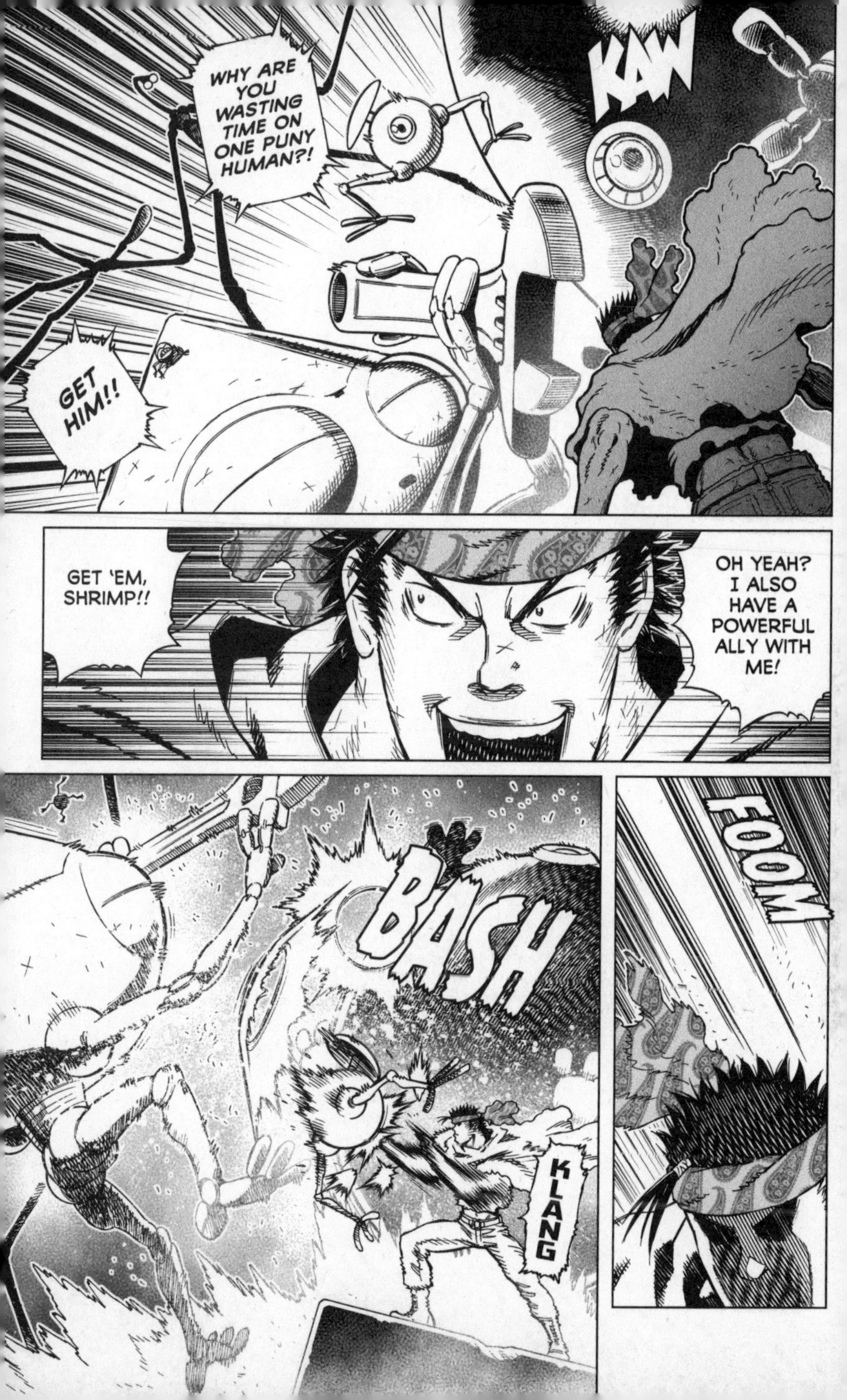
KAW
WHY ARE YOU WASTING TIME ON ONE PUNY HUMAN?!
GET HIM!!
OH YEAH? I ALSO HAVE A POWERFUL ALLY WITH ME!
GET 'EM, SHRIMP!!
FOOM
BASH
KLANG

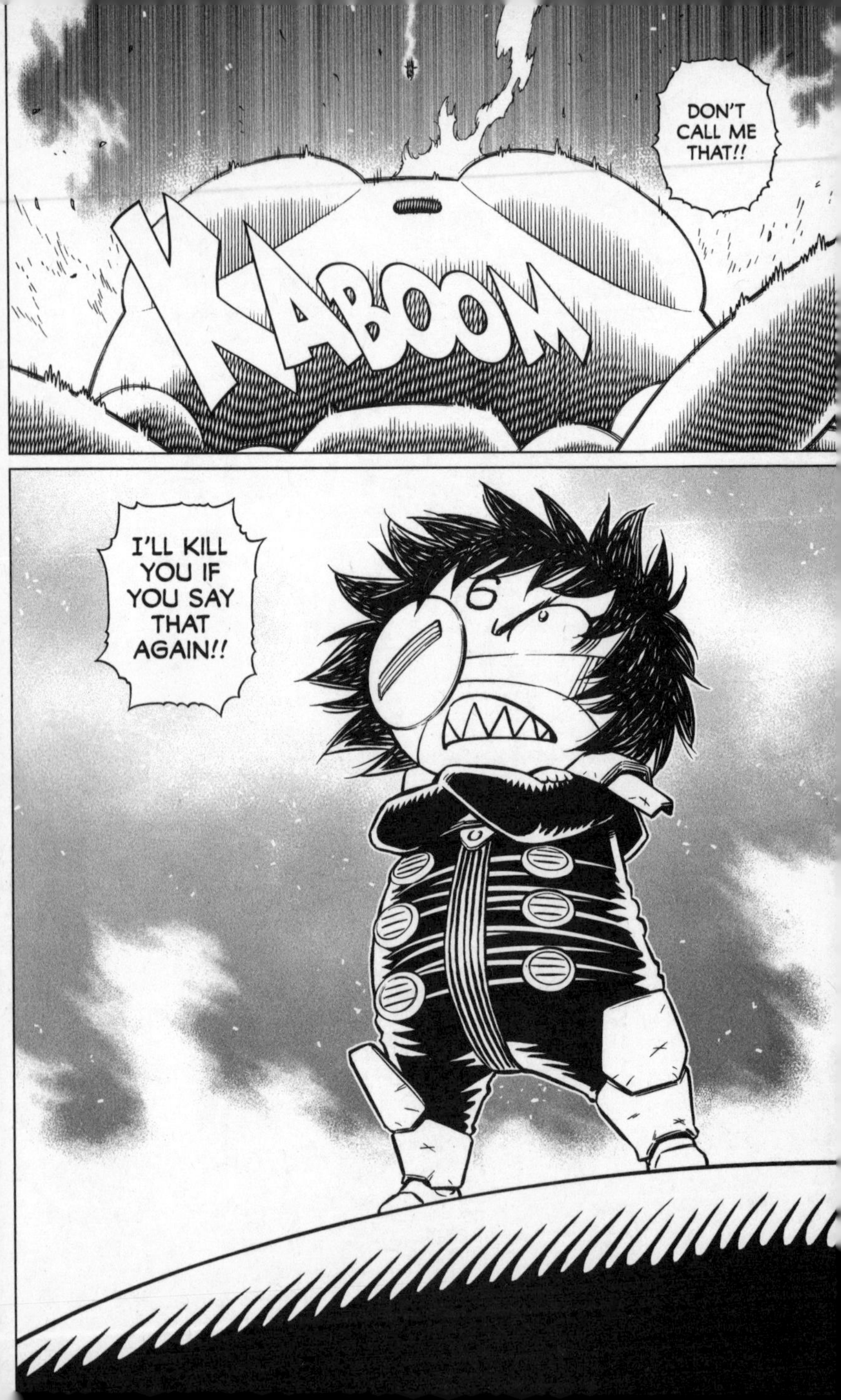
DON'T CALL ME THAT!!
KABOOM
I'LL KILL YOU IF YOU SAY THAT AGAIN!!

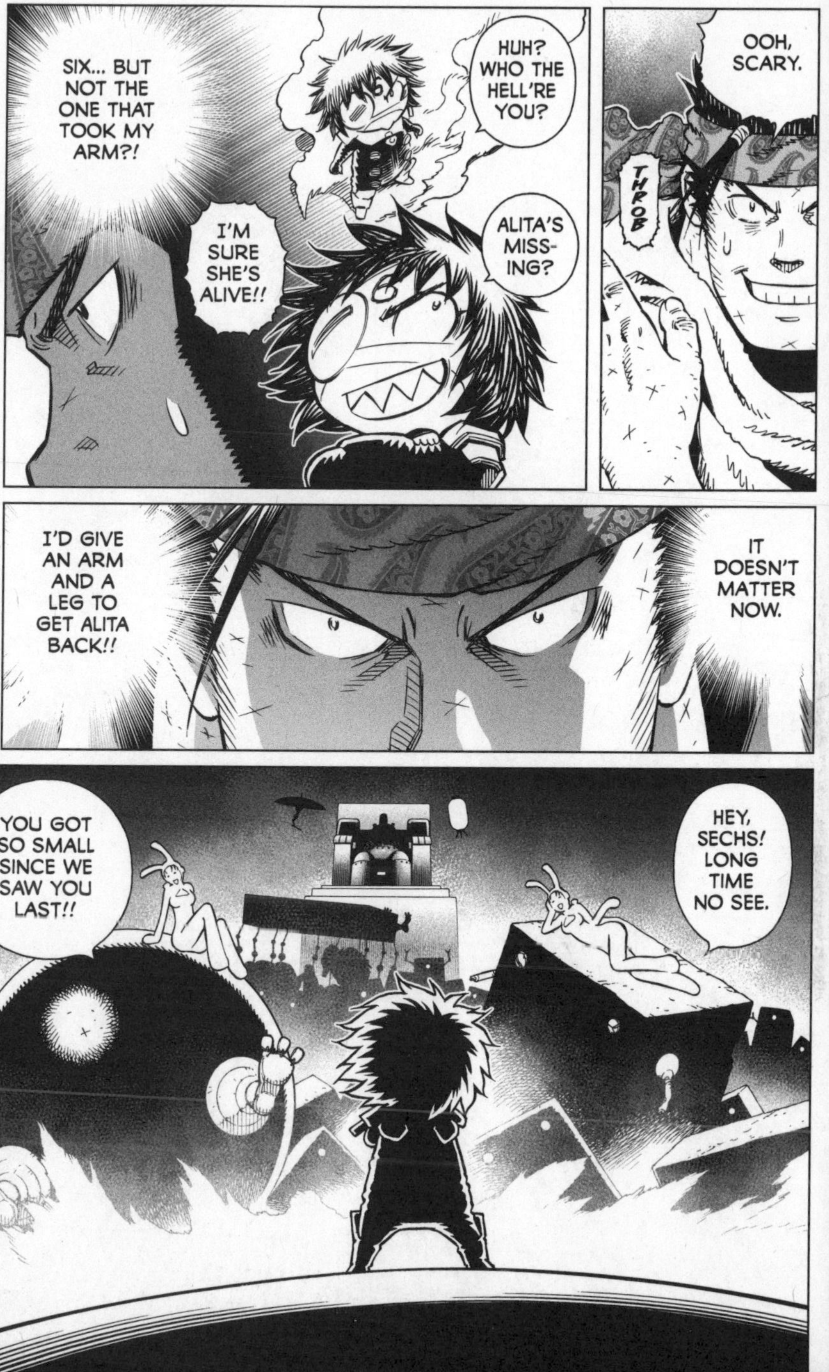
OOH, SCARY.
THROB
HUH? WHO THE HELL'RE YOU?
SIX... BUT NOT THE ONE THAT TOOK MY ARM?!
ALITA'S MISS-ING?
I'M SURE SHE'S ALIVE!!
IT DOESN'T MATTER NOW.
I'D GIVE AN ARM AND A LEG TO GET ALITA BACK!!
HEY, SECHS! LONG TIME NO SEE.
YOU GOT SO SMALL SINCE WE SAW YOU LAST!!

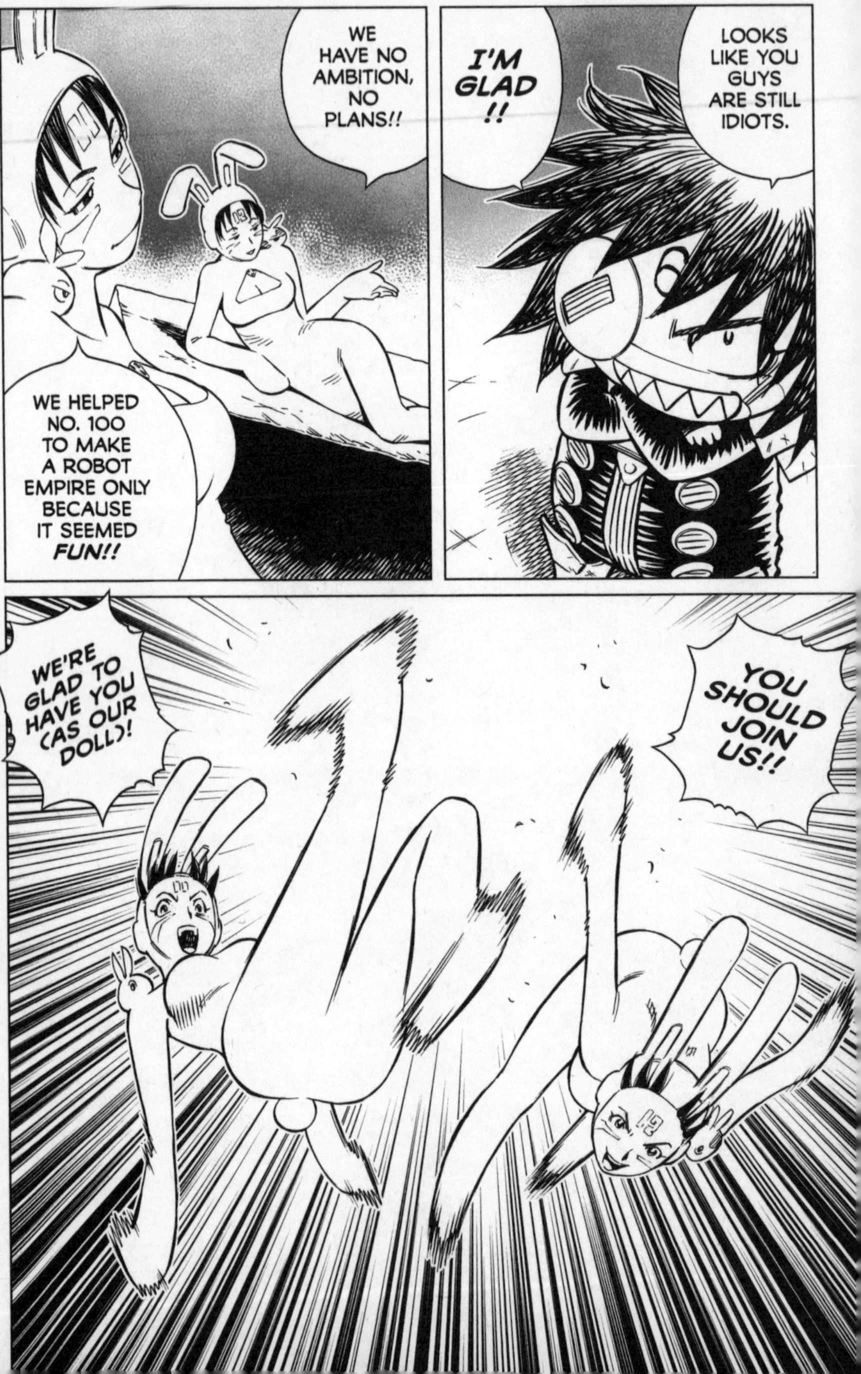

LOOKS LIKE YOU GUYS ARE STILL IDIOTS.
I'M GLAD!!
WE HAVE NO AMBITION, NO PLANS!!
WE HELPED NO. 100 TO MAKE A ROBOT EMPIRE ONLY BECAUSE IT SEEMED *FUN!!*
YOU SHOULD JOIN US!!
WE'RE GLAD TO HAVE YOU (AS OUR DOLL)!

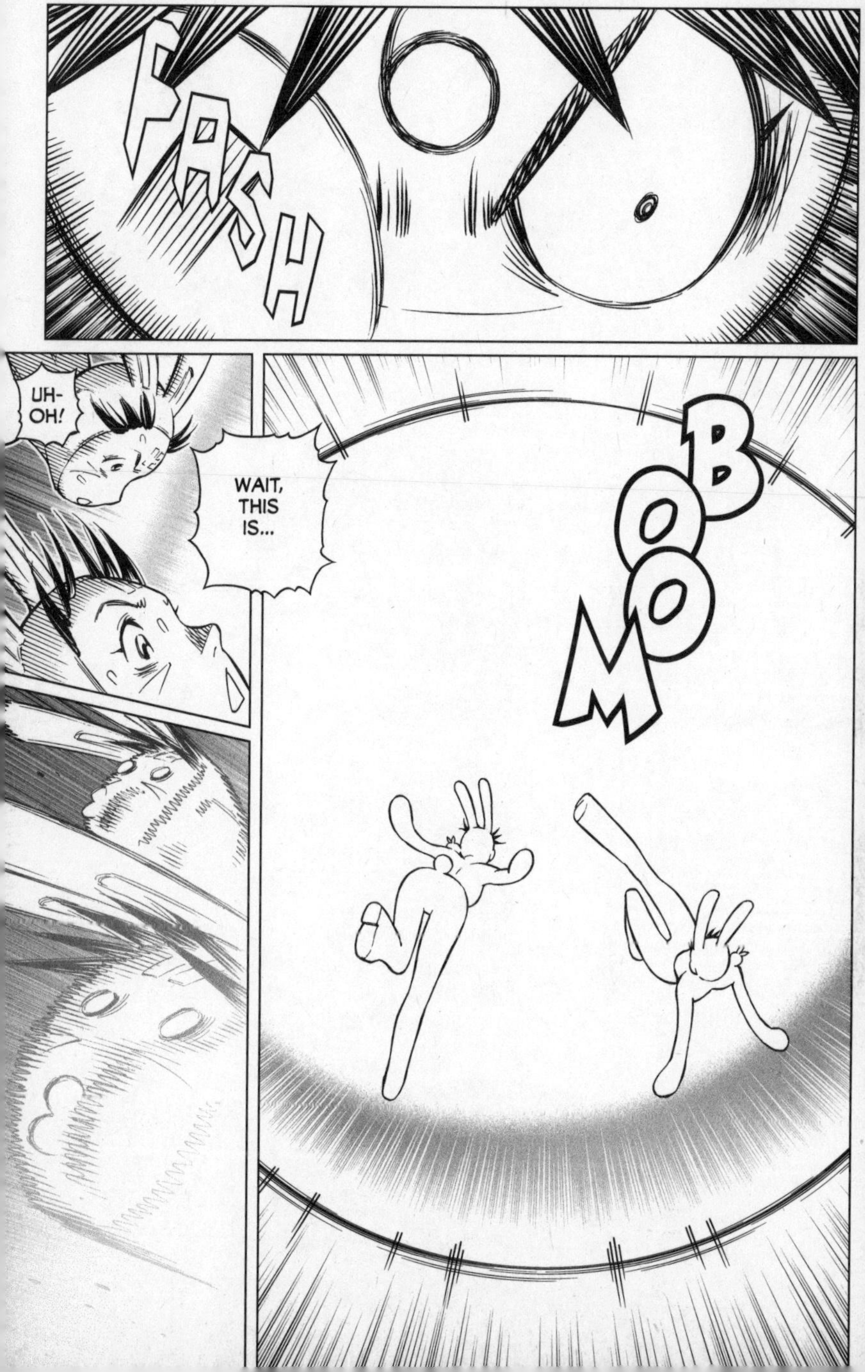
FASH
BOOM
UH-OH!
WAIT, THIS IS...

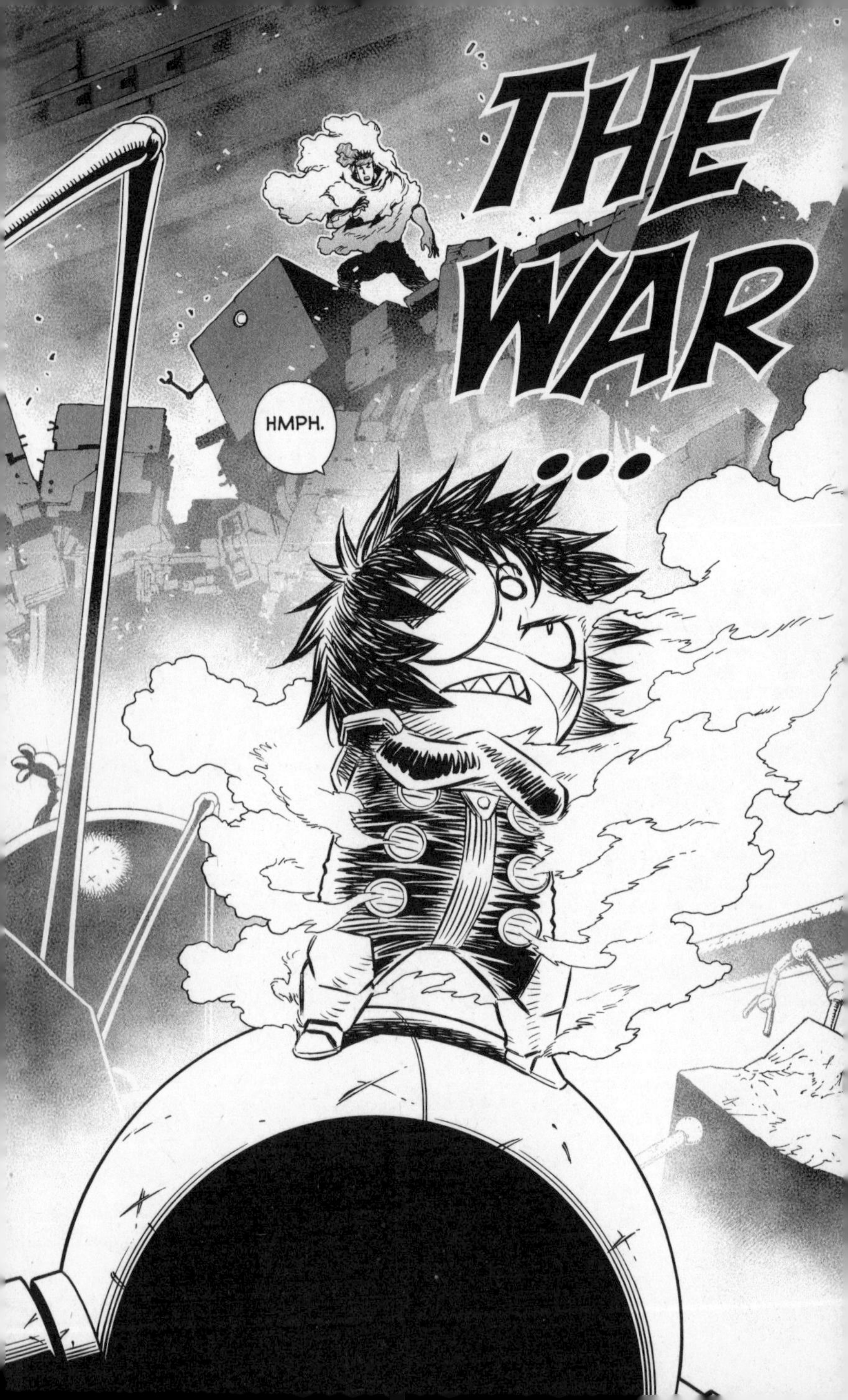
THE WAR...
HMPH.

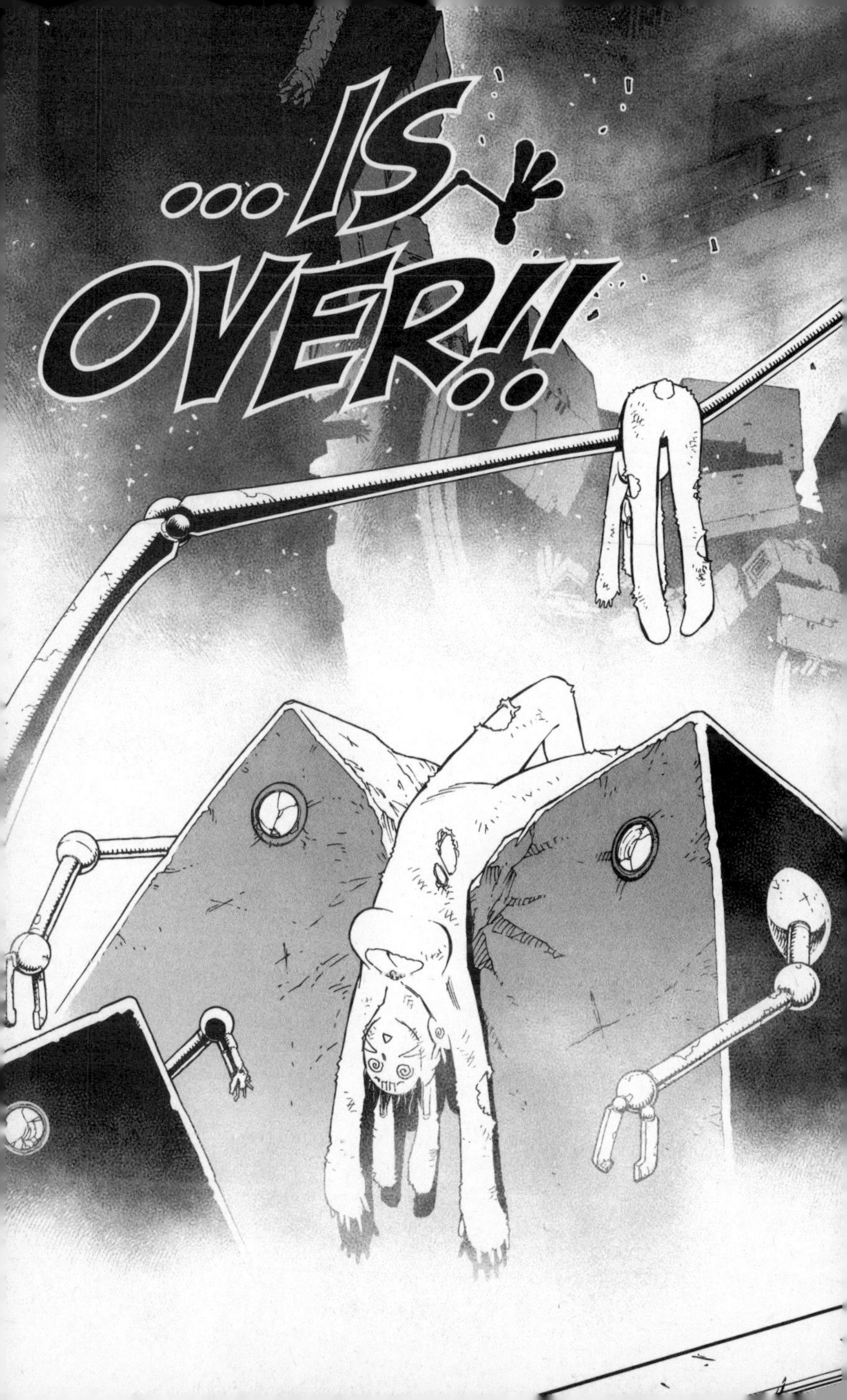
...IS OVER!!

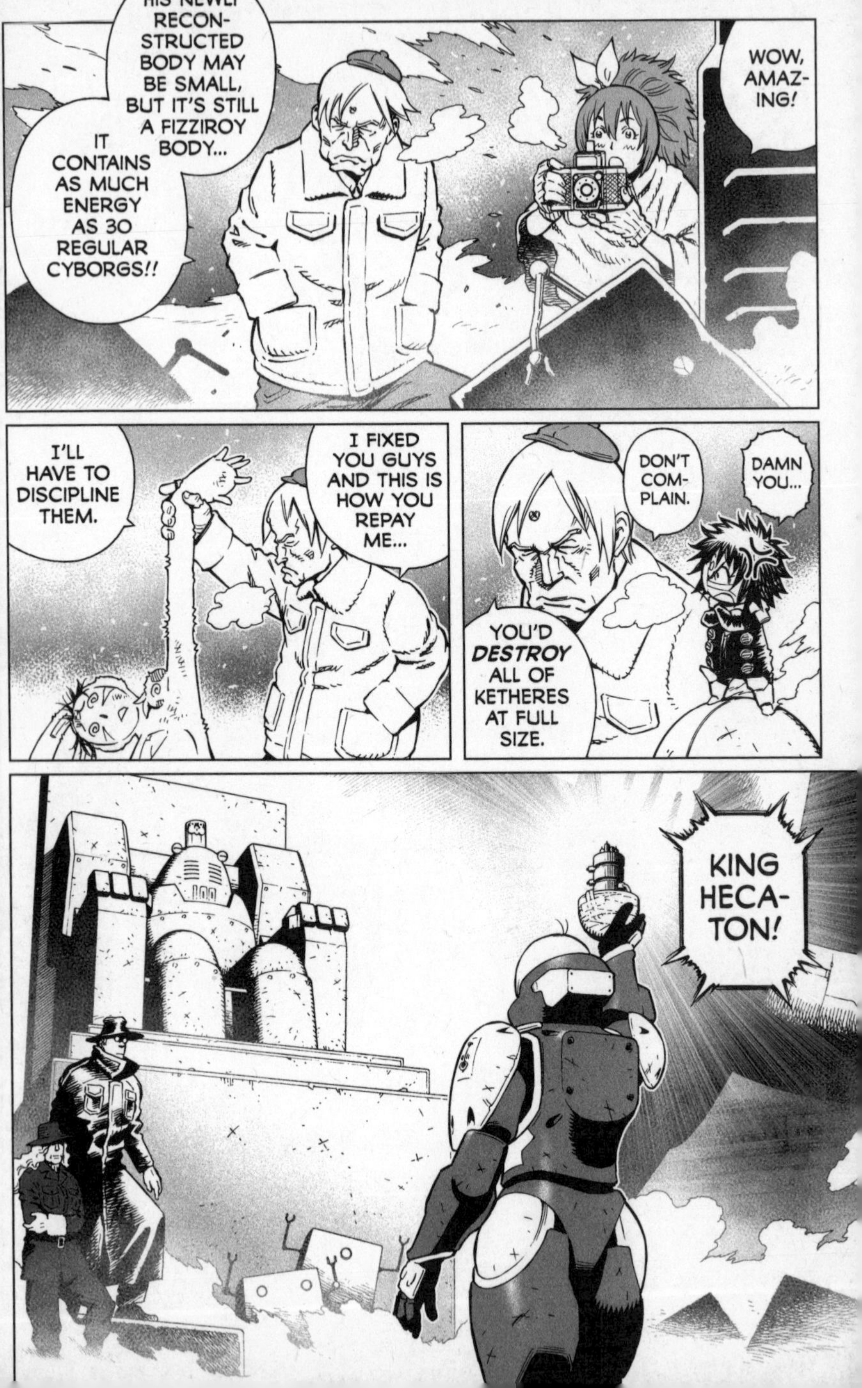
WOW, AMAZ-ING!
HIS NEWLY RECON-STRUCTED BODY MAY BE SMALL, BUT IT'S STILL A FIZZIROY BODY...
IT CONTAINS AS MUCH ENERGY AS 30 REGULAR CYBORGS!!
DAMN YOU...
DON'T COM-PLAIN.
YOU'D *DESTROY* ALL OF KETHERES AT FULL SIZE.
I FIXED YOU GUYS AND THIS IS HOW YOU REPAY ME...
I'LL HAVE TO DISCIPLINE THEM.
KING HECA-TON!

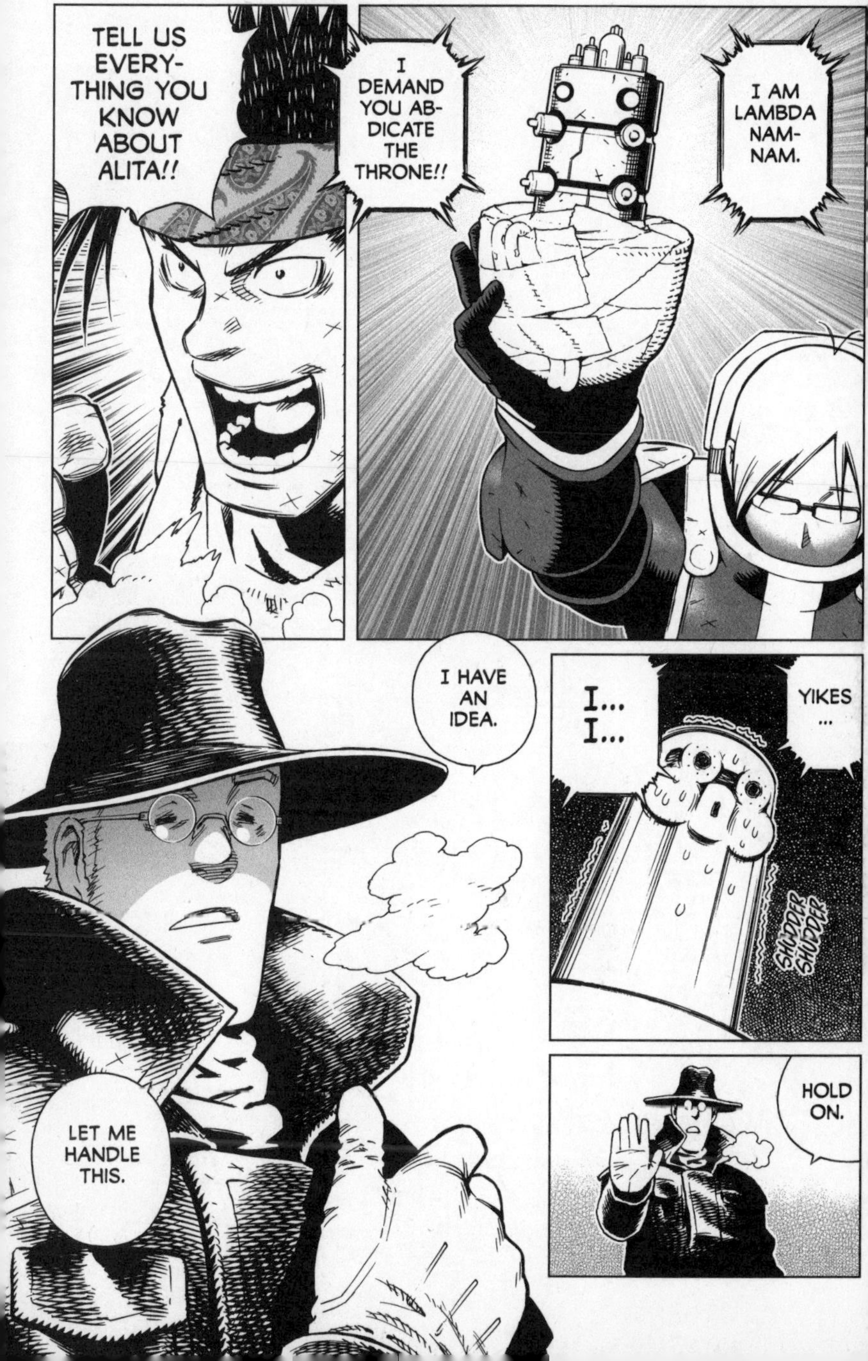
I AM LAMBDA NAM-NAM.
I DEMAND YOU ABDICATE THE THRONE!!
TELL US EVERYTHING YOU KNOW ABOUT ALITA!!
YIKES ...
I... I...
SHUDDER SHUDDER
HOLD ON.
I HAVE AN IDEA.
LET ME HANDLE THIS.

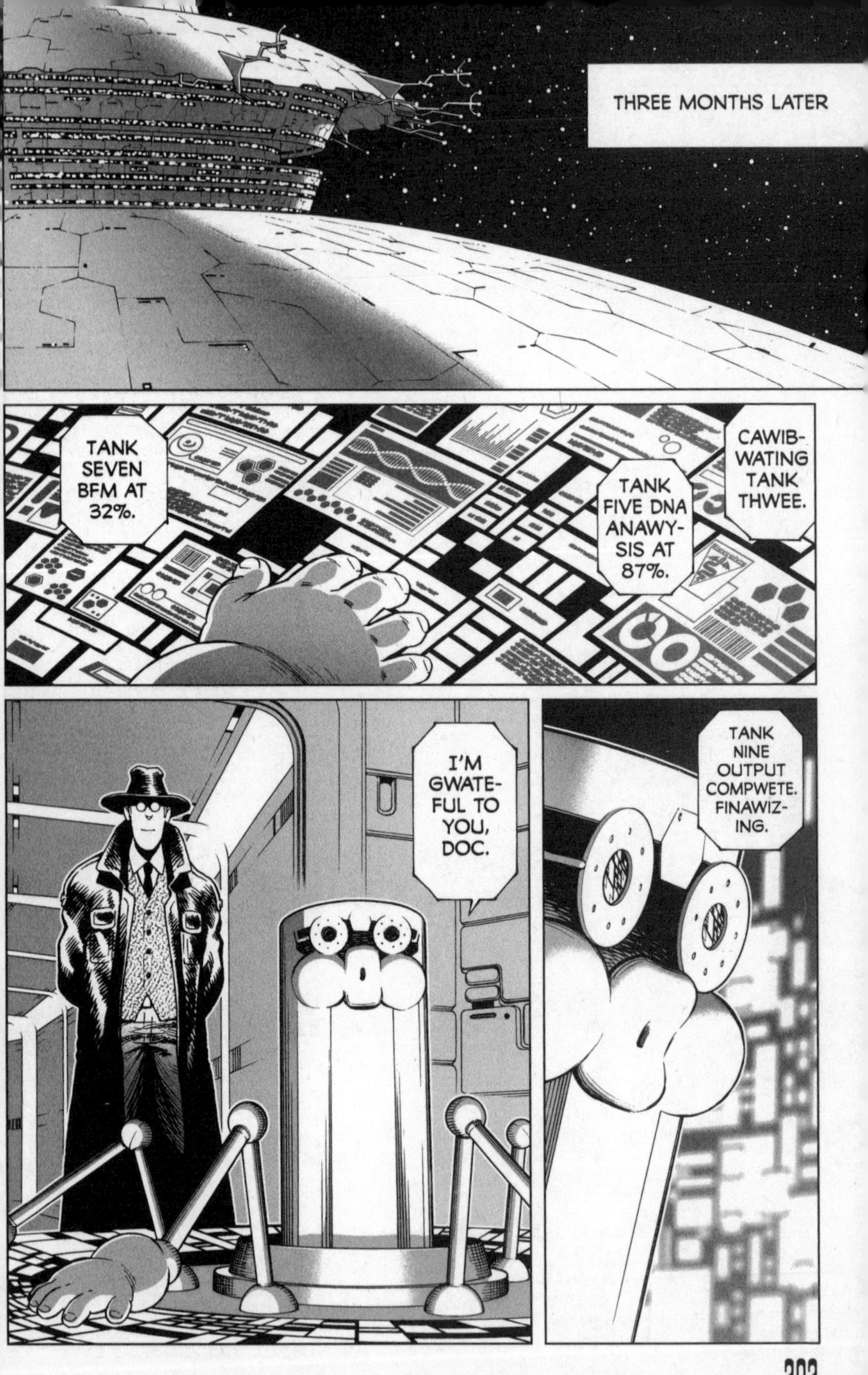
THREE MONTHS LATER
CAWIB-WATING TANK THWEE.
TANK FIVE DNA ANAWY-SIS AT 87%.
TANK SEVEN BFM AT 32%.
TANK NINE OUTPUT COMPWETE. FINAWIZ-ING.
I'M GWATE-FUL TO YOU, DOC.

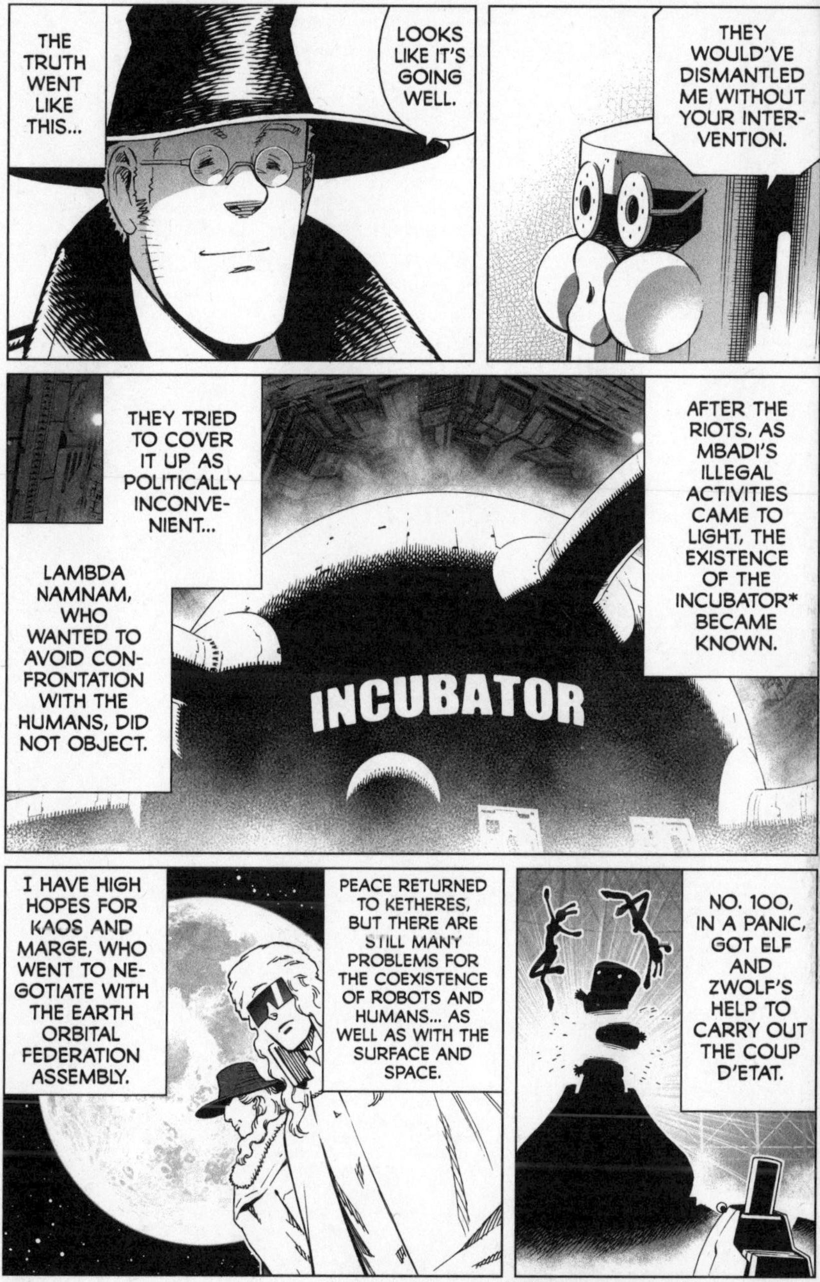
THEY WOULD'VE DISMANTLED ME WITHOUT YOUR INTERVENTION.
LOOKS LIKE IT'S GOING WELL.
THE TRUTH WENT LIKE THIS...
AFTER THE RIOTS, AS MBADI'S ILLEGAL ACTIVITIES CAME TO LIGHT, THE EXISTENCE OF THE INCUBATOR* BECAME KNOWN.
THEY TRIED TO COVER IT UP AS POLITICALLY INCONVENIENT...
LAMBDA NAMNAM, WHO WANTED TO AVOID CONFRONTATION WITH THE HUMANS, DID NOT OBJECT.
INCUBATOR
NO. 100, IN A PANIC, GOT ELF AND ZWOLF'S HELP TO CARRY OUT THE COUP D'ETAT.
PEACE RETURNED TO KETHERES, BUT THERE ARE STILL MANY PROBLEMS FOR THE COEXISTENCE OF ROBOTS AND HUMANS... AS WELL AS WITH THE SURFACE AND SPACE.
I HAVE HIGH HOPES FOR KAOS AND MARGE, WHO WENT TO NEGOTIATE WITH THE EARTH ORBITAL FEDERATION ASSEMBLY.

*Incubator: the device connecting 20,000 brains extracted from the Tiphareans at Initiation. It is used as Ketheres's public order system. See Battle Angel Alita: Last Order ep. 15

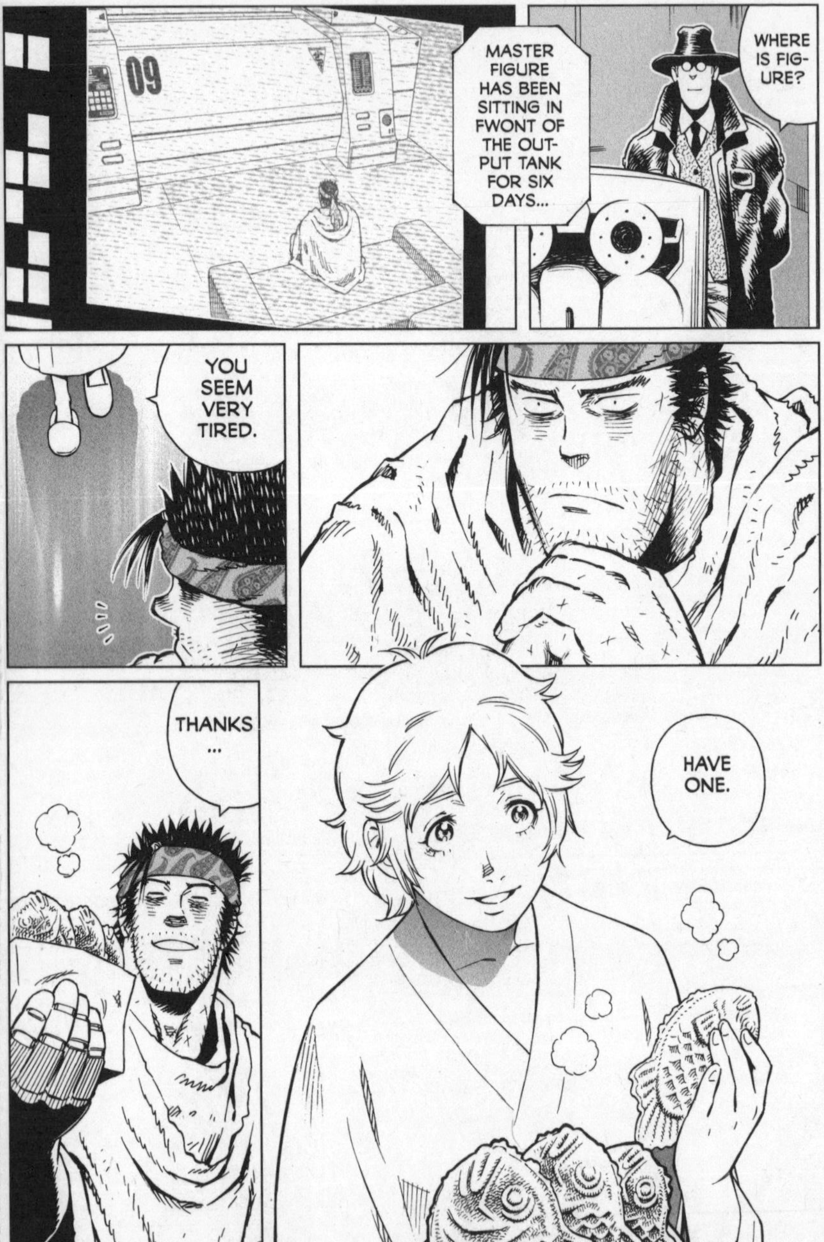

WHERE IS FIG-URE?
MASTER FIGURE HAS BEEN SITTING IN FWONT OF THE OUT-PUT TANK FOR SIX DAYS...
09
YOU SEEM VERY TIRED.
HAVE ONE.
THANKS ...

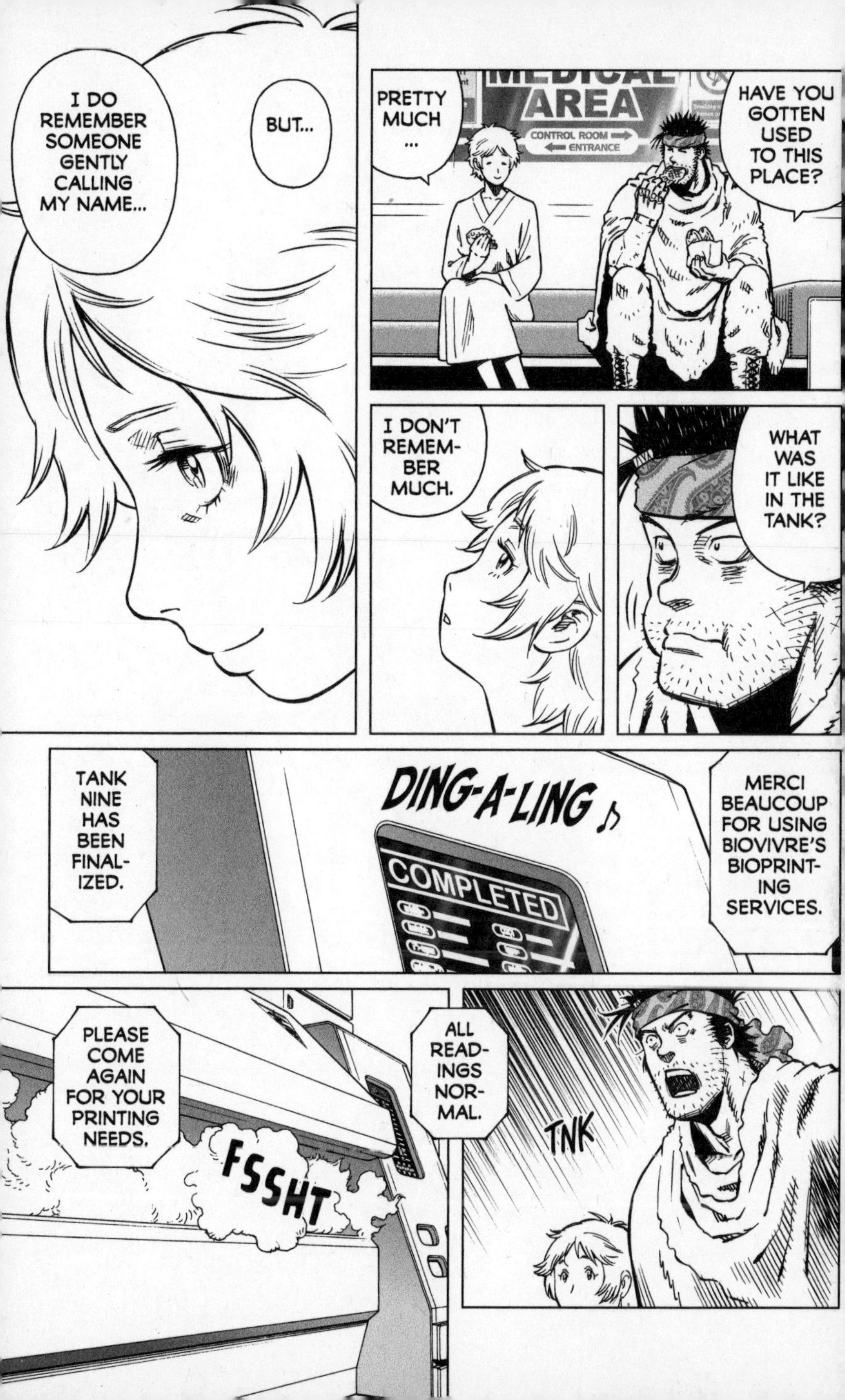
MEDICAL AREA
CONTROL ROOM
ENTRANCE
HAVE YOU GOTTEN USED TO THIS PLACE?
PRETTY MUCH...
WHAT WAS IT LIKE IN THE TANK?
I DON'T REMEMBER MUCH.
BUT...
I DO REMEMBER SOMEONE GENTLY CALLING MY NAME...
MERCI BEAUCOUP FOR USING BIOVIVRE'S BIOPRINTING SERVICES.
DING-A-LING ♪
COMPLETED
TANK NINE HAS BEEN FINALIZED.
TNK
ALL READINGS NORMAL.
PLEASE COME AGAIN FOR YOUR PRINTING NEEDS.
FSSHT

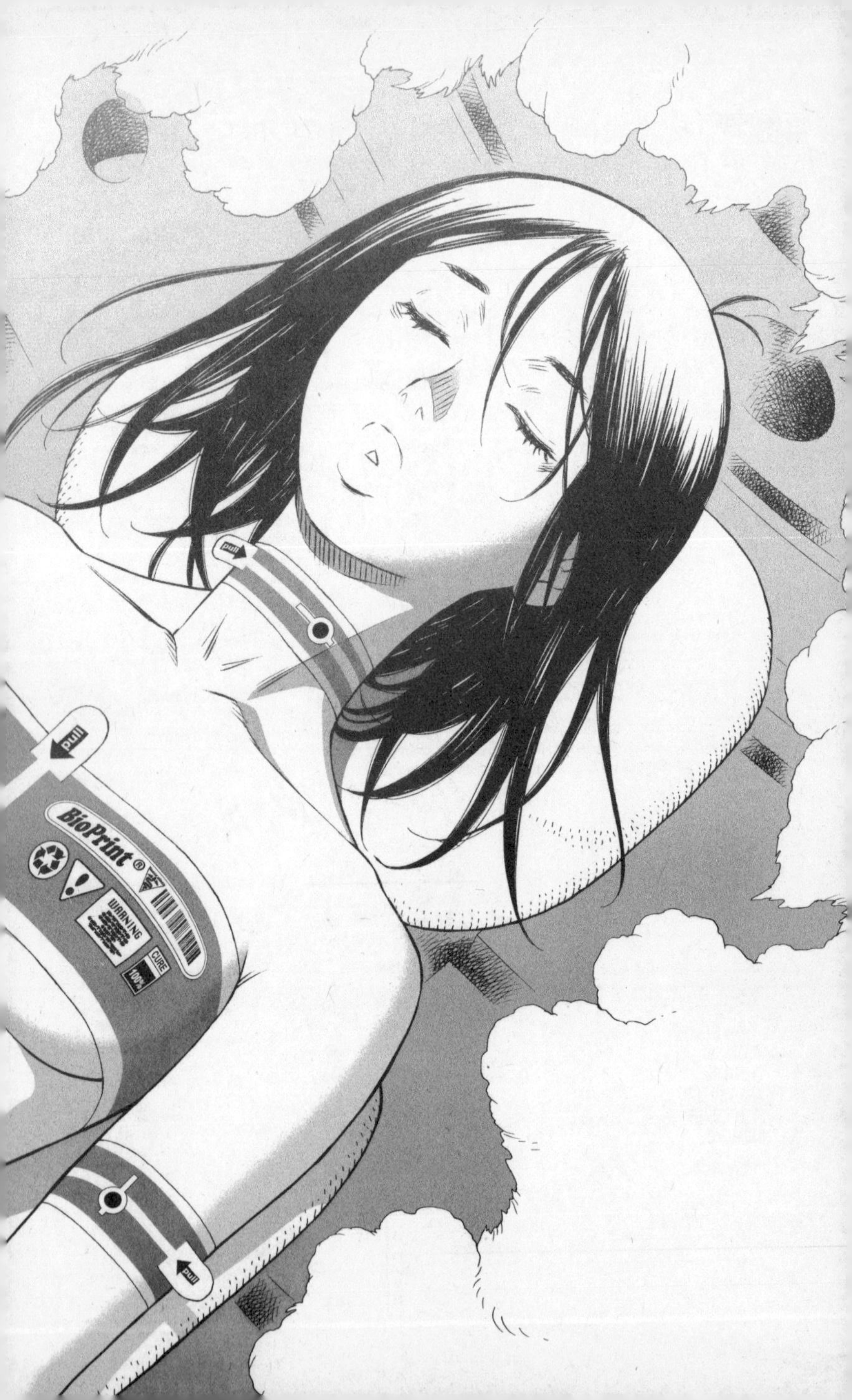
pull
pull
BioPrint ®
WARNING
CURE
100%
pull

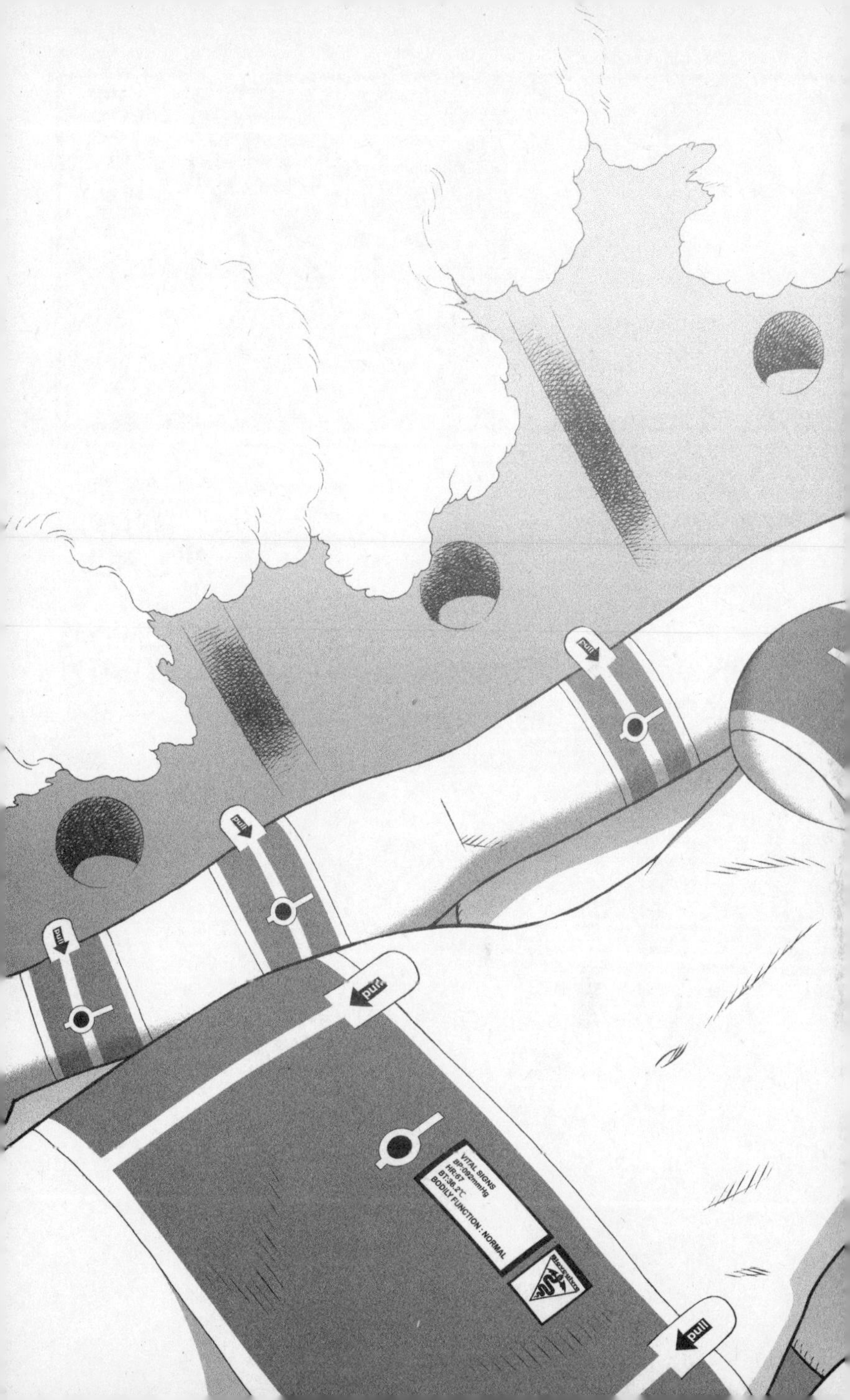
pull
pull
pull
pull
pull
VITAL SIGNS
BP:092mmHg
HR:67
BT:36.2℃
BODILY FUNCTION : NORMAL

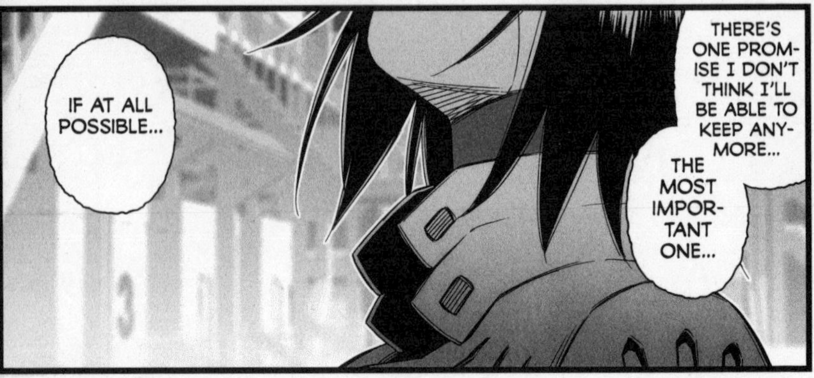
THERE'S ONE PROMISE I DON'T THINK I'LL BE ABLE TO KEEP ANYMORE...
THE MOST IMPORTANT ONE...
IF AT ALL POSSIBLE...

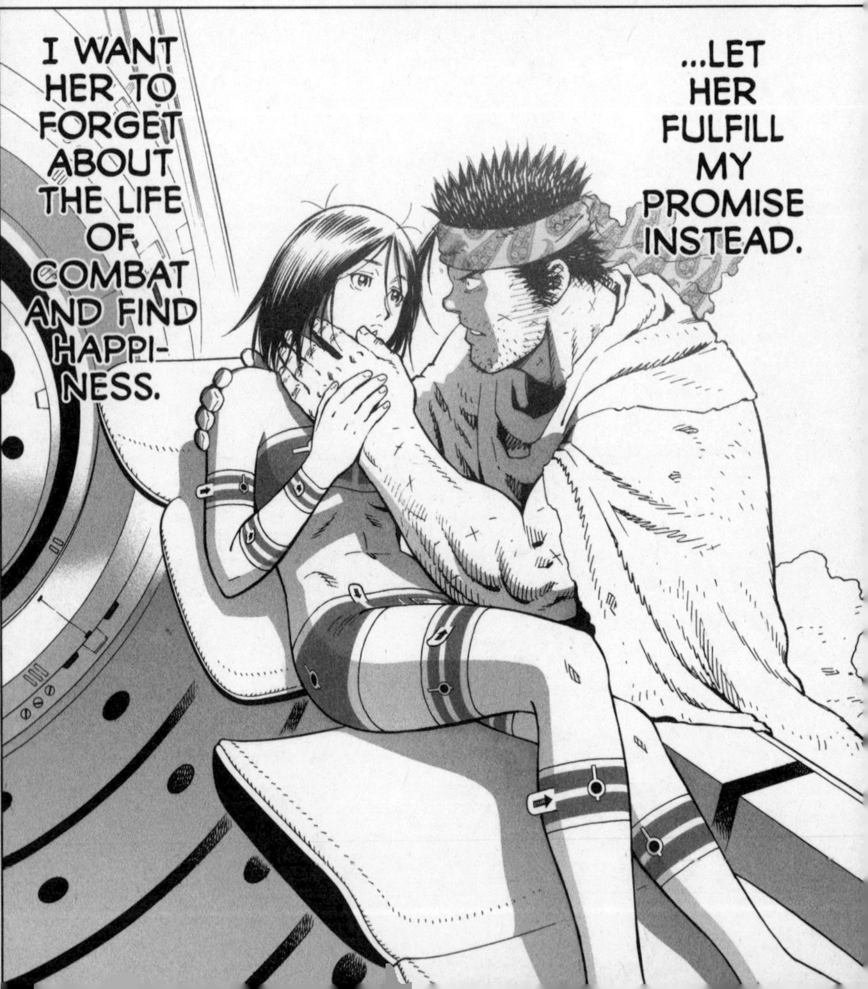
...LET HER FULFILL MY PROMISE INSTEAD.
I WANT HER TO FORGET ABOUT THE LIFE OF COMBAT AND FIND HAPPINESS.

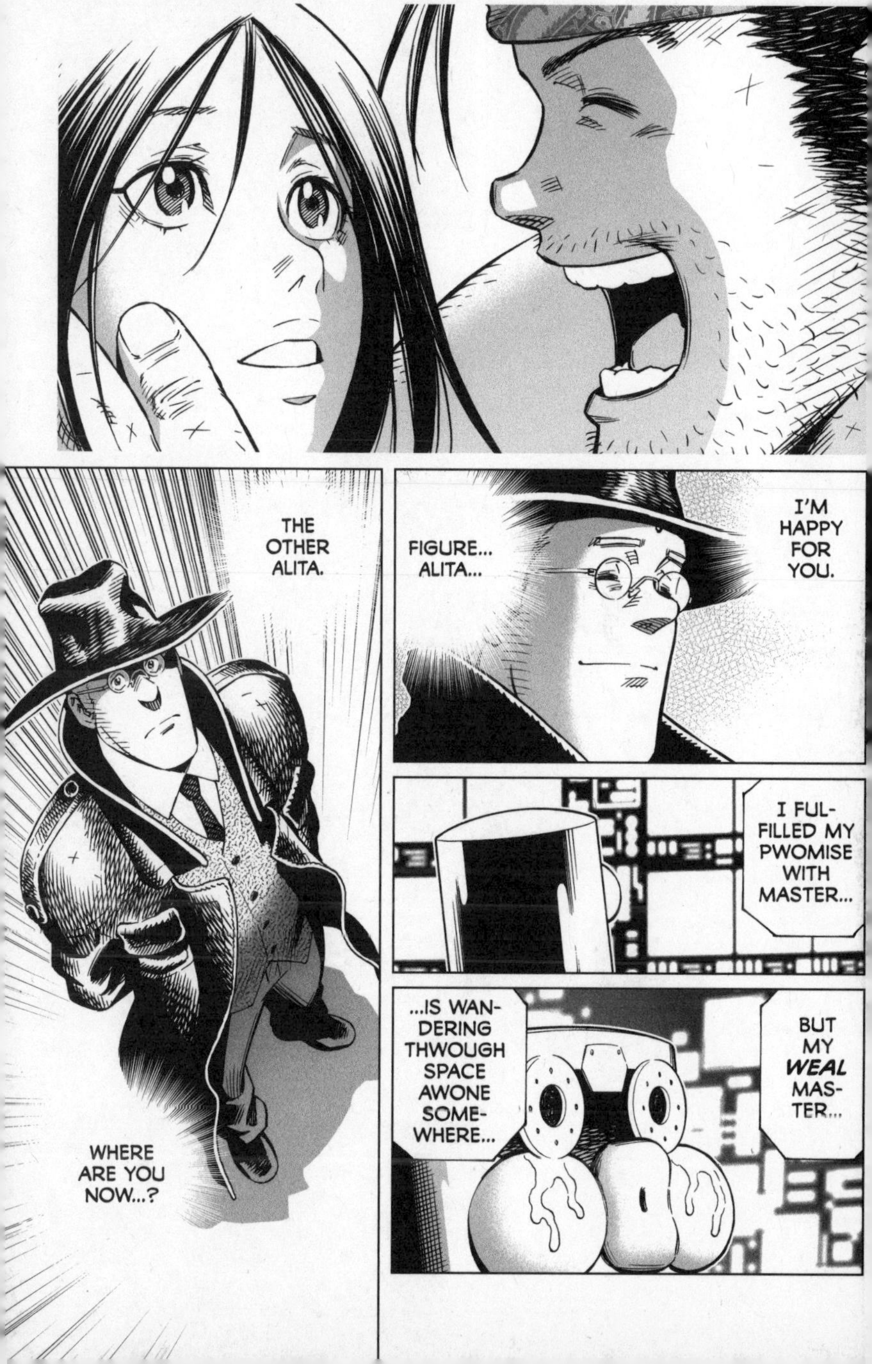
I'M HAPPY FOR YOU.
FIGURE... ALITA...
I FUL-FILLED MY PWOMISE WITH MASTER...
BUT MY *WEAL* MAS-TER...
...IS WAN-DERING THWOUGH SPACE AWONE SOME-WHERE...
THE OTHER ALITA.
WHERE ARE YOU NOW...?

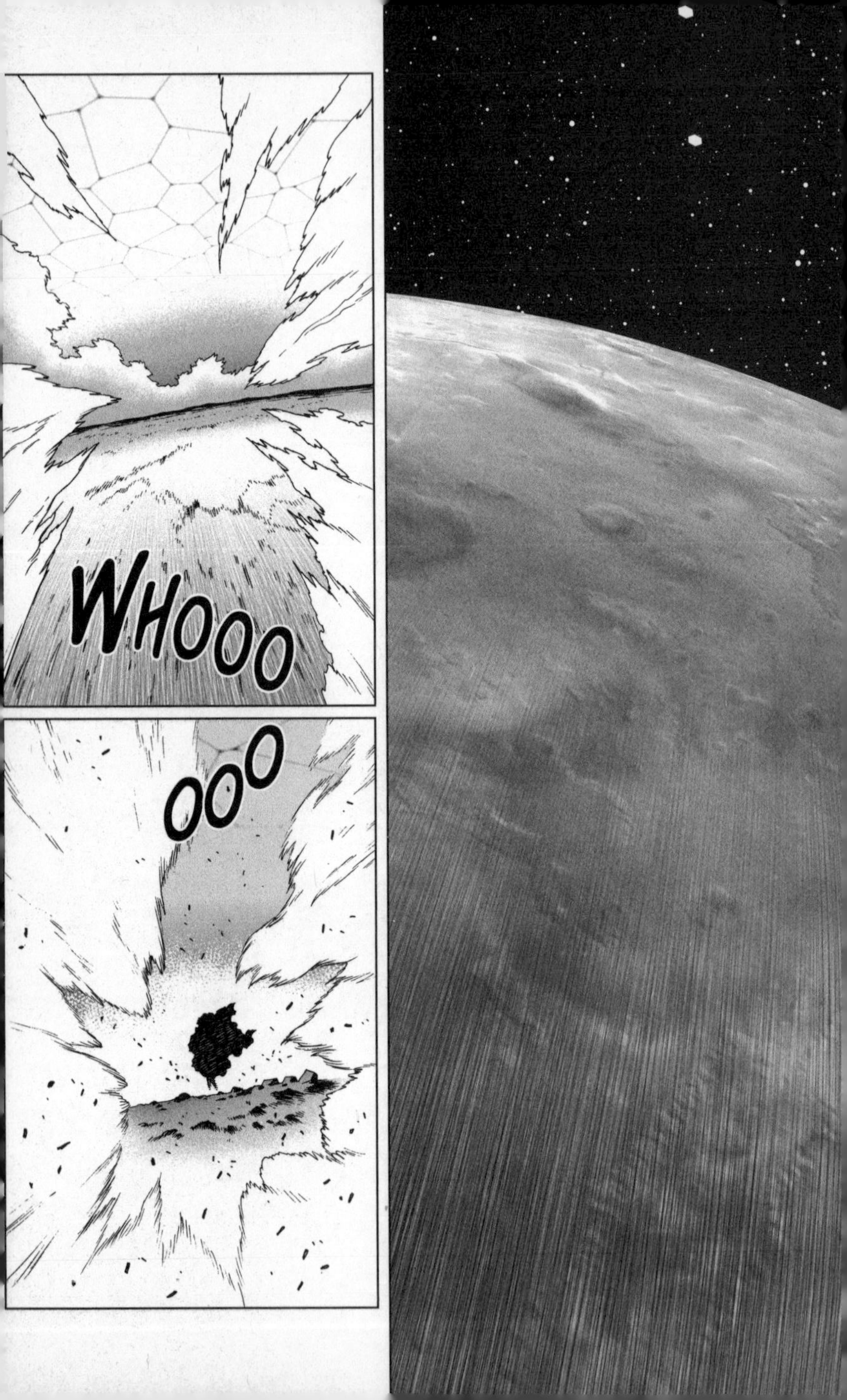
WHOOO
OOO

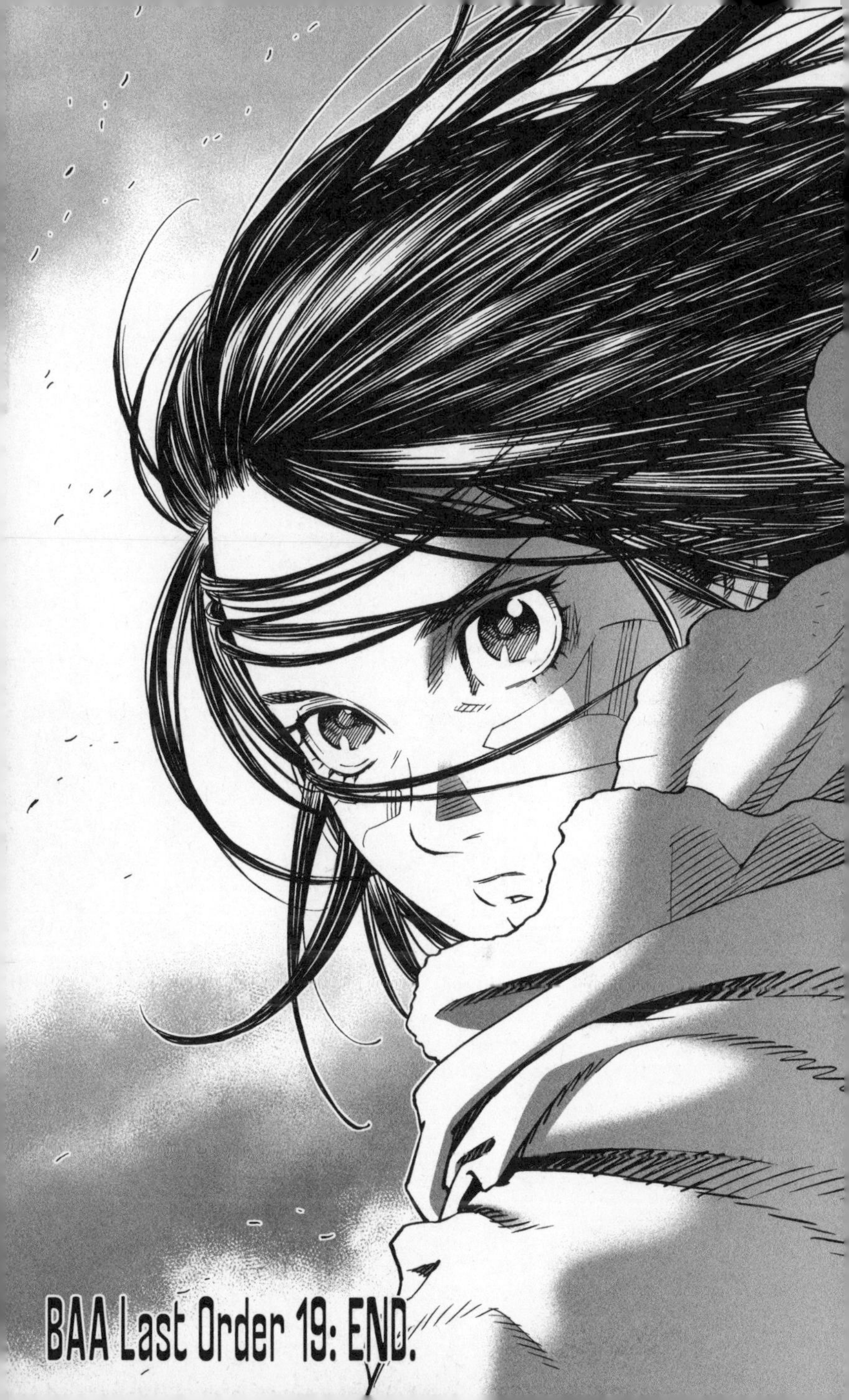
BAA Last Order 19: END.

Human Regeneration Devices

The world of Battle Angel Alita contains multiple regeneration devices. Let's review their features and mechanisms.

Reformation Bath

Cosmetic regeneration via Nova's nanomachine technology. It breaks down the body to the cellular level, removes waste products, and reconstructs it. Eelai used it to maintain her good looks.

Dedekind Clone Regeneration

Regeneration treatment by Tiphatean physician Dedekind appeared in "The Holy Night." He regrew body parts from DNA and transplanted them back into cyborgs.

MIB Regeneration System

Like "Stereotomy" this device utilizes nanomachine technology to reconstruct a sampled life form or object at the molecular level. This system was created by Nova after he repurposed and altered equipment from the medical inspector's office. Because the construction materials are prepared in advance, a human being can be regenerated in approximately three hours.

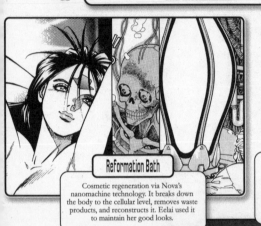

Stereotomy Cocoon

Nova's personal automatic regeneration system. When Stereotomy, the airborne nanomachines in Tiphares, detects Nova's death signal molecules, it automatically begins its process. This process takes six days during which it gathers raw materials from the environment. Nova is faithfully regenerated with his body, memories, clothing and accessories intact as of the time of sampling.

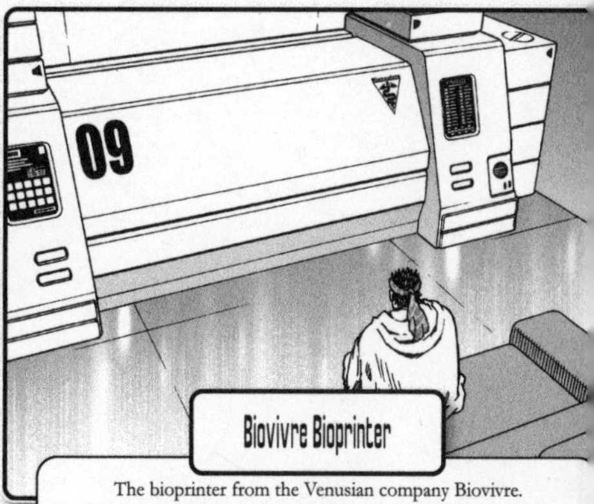
09

Biovivre Bioprinter

The bioprinter from the Venusian company Biovivre. It does not violate the LADDER treaty since it does not use nanomachine technology. It extracts DNA from cell fragments, analyzes it, and after growing cellular ink in a culture, it prints the organism's structure layer by layer. The merit over other methods is the abundance of adjustable parameters. Repair or removal of damaged DNA, adjustment of biological age, height, weight, muscle mass, percent body fat, the color of hair, skin, and eyes, and other modifications or enhancements of body parts are all possible for a total of up to 30,000 parameters. It takes about an average of ten days to print out a whole body.

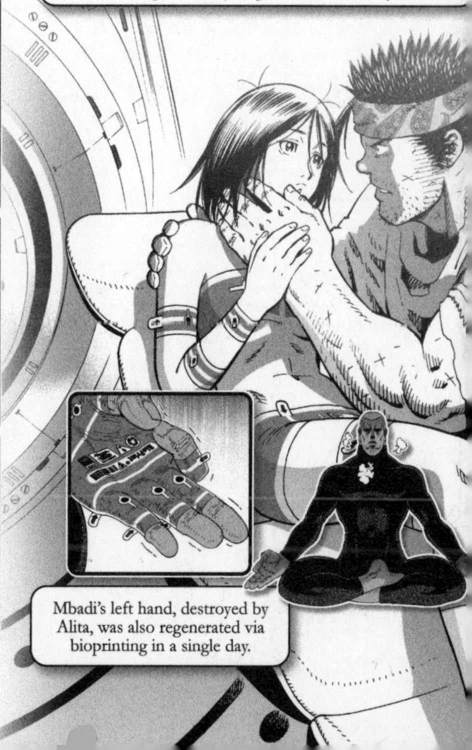

Mbadi's left hand, destroyed by Alita, was also regenerated via bioprinting in a single day.

SAMPLING MYSTERY!!

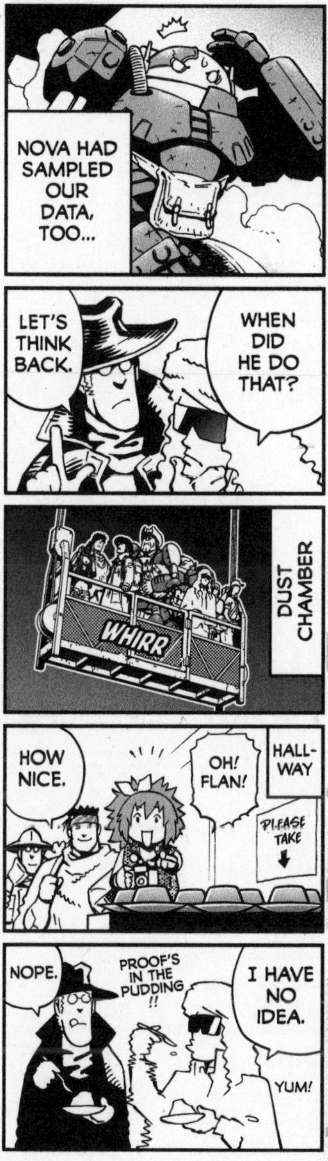
NOVA HAD SAMPLED OUR DATA, TOO...
WHEN DID HE DO THAT?
LET'S THINK BACK.
DUST CHAMBER
WHIRR
HALL-WAY
OH! FLAN!
HOW NICE.
PLEASE TAKE
I HAVE NO IDEA.
PROOF'S IN THE PUDDING!!
NOPE.
YUM!

Yukito Products Staff:

Yukito Kishiro,
Tsutomu Kishiro,
Emiya Kinari

Published in:

Phase 116: Evening vol. 10 2013
Phase 117: Evening vol. 12 2013
Phase 118: Evening vol. 14 2013
Phase 119: Evening vol. 16 2013
Phase 120: Evening vol. 20 2013
Phase 121: Evening vol. 22 2013
Phase 122: Evening vol. 24 2013
Phase 123: Evening vol. 2 2014
Final Phase: Evening vol. 4 2014

Translation Notes

May Buddha have mercy!, page 177

In Japanese, Figure is actually saying *Nanmandabu*, which is a shortened version of *Namu Amida Butsu*. This is a mantra that is recited in Pure Land Buddhism and directly translated, it could be interpreted as "homag to the infinite light," with the infinite light referring to the principle figur of Pure Land Buddhism, *Amida Butsu* (the infinite light Buddha). This is often said as a mantra for meditation or in funeral rites. In this case, Figur is likely using it in the way that it would be used at a funeral, reciting this mantra to send the departed to its next destination.

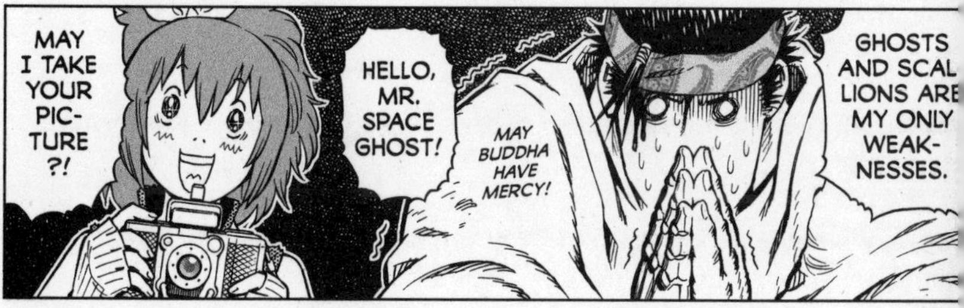
GHOSTS AND SCAL LIONS ARE MY ONLY WEAK- NESSES.
MAY BUDDHA HAVE MERCY!
HELLO, MR. SPACE GHOST!
MAY I TAKE YOUR PIC- TURE ?!

Battle Angel Alita: Last Order volume 19 is a work of fiction. Names, characters, places, and incidents are the products of the author's imagination or are used fictitiously. Any resemblance to actual events, locales, or persons, living or dead, is entirely coincidental.

A Kodansha Comics Trade Paperback Original.

Battle Angel Alita: Last Order volume 19 copyright © 2014 Yukito Kishiro
English translation copyright © 2014 Yukito Kishiro

All rights reserved.

Published in the United States by Kodansha Comics, an imprint of Kodansha USA Publishing, LLC, New York.

Publication rights for this English edition arranged through Kodansha Ltd., Tokyo.

First published in Japan in 2014 by Kodansha Ltd., Tokyo, as *Gunnm: Last Order* 19.

ISBN 978-1-61262-920-9

Printed in the United States of America.

www.kodanshacomics.com

9 8 7 6 5 4 3 2

Translator: Lillian Olsen
Lettering: Scott O. Brown
Editing: Ajani Oloye
Kodansha Comics edition cover design by Phil Balsman